Godly Heretics

ALSO BY MARC DIPAOLO

War, Politics and Superheroes: Ethics and Propaganda in Comics and Film (McFarland, 2011)

Godly Heretics

*Essays on Alternative Christianity
in Literature and Popular Culture*

Edited by MARC DIPAOLO

McFarland & Company, Inc., Publishers
Jefferson, North Carolina, and London

LIBRARY OF CONGRESS CATALOGUING-IN-PUBLICATION DATA

Godly heretics : essays on alternative christianity in literature and popular culture / edited by Marc DiPaolo.
        p.   cm.
Includes bibliographical references and index.

ISBN 978-0-7864-6780-8
softcover : acid free paper ∞

1. Christianity and culture.   2. Popular culture — Religious aspects — Christianity.   3. Christianity and art.   I. Di Paolo, Marc, editor of compilation.
BR115.C8G63 2013
261.0973—dc23   2013006054

BRITISH LIBRARY CATALOGUING DATA ARE AVAILABLE

© 2013 Marc DiPaolo. All rights reserved

No part of this book may be reproduced or transmitted in any form or by any means, electronic or mechanical, including photocopying or recording, or by any information storage and retrieval system, without permission in writing from the publisher.

On the cover: *Jesus Heals the Blind Man* (courtesy Restored Traditions archive of public domain religious art)

Manufactured in the United States of America

McFarland & Company, Inc., Publishers
  Box 611, Jefferson, North Carolina 28640
  www.mcfarlandpub.com

For Mom

Acknowledgments

I would like to thank the contributors to this volume, who were kind enough to respond to my invitation to participate and went on to produce some of the finest academic writing I've yet encountered.

I owe thanks to Christina Wolf, Archivist & Special Collections Librarian at Oklahoma City University, for help acquiring excellent artwork for this text.

I also appreciate the valuable time and feedback the following manuscript reviewers offered: Marc Lucht, Thomas Bierowski, James Røvîrå, and Catherine DiPaolo.

Finally, I'd like to thank the organizers of the March 11, 2012, Southwest Commission on Religious Studies conference — including Katherine Brown Downey and Darren Middleton — who helped introduce our work-in-progress to a larger audience of fellow scholars who reassured us that we were, indeed, onto something special with this project.

Table of Contents

Acknowledgments   vi

Introduction: Authentic vs. Imperialist Christianity in Literature and Film   1

Part I. Rewritten Bibles, Alternative Christs

Revolution by Other Means: Jefferson, the Jefferson Bible, and Jesus (TIM H. BLESSING)   25

Portraying Jesus as Human: *The Last Temptation of Christ* (KATHERINE BROWN DOWNEY)   43

Nietzsche and Tolstoy on Authentic Christianity (MARC LUCHT)   62

Amnesty for the Devil (GERALD S. VIGNA)   79

Lamb Unslain: Nonhuman Animals and Shelley's Panentheism (RUTH VANITA)   98

Shaw's Subversion of Biblical Language (GUSTAVO A. RODRÍGUEZ MARTÍN)   114

Song of Myself: Teaching Whitman's New Bible Today (TRACY FLOREANI)   133

Part II. Angels and Demons Among Us: The Politics and Economics of Heaven and Hell in Popular Culture

The Gospel According to Comic Strips: On *Peanuts* and *The Far Side* (ERIC MICHAEL MAZUR)   143

Religious Discourse in *Lost* and *Battlestar Galactica* (VAL NOLAN)   162

Table of Contents

The Radical Theology of Krzysztof Kieslowski's *Decalogue*
(MATTHEW YDE)   180

Fanaticism and Familicide from *Wieland* to *The Shining*
(DARA DOWNEY)   199

From Bedford Falls to Punxsutawney: Refashioning
A Christmas Carol (GRACE MOORE)   221

Reclaiming the Relation of Religion, Politics, and Economics
(JOERG RIEGER)   239

About the Contributors   255

Index   259

Introduction: Authentic vs. Imperialist Christianity in Literature and Film

> *I distrust those people who know so well what God wants them to do, because I notice it always coincides with their own desires.*—Susan B. Anthony
>
> *Theology without love is the theology of the demons.*—Symeon the New Theologian

It may not be true where you live, but in the rural regions of New York, Pennsylvania, and Oklahoma where I have resided, there is no shortage of preachers and cultural commentators on the local radio and television stations casting aspersions upon public figures and private citizens for not being sufficiently Christian. Certainly, such authoritarian figures can be found on national radio and television programming as well, and many of them make a lucrative living out of decrying the evils of secular humanism and fairweather Christianity regardless of the denomination they themselves are members of. They are often known to wag their fingers at guests on their shows (or at absent, headline-making figures) and exclaim:

"You're not a real Christian because your social views are too trendy."

"You're not a real Christian because you don't go to church enough."

"You're not a real Christian because you are too interested in the historic Jesus."

"You're not a real Christian because you're not into persecuting heretics and demonizing non–Christians."

"You're not a real Christian because your sect of Christianity isn't valid. All members of your sect are destined for hell, sad to say. Nice knowing you."

or

"You're too *alternative* Christian to be *authentic* Christian."

Whether they are self-appointed or representative of some sort of establishment organization with an axe to grind, these policemen of Christianity are tiresome and ubiquitous—on the radio and television, in the pulpits, and in powerful government positions. They act as if they speak directly *to* God, speak directly *for* God, and know exactly what is in the hearts of those whom they are demonizing. In fact, it is abundantly clear that they *do not* speak directly to God, they *do not* speak directly for God, and *they have no idea* what is in the hearts of those whom they are demonizing. Indeed, generally speaking, the only fake Christians are the ones pointing out the fake Christians. These modern-day Cotton Mather figures are often less the "true" worshippers of Christ and more the servants of Mammon and Ares. After all, more often than not they speak and act as the (un)acknowledged public relations voices of Wall Street and the military-industrial complex. Passionate as they are in their views, these modern-day Jeremiahs are judgmental and hypocritical, and I stand in defiance of their misanthropic, fire-and-brimstone message.

This book is about challenging preconceived notions of what constitutes authentic and alternative Christianity. The scholars who have contributed essays to the collection come from a variety of religious, academic, cultural, and political backgrounds, but what links their work is the shared contention that there is not always an oppositional relationship between authentic and alternative Christianity. Sometimes alternative Christianity *is* authentic Christianity. In other words, this book is about how some artists and thinkers, whose views have been long condemned as heretical, demonstrably represent a purer form of Christianity than the establishment Christian churches historically have engaged in and promulgated. Furthermore, when these artists and thinkers are condemned for being heretics, they are identified as such by preachers and religious institutions that have a history of endorsing belief systems and social actions that appear to directly contradict the teachings of Jesus as represented in the Gospels.

Almost invariably, when prominent artists or thinkers point out that the historic Jesus appears to have been a pacifist, anti-establishment, proto-feminist, proto-multicultural figure, certain members of the establishment Church level *ad hominem* accusations at these thinkers, calling into question the legitimacy of their religious views as Christians, non–Christians, apostates, agnostics, or atheists. Of course, these *ad hominem* attacks can easily be reversed, since most Christian churches do not have full credibility when they speak of what Christ did or did not "stand for." After all, many priests, ministers, theologians, and Christian lawyers, businessmen, and heads of state have taken part in, or turned a blind eye to, imperial conquests, autocratic regimes, genocide, institutional torture, endless wars, state economies built upon a foundation of slavery and social Darwinism, and the oppression of women and racial and ethnic minorities. Upon reflection, Jesus appears to endorse none of these aspects of (in)human civilization in his sermons and interactions with Jews and non-Jews alike.

Imagine Jesus himself performing the actions taken in his name by some of his more respected spokesmen in the Church and in government. Picture, if you can, Jesus standing shoulder-to-shoulder with John Hathorne at the Salem Witch Trials, Jesus himself echoing Pope Urban II's calls for the first Crusade, Jesus excommunicating Galileo, Jesus "curing" or lynching gays and lesbians, Jesus mass-slaughtering Jews and Native Americans, Jesus defending corporate personhood, and Jesus cheering Jefferson Davis' assertion that slavery "was established by decree of Almighty God ... is sanctioned in the Bible, in both Testaments, from Genesis to Revelation ... it has existed in all ages, has been found among the people of the highest civilization, and in nations of the highest proficiency in the arts."

The prophets-dubbed-heretics who condemn the organized Christian churches for their history of misrepresenting Christ while promoting imperial and patriarchal interests often exert their moral authority by asserting that, at some time during the development of Christianity, something went "wrong" with Christianity. For Dante Aligheri, the moment of crisis came with "The Donation of Constantine," an infamous—and, as it turned out, forged—document that declared Christianity the official religion of the Roman Empire. For Dante, this document helped transform Christianity from a small, persecuted cult of devoted followers of Jesus who were thrown to the lions by the Romans into an establishment faith whose leaders eventually became the ones ordering people thrown to the lions—Dante metaphorically included.

In a similar vein, feminist historian Marina Warner argued in "Fantasy's Power and Peril" that the early Christian fathers made a tragic error in rejecting Origen of Alexandria's doctrine of universal salvation. According to Warner, in supplanting Origen's views with the theology of Christianized Zoroastrianism, Christians chose to embrace a view of a universe locked in an endless, mystical war between the forces of light and dark. This good/evil polarity encourages endless warfare on our material, human plane to this day and is the fuel that keeps conflict in the Middle East alive, Warner contends.

Though not taken seriously in most quarters, bestselling thriller novelist Dan Brown makes a compelling point in *The Da Vinci Code* (2003) that the cardinal sin of the Roman Catholic Church has been its exclusion of women from the Church hierarchy, distortion of women's historical roles, and an aversion to sex that has prevented it from acknowledging the existence of

Jesus's extended family. The *Da Vinci Code* may be a mere potboiler and its historical assertions may be dubious, but its thesis regarding Church misogyny is sound.

For their parts, both Thomas Jefferson and Nietzsche have asserted that Jesus's biographers, not the least among them St. Paul, distorted his message by placing their own, highly subjective gloss on his life and by waiting too long after his death to set his words down. Jefferson and Nietzsche both attempt to excavate the true message of Christ from underneath the surface texts included in the New Testament in a manner that predicts the scholarship published by members of the Jesus Seminar. Interestingly, four scholars who are part of that seminar — Arthur J. Dewey, Roy W. Hoover, Lane McGaughy, and Daryl D. Schmidt — are not only concerned with the accurate historical representation of Christ but also with that of Paul. In their book *The Authentic Letters of Paul* (2010), these scholars break with the precedent set by Jefferson and Nietzsche and attempt to rescue Paul from the way in which he himself has been misrepresented, first by those who may have edited his original prose or written texts in his name, and then by his later interpreters—Christian thinkers such as Augustine and Martin Luther — who have left an inaccurate and indelible impression on our minds concerning who Paul was.

Such orthodox and alternative theology is often expressed in preaching and encyclicals, or in the scholarly works of historians and theologians, but this book is primarily concerned with the kinds of theological statements made in fiction by writers, poets, artists, and secular thinkers. Many of the popular and literary works of fiction found in these pages are regarded as classics of orthodox Christianity while others are well-known as "heretical" tracts: *The Last Temptation of Christ, The Passion of the Christ, The Jefferson Bible, It's a Wonderful Life, A Christmas Carol, The Decalogue, De Profundis, A Charlie Brown Christmas, Song of Myself, Androcles and the Lion, Lost, War and Peace,* and *Battlestar Galactica*. As this list indicates, for the purposes of this book, we will be discussing manifestations of alternative Christian thought in cultural studies artifacts from a wide variety of genres and media, including narratives constructed as novels, poems, short stories, films, pictorial art, and even radically rewritten and re-edited Bibles as "remixed" or "original" works of fiction. Indeed, to use a word popular in contemporary film and comic book criticism, many of these works were intended to, effectively, "reboot" Christianity by bringing it back to basics, retelling its "origin," and getting the narrative back on track after it wandered to a dead end.

This book is about some of the most famous and infamous efforts that have been made over the years to reboot Christianity.

One of the goals of this book is to involve academics from a variety of disciplines—including theology, literature, history, philosophy, cultural crit-

Tom Hanks as Robert Langdon and Audrey Tautou as Sophie Neveu — a character descended from Jesus himself — in Ron Howard's 2006 film adaptation (Columbia Pictures) of Dan Brown's 2003 novel *The Da Vinci Code*.

icism, and film criticism — in rescuing cardboard prophets and heretics, saints and sinners from their one-dimensionality and helping us to see them anew with fresh eyes, fully aware of their complexity as human beings and thinkers. The end result is a book that suggests that those who have long been considered pure enemies of Christianity, including Thomas Jefferson, Frederick Nietzsche, and George Bernard Shaw, have much to say about what constitutes authentic Christianity, while those who are seen as champions of established churches, including Dante and the screenwriters of the religious television shows *Lost* and *Battlestar Galactica*, have a more complex and anti-establishment religious view than one might think at first.

Let us consider an example of the above from Oscar Wilde, an author whose work is referenced in several essays included in this book. In his epistle "De Profundis" (1897), Wilde describes Christ as the ultimate suffering artist, whose miracles stemmed from his magnetic personality and empathy and capacity for forgiveness, not from any supernatural source:

His miracles seem to me to be as exquisite as the coming of spring, and quite as natural. I see no difficulty at all in believing that such was the charm of his personality that his mere presence could bring peace to souls in anguish, and that those who touched his garments or his hands forgot their pain; or that as he passed by on the highway of life people who had seen nothing of life's mystery, saw it clearly, and others who had been deaf to every voice but that of pleasure heard for the first time the voice of love and found it as "musical as Apollo's lute"; or that evil passions fled at his approach, and men whose dull unimaginative lives had been but a mode of death rose as it were from the grave when he called them; or that when he taught on the hillside the multitude forgot their hunger and thirst and the cares of this world, and that to his friends who listened to him as he sat at meat the coarse food seemed delicate, and the water had the taste of good wine, and the whole house became full of the odour and sweetness of nard [qtd. in Robbins 173].

As Ruth Robbins observed in her 2011 biography of Wilde, "What Wilde is describing of Christ's personality is, of course, very close to the common perception of his own. His conversation, the stories he told others, all acted like a charm on those who heard him. Even [Wilde's arch nemesis] the Marquess of Queensberry, when he met Wilde for the first time, was charmed, writing to Bosie, 'I don't wonder that you are so fond of him. He is a wonderful man' (Ellman 1988: 393). In this text, then, man is not made in the image of God; Christ is remade in the image of Oscar Wilde" (173).

Robbins' observation recalls Susan B. Anthony's admonition to avoid speaking for God when one speaks on one's own behalf. Wilde's depiction of Christ also reminds us of the extent to which Christ has become, over time, a sort of spiritual Rorschach test—people see in Christ what they wish to, employ out-of-context Biblical passages as precedent to justify their own personal theology, and ignore all Bible passages that clash with their preconceived vision of Jesus. In this way, for example, progressive Americans embrace a socialistic, pacifistic interpretation of the Sermon on the Mount and ignore the Christ that warns that those who betray the Son of Man would have been better off if they had never been born (Matthew 26:24), while conservative Christians embrace an authoritarian interpretation of Paul's Epistle to the Romans and forget Christ's admonition to "judge not, that ye be not judged" (Matthew 7:1). On the other hand, one might argue that progressive Christians have focused on one part of the truth of Jesus in the Bible and that conservative Christians have focused on another. Could both depictions of Jesus be true? One more than the other? One more "historically accurate" than another? One more "theologically sound"?

And what of Wilde's depiction of Jesus? As idiosyncratic and self-centered as it appears to be, it is, surprisingly, not without echo in Biblical scholarship.

Introduction 7

Indeed, one of the titular *Profiles of Jesus* (2002), "Jesus as Peasant Artisan" by Jesus Seminar scholar Arthur J. Dewey, portrays Jesus as a "crafty" wordsmith who employs "humorous exaggeration" and a narrative "double focus" to discourage dogmatic thinking and collapse either/or choices and good/bad distinctions in on themselves (77–79). Consequently, Jesus's parables and aphorisms confound his audience by making listeners ponder the ever-expanding ramifications of what he has said. Jesus employed his narrative brilliance and pedagogical skill to teach his audience about social injustice in first-century Palestine. Oscar Wilde used much the same narrative style and pedagogical tactic to instruct his audience about its own moral hypocrisies and social injustice in Victorian England. Living during a socially and politically turbulent time, Wilde employed a double-perspective that simultaneously looked back on Victorian values, anticipated 20th century modernist values, and meshed them together, wittily demonstrating both the relative truths and limitations of both perspectives, Robbins has observed.

Regarding the issue of Christ's double-perspective, Dewey offers as an example the ever-expanding ramifications of Jesus's exhortation to love *everyone*:

> The aphoristic command "Love your enemies" (Luke 6:27b; Matt 5:44b) also plays upon a double-perspective. First, it disputes the conventional wisdom that enjoins primary concern for those within one's social group. Second, it admits the alienation in Palestinian society (village feuding, opposition by the rich, Roman occupation). The audience could easily identify their enemies. Third, it challenges the listeners to replace a simplistic obedience with a radical reconfiguration of their societal categories. As the Seminar rightly puts it in *The Five Gospels*, "Those who love their enemies have no enemies." The challenge of the aphorism is clear: can you imagine acting differently towards those outside the circle of your people? The saying has a concussive effect; it keeps echoing in the resisting areas of the listeners' hearts [80].

In the same essay, Dewey also examines similarly thought-provoking, double-perspective parables and aphorisms of Christ, including "It is easier for a camel to go through the eye of a needle, than for a rich man to enter into the kingdom of God" (79, Mark 10:25, Matthew 19:24, Luke 8:25), "[God] causes the sun to rise on both the bad and the good, and sends rain on both the just and unjust" (81, Matthew 5:45), "You see the sliver in your friend's eye, but you don't see the timber in your own eye. When you take the timber out of your own eye, you will see well enough to remove the sliver from your friend's eye" (77, Thomas 26:12, Matthew 7: 3–5, Luke 6: 41–42).

Though Wilde's pairing of opposites and unexpected reversals of commonly embraced truths seem, at first glance, more frivolous than Christ's assertion to love your enemy, consider Wilde's statement that "anybody can sympathise with the sufferings of a friend, but it requires a very fine nature — it requires, in fact, the nature of a true Individualist — to sympathise with a friend's success." Here he notes well the rivalries and jealousies and egotism that lie at the heart of many friendships and — in pointing them out — prods us to be aware of such dark feelings ourselves and deal with them accordingly. Consider Wilde's similarly provocative observations concerning marriage ("The proper basis for a marriage is mutual misunderstanding"), history ("The one duty we owe to history is to re-write it"), cynicism ("A cynic is a man who knows the price of everything but the value of nothing"), and ambition ("In this world there are only two tragedies; one is not getting what one wants, the other is getting it"). All of these statements, and a seemingly endless parade of similar Wilde aphorisms, seem at once sparklingly humorous and starkly bleak, empathetic and misanthropic, wise and frivolous. They are also in the same subversive genealogy as the aphorisms and parables of Arthur Dewey's "peasant artisan" Christ.

The overlap between Dewey's portrait of Christ and Wilde's suggests that both the historic Jesus scholar and the Victorian decadent are not only offering overlapping Biblical exegesis, but potentially offering a truth about Christ that is not often discussed or pondered by more mainstream depictions of Christ. To this extent, both Wilde and Dewey have something to teach the skeptic and the believer alike about Christ the moralist raconteur.

Another potential source of Christian wisdom that is often overlooked is the wisdom of the atheist. As you will see in the essay on Nietzsche in this collection, atheists are able to examine aspects of theology, organized religion, and the life and teachings of Christ from the valuable perspective of the outsider looking in, and they can see things that those of us within religion cannot. In devout circles, the religious views of atheists are often deemed too dangerous to read since they "believe in nothing" and threaten to kill genuine faith; however, in my experience in discussing religion with atheists, they believe in a great deal and they often act more like bona fide Christians than most devout Christians do in the way they interact with the world around them.

One of the most famous atheist directors in the history of world cinema, and one of the greatest directors who ever lived, Luis Buñuel, made a number of films that criticized religion in general and the Catholic Church in particular, including the classic films *Viridiana* (1961), *Simon of the Desert* (1965), *The Milky Way* (1969), and *The Discreet Charm of the Bourgeoisie* (1972). As in the case of John Lennon's secularist manifesto "Imagine," several of the aforementioned films are so relentlessly cynical, atheistic, and materialist that they achieve an odd religiosity that is difficult to describe, especially to the skeptical, incredulous, conservative Christian. In an essay on Luis Buñuel,

"Damned If You Do...," Michael Wood offers his own take on Buñuel's odd relationship with God:

> A good friend of Luis Buñuel's suggested in conversation that the director was likely to be damned twice: once for being an atheist, and once for joking about it on his deathbed. The friend, a priest, certainly knew what he was talking about, but I don't believe he really thought Buñuel would be damned. God can't ultimately condemn serious atheists. They pay far more attention to him than half-hearted believers do, and they help keep him in business. On the soundtrack of Buñuel's film *Nazarin* (1959), we hear a barrel organ playing an old song called "Dios nunca muere" (God Never Dies). The song itself is a bit of popular piety, an assertion of enduring faith. In Buñuel's movie, it is an ironic tribute to the director's everlasting antagonist, a correction of Nietzsche's premature announcement of God's death. And when Buñuel says, as he frequently and famously did, "Thank God I'm still an atheist," the remark is not only a witty paradox, it is a form of courtesy. Why wouldn't an atheist want to show gratitude to the nonexistent deity who never lets him down? [5].

Buñuel's friend was a Catholic priest and many of his fans were — and are — devout Christians who, nevertheless, believe that his film art has much to say about life and religion that is worth contemplating. In a similar vein, many of Federico Fellini's devotees are religious Catholics who enjoy his work despite — or, in part, because of — his biting satire of the Church in films such as *Roma* (1972), *La Dolce Vita* (1960) and *Nights of Cabiria* (1957).

None of the above films are lives of Christ, but "Jesus movies" have been fascinating and still more controversial than the aforementioned classics thanks to the narrative content of the films themselves and the religious beliefs of the filmmakers. For example, it is interesting to note that some critics and scholars believe that Pier Paolo Pasolini's film *The Gospel According to St. Matthew* (1964) is morally and spiritually superior to Mel Gibson's *The Passion of the Christ* (2004) because Pasolini focuses on the words and deeds of Jesus the teacher and healer while Gibson's film is concerned primarily with Jesus's death — and with graphically recreating the historical methods that soldiers would use to torture and execute the Roman Empire's political prisoners. That Gibson is a devout conservative Catholic and Pasolini is a Marxist, atheist, and homosexual makes this contrast between the focus and dramatic effect of their two filmic lives of Christ all the more intriguing. Commenting on the fruits of Pasolini's labor, film critic Roger Ebert observed: "Pasolini's is one of the most effective films on a religious theme I have ever seen, perhaps because it was made by a nonbeliever who did not preach, glorify, underline, sentimentalize or romanticize his famous story, but tried his best to simply record it." Ebert added *The Gospel According to St. Matthew* to his online list of Great Movies in March 14, 2004, in response to the popularity of Gibson's

In Federico Fellini's *La Dolce Vita* (1960, Koch-Lorber Films), Marcello Mastroianni (Marcello Rubini) is a dispirited journalist who looks for love and spiritual fulfillment in the wrong places. He flirts with a glamorous Hollywood actress (Anita Ekberg as Sylvia), covers two small children who are pretending to see visions of the Virgin Mary, and lives vicariously through an intellectual friend who only seems to be living the perfect life.

recently released opus. Ebert thought the story of how Pasolini came to make the film was particularly noteworthy. The filmmaker "had accepted [an] invitation [to attend a seminar at a Franciscan monastery in St. Francis' hometown of Assisi] after Pope John XXIII called for a new dialogue with non–Catholic artists." During the course of his stay in Assisi, Pasolini read the Gospels through and was enraptured by the figure of Jesus, whom he saw as a counterculture figure with stunning contemporary relevance. He was then inspired to make a film based on the most socially aware Gospel.

Again comparing Pasolini's film to Gibson's, Ebert writes: "To see [this] film a few weeks after seeing Gibson's is to understand that there is no single version of his story. It acts as a template into which we fit our ideas, and we see it as our lives have prepared us for it. Gibson sees Christ's suffering as the overwhelming fact of his life, and his film contains very little of Christ's teachings. Pasolini thought the teachings were the central story. If a hypothetical

Introduction

Jim Caviezel as Jesus Christ in *The Passion of the Christ*, a 2004 film (Newmarket Films) directed by Mel Gibson. The mirror image of *The Last Temptation of Christ* (1988), this movie was enormously popular with many of the same conservative Christians who hated Scorsese's epic and criticized by liberals who felt that the film was offensive due to its extreme violence and anti–Semitic undertones.

viewer came to *The Passion* with no previous knowledge of Jesus and wondered what all the furor was about, Pasolini's film would argue: Jesus was a radical whose teachings, if taken seriously, would contradict the values of most human societies ever since."

Go tell it on the mountain, Roger.

Admittedly, theology presented as a narrative is particularly controversial because it makes potentially subversive forms of Christianity more available to the public. Furthermore, these narratives often compound the problem by violating the Hebraic law against making graven images found in the Pentateuch. Despite the understandable anxieties caused by these narratives, those that are classic stories of elite and popular culture deserve better than to be dismissed out of hand or censored, especially since some of these narratives, and their creators, can potentially teach their audiences important truths about Christ and Christianity. However, more often than not, priests and ministers do not want their interpretation of the word of God to be challenged or supplanted by a work of popular art or literature that has the power to reach a much broader audience than any individual sermon. They fear not only a loss of power and authority over their brothers and sisters, but also that a popular and wildly inaccurate new reading of the Bible will corrupt the faith of the individual Christian, or the integrity of Christianity itself. They recall Christ's warning against false prophets and stand guard against any and all who appear to be such figures. Hence, out of fear, churches and individual preachers tend to condemn unauthorized Christian narratives out of hand, even when the moral of these narratives can be safely summarized as "thou shalt love thy neighbor as thyself." These moral condemnations sometimes lead to efforts at censorship — either direct or indirect (including calls for the cutting of funding for the National Endowment for the Arts) — consequently placing conservative Christian values at odds with freedom of speech and the First Amendment, adding another troubling layer to an already emotionally fraught conflict of values. Some of the most famous examples of these controversies include the outcry against Andres Serrano's "Piss Christ" and Chris Ofili's elephant dung-covered painting "The Holy Virgin Mary," the latter of which outraged Mayor Rudolph Giuliani and many New York Catholics in 1999. (For a particularly insightful essay on the ramifications of the Ofili controversy, see Andrea Fraser's "A 'Sensation' Chronicle.")

To paraphrase an oft-asked question during the 2008 presidential election: "Is America ready for a black depiction of God?" If it is Morgan Freeman, then yes! Freeman plays God in the film comedies *Bruce Almighty* (2003) and *Evan Almighty* (pictured above, 2007, Universal Pictures).

Some of the books, films, television programs, and works of art examined in this book were deliberately designed to provoke a strong reaction from a Puritanical audience on principle, others were intended to generate controversy to generate profits, and still others are seriously intended religious statements. Sometimes it is difficult to separate these motivations, and some pieces were crafted for all of the above reasons. For example, should Dan Brown's work be treated as serious theological statements when they are clearly, first and foremost, thriller novels? And what of the disclaimers attached to both Chaucer's *Canterbury Tales* and Kevin Smith's *Dogma*? Do they show an eleventh hour repentance that undermines the power of a work originally intended to be taken totally seriously, or should we all just pretend that those disclaimers were never written? By and large, the scholars who have written essays for this collection have decided to take apologetic views of the works and their creators, discussing original intentions, offering serious and nuanced critiques of their controversial theology. Some scholars come to strong and controversial conclusions, while others leave the solution to an arguably unsolvable puzzle to you, the reader, to determine.

For my part, as the editor, one of my chief concerns in collecting essays from this variety of genres, time periods, nationalities, and religious sects is that I believe all of these works have something to teach American readers in particular about Christianity. Since the birth of the nation, the darker side of American religious belief has been unduly influenced by the worldview evident in Jonathan Edwards' "Sinners in the Hands of an Angry God." Many of the critics whose essays are included in this collection share my desire to see the misanthropy inherent in the worldview mitigated. After all, this kind of religion underlies some of the greatest historical and cultural sins committed in America in the name of religion. Frederick Douglas and Martin Luther King both wrote strong statements about the role Christianity played in supporting the institution of slavery and of the hypocrisy of Christians who did not support abolition or equality for blacks in America. Norman Dain observed in "Madness and the Stigma of Sin in American Christianity" that one of the reasons that public funding for treatment for individuals with mental illnesses is entirely inadequate is because individuals with such conditions are falsely believed to be sinners and unworthy of treatment.

Authors and cultural critics from overseas have matched these criticisms made by American citizens. As a case in point, Anthony Burgess, author of the classic British science fiction novel *A Clockwork Orange* (1962), wrote a defense of his censored work that was, in its way, illustrative of the differences between British and American religious and political values. His novel was originally intended to be a redemption story that concerned the reform of a young gangbanger who ultimately "grows bored with the violence and recognizes that human energy is better expended on creation than destruction" (vii). While the book was published around the world in its unedited form, Burgess was horrified to discover that his American publisher refused to include his intended ending and, instead, omitted the final chapter that featured the redemption segment. Consequently, the American version of the book ended at precisely the point when protagonist Alex DeLarge declares himself an unrepentant rapist and evildoer. The film adaptation directed by Stanley Kubrick also followed the lead of the American publisher, joining the eviscerated American version of the novel in inverting Burgess' intended moral.

As Burgess wrote in his introduction to the 1986 edition of the book, "A Clockwork Orange Resucked,"

> My New York publisher believed that my twenty-first chapter was a sellout. It was veddy, veddy British, don't you know. It was bland and it showed a Pelagian unwillingness to accept that a human being could be a model of unregenerable evil. The Americans, he said in effect, were tougher than the British and could face up to reality. Soon they would be facing up to it in Vietnam. My book was Kennedyan and accepted the notion of moral progress. What was really wanted was a Nixonian book with no shred of optimism in it. Let us have evil prancing on the page and, up to the very last line, sneering in the face of all the inherited beliefs, Jewish, Christian, Muslim and Holy Roller, about people being able to make themselves better. Such a book would be sensational, and so it is. But I do not think it is a fair picture of human life.
>
> I do not think so because, by definition, a human being is endowed with free will. He can use this to choose between good and evil. If he can only perform good or only perform evil, then he is a clockwork orange — meaning that he has the appearance of an organism lovely with colour and juice but is in fact only a clockwork toy to be wound up by God or the Devil or (since this is increasingly replacing both) the Almighty State. It is as inhuman to be totally good as it is to be totally evil. The important thing is moral choice [viii–ix].

Burgess's sentiments seem to me to be very Christian and very much in the spirit of Origen (see Vigna). They also speak to the main themes of several of the essays included here, especially the intersection of Christianity and art.

In a similar vein, the dark side of American Christianity has been criticized by those who arrive to the country as immigrants and find themselves victims of racially and religiously motivated bigotries that point to larger problems at the heart of American Christianity. One of the most historically significant victims of anti-immigrant sentiment was Bartolomeo Vanzetti — an anarchist who may have been wrongly convicted of murder and executed primarily on the basis of his ideological beliefs and immigrant status. While Vanzetti's outspoken supporters included Albert Einstein, Dorothy Parker, H.G. Wells, and George Bernard Shaw, his left-wing views and ethnic background did not inspire empathy from most American conservatives then or now. Indeed, one could see where his inflammatory views would have the potential to offend a great number of 21st century American readers, especially the portrait he paints of American culture, and American justice, in a January

12, 1911, letter to his sister, Luigia. The letter is damning to the point of sounding wholly anti–American, but one might wonder what experiences he had that compelled him to develop such feelings about the United States. He wrote:

> Here, public justice is based on force and brutality, but not that the foreigner, and in particular, the Italian, should dare to enforce it with energetic means: for him there are the police batons, prisons and the penal code. Don't think that America is so civil, though there are no qualities missing in the American people and more yet in the cosmopolitan population, if you take away their dollars and the elegance of their dress, you'll find semi-barbarians, fanatics and delinquents. No country in the world hosts so many religions and religious extravagances like the holy United States. Here, he who makes money is good, it doesn't matter if he steals or poisons. Many have and are making their fortune by selling their dignity, spying on and persecuting their compatriots. Many reduce morality to a level lower than that which nature bestowed on animals [qtd. in Muscio 28].

These words are cruel, but there is truth in them worth pondering. When Christian values take second place to the concerns of white privilege, the amassment of wealth and prestige, then the religion of Mammon has both supplanted authentic Christianity and masqueraded as the religion of Jesus of Nazareth. However, this is not to say that American religion and American culture is beyond remedying. The patient is critically ill, but has not flatlined yet. Like Burgess, I believe that living, breathing people are capable of change, and if good examples of true Christianity taken from art, literature, history, film, music, and theology can be placed before individuals who have embraced a broken form of Christianity, there is always the hope that they will see the error of their ways and consider reforming their own religious views. If enough individuals are inspired by this book to look within themselves to determine for themselves the extent to which they are embracing a healthy or unhealthy religion, an authentic or a corrupt inversion of Christianity, then there is hope. There is hope that those Americans who have embraced fire-and-brimstone Christianity may, at long last, learn to love themselves, love their neighbors, love their enemies, and love God—even if God turns out to be a big old softie and not the hanging judge they had been raised to worship and fear.

This is by no means the first and only book to analyze the extent to which works of classic literature are orthodox or not and authentically Christian or not. *Milton and Heresy* (2009), edited by Stephen B. Dobranski and John P. Rumrich, asks why an author who supported the execution of Charles I, opposed infant baptism, and supported divorce and polygamy could be deemed a religious conservative. *Dante and the Unorthodox* (2005), edited by James Miller, examines Dante's anticlericalism, female prophet figures, and the pagans that he places in Heaven in the *Commedia* (one of whom, ultimately, may be Virgil, should Beatrice's prayer on his behalf be heeded). *Dante and the Unorthodox* also deals heavily with the writings of T.S. Eliot, which is why he is not covered in this text. A similar book has been written about the influence of the Wycliffite heresy on Chaucer and his contemporaries— Andrew Cole's *Literature and Heresy in the Age of Chaucer* (2008).

Just as these books have asked literary scholars to reconsider their rarified visions of the three most venerable Christian authors of the Western literary canon, other books have asked readers to see that which is "religious" in secularist or heretical figures. In *Myth* (1997), Laurence Coupe argues that even those who attempt to start new religions or eliminate religions altogether are ultimately doomed by the "anxiety of influence" to reflect the belief system that has come immediately before and start a new myth for a new generation. Consequently, Sigmund Freud not only founded a new science and academic discipline but a new religious worldview based on an unsubstantiated prehistoric fratricide myth. Similarly, Coupe argues, Karl Marx not only founded a political party but also wrote a secularized Christian myth that prophesized an earthbound Socialist paradise in an eschatological future. (Coupe did not use this example, but I wonder if his reasoning might also explain why John Lennon's "Imagine" calls for a world without religion yet seems to be the most fervent of hymns.)

Other works of cultural criticism have found theological ideas embedded in popular culture artifacts that are worth serious academic attention. Eric Michael Mazur's *Encyclopedia of Religion in Film* (2011) is a superb reference book replete with insightful essays that examine the full scope of film history to uncover the most culturally significant religious films representing all of the major world religions produced by the most prominent international film communities. I, myself, am proud to have included essays on the unorthodox Catholicism found in vampire films and the works of Sergio Leone and Luc Besson. Of course, Mazur's text is only one of the most recent and most comprehensive efforts in the project of examining religion and film. While it is not a book that is solely about film, Chris Hedges's *Losing Moses on the Freeway: The 10 Commandments in America* (2006) explores how *The Decalogue*, Krzysztof Kiéslowski's television miniseries about the Ten Commandments in the modern day, offers a more compelling and loving model of how contemporary Christians should follow God's laws than the self-righteous and authoritarian model offered by Bible-thumping fundamentalist Christians and neoconservatives. (This is a theme he explores further in *American Fascists: The Christian Right and the War on America* [2008], a Christian book that condemns the reactionary followers of Pat Robertson who wish to transform America from a democracy into a super-nationalist theocracy.)

Introduction   17

In addition to these texts, several books on religion in comic books and graphic novels have appeared recently, including Ben Saunders's monograph *Do the Gods Wear Capes? Spirituality, Fantasy, and Superheroes* (2011) and the anthology *Graven Images: Religion in Comic Books and Graphic Novels* (2010), edited by A. David Lewis and Christine Hoff Kraemer. Similar books have also examined religion in television, popular music, art, and so on, and they are too many to enumerate here. However, a great number of them are *Gospel According to _____* books (such as *The Gospel According to Oprah* and *The Gospel According to Peanuts*) that are examined in greater detail by Mazur in the essay he wrote for this collection. In focusing on the religious messages of popular art, these books collectively elevate the literary and theological significance of what was once deemed "trash" culture—with fascinating results.

As comprehensive as the above-mentioned books are, they are limited by their focus on genre and time period. One of the goals of this anthology is to collapse the difference between literary and popular culture studies, and the walls standing between academic disciplines, thereby offering a truly interdisciplinary study of authentic and alternative Christianity in fiction that covers both popular and elite texts and eschews snap qualitative judgments. Indeed, as A. David Lewis and Christine Hof Kraemer have argued, "particularly in light of Americans' increasing detachment from mainline churches, the religious explorations taking place in and around popular culture should be taken seriously as one of the ways Americans express their religiosity" (3–4). Of course, the scope of this anthology, and its interdisciplinary leanings, make it an ideal secondary source for undergraduate Western literature and humanities courses that include the subjects of many of these essays on their syllabi (i.e., Dante, Milton, Wilde, Whitman, Dickens, the Founding Fathers, etc.).

In recent years, excellent work has been done within academia and for the popular market on the very socially relevant, very contested, and very political topic of authentic Christianity in America. Robin Meyers, for one, has written several books arguing that Americans adopt a more progressive view of Christianity (which he calls "underground Christianity" instead of authentic Christianity, but the concepts are similar). Among his works are *The Underground Church: Reclaiming the Subversive Way of Jesus* (2012), *Saving Jesus from the Church: How to Stop Worshiping Christ and Start Following Jesus* (2010), and *Why the Christian Right Is Wrong: A Minister's Manifesto for Taking Back Your Faith, Your Flag, Your Future* (2008).

Joerg Rieger's scholarship concerns the history of progressive forces in Christianity, including historical liberation movements in the United States. He has argued recently that still more Christians should embrace the economic justice causes underlying the Occupy Wall Street movement. (Notably, some members of the Occupy movement agree, as one headline-making sign held aloft by a protestor read; "Obama is not a dark-skinned socialist. You're thinking of Jesus.") Among Rieger's works are *Christ & Empire: From Paul to Postcolonial Times* (2007), *No Rising Tide: Theology, Economics, and the Future* (2009), *Globalization and Theology* (2010), and an upcoming book co-authored with Kwok Pui-Lan called *Occupy Religion: Theology of the Multitude*.

Interested parties should also consider consulting the other works written by contributors to this collection, most of which speak to themes that this book explores. They are noted in the About the Contributors section at the end of the book.

This collection of essays is a continuation of the work scholars such as these have already done, but it involves the application of the principle of authentic Christianity to narratives from other disciplines — works of literature, films, TV shows, comic strips, personal manifestos, and other narratives. During my formative years, my parish priest admonished me to stay away from works of art and literature that had been condemned by the Catholic Church. I listened to him for several years and I regret that I did. Later I decided that — as a literate, thinking person — I needed to seek out at least some of these condemned works to see just how "evil" they really were. When several such works turned out to be not only *not* evil but, indeed, quite moral, I knew it was time to go on safari and examine every classic work that I had been hitherto avoiding on the grounds of its suspect Christianity. These days, the only artistic works I avoid exposing myself to are those that appear, from a distance, to have no artistic or moral merit whatsoever (i.e., advertising, television news, *The Human Centipede* films of Tom Six, and the in-name-only adaptation of *Dante's Inferno* video game), not those that authority figures have told me to avoid for suspect reasons.

As I designed this book, I invited scholars to help me complete my odyssey through landmark works of fiction and nonfiction that have been dubbed morally suspect by Church authorities and consider the extent to which these judgments have been fair. Together, we will also examine several landmark works that the Church has deemed "safe" for public consumption that may also, to a degree, undermine the very authority the establishment Church guards so jealously.

While I was once tempted to write this whole book myself, I was worried that attempting to do so would brand me a dilettante and an egomaniac. I was not an expert in all of the academic disciplines that I would be engaged with throughout — theology, political science, theater, art, literature, history — nor did I know all of these writers and storytellers, the history of these works, or the cultural context in which these works existed. It was apparent that I would need help from an array of Virgils and Beatrices to guide me through all of these sacred and profane texts and to help me give them the fair chance that they may have been denied by the anti-intellectual contingent of Christian thinkers and believers. It would also be interesting to see such an eclectic mix of texts examined from so many methodological angles. Of further interest would be the varying political and religious perspectives of the contributors, many of whom never disclosed their ideologies to me in advance of being commissioned to write an essay. I have disclosed my biases to you here, in this introduction. I know for a fact that several of the contributors do not share my political party or Christian denominational allegiance, so each scholar's work should be judged on its own terms and not solely as a piece of the overall argument made by me here or as a part of the narrative thrust of the book as a whole.

The essays are divided into two parts, "Rewritten Bibles, Alternative Christs" and "Angels and Demons Among Us: The Politics and Economics of Heaven and Hell in Popular Culture." The first part deals with authors, philosophers, poets, and thinkers who have dared to edit, update, modernize, or replace the Bible, and who have presented their own interpretations of the values Jesus Christ represented and what humans should do to imitate him. The second part examines representations of evil in the Bible, literature, and popular culture and considers how religious Christians could strive to be better themselves and the extent to which they are called to combat corruption in society or forgive it in their enemies.

Part I begins with perhaps the most famous alternative Bible ever written. Presidential historian Tim H. Blessing examines Thomas Jefferson's perennially controversial religious views alongside those of other foundational American leaders, including George Washington and Andrew Jackson, in his essay "Revolution by Other Means: Jefferson, the Jefferson Bible, and Jesus." Jefferson famously created his own Gospel Harmony by melding the four canonical gospels into one coherent narrative and — in the process — took it upon himself to excise passages that he felt were unhistorical or corrupted Jesus's message. While some commentators have argued that the endeavor reveals Jefferson to be a secularist humanist, Blessing demonstrates that Jefferson was clearly a religious man who believed in angels, heaven, and hell, and who sought to rescue Christ from being defined solely by his foolish Biblical biographers. Blessing also discusses the nature of Jefferson's anti–Semitism and its troubling but fascinating role in inspiring the Founding Father to complete not one but two versions of his Gospel Harmony.

The second essay is "Portraying Jesus as Human: *The Last Temptation of*

Christ," Katherine Brown Downey's case study of one of the most controversial rewritings of the Christ story. She considers all that is authentically Christian about both the classic novel by Nikos Kazantzakis and the film adaptation directed by Martin Scorsese, as well as the political and theological firestorms surrounding the film's release in 1988.

Marc Lucht's essay, "Nietzsche and Tolstoy on Authentic Christianity," challenges preconceived notions of Nietzsche's religious beliefs by demonstrating how the philosopher's harsh criticisms of establishment Christianity do not extend to the historical Jesus, whom Nietzsche admired. Nietzsche's views emerge as strikingly similar to Leo Tolstoy's post-conversion writings about Jesus as the ultimate peacemaker.

In "Amnesty for the Devil," Gerald S. Vigna writes about the theological proposition that, at the end of time, God may abolish hell and allow all humans and angels entrance into Heaven. Vigna examines the treatment of the doctrine of apokatastasis (a.k.a. universalism) in the theological writings of Origen of Alexandria and Hans Urs von Balthasar, in C.S. Lewis' novel *The Great Divorce*, and in the Clint Eastwood film *Unforgiven*. The essay also considers the socio-political ramifications of a theology that posits eternal damnation for sinners by examining the harshness of the American criminal justice system.

Co-writer and director Franco Zeffirelli collaborated with Anthony Burgess and Suso Cecchi d'Amico to tell a story of the life of Christ synthesized from the Gospels and historical research in the miniseries *Jesus of Nazareth* (1977, Incorporated Television Company). Pictured above is Jesus (Robert Powell) in his crown of thorns, shortly before the crucifixion. Zeffirelli was one of Martin Scorsese's most outspoken critics following the release of *The Last Temptation of Christ* (1988).

In "Lamb Unslain: Non-human Animals and Shelley's Panentheism," Ruth Vanita argues that Hindu philosophical texts influenced Percy Shelley's worldview and passionate opposition to cruelty against non-human animals. Shelley rereads the Bible in an attempt to expand Christian compassion and ultimately envisions non-violence to humans as impossible without non-violence to non-humans, and human dignity as inseparable from animal dignity.

Gustavo A. Rodríguez Martín demonstrates how George Bernard Shaw's religious beliefs were informed by his life and politics in "Shaw's Subversion of Biblical Language." Rodríguez Martín provides textual evidence drawn from Shaw's personal writings, essays, and several of his plays, including *Androcles and the Lion*, *Man and Superman*, and *Back to Methuselah*. Those who read this essay after Lucht's will see parallels between Shaw's view of Christianity and Tolstoy's and Nietzsche's, and will understand the reasoning behind Shaw's oft-made joke that "Christianity might be a good thing if anyone ever tried it."

In *"Song of Myself*: Teaching Whitman's New Bible Today," Tracy Floreani demonstrates how Walt Whitman's nineteenth-century opus *Leaves of Grass* appeals to a modern, pluralistic American sensibility and has much to offer twenty-first century students from a variety of religious, ethnic, and political backgrounds. She concludes that, in numerous cases, Whitman's theology has provided an alternative, liberating faith to students who have struggled with the sexual, intellectual, and social restrictions placed upon them by traditional Christianity.

The second part begins with a brief history of Christianity in popular culture since the 1960s. As Eric Michael Mazur observes in his essay "The Gospel According to Comic Strips: On *Peanuts* and *The Far Side*" the best-selling book *The Gospel According to Peanuts* (1965) helped launch a cottage industry of books that explored Biblical themes in popular culture, including 798 similar works offering *The Gospel According to*—among others—Bob Dylan, Oprah Winfrey, The Beatles, *Twilight*, *Harry Potter*, and J.R.R. Tolkien. Mazur contends that this phenomenon can be explained, in part, by the enormous changes in American culture from the 1960s to the present. The result has been a growing comfort with, and increasing informality of, religious expression, which can be seen in the plethora of books exploring theological concepts and conventions in popular culture, not only in *Peanuts* and *B.C.* but in the edgier, more satirical commentaries on religion provided by Gary Larson's *Far Side* cartoon library.

Val Nolan's "Religious Discourse in *Lost* and *Battlestar Galactica*" considers the cultural significance of two recent, popular genre shows in a post–9/11 television landscape and explores their subversive theological underpinnings. While viewers who like their science fiction and fantasy free of the taint of theology tended to reject the religious content of the two shows as half-baked, Nolan explains that *Lost* and *Battlestar Galactica* both had profound messages to communicate about life, belief, community, and the dangerous tendency of religion to divide rather than unite.

"The Radical Theology of Krzysztof Kieslowski's *Decalogue*" is Matthew

Yde's essay about the classic 10-hour Polish film named by Roger Ebert as one of the best films ever made. According to Yde, *The Decalogue* shines a light on the most fundamental questions of what it means to be a human being, illuminating the relevance and even the complexity of the Ten Commandments within the context of our modern world in unparalleled and unconventional ways. Yde also shows how *The Decalogue* calls upon us to view the Commandments as encouragement to feel empathy for our fellow human beings and fellow sinners instead of as a justification for our own tendency towards judgmentalism and misanthropy.

In "Fanaticism and Familicide from *Wieland* to *The Shining*," Dara Downey examines Gothic fiction's portrayal of religious fanaticism in the domestic sphere from the first American Gothic novel through Stephen King's landmark bestseller up to the 2001 Bill Paxton film *Frailty*. Downey notes that all these narratives feature a mentally unhinged patriarch who has visions of supernatural beings that prompt him to murder members of his own family. She considers how some of these stories grant the insane religious figure charisma and gravitas while others seek to undercut his legitimacy and narrative centrality by challenging his theological worldview and empowering his (often female) adversaries.

In "From Bedford Falls to Punxsutawney: Refashioning *A Christmas Carol*" Grace Moore explores how Charles Dickens hoped to make a fortune from his novella, but also firmly believed that it could play an important role in bringing about social reform. Ebenezer Scrooge's tale has been adapted into numerous stage plays, cartoons, and films, and has inspired radically different re-imaginings that have themselves become classic holiday films about personal redemption, including *It's a Wonderful Life* (1946), *Scrooged* (1988) and *Groundhog Day* (1993). While Frank Capra's film shares Dickens's concerns regarding the vulnerability of families and communities in the face of risk, bank fraud, and finance capitalism, later adaptations—like *Groundhog Day*—focus their attention on romantic subplots and the rehabilitation of the individual Scrooge-figure, rather than on what "Scrooge" might do for his community once he has been re-claimed.

Finally, Joerg Rieger's essay "Reclaiming the Relation of Religion, Politics, and Economics" acts as a closing argument for the book as a whole, explaining how the legacy of progressive Christianity and the example of Occupy Wall Street can help contemporary Christians bring an end to dogmatic thinking in politics, religion, and economics, and to restore practical, humanist, and compassionate real-world concerns to primacy in all of these areas of life worldwide.

Collectively, these essays consider how some of the greatest thinkers and storytellers in the history of Western philosophy, literature, film, and television have wrestled with the message of Jesus of Nazareth. The essays touch upon a broad range of topics, some dealing with issues of faith, economics, human sexuality, and "just war" theory, but they are united by their interest in what Jesus really preached, who has the authority to interpret Jesus's message, and how one might best live a life that embraces and reenacts Jesus's value system in twenty-first-century context. These essays consider what Jesus's message truly was. They consider the extent to which the churches founded in his name have and have not accurately represented his values and behaved in a truly Christian fashion. Finally, they consider the extent to which the individual Christian should have the right and the freedom to defy authority figures within the establishment Christian churches whenever those authorities seem to have strayed from the path of righteousness and asked their followers to think and act in ways that are not authentically Christian. Some essays even consider the possibility that Christianity's day is done and assert that the Christian faith needs discarding altogether. Asking difficult questions about the nature of Christian faith and its role in global and domestic politics may be dangerous, but it is still more dangerous asking no questions whatsoever. Just as Socrates maintained that the unexamined life is not worth living, it is equally true that the unexamined faith is not worth practicing. The questions this book raises are fraught with controversy and the possible answers the authors herein provide may be more controversial still. In many ways this is, admittedly, a dangerous book. However, the contents of this collection should provide food for thought and prayer that will, hopefully, help inform any intelligent, moral, and devout discussion of the role of Christianity in the modern world. It may shake some readers up, but I believe Jesus would support shaking some readers up. After all, he certainly was adept at shaking up *his* audiences.

Works Cited

Anthony, Susan B. "Susan B. Anthony." *The Quotable Atheist: Ammunition for Non-Believers, Political Junkies, Gadflies, and Those Generally Hell-Bound.* Ed. Jack Huberman. New York: Nation Books, 2006.
Brown, Dan. *The Da Vinci Code.* New York: Anchor, 2009.
Burgess, Anthony. "Introduction: A Clockwork Orange Resucked." *A Clockwork Orange.* New York: W. W. Norton, 1995. v–xi.
Cole, Andrew. *Literature and Heresy in the Age of Chaucer (Cambridge Studies in Medieval Literature).* Cambridge: Cambridge University Press, 2008.
Coupe, Laurence. *Myth.* London: Routledge, 1997.
Dain, Norman. "Madness and the Stigma of Sin in American Christianity." *Stigma and Mental Illness.* Ed. Paul Jay Fink and Allah Tasman. Washington, D.C.: American Psychiatric Press, 1992.
David, Jefferson. *Inaugural Address as Provisional President of the Confederacy.* Montgomery, Alabama, February 18, 1861.

Dewey, Arthur J. "Jesus as a Peasant Artisan." *Profiles of Jesus*. Ed. Roy W. Hoover. Santa Rosa, CA: Polebridge Press, 2002. 73–86.

_____, Roy W. Hoover, Lane McGaughy, and Daryl D. Schmidt. *The Authentic Letters of Paul*. Salem, OR: Polebridge Press, 2010.

Dobranski, Stephen B., and John P. Rumrich, eds. *Milton and Heresy*. Cambridge: Cambridge University Press, 2009.

Ebert, Roger. "Great Movies: The Gospel According to St. Matthew (1964)." *Roger Ebert.com*. February 24, 2004. http://rogerebert.suntimes.com/apps/pbcs.dll/article?AID=/20040314/REVIEWS08/403140301/1023.

Edwards, Jonathan. "Sinners in the Hands of an Angry God." *Sinners in the Hands of an Angry God and Other Puritan Sermons (Dover Thrift Editions)*. Mineola, NY: Dover, 2005. 171–185.

Fraser, Andrea. "A 'Sensation' Chronicle." *Museum Highlights: The Writings of Andrea Fraser (Writing Art)*. Cambridge: MIT Press, 2007. 179–212.

Hedges, Chris. *American Fascists: The Christian Right and the War on America*. New York: Free Press, 2008.

_____. *Losing Moses on the Freeway: The 10 Commandments in America*. New York: Free Press, 2006.

Lewis, A. David, and Christine Hof Kraemer. "Introduction." *Graven Images: Religion in Comic Books & Graphic Novels*. London: Continnum, 2010.

Mazur, Eric, ed. *Encyclopedia of Religion and Film*. Santa Barbara, CA: ABC-CLIO, 2011.

Miller, James, ed. *Dante and the Unorthodox*. Waterloo, Ontario: Wilfrid Laurier University Press, 2005.

Muscio, Giuliana, Joseph Sciorra, et al. *Mediated Ethnicity: New Italian-American Cinema*. New York: John D. Calandra Italian American Institute, 2010. 28.

Robbins, Ruth. *Oscar Wilde: Writer's Lives*. London: Continuum, 2011.

Saunders, Ben. *Do The Gods Wear Capes? Spirituality, Fantasy, and Superheroes (New Directions In Religion & Literature)*. London: Continuum, 2011.

Warner, Marina. "Fantasy's Power and Peril." *The New York Times*. Dec. 16, 2001. June 25, 2010.

Wood, Michael. "Damned If You Do...." *Simon of the Desert: Criterion Collection Vol. 450*. DVD. Criterion Collection, 2009.

PART I. REWRITTEN BIBLES, ALTERNATIVE CHRISTS

Revolution by Other Means: Jefferson, the Jefferson Bible, and Jesus

TIM H. BLESSING

It would be difficult to dispute that Thomas Jefferson was, at times, a ruthless, amoral, and unscrupulous politician. While Secretary of State, he secretly helped create a newspaper to attack his boss, President Washington, he supported the paper (and its editor) with funds drawn from State Department accounts; and he leaked secret information taken from State Department files so that the paper (the *National Gazette*) could publicize Jefferson's views without Jefferson actually having to confront Washington (Burns; see, however, Malone, 423–427). Once he had assumed the presidency, himself, Jefferson pushed his followers to find ways to impeach politically inconvenient judges (Bernstein). Later, despite having won the presidency, in part, by charging President Adams and his followers with violating the press's liberties, he urged his followers to use local and state laws to harass newspapers that opposed him with a few "wholesome punishments" (Levy; Jefferson, "Second Inaugural," avalon.law.yale.edu).

While acknowledging Jefferson's duplicity and ruthlessness in politics, most historians have been willing to accept at face value his protestations regarding religion. He, after all, had placed on his tombstone "HERE WAS BURIED THOMAS JEFFERSON [—] AUTHOR OF THE DECLARATION OF AMERICAN INDEPENDENCE[;] OF THE STATUTE OF VIRGINIA FOR RELIGIOUS FREEDOM[;] AND FATHER OF THE UNIVERSITY OF VIRGINIA...."

His tolerance, his deism, his belief in a rational approach to religion are writ large in accepted history — and this essay will not challenge the broad outline of this dogma. There are, however, devils in the details of Jefferson's religious beliefs and the accepted texts of his beliefs must, in some instances, be tinted and footnoted.

We need to turn first to the religious shades cast by many American leaders during the time of the American Revolution and the Early Republic. As Gordon Wood has noted, "most of the founding fathers had not put much emotional stock in religion.... As enlightened gentlemen, they abhorred the 'great gloomy superstition disseminated by ignorant illiberal preachers' and looked forward to the day when 'the phantom of darkness will be dispelled by the rays of science, and the bright charms of rising civilization'" (Wood, 330).

The leading founders embodied their views in their actions. On June 7, 1797, for instance, the Senate of the United States unanimously passed a "Treaty of Peace and Friendship" with the pasha of Tripoli, a so-called "Barbary pirate" who had been raiding American ships and holding American sailors hostage. The eleventh article of this treaty has, deservedly, attracted attention over the years. It reads:

> As the Government of the United States of America is not, in any sense, founded on the Christian religion, — as it has in itself no character of enmity against the laws, religion, or tranquility, of Mussulmen, — and as the said States never entered into any war or act of hostility against any Mahometan nation, it is declared by the parties that no pretext arising from religious opinions shall ever produce an interruption of the harmony existing between the two countries [avalon.law.yale.edu].

Article 11 did not, at the time, excite consternation. The treaty was widely available in newspapers and it had been read on the floor of the Senate. The vote, outside of its unanimity, was not exceptional in any way and the Senate moved onto other business. Retrospectively, its implications regarding the founding generation's "original intent" are, here in the early twenty-first century, significant. Within less than a decade of the writing of the United States Constitution, the Senate, in very humdrum fashion, put the government on record as not being "in any sense" a Christian nation (Gould, stephenjaygould.org).

Seven years earlier, George Washington had undertaken a tour of New England as a "goodwill tour" promoting the new government he now headed. The Touro congregation at the Sephardic synagogue in Newport, Rhode Island, anticipating Washington's arrival in their area, had expressed their pleasure at being included in "a Government, which to bigotry gives no sanction, to persecution no assistance — but generously affording to all Liberty of conscience, and immunities of Citizenship: — deeming every one, of whatever Nation, tongue, or language equal parts of the great governmental Machine" (avalon.law.yale.edu).

Washington responded that year with what has become one of the most famous of his letters— now called the "Touro Synagogue Letter":

The Citizens of the United States of America have a right to applaud themselves for having given to mankind examples of an enlarged and liberal policy: a policy worthy of imitation.... It is now no more that toleration is spoken of as if it was by the indulgence of one class of people that another enjoyed the exercise of their inherent natural rights, for happily, the Government of the United States, which gives to bigotry no sanction, to persecution no assistance, requires only that they who live under its protection should demean themselves as good citizens, in giving it on all occasions their effectual support ... every one shall sit in safety under his own vine and fig tree, and there shall be none to make him afraid [George Washington Papers, Library of Congress, Series 2 Letterbooks, Letterbook 39].

In fact, the George Washington who has been pictured in innumerable (and romanticized) etchings, sketchings, posters, and tourist trinkets as kneeling in prayer at Valley Forge quite likely did not exist. On February 1, 1800 (or forty-nine days after Washington's death), Jefferson recorded in his private notes:

[Benjamin] Rush tells me that he had it from Asa Green that when the clergy addressed Genl. Washington on his departure from the govmt, it was observed in their consultation that he had never, on any occasion said a word to the public which showed a belief in the Xn religion and they thot they should so pen their address as to force him at length to declare publicly whether he was a Christian or not. They did so. However he observed the old fox was too cunning for them. He answered every article of their address particularly except that, which he passed over without notice. Rush observes he never did say a word on the subject in any of his public papers except in his valedictory letter to the Governors of the states when he resigned his commission in the army, wherein he speaks of the benign influence of the Christian religion. "I know that Gouverneur Morris, who pretended to be in his secrets & believed himself to be so, has often told me that Genl. Washington believed no more of that system [Christianity] than he himself did" [Jefferson in Bergh, ed., 433–434].

The import of Jefferson's notes is supported by a pastor of the Episcopal Church in Philadelphia which the Washingtons attended during Washington's presidency:

I can only state the following facts: that, as Pastor of the Episcopal Church, observing that, on Sacrament Sundays, George Washington, immediately after the desk and pulpit services, went out with the greater part of the congregation ... I considered it my duty, in a Sermon on Public Worship, to state the unhappy tendency of example, particularly of those in elevated stations, who uniformly turned their backs upon the celebration of the Lord's Supper.... A few days after, in conversation ... with a Senator of the United States, he [the Senator] told me he had dined the day before with the President, who, in the course of conversation at the table, said that ... he had received a very just rebuke from the pulpit for always leaving the church before the administration of the Sacrament; ... that he had never sufficiently considered the influence of his example, and that he would not again give cause for the repetition of the reproof; and that, as he had never been a communicant, were he to become one then, it would be imputed to an ostentatious display of religious zeal, arising altogether from his elevated station. Accordingly, he never afterwards came on the morning of sacrament Sunday, ... [James Abercrombie, qtd. in Sprague, 394].

Even the most religious and, by far, the most enthusiastically devout of the early presidents, Andrew Jackson, not only refused to support a movement to form a Christian (read Protestant) Party, he, perhaps more importantly, also refused to halt mail deliveries on Sunday. In response to a call by a supporter, the Evangelical minister Ezra Stiles Ely, to form a Christian (read Protestant) party, Jackson wrote to Ely: "Amongst the greatest blessings secured to us under our Constitution is the liberty of worshipping God as our conscience dictates" (Andrew Jackson to Ezra Stiles, qtd. in Haskell, 406; for Ely sermon see *The Reformer*, 7:135–137).

Jackson's point of view indicates that even the more religious of American political leaders were not so quick to call for religious obedience *supra* the Constitution or America's libertarian past. Congress simply refused to listen to those Protestants who wanted a stricter observance of the Sabbath. After more than a decade of petitions from evangelicals on the subject and with almost two full decades in which the voters could have made their preferences known, the Senate's "1829 Report on the Subject of Mails on the Sabbath" declared that the Senate was "a civil institution, wholly destitute of religious authority" and concluded that "the line cannot be too strongly drawn between church and state" (U.S. Senate Report, qtd. in Lambert, 2010; "Review of a report of the Committee, to whom was referred the several petitions on the subject of mails on the Sabbath; presented to the Senate of the United States, January 16, 1829, by the Hon. Mr. Johnson, of Kentucky, chairman of said committee").

There was, however, another side to American political life in the founding decades. While Minister Ely had little luck with his crusade against Sunday mail deliveries, the cultural magnet of religion grew ever more powerful.

During the Constitutional era, several states decided to rewrite their constitutions. Generally, this has been seen as a conservative reaction against state constitutions which were either perceived as too radical, too threatening to coastal elites, or simply too unworkable (or some combination thereof). The most important of the rewrites was almost certainly the one undertaken by Pennsylvania. Pennsylvania's 1776 Constitution had been the most radical of the state Revolutionary era constitutions; in fact, it was known as the "Radical" Constitution. It had been put into place without ratification, without consultation with the populace, and without even much deliberation. When Pennsylvania wrote a new constitution in 1789–1790, its constitutional convention wrote the new constitution in a very deliberate fashion, debated it at considerable length, and enacted it only after a pause of a number of months in which delegates returned to their districts to sample their constituents' opinions. Despite a period of furious debate over the provisions for the State Senate during December and early January, by late January the people of Pennsylvania seem to have found the process so unexceptional that they lost interest in it. Even the more radical newspapers in Pennsylvania stopped reporting on it by early February. The populace accepted its installation without murmur in September of 1790.

Yet, in the convention's debates over religious qualifications for officeholding, something odd had occurred — something which suggests that the skepticism and deistic coloration of America's leaders did not quite match what was occurring at lower political levels. A committee of distinguished state leaders had created the first draft of the new state constitution in December of 1789 and reported a bill of rights that had as its fourth section: "That no person who acknowledges the being of a God, and a future state of rewards and punishments shall, on account of his religious sentiments, be disqualified to hold any office of trust or profit under this commonwealth" (Pennsylvania State Constitutional Convention, 1789–1790).

By European standards, this was remarkably liberal; it opened the door to political office not only to Christians, but to Jews and Moslems. Some delegates, nevertheless, felt that it was not sufficiently liberal. On February 3, one Philadelphia County delegate, William Robinson, Jr., moved to strike "and a future state of rewards" from the draft. Apparently before a vote on that motion could be held (parliamentary procedure being somewhat looser in the eighteenth century), he made a second motion to also strike "who acknowledges the being of a God, and a future state of rewards and punishments." Robinson's motion was defeated 13–47. Most of the votes in favor of Robinson's motion came from (supposedly conservative) Federalists, while those who were later to be identified with "liberal" Jeffersonian agrarianism, and certainly with Jefferson, himself generally voted to keep the restrictions (Minutes of the Grand Committee, 84).

There was something of the future in this vote. Gordon Wood, in his *Radicalism of the American Revolution*, notes that by the 1820s even such a profoundly anti–Christian jurist as the New York chancellor, James Kent, found it necessary to recognize Christianity as being at the core of the body politic (Wood, 331). In the case of *New York v. Ruggles* (8 Johns. R. 290 N.Y.

1811), Kent found that Ruggles, in saying that "Jesus Christ was a bastard, and his mother must be a whore," had threatened the basic tenets of ordered civilization:

> We stand equally in need, now as formerly, of all the moral discipline, and of those principles of virtue, which help to bind society together. The people of this state, in common with the people of this country, profess the general doctrines of christianity, as the rule of their faith and practice; and to scandalize the author of these doctrines is not only, in a religious point of view, extremely impious, but, even in respect to the obligations due to society, is a gross violation of decency and good order.

Christianity had, by the mid–1800s, not become the religion of society; it had become society itself. Admittedly it was, by and large, a very accepting Christianity, one capable of tolerating wide variation. The general society neither disdained nor hindered skeptics such as the young Abraham Lincoln. Religious orthodoxy, admittedly a wide orthodoxy, had found a respect, if not a foothold, among the most religiously liberal. Even those who were not religious, could not ignore the ordering and stabilizing effects of Christianity.

The country may have treasured orthodoxy but it still tolerated attacks on that orthodoxy (assuming a certain level of civility). Jews might not be Christians, but Judaism was tolerated so long as it did not stand in active opposition to the Christian orthodoxy. Skeptics could and did profess their disbelief, but they were generally left unchecked so as long as they did not attempt to savage the broad religious consensus. If one can have a profound but vaporous orthodoxy, then such can be said of the United States. In such a society, it is all but unremarkable, so far as a national history goes, that Jefferson created his own Bible (or, to be more correct, "Bibles")—with a cutting tool and with paste. The Bible appears, at the least, to be the third president's own existential testimony to freedom of conscience. Historians have tended to treat the Jefferson Bible as no more than an intellectual exercise, a quaint tinkering, as it were, with Christianity by slicing out all the mysticism found in it. In a land, however, that held what may seem religiously oxymoronic— a land that possessed a profoundly vaporous orthodoxy—we should be alert that not all may be quite as it seems.

First, Jefferson composed not one but two "Jefferson Bibles." In both instances, Jefferson simply took several bibles, cut from them various verses, and then pasted these verses onto pages that he later bound into what were essentially devotionals. Jefferson, probably a little disingenuously, stated that he compiled the first Bible during a few nights in the late winter of 1804. Using two bibles (which are still preserved) from which he cut the wanted verses, Jefferson pasted them onto 46 octavo sheets. It is at this point that we step into the long strange journey that we name the "Jefferson Bible." What happened to this first "Jefferson Bible" is unknown (D. Adams, ed., 45–53). Jefferson mentioned this first effort in several letters that are still extant. The key one, at least for our understanding, is a letter of April 25, 1816, to Francis Adrian Van der Kemp—a Dutch political radical and minister who had fled from Europe to escape imprisonment by the Prussians and an intellectual considered to be one of the most learned men in the United States (D. Adams, ed., 368–370; Schama). It is in this letter that Jefferson states that the first Jefferson Bible was "hastily done, however, being the work of one or two evenings only...."

While we know that Jefferson created his first Bible quickly, the reality is that it could not have been the work of only one or two evenings. The reader is invited to do the following: first, become very learned in Christian scripture, then create some type of index to guide your selection of verses (making certain that you literally have several hundred verses in your index—enough, in fact, to make a Gospel), now make selections so that you can form reasonable sentences and shape those sentences into reasonable paragraphs, all the while keeping in mind that your paragraphs must finally be formed into reasonable Biblical chapters. You must do all this before you begin your cutting. (In some instances, by the way, you will probably need to split verses in two to create better sentences.) You must, also, locate the verses you want using two different Bibles—you must use two different Bibles since cuts on one side of a page may accidentally delete verses on the other side of the page. Having performed this rather lengthy undertaking, cut your chosen verses out of the Bible, and paste them onto octavo sheets. You must use a glue pot or other gluing items available in 1804 (hence no glue sticks or whatever the present most modern gluing instrument is) and you must use the scissors or shears available in 1804. You will quickly find that even the indexing is not the work of one or two nights. While we do not have anything which tells us how long Jefferson spent on this first effort, it was clearly something on which he expended a great deal of energy. We know that he did it quickly, receiving the Bibles he used on or immediately after February 4, 1804 (although the mere ordering of the Bibles, and the fact that he had thought through the necessity to use two [!] Bibles suggests that Jefferson may have already had a draft index in hand), and having the resultant tome bound no later than March 10, 1804 (D. Adams, ed., 27, please note, in particular, footnote 83). This suggests a considerable amount of energy and concentration expended in a short period. This energy and concentration, in turn, suggests quite significant amounts of intentionality.

Jefferson's second effort, in 1820, has been preserved and, as of this writing (January 2012), is in the Smithsonian Institution in Washington, D.C. The 1820 effort, if we are to judge by the excisions found in the two earlier Bibles and compare them to the 1820 "Jefferson Bible," must have been very similar to the 1804 effort. This 1820 "Jefferson Bible" demonstrates that Jefferson exercised considerable meticulousness in delineating exactly what he believed to be believable. Moreover, Jefferson clearly tried to create a pleasing harmony among sentences. There are a number of places where Jefferson clipped out part of a verse and then joined it to another verse when no verse, in its entirety, quite fit what he wanted to say. For instance, on page 15 of the 1820 manuscript, Jefferson began with Matthew 7:26–29 and 8:1, followed by Mark 6:6, of which he used only the second half of the verse. The Mark snippet formed the bridge to verses pulled from Matthew (11:28–30) and then Luke (7:36–38). The analysis performed by Dickinson Adams of that manuscript indicates that Jefferson snipped individual verses into parts 46 times (D. Adams, ed., 51; see also Charles T. Cullen's "Foreword" to D. Adams). The ability to use so many different verses to construct one column on one page makes it clear that Jefferson was in total control of his material–the King James Bible—and that he took considerable effort in the selection and joining of his verses. Jefferson, however, did not simply cut apart two or more King James Bibles. He also sliced into pieces Greek Bibles, French Bibles, and Latin Bibles; the 1820 Jefferson Bible is a columnar Bible with Greek, French, and Latin columns corresponding to the English versions (photographic reproduction, D. Adams, ed., 127–297). Anyone who has ever tried to align Greek translations precisely with English translations will realize what a strenuous intellectual undertaking such an effort would be. To do it not just for Greek verses but also for Latin and French verses and to have all them align would be an undertaking of staggering dimensions. It is, therefore, clear that the 1820 Jefferson Bible holds only what Jefferson, after much intellectual endeavor, intended it to hold.

The reality that Jefferson was in total control of his material allows us to examine, in detail, Jefferson's intentions and, if we may dare to use the word "faith," faith. Since Jefferson would have excised anything that he did not believe to have a strong potentiality of being true, we can determine, precisely, specific elements of Jefferson's beliefs. An author will not include demons after such an earnest and demanding exercise unless he or she believes that the universe is likely arranged in such a way as to include demons. In short, while many have plumbed Jefferson's letters to determine his belief system, the actual physical cuts—into a number of Bibles—more surely delineate what Jefferson believed than those letters written to audiences besides himself.

First and foremost, the Jefferson Bibles certainly indicate that he believed that there was a God. There is nothing odd about this observation — Deists, by definition, believe in a God. But Jefferson quite apparently meant to refer to a "Christian God" — in distinct contradiction to a "Jewish God." From Jefferson's point of view, the Jews had somehow come to believe, correctly, Jefferson believed, that the arrangement of the universe included one and only one God. His letters, however, indicate that Jefferson believed that Jewish theology was simply incorrect — their one God was not the one that existed. In an 1819 letter to the evangelist Ezra Stiles, Jefferson wrote:

> I am not a Jew; and therefore do not adopt their theology, which supposes that the god of infinite justice to punish the sins of the fathers upon their children, unto the 3d. and 4th. Generation; and the benevolent and sublime reformer of that religion [Jesus] has told us only that God is good and perfect, but has not defined Him. I am, therefore, of His theology ... [Thomas Jefferson to Ezra Stiles, June 25, 1819 in Henry Augustine Washington, ed., 125].

Although not quite adopting a Marcionite[1] position, Jefferson drew a sharp contrast between the Jewish conception of God and the Christian conception of God and believed that Jesus had come to teach the Jews that they had erred in their understanding of God. In a letter written in 1820, Jefferson was even blunter regarding the theology of the Jews: "The whole religion of the Jews, inculcated on him [sic] from his infancy, was founded on the belief of divine inspiration. The fumes of the most disordered imaginations were recorded in their religious code, as communications of the deity.... (Thomas Jefferson to William Short, August 4, 1820, in Washington, ed., 167).[2]

References to Jefferson's God lead to Jefferson's views on heaven. The 1820 manuscript is replete with both references to heaven and, what is more important, given the term's connection with Jesus, the "kingdom of heaven."[3] The exact phrase "kingdom of heaven" occurs 20 times in the manuscript. "Heaven" is referred to 49 times. There are numerous instances where the word "kingdom" is used alone — but clearly referring to the "kingdom of heaven." Jefferson, moreover, includes three instances of Jesus referring to "my kingdom" while angels are explicitly referenced nine times. Jefferson, incidentally, included references to the "devil" three times and to "Hell" nine times. Strikingly, Jefferson included (from Matthew 13):

> He that soweth the good seed is Son of man; The field is the world; the good seed are the children of the kingdom; but the tares are the children of the wicked one; The enemy that sowed them is the devil; the harvest is the end of the world; and the reapers are the angels. As therefore the tares are gathered and burned in the fire; so shall it be in the end of this world. The Son of man shall send forth his angels, and they shall gather out of his kingdom all things that offend, and them which do iniquity; And shall set them into a furnace of fire: there shall be wailing and gnashing of teeth.... So shall it be at the end of the world: the angels shall

come forth, and sever the wicked from the just, And shall cast them into the furnace of fire: there shall be wailing and gnashing of teeth [37–42, 49–50].

The "wicked one," "the devil," the apocalypse, angels, the sinners tossed into the "furnace of fire" and the angels "sever[ing] the wicked from the just"— the reality is that Jefferson placed these mystical elements into his own personal devotional; the Jefferson Bible was, after all, not *the* "Jefferson Bible" to him, but his own personal guide to his own personal religion — and one he kept to himself until his death.

The "textbook Jefferson," the one who is credited with being a prime example of a Deist, is, to most who believe themselves aware of Jefferson's beliefs, a person whose religious views were based on extremely rational approaches to religion — a sort of religion with all the energy of the mystical and the unknown drained away and only philosophy and reason left. Yet the above examples illustrate that, by the time he had advanced in years, Jefferson had become anything but a person whose religious model was based on a rational examination of the world and whose relationship with Christianity enclosed only its moral precepts. If we accept the idea that actions speak louder than words, Jefferson's Bible states that Jefferson believed in — or at least accepted the strong possibility of — a wide range of items that twenty-first century members of Western culture would term either spiritual or superstitious.

If the Jefferson Bible is not a demystified and desiccated collection of biblical verses, then what was it? More than anything else, it is a variation (albeit with a considerable twist) of a Gospel harmony; that is, an attempt to create a text that takes the four gospels, removes (in Jefferson's case quite literally) contradictions and obscurities to create a harmonious single gospel. The idea dates back at least to Justin Martyr (103–165 C.E.) who created (or, maybe, had access to) a harmony or harmonies of the Mark, Matthew, and Luke traditions.[4] Justin's harmony has been lost, if it ever existed in one single written form, but Justin's follower, Tatian (died c. 190), created a written gospel harmony using all four Gospel traditions. Copies, although at least somewhat incomplete, of Tatian's harmony, the Diatessaron, have been preserved in a number of manuscripts and, although we cannot know, at the most granular level, Tatian's precise ordering of passages from the different gospel traditions, the different manuscripts indicate that Jefferson and Tatian followed very much the same method of composition.[5] Tatian and Jefferson both linked passages from different gospels by using short passages from other gospels. Several centuries after Tatian, the idea of creating a harmony among the different gospels probably reached its peak in an exhaustive, and even daunting, treatise by St. Augustine who wrote to repel attacks by non-Christians on the texts of the Christian scriptures. Augustine wrote his harmony in response to non–Christians who used the many differences between the Gospels as demonstrating that not even Christians knew the truth about their narrative.[6] In short, the idea of a harmony, which is what Jefferson's Bible is, lies well within the Christian tradition.

While some ancient writers continued the tradition of Justin Martyr and Tatian, there were few, if any, attempts to write harmonies during the Western Middle Ages. At the beginning of the modern era, the tradition revived. Charles Cullen came to the conclusion that Jefferson followed, in rough fashion, a harmony in Greek of the Gospels, prepared by William Newcome, who was probably bishop of Dromore (Ireland) when he compiled his particular harmony. Certainly Bishop Newcome's book was in Jefferson's library when Jefferson died and it seems reasonable to suppose that Newcome's version had at least some influence on Jefferson's arrangement of data (D. Adams, ed., 37).

Nevertheless, Jefferson's harmony was not the harmony of Tatian or St. Augustine or Bishop Newcome or anyone else. They wrote their harmonies from the point of view that "received" Christianity, the "old-time religion," as it were, was correct and that harmonies were needed mostly for reasons of simplification or, in Augustine's case, defense of what had become "mainstream Christianity"—their attempt was to include, not exclude. Jefferson, on the other hand, built his harmony on his belief that the Gospels had to be harmonized through paring the text(s)—through exclusion rather than inclusion. Having determined for himself that the Gospels were corrupt, he sought to remove their impurities through an exclusive harmony. Jefferson, moreover, clearly believed that he was the one that had the intellectual ability to remove such corruptions, creating a new harmony. Certainly Jefferson was not shy about his abilities to discern the sayings of the "true Jesus": "[Jesus's words are] as distinguishable as diamonds in a dunghill" and "It is as easy to separate [out the words of Jesus] as to pick out diamonds from dunghills" (Thomas Jefferson to John Adams, October 12, 1813; Jefferson to Adams, January 24, 1814; D. Adams, ed., 352; Broden, ed.). Anything which implied that Jesus was, in some mystic way, united with God, had been, Jefferson reasoned, entered in error and therefore had to be excluded. Certainly such a mix of the rational and the mystical was revolutionary; no one had ever thought to "demythologize" Jesus while keeping the rest of the Christian framework of myth[7] and spirituality. Despite his acceptance of a Christian God and almost all the Christian framework of the spiritual world, the political revolutionary had become a religious revolutionary.

The Jefferson Bible and Jefferson's letters indicate that Jefferson believed that Jesus had set out to create a religious-cultural revolution. Jefferson saw Jesus as reacting (rebelling against, if you will) the base, corrupt, amoral, and intolerant rigidities that Jefferson believed had become part of Jewish society — much as Jefferson had when he listed, in the Declaration of Independence, the base, corrupt, amoral and intolerant rigidities that the British government had fallen into. Moreover, he believed Jesus had a vision of society that was far superior to those of his fellow Jews and much more closely aligned with, the thoughts of the original creator of the world — again much as Jefferson saw the American Revolution as aligning America with the ideals of that original creator ("that all men are created equal ... that they are endowed by their Creator with certain inalienable Rights..."). Jefferson's Bible and his letters express his belief that he, Thomas Jefferson, could rescue Jesus from still another set of base, corrupt, amoral, and intolerant authorities who had seized Jesus's message (in essence his constitution) and used it to further their own ignorant or selfish ends.

In Jefferson's mind, Jesus and Jefferson and his Bible expressed a resistance against three tyrannies. First, Jefferson believed that the Jewish culture of the Second Temple period and more recent Jewish cultures were corrupt and horribly misshapen.

> The reformation of ... [Jewish] blasphemous attributes, and substitution of those more worthy, pure and sublime, seems to have been the chief object of Jesus in his discources [sic] to the Jews ... [Thomas Jefferson to John Adams, April 11, 1823, in Washington, ed., 283].
>
> The deism and ethics of the [Second Temple] Jews ... shew in what a degraded state they were and the necessity they presented of a reformation [which would be provided by Jesus] [Thomas Jefferson to Joseph Priestley, April 9, 1803, in D. Adams, ed., 327–329].
>
> But the greatest of all the Reformers of the depraved religion of his own country, was Jesus of Nazareth [Thomas Jefferson to William Short, October 31, 1819, in Washington, ed., 139].
>
> Jews:
>
> 1. Their system was Deism; that is, the belief of one only god. But their ideas of him and of his attributes were degrading and injurious.
>
> 2. Their Ethics were not only imperfect, but often irreconcilable with the sound doctrines of reason and morality, as they respect intercourse with those around us; and repulsive and anti-social, as respecting other nations. They needed reformation, therefore, in an eminent degree [Thomas Jefferson, syllabus sent to Benjamin Rush, April 21, 1803, in D. Adams, ed., 331–334].
>
> [Quoting William Enfield's *History of Philosophy*] "Ethics were so little studied among the Jews, that, in their whole compilation called the Talmud, there is only one treatise concerning moral subjects. [A long list of objections to Jewish maxims then follows.] What a wretched depravity of sentiment and manners must have prevailed before such corrupt maxims could have obtained credit [i.e., in pre-Talmudic Judaism, including Second Temple Judaism]! It is impossible to

collect from these writings a consistent series of moral Doctrine." It was the reformation of this "wretched depravity" of morals which Jesus undertook [Thomas Jefferson to John Adams, October 12, 1813, in Baden, ed.; Enfield, p. 409, 1792].

This list of quotes could be multiplied. Jefferson clearly saw Jews as being ethically flawed in the most desperate of manners and Jesus as being the person who attempted to rescue his people from their degradation. Jefferson, with his massive erudition, apparently took common points of view, loosely held by most of those who lived in Western civilization, and burnished them to sharp tines on which to impale Judaism and Jews.

Second, Jefferson saw Christianity, as it had come to exist in its organized persona, as being great, but evil, and oppressive.

The Christian priesthood, finding the doctrines of Christ levelled to every understanding, and too plain to need explanation, saw in the mysticisms of Plato, materials with which they might build up an artificial system which might ... admit everlasting controversy, give employment for their order, and introduce it to profit, power, and pre-eminence [Thomas Jefferson to John Adams, July 5, 1814, in Baden, ed.].

[Speaking of a bill before the English Parliament to allow anti–Trinitarians religious freedom and the opposition of the English church leaders to the bill] This constitutes the craft, the power and the profit of the priests. Sweep away their gossamer fabrics of fictitious religion, and they would catch no more flies [Thomas Jefferson to John Adams, August 22, 1813, in Baden, ed.).

On theological subjects, as mangled by our Pseudo-Christians.... It is the mere Abracadabra of the mountebanks calling themselves the priests of Jesus [Thomas Jefferson to Francis Adrian Van der Kemp, July 30, 1816, in D. Adams, ed., 374– 375].

[Toleration] does not satisfy the priesthood. They must have a ... declared assent to all their ... absurdities.... The artificial structures they have built on the purest of all moral systems [i.e., that of Jesus], for the purpose of deriving from it pence and power..." [Thomas Jefferson to Margaret Bayard Smith or B. Harrison Smith, August 16, 1816, in Washington, ed., 28].

Third, Jefferson simply dismissed, more or less as knaves and fools, the writers of the Gospels and other early Christian writers.

To do [Jesus] justice it would be necessary to remark the disadvantages his doctrines have to encounter, not having committed [his doctrines] to writing himself, but [having his writings committed to print] by the most unlettered of men, by memory, long after they heard them from him; when much was forgotten, must misunderstood, and presented in very paradoxical shapes [Thomas Jefferson to Joseph Priestley, April 9, 1803, in D. Adams, ed., 327–329].

[Referring to the Bible] I separate ... the gold from the dross; restore to [Jesus] the former, and leave to the stupidity of some, and roguery of others of his disciples. Of this band of dupes and imposters, Paul was the great Coryphaeus [leader of the chorus], and first corrupter of the doctrines of Jesus [Thomas Jefferson to William Short, April 13, 1820, in Washington, ed., 156].

We must reduce our volume to the simple evangelists, select, even from them, the very words only of Jesus, paring off the Amphibologisms [in this instance, probably meaning dogmatic, if unfounded and ill-conceived, statements] into which they have been led by forgetting often, or not understanding what had fallen from [Jesus], by giving their misconceptions as his dicta, and expressing unintelligibly for others what they did not understand themselves [Thomas Jefferson to John Adams, October 12, 1813, in Baden, ed.].

No historical fact is better established than that of the doctrine of one god, pure and uncompounded, was that of the early ages of Christianity; and was among the most efficacious doctrines which gave it triumph over the polytheism of the antients.... Nor was the unity of the supreme being ousted from the Christian creed by the force of reason, but by the sword of civil government wielded at the will of the fanatic Athanasius[8] [Thomas Jefferson to James Smith, December 8, 1822, in Washington, ed., 269].

The Jefferson Bible, thus, was not the simple product of a deist eliminating whatever seemed mystical, but the outpouring of something far stronger — An almost fanatical dedication to the "pure doctrines" of Jesus of Nazareth; a repudiation and distaste for all things Judaic; a hatred of the clergy that carried back over 1700 years; and a belief that Jesus's near followers had either not understood what Jesus said or that they had forgotten or that they corrupted Jesus's sayings for their own vain and selfish ends.

We need here to take a step back. Jefferson had been the leader of the anti-authoritarian faction in the American Revolution. Whatever his relationship with his slaves, he believed in, if not constant revolution, at least punctuated revolution. He was, after all, the American leader who said that the tree of liberty must be refreshed from time to time with the blood of patriots and tyrants" (Thomas Jefferson to Colonel [William S.] Smith, November 13, 1787 in Randolph, ed., 268); that "no society can make a perpetual constitution.... The earth belongs always to the living generation" (Thomas Jefferson to James Madison, September 6, 1789 in Smith, ed., 30); that "the spirit of resistance to government is so valuable on certain occasions that I wish it to be *always* [emphasis mine] kept alive" (Thomas Jefferson to Abigail Adams, February 22, 1787, in Golden and Golden, 60).

Revolutionary leaders, of course, have never been noted for their restraint and moderation. In 1921, Trotsky told the All-Russian Congress of Peasant Deputies, in defense of acts of terrorism and repression, that "we shall not enter the kingdom of socialism in white gloves on a polished floor" (Johnson, 77). As Maximilian Robespierre said to the French Convention in 1794: "Terror is nothing other than justice, prompt, severe, inflexible justice; it is therefore an emanation of virtue. It is not so much a special principle than a consequence of the general principle of democracy applied to our country's most urgent needs" (Halsall). Or, as Oliver Cromwell is believed to have noted upon the execution of Charles I: "cruel necessity" (Morrill and Baker, 36).

Faced with his countrymen "descending" into ecstatic and emotional and "simplistic" religion Jefferson did what was unthinkable in his day and age. To rescue Jesus, to defy the Jews (at least of the Talmudic era and before), to defy the clergy, and even to defy Jesus's early followers, he took a sharp object and physically cut several Bibles into pieces — and he did so not once, but twice. Compared to ordering massacres and terror and executions, this might seem child's play — but those reading this should think how comfortable even secular academics would feel if someone were to hand them scissors and paste and tell them to begin cutting into their own heritage's sacred texts. Even someone without religion, here at the beginning of the 21st century, might feel a hitch, a pause, a moment of hesitation before cutting into a Bible, into the Torah, into the Qur'an. Had the general populace — and all but a few of his revolutionary colleagues — known that he was doing so, it can be surmised that his activities would have taken them aback. With 1804 being an election year, one can imagine that common knowledge of his first attempt would have revived the Federalist Party.

And yet he did undertake the revolutionary effort of taking the Christ out of Jesus and out of Christianity while leaving the other unseen or spiritual entities in. At least at this distance, the early twenty-first century, it appears that Jefferson believed that he had struck a blow for his fellow revolutionary, Jesus.

Trotsky, of course, died with an ice pick in his head as delivered by one of Stalin's henchmen. Robespierre made his own trip through the valley of the Terror and then to the scaffolding of the guillotine. Cromwell died in 1658 in his own bed. Within less than three years, though, his remains were dug up by a restored royalty, his body beheaded with the head stuck on a pike outside Westminster Hall (where it rotted beneath the sky and the birds until 1685), and his headless body hung in chains in London. (His head, in fact, was not taken to its final resting place at Cambridge until 1960.)

Jefferson died in bed, surrounded by his family, and beloved by his country which, seventeen years before Cromwell's head finally found a home (in a manner of speaking), opened a beautiful monument to him, surrounded by blossoming trees and near a quietly flowing river, in its capital city. As indicated above, Jefferson was a man who, by United States standards, was a Nixonian politician — stealing, libeling, and harassing in his pursuit of political power. But Jefferson attacked Bibles in what most Americans would have contended then and would contend now as supremely sacrilegious actions. While Watergate was sufficiently harmful to Nixon's image and reputation in and of itself, the reader is left to imagine what would have been made of the 37th president — the charges of megalomania — if Nixon had been discovered hacking apart Bibles and rearranging the verses to fit his fantasies late at night in the secrecy of the family quarters. Yet Jefferson, to the end, conducted revolution by other means and his reputation has lived to tell the tale.

On reflection, Jefferson did not live in a land where cold-blooded executions such as accompanied the French and Russian revolutions and the English civil war were likely to occur. While spies and, occasionally, collaborators, were executed during the American Revolution, and summary justice often meted out to pro–British guerillas, the massacres of groups according to status or association did not occur and, so far as we know, the thought of which did not occur. With the Jefferson Bible, Jefferson emerges as both the most radical of the American revolutionaries and the most violent; but that the violence was done with paste and scissors suggests how far America had departed from the continent which produced Trotskies, Robespierres, and Cromwells.

Notes

1. Any number of authors may be consulted to explain the position of Marcion on the Jewish God. Marcion was an influential Christian (held as a heretic by those who formed what would eventually become the mainstream of Christianity) who believed that the vengeful and apparently blood-thirsty God of the Hebrew Scriptures could not possibly be the God to whom Jesus had directed his followers. I suggest Helmut Koester, *Introduction to the New Testament: History and Literature of Early Christianity*, vol. 2 (New York: Walter De Gruyter, 1982), 324–334.

2. Was Jefferson an anti–Semite? There are 41 references to "Jews" in the correspondence between Jefferson and John Adams that began late in their lives. Although none of the references may be considered to be positive references to "Jews," a goodly number are neutral, but the majority are negative, even sneering. None are racial in the sense of seeing Jews as physically inheriting a deficiency. It might be more appropriate to say that Jefferson saw Jews as people who had been corrupted by Judaism. I performed this analysis through a word search for "Jew" and Judaism in the Kindle edition of *"Ye will say I am no Christian": The Thomas Jefferson/John Adams Correspondence on Religion, Morals, and Values*, ed. Bruce Broden (Amherst, NY: Prometheus, 2006).

3. The debate over the phrase "kingdom of heaven" or "kingdom of God" has been a long and rich one. The phrase is certainly one of the key phrases Jesus used — some would contend that it is the key phrase in Jesus's teachings.

4. The question of the harmonies relating to Justin Martyr is another rich field for scholarly disagreement. I refer the reader to Kroeger, 342–343. However, see also Oskar Skarsaune, "Justin and His Bible," *Justin Martyr and His Worlds*, ed. Sara Parvis and Paul Foster (Minneapolis: Fortress Press, 2007).

5. Our knowledge of the Diatessaron is imperfect since such evidence as we have on it is based on Syriac, Greek copies, and Arabic fragments which are manifestly flawed. Still, the reconstructions of Tatian's work allows us to see a compositional consistency which suggests that Tatian's manner of arranging his material must have been close to Jefferson's manner — although with quite different results and without the glue and scissors. A good discussion of the difficulties in disentangling the threads of the Diatessaron is found in a reprint of a 1904 University of Chicago dissertation, A.A. Hobson, *The Diatessaron of Tatian and the Synoptic Problem[:] Being an investigation of the Diates-*

saron for the Light which it throws upon the solution of the problems of the origin of the synoptic gospels (www.forgottenbooks.org).
  6. "Its great object is to vindicate the Gospel against the critical assaults of the heathen. Paganism, having tried persecution as its first weapon, and seen it fail, attempted next to discredit the new faith by slandering its doctrine, impeaching its history, and attacking with special persistency the veracity of the Gospel writers. In this it was aided by some of Augustin's heretical antagonists, who endeavored at times to establish a conspicuous inconsistency between the Jewish Scriptures and the Christian, and at times to prove the several sections of the New Testament to be at variance with each other. Many alleged that the original Gospels had received considerable additions of a spurious character. And it was a favorite method of argumentation, adopted both by heathen and by Manichæan adversaries, to urge that the evangelical historians contradicted each other. Thus, in the present treatise (i. 7), Augustin speaks of this matter of the discrepancies between the Evangelists as the primary argument wielded by his opponents. Hence, as elsewhere he sought to demonstrate the congruity of the Old Testament with the New, he set himself here to exonerate Christianity from the charge of any defect of harmony, whether in the facts recorded or in the order of their narration, between its four fundamental historical documents" (Augustine of Hippo, in Schaff, ed.).
  7. By using "myth" I do not mean to imply "falsehood" or "fantasy." I here am using "myth" in all its mystical, cosmological, sociological and pedagogical senses. See Joseph Campbell, *The Power of Myth* (New York: Doubleday, 1988).
  8. Athanasius (c. 296–378 C.E.), Bishop of Alexandria, was the great proponent of Trinitarianism during the time when Christianity was becoming the recognized religion of the Roman Empire. Although it is very unlikely that Athanasius was the writer of the Athanasian Creed used by most Christian churches, the Creed's content strongly reflects Athanasius's unrelenting Trinitarianism.

Works Cited

Abercrombie, James. Letter to a friend dated 1831 quoted in *Annals of the American Pulpit: Episcopalianism*. Ed. William Bell Sprague. Washington, D.C.: Robert Carter and Brothers, 1858. Vol. 5 of 9. This volume's date is often incorrectly cited as 1859.

Adams, Dickinson, ed. *Jefferson's Extracts from the Gospels: The Papers of Thomas Jefferson*, Second Series. Princeton: Princeton University Press, 1983.

Augustine of Hippo. *St. Augustine: Sermon on the Mount; Harmony of the Gospels; Homilies on the Gospels*, First Series, Vol. 6 of 14. Ed. Philip Schaff. Edinburgh: T & T Clark, 1887.

———. *A Select Library of the Nicene and Post-Nicene Fathers of the Church*. New York: The Christian Literature Co., 1886.

Bernstein, Richard B. *Thomas Jefferson*, Kindle ed. New York: Oxford University Press, 2003.

Burns, Eric. *Infamous Scribblers: The Founding Fathers and the Rowdy Beginnings of American Journalism*, Kindle ed. New York: Public Affairs, 2007.

Campbell, Joseph. *The Power of Myth*. New York: Doubleday, 1988.

Cullen, Charles T. Foreword. *Jefferson's Extracts from the Gospels: The Papers of Thomas Jefferson*, Second Series. Ed. Dickenson Adams. Princeton: Princeton University Press, 1983.

Dumas, Malone. *Jefferson and the Rights of Man*, vol. 2 of 6 of *Jefferson and His Times*, 1948–1981. Boston: Little, Brown, 1951.

Enfield, William. *The History of Philosophy, from the Earliest Periods: Drawn Up from* [Johann Jakob] *Brucker's* ["]Historia critica Philosophiae["]. 1791. London: Thomas Tegg and Son, 1837.

Ely, Ezra. "The Duty of Christian Freeman to Elect Christian Rulers." *The Reformer: A Religious Work*, vol. 7 of 8 (1820–1826). Philadelphia: Printed by J. Rakestraw, 1826.

Golden, James L., and Alan L. Golden. *Thomas Jefferson and the Rhetoric of Virtue*. New York: Rowman & Littlefield, 2002.

Gould, Stephen Jay. http://www.stephenjaygould.org/ctrl/buckner_tripoli.html. Accessed December 27, 2011.

Halsall, Paul, ed. *Modern History Sourcebook*. "Maximilien Robespierre: Justification of the Use of Terror." http://www.fordham.edu/halsall/mod/robespierre-terror.asp. Accessed March 18, 2012.

Haskell, S.C. *Andrew Jackson and Early Tennessee History*. Nashville: Ambrose, 1920. Print.
Hobson, A.A. *The Diatessaron of Tatian and the Synoptic Problem[:] Being an investigation of the Diatessaron for the Light which it throws upon the solution of the problems of the origin of the synoptic gospels*. www.forgottenbooks.org.
Jefferson, Thomas. *Memoir, Correspondence, and Miscellanies from the Papers of Thomas Jefferson*, vol. 2 of 4. Ed. Thomas Jefferson Randolph. Charlottesville: F. Carr, 1829.
_____. *The Papers of Thomas Jefferson*, vol. 11 of 36 to date (1950–2012). Ed. Julian Boyd. Princeton: Princeton University Press, 1955.
_____. "Second Inaugural." 1805. http://www.bartleby.com/ 124/pres17.html. Accessed February 19, 2012.
_____. *The Works of Thomas Jefferson*, Federal ed., vols. 1 and 4 of 12. Ed. Paul Leicester Ford. New York: G.P. Putnam's Sons, 1904–1905.
_____. *The Writings of Thomas Jefferson*, Monticello ed., vol. 1 of 2. Ed. Albert Ellergy Bergh. Washington, D.C.: Issued under the ouspices of the Thomas Jefferson Memorial Association of the United States, 1903–1904.
_____. *The Writings of Thomas Jefferson: Being his Autobiography, Correspondence, Reports, Messages, Addresses, and Other Writings, Official and Private*, vol. 7 of 9. Ed. Henry Augustine Washington. New York: Darby & Jackson, 1859.
_____, and John Adams. *"Ye will say I am no Christian": The Thomas Jefferson/John Adams Correspondence on Religion, Morals, and Values*, Kindle ed. Ed. Bruce Broden. Amherst, NY: Prometheus, 2006.
Johnson, Paul. *Modern Times: The World from the Twenties to the Nineties*, rev. ed. New York: HarperCollins, 1991.
Koester, Helmut. *Introduction to the New Testament: History and Literature of Early Christianity*, vol. 2 of 2. New York: Walter De Gruyter, 1982.
Lambert, Frank. *Religion in American Politics: A Short History*. Princeton: Princeton University Press, 2010.
Levy, Leonard. *Jefferson and Civil Liberties*. Chicago: Ivan R. Dee, 1989.
Morrill, John, and Phillip Baker. "Oliver Cromwell, the Regicide, and the Sons of Zeruiah." *Cromwell and the Interregnum: The Essential Readings*. Ed. David Smith. Malden, MA: Blackwell, 2003.
New York v. Ruggles. 8 Johns. R. 290 N.Y. 1811.
Pennsylvania State Constitutional Convention, 1789–1790. "Minutes of the Grand committee of the whole Convention of the commonwealth of Pennsylvania, which commenced at Philadelphia, on Tuesday, the twenty-fourth day of November, in the year ... one thousand seven hundred and eighty-nine, for the purpose of reviewing, and, if they see occasion, altering and amending the constitution of this state." Philadelphia: Printed by Zachariah Poulson, 1790.
Schama, Simon. *Patriots and Liberators. Revolution in the Netherlands, 1780–1813*. New York: Knopf, 1977.
Skarsaune, Oskar. "Justin and His Bible." *Justin Martyr and his Worlds*, Kindle ed. Ed. Sara Parvis and Paul Foster. Minneapolis: Fortress Press, 2007.
Smith, James Morton. *The Republic of Letters: The Correspondence Between Thomas Jefferson and James Madison*. New York: W.W. Norton, 1995.
Treaty of Peace and Friendship, Signed at Tripoli November 4, 1796. http://avalon.law.yale.edu/18th_century/bar1796t.asp. Accessed December 27, 2011.
United States Senate. "1829 Report on the Subject of Mails on the Sabbath." *Religion in American Politics: A Short History*. Ed. Frank Lambert. Princeton: Princeton University Press, 2010.
Washington, George. George Washington Papers, Library of Congress, 1741–1799: Series 2 Letterbooks, Letterbook 39. www.memory.loc.gov.
Wood, Gordon. *The Radicalism of the American Revolution*. New York: Vintage, 1991.

Portraying Jesus as Human:
The Last Temptation of Christ

KATHERINE BROWN DOWNEY

The struggle with God and against temptation is foundational to Judeo-Christian thought and inspires a long tradition of storytelling that represents this abiding human experience. "Israel" in Hebrew means "one who wrestles with God" or "God struggler," coined after Jacob wrestled with God's angel: "Your name will no longer be Jacob, but Israel, because you have struggled with God and with men and have overcome" (*NRSV*, Gen 32:28). Israel becomes, in the prophetic tradition, the suffering servant of God, appearing four times in Isaiah: as the chosen one, given the Spirit to establish justice through the world (42:1-4), who speaks to the entire world and identifies himself as one called by God before birth (49: 1-6), declaring his confidence in divine help even in the face of physical persecution (50:4-11), and oppressed "like a lamb that is led to the slaughter" (52:113-53:12). In his 1955 novel *The Last Temptation* (translated into English by P.A. Bien and published in 1960 as *The Last Temptation of Christ*), Nikos Kazantzakis followed the Christian tradition of representing Jesus as Israel, chosen, called before birth, persecuted and oppressed, the redemptive scapegoat. If Jesus was fully human, as Christian orthodoxy claims, then he must have struggled as all humans do, with God and against temptation. Kazantzakis's novel portrays that life subjectively, exploring Jesus's experience, what it might feel like to be Christ. Kazantzakis was keenly interested in the struggle Jesus must have had with his calling by God to be Christ, for in that struggle he found a model for the faithful struggle with God.

That Jesus was tempted by the devil is reported in Mark, Matthew, and Luke, and the temptations are fleshly, worldly, and spiritual: to eat while fasting, to assume power over the kingdoms, and to test God's protection. These Biblical accounts, though, merely report what the devil offered and what Jesus said in reply. In the Bible's narrative economy, Jesus's reply appears after no interval and, therefore, seems immediate. For temptation to be real, it needs to be really tempting. What would really tempt a fully human Jesus called to be the Christ, and how would he struggle against those temptations? Just as Kazantzakis experienced the "merciless battle between the spirit and the flesh" (1), so also does the Jesus in his novel. For, he asserts in the novel's prologue,

> every man partakes of the divine nature in both his spirit and his flesh. That is why the mystery of Christ is not simply a mystery for a particular creed: it is universal. The struggle between God and man breaks out in everyone, together with the longing for reconciliation.... Struggle between the flesh and the spirit, rebellion and resistance, reconciliation and submission, and finally — the supreme purpose of the struggle — union with God: this was the ascent taken by Christ, the ascent which he invites us to take as well, following his bloody tracks [2].

The novel's 500 pages depict a fully human Jesus struggling with God and subsequently confronted by real temptations, fictionalizing the experience that the Biblical text reports in two sentences (Mark 1:12–13). The Roman Catholic Church indexed *The Last Temptation of Christ*, and the Greek Orthodox Church refused Kazantzakis a Christian burial.

The Church might have provenance over Kazantzakis's earthly remains, but it does not enjoy the power it once had in our pluralistic world. There is, frankly, for many people living in it, nothing like banning a book to make it a must-read, increasing sales, translations, discussions of and general interest in it. Since the late twentieth century, though, there is no greater boon for a book than for it to be adapted to film. The popular appeal of movies is vastly greater than that of books. We also worry about them more, censoring films through the rating system, while scoffing at the book banning of the olden days. So, when Martin Scorsese adapted *The Last Temptation of Christ* to film, thereby fulfilling a long-held interest in making a "Jesus film," now a film genre, he transformed through the power of Hollywood a Greek novel of the 1950s into a late 20th century cultural phenomenon of startling intensity, breadth, and proportion.

More than fifty years after the novel's publication and nearly 25 years after Scorsese's film adaptation of it, the controversies ensuing from both of them, especially the film, seem, however, to have become mere history. Recent scholarship suggests so. Those interested in Jesus films enjoyed a spate of controversy in 2004 when Mel Gibson released *The Passion of the Christ*, drawing comparisons between this firestorm and the last one, thereby revisiting *The Last Temptation of Christ* after nearly a decade of scholarly silence. In *Scandalizing Jesus? Kazantzakis's The Last Temptation of Christ Fifty Years On*, an anthology edited by scholar of literature and theology Darren Middleton, specialists in literature, religion, and film seem to have pulled all the threads and tied up all the loose ends in a comprehensive work of review, analysis, criticism, historical and theological reflection, and concluding assessment. A webliography and "for further reading" bibliography together summarize the literature on the novel, film, and cultural phenomenon.

Since then, the novel and film receive mention in scholarly works of a more general nature, those on Kazantzakis's *oeuvre*, for instance, or studies of Jesus films. Though Blockbuster refused to carry the film, it is available now even for streaming from Netflix. The novel remains in print, copyright renewed the year the film was released, and in a new paperback edition released ten years later, as the scholarly treatments waned. Yet, both the novel and the film are largely unknown to a new generation. Indeed, if you were born before 1974, you likely remember much of this, but most of those born after 1974 know little about the film and the firestorm of controversy it ignited, and even less about the novel, acknowledging vaguely that they have heard something about them, probably from their parents, sort of the Viet Nam of film, the Galileo of literature.

At least, that has been my observation since I wrote on the film in the last chapter of my 1998 doctoral dissertation on Biblical drama. Indeed, when I revised that for publication, I excised the portion of the chapter treating *The Last Temptation of Christ*, thinking that it dated the work. Little did I know that the same year my book was published Gibson's film would renew interest in *The Last Temptation of Christ*. With this renewed, if antiquarian, interest, the Middleton anthology, recent studies of Jesus films, and the nearing 25th anniversary of Scorsese's film, I find myself in conversation with younger scholars who respectfully ask questions about this as a, well, *historical* event. Are the novel and film still relevant or merely cultural artifacts? At a time when Christian, Jewish, and Islamic fundamentalists make claims to orthodoxy, and do so with the power to suppress and oppress, when a cartoon depicting Mohammed can foster a fatwa, when Americans with political aspirations feel a need to define publically their religious allegiances and convictions, and when films like Gibson's can inspire popular controversy and scholarly criticism, *The Last Temptation of Christ* still serves as a potent example of fiction's capacity to challenge putative orthodoxy.

I came to thinking about *The Last Temptation of Christ* through my argument in *Perverse Midrash: Oscar Wilde, Andre Gide, and Censorship of Biblical Drama* that Wilde's and Gide's *fin de siècle* plays had been mistreated by the critical literature, that both plays were indeed the religious works their authors claimed them to be, albeit unorthodox ones. Though they "perverted" the Biblical texts (adding, subtracting, and changing narrative, characterization, and thematic elements), as their early critics decried, they did so, I argued, in order to restore to these narratives their originary, spiritual, inspiration. That is, they changed the stories in order to reveal to audiences the spirit infusing them that had been lost by ecclesiastical reading and, in so doing, they return us to those original texts refreshed.

Characterizing them as midrashic, as imaginative retellings that seek to regain the significative function of their Biblical sources, I noted, however, that unlike traditional midrash, which is conservative in purpose, these plays do not smooth textual anomalies as much as they highlight what was elided by orthodoxy. In perverting the Biblical texts, the plays open them up to explore the experiences inspiring them, particularly of separation and abandonment, desire for union with God, the plight of humanity. The plays also "exposed the secret that Western culture's most sacred document does not sustain its myths and values, that the referent for so-called blasphemy is the cultural myth and not the text itself, and that the Bible, in its perplexities and perversities, is in fact a subversive challenge to that culture's most cherished beliefs" (Downey 159). So also is *The Last Temptation of Christ*, I thought, an example from our own *fin de siècle* of the cultural phenomenon I observed at work in Wilde's and Gide's.

Religionists, scholars, and artists represent three distinctive interpretive stances toward the Biblical texts. Consider, for instance, the case of the first king of Israel, chosen and then completely abandoned by God, both for unclear reasons, the subject of 1 Samuel and Gide's play *Saul*. For the commentary tradition of both Jewish and Christian thought, the essential question is the nature of Saul's sin: What exactly was it? And how are we then to behave or not to behave? For Biblical scholars since early in the nineteenth century, the question is why Saul's sin was sinful. They study the cultural context to understand why Saul did what the text reports he did, and why Samuel and God did as the text reports they did. More recent scholars trained in literary criticism seek a similar understanding but from within the text itself. Though their stance differs from the religious readers of the commentary tradition, these scholarly critics' project remains the same: to explain (or to explain away) a difficult text so we might not become guilty of the same sin as Saul, or so that we might contextualize his sin in a world not our own, in either case to create distance between reader and text.

The artistic community, however, tends to take a different approach and to ask different questions. Typically reading the biblical text as expressing the human condition, artists treating Saul's story ask how it *feels* to be rejected by God, how rejection by God is *experienced*. They make no attempt to explain the situation; rather, in Saul's case, they protest against its injustice. Kazantzakis's thought was characterized by struggle, to which he refers repeatedly in the prologue to his novel, and it is its central theme, specifically Jesus's struggle with becoming the Christ: "We struggle, we see him struggle also, and we find strength. We see that we are not all alone in the world: he is fighting at our side" (3). The artist's interpretive approach is especially compelling if it subverts the Church's story that is infused by interest in religious dogma and appropriate behavior. As Kazantzakis explained in a letter,

> I wanted to renew and supplement the sacred Myth that underlies the great Christian civilization of the West. It isn't a simple "Life of Christ." It's a laborious, sacred, creative endeavour to reincarnate the essence of Christ, setting aside the dross—falsehoods and pettinesses which all the churches and all the cassocked representatives of Christianity have heaped upon His figure, thereby distorting it [Kazantzakis 505–6].

Greek scholar Vrasidas Karalis observes of *The Last Temptation of Christ* that it occupies the "gray area between religion and literature," yet seems to receive more critical attention to its religious side than to its literary merits or demerits (73). He argues for an understanding of it as a "narrativized elaboration of a major christological statement—a hybrid form of an anthropological investigation in Christology employing both imagination and history," composed in "a style that consciously emulates the narrative practices of the canonical Gospels, especially Matthew" (73). Like Matthew, it is midrashic, employing Biblical material to narrate its story. But, like Wilde's and Gide's plays, Kazantzakis's novel is perversely midrashic, seeking not to support an ecclesiastical reading, but instead to open the text up to exploration of subjective experience, the "anthropological investigation" of what it feels like to be the Christ.

Artists' interpretive approaches differ from those of religionists and scholars, but they are not separated from the community; indeed, art both serves and needs community. While we might remind religious or scholarly critics that art pursues a distinctive task in portraying an imagined subjective experience, that is, then, *just* art, we must acknowledge that art has power, and we might caution artists to recognize that one does not "renew and supplement" the Church's story, calling it false, petty, and distorting, without consequences.

The arts, of course, comprise literary, visual, and performative works. Though Kazantzakis's novel appeared on the Catholic index, it in no way provoked the kind of storm that the film adaptation of it did. One of the points that had been made in the 19th-century discourse about censoring the stage was that performance differs from a book, that an event narrated in a book might take on a quite different nature when enacted on stage. The often-invoked example was of a woman rising from her bath, quite unremarkable in narration yet scandalous and worthy of censorship when portrayed on stage. The report in a book that something has transpired has a quite different effect on readers than the enactment of an event does on an audience. Kazantzakis's novel had been on bookshelves, even in translation, for some thirty years before Scorsese adapted it, fostering little controversy and a comparative modicum of interest.

The narrative of the novel and the film exploits gaps in the Biblical text, such as the relationship between Mary Magdalene and Jesus, Jesus's erratic behavior, his desire to relinquish his role, and his friendship with Judas. It also employs an idea that Gide had used in one of his Biblical plays, *Bathsheba*. As a retelling of the story of King David, the play portrays David as coveting not the wife of Uriah but the *life* of Uriah. When David visits Uriah in his home and Bathsheba serves them dinner, David envies Uriah his normal and happy life at home with wife and family. It is this that Gide's King David tries to appropriate, not the sexuality of Bathsheba. Kazantzakis developed this same theme of the hero desiring a normal human life, and this interested Scorsese: "The last temptation is for Christ to get off the cross and live the rest of His life as a normal human being" (124). Scorsese observed that as a student in Catholic schools that placed emphasis on the divine side of Jesus, such that if he "walked into a room, you'd know He was God because He glowed in the dark," it occurred to him that it would be easy for a divine Jesus to reject temptation. "He could reject especially the temptation of sex; and He could undergo the suffering on the cross, because He knew what was going to happen, what death is all about" (124). Indeed, the temptation would not in fact be tempting at all. In Kazantzakis's novel Scorsese found engagement with the two natures of Jesus:

> I found this an interesting idea, that the human nature of Jesus was fighting Him all the way down the line, because it can't conceive of Him being God. I thought this would be great drama and force people to take Jesus seriously — at least to re-evaluate His teachings.... So through the Kazantzakis novel I wanted to make the life of Jesus immediate and accessible to people who haven't really thought about God in a long time [124].

Like Wilde's and Gide's plays, Kazantzakis's novel and Scorsese's film did not merely enact Biblical material but rather created new meaning with it. The narrative is midrashic: it exploited gaps in the Biblical text and made changes to it to explore an idea that was in the end christologically correct, had been, in fact, since the Council of Chalcedon decision in 451 that established the

Christian doctrine that a fully human Jesus struggled against and conquered real temptation.

Despite numerous production obstacles, the film was released in 1988 to considerable protest, which has been well documented, even by Scorsese himself in *Scorsese on Scorsese* published a year later, as well as by critics, sympathetic ones such as Randy Pitman in scholarly journals, and unsympathetic ones such as Michael Medved in both popular journals and his book *Hollywood vs. America*. Though there was no official censorship in the late 20th century, the discourse about Scorsese's film echoes remarkably that about Wilde's play a century before, and suppression of the film was startlingly effective.

Those who protested against the production and then release of the film did so on the grounds of blasphemy and immorality, most of them without having seen it. What they knew about it was that it had made changes to the "historical" account in the Bible. They considered these changes offensive to religious people because, they claimed, the film held religion up to ridicule. These criticisms, that would have sounded familiar to Wilde and Gide, were lodged by a conservative coalition (calling themselves "mainstream") of Catholic clergy, Southern Baptists, and various Christian fundamentalists. According to Medved, this coalition comprised the National Council of Catholic Bishops, the National Catholic Conference, the Southern Baptist Convention, the Eastern Orthodox Church of America, the Archbishop of Canterbury, twenty members of the U.S. House of Representatives (who cosponsored a bipartisan resolution condemning the film), the Christian Democratic Party of Italy, and Mother Teresa. Medved, who actually saw the film and wrote about it in *Christianity Today* and *Hollywood vs America*, is a practicing Jew.

Liberal religious groups and scholars saw theological correctness in the film and an explanation of ideas consistent with the current scholarship that emphasized first-century Palestinian culture, the real life of Jesus and his actual words, and indications of the human experience of Jesus. While conservatives pointed to blasphemy, religious liberals pointed to the heresy of ignoring the humanity of Christ in favor of his divinity. Non-religious liberals, meanwhile, asserted First Amendment rights and warned about the dangers of censorship. As most of this back-and-forth transpired prior to the film's release, it could not treat what the film had actually done, and few people had read Kazantzakis's 500-page novel.

Even after the film's release, most of the discussion had very little to do with the film itself. As Randy Pitman, now editor of *Video Librarian*, put it, "Neither side, defenders or censors, had much to say about the film as film. Neither side was prepared to look at the movie in historical context. Neither side was particularly interested in the ideas with which Scorsese grappled. For each side, it was a black-and-white issue — either 'censorship' or 'no censorship.'" Pitman concluded, "That is why I often find these kinds of debates to be both boring and meaningless" (136). For my purposes, though, that is what made the debate so interesting.

What the conservative critics called blasphemous were the changes Kazantzakis and Scorsese had made and the ideas they explored, chiefly the suggestion that Jesus would have been tempted by sexuality, marriage, and family to the point of being willing to come down from the cross to enjoy them. Critics objected to Jesus's sexual interest in Mary Magdalene, represented in two scenes in the film. In the first of these, very early in the film, Jesus visits Mary's tent where as a prostitute she receives her customers, and he voyeuristically observes these transactions while recalling her having blamed him for her vocation because of his rejection of her love when they were younger. In the second, in the latter portion of the film, after an angel, portrayed as a young girl, tells Jesus that he has done enough and may come down from the cross, he makes love to Mary, now his wife, in their home under the sympathetic observation of the angel. Mary dies shortly thereafter, though, stoned to death by the community. Jesus then marries the sisters Mary and Martha and fathers children by them. The stoning death of Mary received no comment from critics.

Conservative critics also objected to an encounter between Jesus and Paul in which Jesus, having heard Paul preaching, confronts him with the untruth of his death and resurrection, with the reality of his normal life. Kazantzakis's Paul responds, "Shut your shameless mouth!" And he goes on: "In the rottenness, the injustice and poverty of this world, the Crucified and Resurrected Jesus has been the one precious consolation for the honest man, the wronged man. True or false — what do I care! It's enough if the world is saved!" And then his thought takes flight: "What is 'truth'? What is 'falsehood'? Whatever gives wings to men, whatever produces great works and great souls and lifts us a man's height above the earth — that is true." He might have been commenting about art, but he is not. Rather, he rants: "I don't give a hoot about what's true and what's false, or whether I saw him or didn't see him, or whether he was crucified or wasn't crucified. I create the truth, create it out of obstinacy and longing and faith. I don't struggle to find it — I build it" (477). Clearly, this scene implies comment on the belief in Paul over belief in Jesus that characterizes rigid adherence to Church doctrine and on the credibility of the sources of that doctrine. Similarly, in the scene where Jesus raises Lazarus from the dead, Saul (not yet Paul) asks Lazarus what death was like, whether it is better than life, and he responds, "I was a little surprised ... there wasn't that much difference" (Memorable Quotes), dispiriting news for those expecting something quite different of an afterlife, provocative to those promised that by ecclesiastical authorities.

The narrative in the novel and the film opens with Jesus as an adult, depicting him as a carpenter who builds crucifixes with which the Romans execute Jews. The novel is especially replete with people addressing him with vitriol as the Cross Maker. His best friend Judas, a zealous Jewish rebel, confronts and argues with Jesus with increasing severity, asking how Jesus can be engaged in this appalling work. From this dialogue, we gather that Jesus is struggling against the voices he hears in his head, fighting the god calling him, doing his vilest work in order to alienate that god, but to no avail. "Who is tormenting you?" Judas asks. Kazantzakis's narrator reports,

> The young man laughed feebly. He was about to reply that it was God, but he restrained himself. This was the great cry within him, and he did not want to let it escape his lips.
> "I am wrestling," he answered.
> "With whom?"
> "I don't know. I'm wrestling."
> The redbeard plunged his eyes into those of the youth. He questioned them, implored them, threatened, but the pitch-black inconsolable eyes, full of fear, did not answer [21–2].

The narrative subjectivizes Jesus's experience, the film showing us what Judas sees, the novel providing direct access to Jesus's mind so the reader knows here what he wants to but does not say. Indeed, the narrator in the novel has presence and voice, often opening a chapter with a reflection, such as the following:

> The foundations of the world were shaken because man's heart was shaken, crushed under the stones which men called Jerusalem, under the prophecies, the Second Comings, the anathemas, under the Pharisees and Sadducees, the rich who ate, the poor who were hungry, and under the Lord Jehovah, from whose beard and mustaches the blood of mankind had been running for centuries upon centuries into the abyss. No matter where you touched this God, he bellowed [364].

In any case, the premise that Jesus fought his divine calling and that Judas was his closest friend conservative critics found objectionable and blasphemous.

The Last Temptation of Christ obviously perverted the Biblical text, but like Wilde's and Gide's plays, it exploited gaps actually present in the text. The nature of the relationship between Jesus and Mary Magdalene, for instance, is notoriously undefined. That she appears in the novel and film as a prostitute did not trouble critics, despite the absence of this in the Biblical account, for she had already acquired this reputation in the post–Biblical tradition. Kazantzakis's incorporation into his narrative of the many such accretions to the Biblical accounts in Christian tradition — and the novel is comprehensive in this respect — is, for the reader who can recognize them, astonishing in its deft and clever integration. Kazantzakis's wide knowledge of the Biblical texts, Christian theology, and the tradition's mythology is vividly evident, and his craft in employing them meaningfully subtle.

The relationship between Jesus's and Paul's ministries is complicated. The Biblical Paul, of course, did not know the human Jesus, and his own report of his conversion experience (as distinguished from the account found in Acts) mentions only that the risen Christ was revealed to him. Paul's writing seems largely unconcerned with the life and ministry of Jesus, focused rather on the atoning function of his death and resurrection. Paul's attention was on building the Church in anticipation of the parousia, while Jesus's was on raising up the socially marginalized and downtrodden and calling Jews from rigid legalism to live the spirit of Torah in the here and now.

Similarly, the relationship between Jesus and Judas is odd and unresolved in the Biblical accounts. This textual problem intrigued Scorsese and provided a focus for creative expansion.

> I never really quite believed the representation of Judas in films based on the Gospels. It was too easy either to make him totally political or to make us believe he betrayed Jesus for thirty pieces of silver.... I think everybody who worked on the film, and everybody who's read the book over the years, feels it's the first time you can really believe in this relationship — that Judas did not want to betray him, but had to go through with being God's instrument for the sacrifice of Jesus.... While we're not saying our version is the whole truth, it makes you question and maybe understand the concept of loving a little better [130].

In response to protests, Scorsese expressed his motivation, similar to Wilde's and Gide's, in a public statement:

> My film was made with deep religious feeling. I have been working on this film for fifteen years; it is more than just another film project for me. I believe it is a religious film about suffering and the struggle to find God. It was made with conviction and love and so I believe it is an affirmation of faith, not a denial [xxii].

Kazantzakis made a similar statement in his prologue to the novel:

> This book is not a biography; it is the confession of every man who struggles. In publishing it I have fulfilled my duty, the duty of a person who struggled much, was much embittered in his life, and had many hopes. I am certain that every free man who reads this book, so filled as it is with love, will more than ever before, better than ever before, love Christ [4].

The last temptation for Kazantzakis's Jesus is to come down from the cross, and fifty pages before the end of the 500-page novel he does. Forty pages later, though, Judas confronts him with the truth of the angel: it is Satan, and Jesus has succumbed to his temptation. In the last ten pages, Jesus makes his way back up to and onto the cross, and when he awakens from a faint we realize this has been a hallucination, a "dream," as most critics and scholars refer to this portion of the novel and the film. Jesus dies uttering "a triumphant cry: IT IS ACCOMPLISHED!" Kazantzakis's narrator concludes, "And it was as though he had said: Everything has begun" (496).

In their introductory essay to *Scorsese on Scorsese*, "Living Cinema— The Passion of Martin Scorsese," editors David Thompson and Ian Christie, demonstrate through their review of the events that transpired around the release of *The Last Temptation of Christ*, the making, releasing, and defending of this film, to be the singular influential experience of Scorsese's career. In the months before the film's release, protests against it accelerated. On July 15, 1988, evangelist Bill Bright offered MCA reimbursement for the cost of the film if Universal Studios would hand it over for destruction. The next day two hundred members of the Baptist Tabernacle of Los Angeles, led by Reverend R. L. Hymers, picketed Universal carrying banners saying "Universal are Like Judas Iscariot," "The Greatest Story Ever Distorted," and "Wasserman [chairman of MCA] Endangers Israel," and staged a mock crucifixion. The following week, after a screening of the film for religious leaders that resulted in some clergy observing "nothing blasphemous about it" (Episcopal Bishop of New York Paul Moore) and others finding it "morally offensive" and to be avoided (Episcopal Archbishop of Los Angeles Roger M. Mahony), Mother Angelica, head of The Eternal Word television network, characterized it as "the most satanic movie ever made," declaring it "will destroy Christianity." When Universal decided to release the film early, Bill Bright, Jerry Falwell, and Donald Wildman called for a boycott on voting for Democrats on the grounds that the party had connections with MCA. The U.S. Catholic conference pronounced that its forty million followers should not see the film. And on the day before its August 12 release, 25,000 protesters marched around Universal Studios. Upon its opening the next day on nine screens, there were further protests conducted outside these sell-out performances. Hundreds of theatres across the country decided not to show the film, some merely nervous about the potential damage to their facilities, and others joining the coalition in protest (xxi–iv). Though there was no official censorship in force, *The Last Temptation of Christ* was nonetheless quite effectively censored by an enormous grassroots, conservative effort to suppress it.

In May 1989, MCA released a video of the film with only a low-key announcement and no promotion. Boycotts of sales of MCA's video release of another film, *E.T.*, were organized, though these foundered (xxvi). Video stores blackballed the release of *The Last Temptation of Christ*, purchased by more libraries than retail outlets. In October, when Cinemax announced three scheduled showings, numerous newspaper articles denounced the plan, and local cable companies blacked out the showings (Pitman 86). Blockbuster, the largest video rental retailer in the U.S. before Netflix, refused to carry the film in any of its stores.

There was a similar storm of protest in Europe. Guglielmo Biraghi, director of the Venice Film Festival, screened the film out of competition, describing it as "a very Catholic film," while Italian filmmaker Franco Zeffirelli, who had directed a 1977 television mini-series titled *Jesus of Nazareth* that premiered in the U.S. as an N.B.C. Easter special, campaigned with other Catholics to bar it entirely. In England Mary Whitehouse threatened to invoke the law of blasphemy against the film in her protest to the British Board of Film Classification, and Basil Cardinal Hume announced that the Catholic community should not see the film because parts of it would shock and outrage believers. When it opened in Paris in September, the film met with violent demonstrations, a riot in the foyer of the Odeon, Molotov cocktails, tear gas, and injuries. Similar incidents occurred in Avignon, Besancon, and Marseilles. A fire gutted a cinema in October, injuring more people, and the distribution of the film in France was rapidly curtailed. It met with similar violence in Brazil, and was banned in Israel and Greece (xxiii–vi).

The outcry and violence the film provoked suggests that there was something large at stake. *The Last Temptation of Christ* was a turning point in the careers of both Scorsese and Michael Medved, who had become the opposition's most articulate and coolheaded exponent. Medved was a PBS film critic who had grown increasingly uncomfortable with the movies that Hollywood was producing and distributing to the American public. But it was *The Last Temptation of Christ* that became for him the watershed moment, and though his *Hollywood vs America* treats that general concern, it is to *The Last Temptation of Christ* that he continually returns, and which represented for him all that is wrong with the entertainment industry.

Medved claims that "tens of millions of Americans now see the entertainment industry as an all-powerful enemy, an alien force that assaults our most cherished values and corrupts our children" (3). Hollywood, he argues, is hopelessly out of touch with "mainstream" Americans and, therefore, no longer (because he claims that at one time it did) reflects the values of American families. The principal value, as is clear from this claim, is "family." The others he itemizes:

> Our fellow citizens cherish the institution of marriage and consider religion an important priority in life....

> In our private lives, most of us deplore violence....
> Americans are passionately patriotic....
> Nearly all parents want to convey to their children the importance of self-discipline, hard work, and decent manners....

And, he concludes, "as a working film critic, I've watched this assault on traditional values for more than a decade" (10).

So, the real problem with *The Last Temptation of Christ* was that it assaulted "our most cherished" and "traditional" values. Now, this is an interesting claim about a film that portrayed the family and marriage as the ultimate temptation, a life-long struggle with God and the problem of how to live faithfully, violence as sacrificial suffering, the acceptance of the most difficult life calling, the commitment to follow through with it, and a loving concern for all human beings. The problem here is that the Biblical story does not in fact support the cultural myth underlying these so-called traditional mainstream values.

This cultural myth was characterized by Robert Jewett and John Shelton Lawrence as the "American Monomyth" in an intriguing study of that same title. Analyzing American literature, film, and television, they uncovered a peculiarly American version of the monomyth of the mysterious stranger who passes by, coming from nowhere and going to nowhere, asking nothing in return, and putting everything wrong to rights. Every culture invents such a figure. The classical version is the hero who ventures from the common world to the world of supernatural wonder, encountering fabulous forces, winning decisive victories, and bringing back to the common world powers that will benefit man. In the American version, evil threatens the community of harmonious paradise, and its normal institutions all fail to contend with it. A selfless superhero emerges to renounce temptations and carry out the redemptive task; victory restores the community to its edenic condition, and the superhero recedes into obscurity (xvii–xxi). Sexual renunciation is imperative for the superhero's continued fight against evil; once married with a family he would be unable to conduct his work (169–85).

> By elaborate conventions of restraint, his desire for revenge is purified. Patient in the face of provocations, he seeks nothing for himself and withstands all temptations. Sexual fulfillment is renounced for the duration of the mission. The purity of his motivations ensures moral infallibility in judging persons and situations.... In these conventions the monomyth betrays an aim to deny the tragic complexities of human life. The American monomyth offers vigilantism without lawlessness, sexual repression without resultant perversion, and moral infallibility without use of intellect. It features a restoration of Eden for others, but refuses to allow the dutiful hero to participate in its pleasures [195–6].

This sounds very much like the version of the Biblical story that those who objected to Scorsese's film espoused. Jewett and Lawrence are themselves interested in how the myth provides escapism from the realities of life and responsibility for having to confront them. The key here is that "families are too demanding to accommodate redemptive crusades..." (212). Medved's argument is an articulation of the American monomyth: the American family and its "traditional" values are under "assault" by Hollywood, and democratic processes are no help against this evil. His objection to Scorsese's film is that it portrays a Jesus different from the Christ of the American monomyth: Scorsese's Jesus was tempted by family life, and he struggled against becoming a superhero.

The Biblical story of the life and teaching of Jesus the Christ does not seem to support the cultural myth underlying the values Medved and others held to be traditional and under attack by *The Last Temptation of Christ*. The Jesus of the Biblical accounts engaged in frequent and escalating resistance to institutional power and religious authority, and lived in solidarity with the poor. It is difficult to overlook that he spent a lot of time with sinners, viewed the moral questions of his time with quite a critical eye, and had comparatively little interest in the afterlife. Though Jesus's parables all address the subject of "the kingdom," New Testament scholar Bernard Brandon Scott demonstrates that his central premise was that the kingdom is here and now, not elsewhere and in some future, that Jesus's sense of urgency comes from his being thoroughly rooted in the present. Importantly, it is tough to ascribe to the Biblical Jesus any kind of commitment to marriage and family, given the passages in which he admonishes people to leave family behind and argues that those he has chosen to be around him are now his family. Though he clearly enjoyed and respected children, they seem to be more a part of the group of people for whose welfare he was concerned than they are a group about whose corruption he specifically feared.

Traditional readings, liberation theologians point out, tend to support the perspective that claims universality and enjoys cultural hegemony and power. Claiming God's preferential option for the poor and oppressed based upon the Biblical accounts, these theologians working in Latin American "base camp communities" conduct readings of the Bible from the unprivileged perspectives of poverty and marginality, having come to suspect all scriptural readings that support the dominant culture's values. The response to liberation theology within the dominant culture in Latin America has been dramatic, from Papal denunciation to political suppression and violence, for it challenges both religious and political authority and the tenuous grounds on which they are claimed. Such readings are subversive and worthy of suppression, violently if need be. Similarly, Scorsese made very public a reading of scripture that did not endorse and perhaps exposed the dubious basis of the mainstream, traditional, culturally hegemonic values, and in doing so exposed the secret that the story, in fact, as it appears in the Bible — Western culture's sacred book — does not support that culture's values.

Much of the controversy around Scorsese's *The Last Temptation of Christ* centers on the issue of fidelity. Critics pointed to perversions and distortions in its narrative and characterizations of events reported by the Gospels, and of persons appearing in the Biblical accounts, as blasphemous because they were unfaithful to these sources. Supporters, on the other hand, celebrated the film's depictions of the characters and events for their fidelity to the spirit of these accounts, making them fresh, provocative, and accessible, they argued. But, Scorsese adapted Kazantzakis's novel to film, not the Gospels themselves.

It is a commonplace for audiences to lament a film's adaptation of a much-loved book, and, as Robert Stam points out in his introduction to *Literature and Film: A Guide to the Theory and Practice of Film Adaptation*, they employ quite moralistic language to characterize the disservice the film has done the novel:

> Terms like "infidelity," "betrayal," "deformation," "violation," "bastardization," "vulgarization," and "desecration" proliferate in adaptation discourse, each word carrying its specific charge or opprobrium. "Infidelity" carries overtones of Victorian prudishness; "betrayal" evokes ethical perfidy; ... and "desecration" intimates religious sacrilege and blasphemy [3].

Indeed, one of Gibson's significant missteps, in my opinion, was to claim fidelity, for, as Paula Frederiksen, one of the scholars gathered by officers of the United States Conference of Catholic Bishops and by the Anti-Defamation League to evaluate Gibson's script (with his knowledge), apprised, he

> championed his film's historical realism, and its fidelity to the Passion narratives in the New Testament gospels. *The Passion of the Christ*, Gibson has proclaimed, was Jesus' story as it "really was," ... he has insisted, loudly and often, that his film is the most historically accurate of any Jesus-film ever made.... In our culture, to claim that something is "historically accurate" is to claim "This is what *really* happened." Viewers watching his movie are invited to see its (erroneous) ancient languages, its idiosyncratic selection of gospel themes, and its simulacra of pain and blood as attesting to its "realism." They are thereby encouraged to think that the story they are watching is, somehow, also "what really happened" [Frederickson].

Like all Biblical narratives, the Gospels are startlingly concise, providing scant detail useful to a film maker: "They crucified him" is the sum of the narrative. All those who portray this event, from the earliest icons and passion plays to the Jesus films of today, confront the problem of how to dramatize an event merely reported as having transpired in the source text, a problem that vexes notions of fidelity.

To what should a filmmaker be faithful? If not fidelity, then against what criteria should critics evaluate the success of a film? Stam proposed a model for analysis of film adaptations that pays "attention to 'transfers of creative energy,' or to specific dialogical responses, to 'readings' and 'critiques' and 'interpretations' and 'rewritings'" for analyses that "take into account the gaps between very different media and materials of expression" (46). The model employs new metaphors for speaking about adaptation, for "the translation of one 'text' into a new format," as a "transcoding" (11–12). A critic, then, of *The Passion of the Christ* or of *The Last Temptation of Christ* might profitably discern from analysis of the film the criteria the film maker employed in the adaptation, comprising a "series of operations: selection, amplification, concretization, actualization, critique, extrapolation, popularization, reaccentuation, transculturalization" (45), etc., to assess how the film transcoded the source.

The sources of these two films, though, differ. The criteria Gibson employed in transcoding the Gospel sources "tend in a particular direction," as Frederiksen observed of what she called his "errors," his "misreading of the Gospels" (Frederiksen), one reflecting his film career and adherence to a peculiar brand of Catholic faith. Similarly, the criteria Scorsese employed in his film adaptation also tend in a particular direction, one reflecting his film career and personal concerns. Scorsese's source, though, was Kazantzakis's novel, not the Bible.

In Stam's argument against traditional film adaptation criticism, he observes that the problem of fidelity is unique to film, that other media seem not to be held to such an impossible standard, media such as music or painting, for instance. "While filmic rewritings of novels are judged in terms of fidelity, literary rewritings of classical texts, such as Coetzee's rewriting of *Robinson Crusoe* are not so judged—change is presumed to be the point!" (15–16). Sacred texts, however, seem a major exception to Stam's generalization; certainly Kazantzakis's novel was, for he suffered meaningfully from judgments made about its fidelity to its source.

In their study of his thought and *oeuvre*, Middleton and Bien characterized Kazantzakis concisely by their title, *God's Struggler*. So also is the Jesus of Kazantzakis's novel a struggler with God, and the novel portrays that struggle as subjective experience, one necessarily fictionalized, for we have no record of what Jesus felt or thought. Indeed, it is a peculiarity of the Gospel narratives that they objectify his experience, narrating what transpired and reporting how others responded. Characterized variously as historical or mythopoeic, the Gospels uniquely comprise a literary genre that narratively expresses the beliefs of a believing community about the meaning of the life and death of Jesus of Nazareth. Though they are literary and narrative, they are also doctrinal, christological. Kazantzakis's novel synthesized an extraordinary breadth of Biblical, ecclesiastical, and traditional narrative details, organized to explore Jesus's experience subjectively. In configuring these details, he constructed a fictional experience, the dream portion portraying Jesus's temptation to descend from the cross and to live a normal life, the most fictionalized. For there, not only does the reader encounter the temptation as a fully developed experience, but also Kazantzakis's revisioning of characters, importantly Judas and Paul. These characterizations are some of the most provocative features of Kazantzakis's novel, transforming Judas from the loathsome betrayer of Jesus into his greatest friend, and Paul from the inspired interpreter of Christ into Jesus's most fearsome enemy.

Despite Kazantzakis's title, *The Last Temptation,* the dream portion depicting that comprises only ten percent of the novel, though indeed appears last in it. That is, it concludes the narrative of Jesus's journey from Cross Maker to crucified, from struggler against God to Christ. Kazantzakis's principal interest was in that struggle, and for his Jesus the ultimate temptation was to give it up, to believe that God had relinquished him from it: "Jesus's face shone. 'I've finished wrestling with God,' he said. 'We have become friends. I won't build crosses any more. I'll build troughs, cradles, bedsteads'" (461). The dream portion in Scorsese's adaptation, though, is almost a third of the film, suggesting that the principle guiding Scorsese's "selection, amplification, concretization, actualization, critique, extrapolation, popularization, reaccentuation, transculturalization," his transcoding of the novel, was an interest in temptation. The proportion of treatment of it in the film is three times that of the novel. It is the most fictionalized portion of both the novel and the film, the least faithful to Biblical and traditional sources, and the most provocative, for conservative critics blasphemous and for liberal critics inspiring, for what it suggests.

This suggestive capacity of fiction, whether literary or performative, is the source of its abiding value. For, we might recall that the Biblical sources themselves, the Gospels, are imaginative retellings of events in the life and death of Jesus and those who encountered him. That four Gospels were canonized in the Bible yet disagree with each other in narrative detail, sequence, characterization, and thematic emphasis, manifests acknowledgement by the institution that canonized them of their inspirational capacity as fictions. That is, there is not one account of the life and death of Jesus that orthodoxy holds authoritative, rather there are four narratives that each tell a story of the good news of the meaning of that life and death. None is held to be more or less faithful than the others are.

Since the composition of the Gospels, there have been countless retellings of their stories in the passion plays of the Middle Ages, in iconography, in oratorio, in Biblical poetry and drama, in Life of Jesus novels, and in Jesus films. Scorsese's, produced by the world's greatest fiction factory, Hollywood, raised up to the world a comparatively obscure retelling, composed in a comparatively obscure place in an obscure language by a significant but relatively obscure author. Without Scorsese's film, Kazantzakis's novel would not have come to the world's notice.

Likewise, the Gospels raised up for the world, a generation or two after the events they narrate, the story of an obscure man, a Jewish martyr among thousands of Jewish martyrs, who in the last three years of his life challenged ecclesiastical authority, deplored adherence to the letter of the law, and restored the spirit of the sacred texts through the commitment of his life to the redemption of "the least of these" (Matt 25:45). At an apocalyptic moment in Israel's history, there was no shortage of putative prophets and messiahs. But the stories told about one of them, stories that weave together details of his life in varying ways reflecting varying interpretations of the meaning of that life, inspired a movement that became a religion that two thousand years later enjoys cultural hegemony. It was a new ecclesia, a new dogma, and a new scripture that Kazantzakis and Scorsese challenged, fostering controversy that inspired riots. But they join a long tradition of telling and retelling stories to challenge orthodoxy and inspire new faith. This is the power of fiction.

Works Cited

Downey, Katherine Brown. *Perverse Midrash: Oscar Wilde, Andre Gide, and Censorship of Biblical Drama*. New York: Continuum, 2004. Print.

Frederiksen, Paula. " History, Hollywood, and the Bible: Some Thoughts on Gibson's Passion." *SBL Forum*. March 2004. Web. 3 Sept. 2010. http://sbl-site.org/Article.aspx?ArticleID=225.

Gide, Andre. "Bathsheba." *The Return of the Prodigal Preceded by Five Other Treatises with "Saul," a Drama in Five Acts*. Trans. Dorothy Bussy. 105–122. London: Secker & Warburg, 1953. Print.

_____. "Saul." *The Return of the Prodigal Preceded by Five Other Treatises with "Saul," a Drama in Five Acts*. Trans. Dorothy Bussy. 151–304. London: Secker & Warburg, 1953. Print.

Jesus of Nazareth. Dir. Franco Zefirelli. Incorporated Television Company, 1977. TV Miniseries.

Jewett, Robert, and John Shelton Lawrence. *The American Monomyth*. New York: Anchor Doubleday, 1977. Print.

Karalis, Vrasidas. "The Unreality of Repressed Desires in *The Last Temptation*." *Scandalizing Jesus? Kazantzakis's* The Last Temptation of Christ *Fifty Years On*. Ed. Darren J.N. Middleton. 73–83. New York: Continuum, 2005. Print.

Kazantzakis, Nikos. *The Last Temptation of Christ*. Trans. P.A. Bien. New York: Simon & Schuster, 1998. Print.

_____. *Nikos Kazantzakis: A Biography Based on His Letters*. Trans. Amy Mims. New York: Simon & Schuster, 1968. Print.

The Last Temptation of Christ. Dir. Martin Scorsese. Universal Pictures, 1988. Film.

Medved, Michael. *Hollywood vs America: Popular Culture and the War on Traditional Values*. New York: Zondervan, 1992. Print.

___. "The Thorn in Hollywood's Side." *Christianity Today.* April 27, 1992. Print.
"Memorable Quotes for *The Last Temptation of Christ.*" IMDb.com. Web. 4 Sept. 2011.
Middleton, Darren J.N., ed. *Scandalizing Jesus? Kazantzakis's* The Last Temptation of Christ *Fifty Years On.* New York: Continuum, 2005. Print.
Middleton, Darren J.N., and Peter Bien. *God's Struggler: Religion in the Writings of Nikos Kazantzakis.* Macon: Mercer University Press, 1996. Print.
The New Oxford Annotated Bible with Apocrypha: New Revised Standard Version. Eds. Michael Coogan, Marc Z. Brettler, Carol Newsom, and Pheme Perkins. New York: Oxford University Press, 2010. Print.
The Passion of the Christ. Dir. Mel Gibson. Icon Productions, 2004. Film.
Pitman, Randy. "Censorship and *The Last Temptation of Christ.*" *Wilson Library Bulletin* 64, No. 5 (January 1990): 85–86, 136. Print.
Scorsese, Martin. *Scorsese on Scorsese.* Eds. David Thompson and Ian Christie. Boston: Faber & Faber, 1989. Print.
Scott, Bernard Brandon. *Hear Then the Parable: A Commentary on the Parables of Jesus.* Minneapolis: Fortress, 1989. Print.
Stam, Robert, and Alessandra Raengo, eds. *Literature and Film: A Guide to the Theory and Practice of Film Adaptation.* Malden, MA: Blackwell, 2005. Print.
Thompson, David, and Ian Christie, eds. "Living Cinema — The Passion of Martin Scorsese." *Scorsese on Scorsese.* Boston: Faber & Faber, 1989. xix–xxvii. Print.

Nietzsche and Tolstoy
on Authentic Christianity

MARC LUCHT

At first glance, the philosophical stances of Friedrich Nietzsche and Lev Tolstoy could not seem to be more sharply opposed. Tolstoy is the consummate Christian moralist, indicting modern culture for its corrupted inversion of the norms articulated by Christ. For Tolstoy, the life committed to Jesus's authentic message is the life of truth. Nietzsche inveighs against moralizers, diagnosing the hypocrisy and danger connected with the commitment to traditional conceptions of the good. For him, Christian values all too often are motivated by resentment and the desire for revenge, and threaten to result in herd-like conformity and pessimism. Nietzsche rejects the dogmatic adherence to Christian morality most typically in favor of an aesthetic individualism and retrieval of ancient pagan values. Tolstoy is the champion of universal brotherhood, unconditional love, anarchic pacifism, and kindness to all, including to all humanity and non-human animals. Nietzsche is well aware of the various ways in which suffering can strengthen and enhance an individual or a community, and he does not shrink from claiming that such suffering at times may be necessary. He shows very little interest in the material conditions of the poor and, as he regards contest and strife as conditions for growth, sees great benefit in hierarchical and exploitive social orders. Tolstoy's Christianity commits him to the idea that the best manner of life for humanity is to be found in participation in or communion with the source of life, God the Father, and in the attempt to realize the kingdom of God by promoting loving harmony among all living human beings and animals. Tolstoy advocates political equality and the abolition of private property, and excoriates the military, the wealthy, and the state for fostering conditions of strife, inequality, and suffering. Spiritual maturity is to be found within a life of simple piety and manual labor, and he urges upon us a patient endurance of life's sufferings oriented by the recognition that our lives do not belong to us, but to God. Nietzsche argues that the Christian churches' belief in an immortal, non-material soul and their pursuit of a transcendent ideal (such as God or an eternal, non-earthly afterlife), are motivated by a poisonous need to devalue the body and our earthly existence, and thus contribute to a life-denying nihilism. For him, something like redemption is to be found instead in the recognition of the tragic nature of life while at the same time committing oneself affirmatively to earthly existence with the exuberance of self-assertion, aesthetic creativity, and world-historical mission. Nietzsche would have indicted Tolstoy's late commitment to absolute chastity as symptomatic of precisely the kind of perverse hostility to the body and its drives that motivates religion's nihilistic stance against reality and nature and leads to a decadent morality of "un-selfing."[1]

Indeed, Tolstoy and Nietzsche, to the extent that each was aware of the other, were mutually quite hostile. Tolstoy found Nietzsche's works to be depraved nonsense. He judged *Thus Spoke Zarathustra* to be the work of someone "completely insane," and took Nietzsche's thought to endorse "egoism, evil and hatred."[2] The aestheticist indifference to morality that Tolstoy regarded as the degradation of art and a contributing factor to the corruption of especially the upper social classes, and that is the primary concern of his book *What Is Art?*, he attributes to "Nietzsche and his adherents, and with the decadents, and aesthetes of the type at one time represented by Oscar Wilde, select as a theme for their production the denial of morality and the laudation of vice."[3] In a short discussion of what he understood to be Nietzsche's doctrine of the "overman," namely, that "a man truly free is under no obligation to obey any injunction, human or divine," Tolstoy writes,

> Expressed in the form of a doctrine these positions startle us. In reality they are implied in the ideal of art serving beauty[...]. It is this supplanting of the ideal of what is right by the ideal of what is beautiful, i.e., of what is pleasant, that is the fourth consequence, and a terrible one, of the perversion of art in our society. It is fearful to think of what would befall humanity were such art to spread among the masses of the people.[4]

For his part, though never engaging with Tolstoy's works in any detail, Nietzsche expresses no admiration for Tolstoy. He found in Tolstoy a representative of the "morality of pity" arising out of a pathological hostility to life and characterizing "our entire literary and artistic decadence from St. Petersburg to Paris, from Tolstoi to Wagner[...]."[5] In an unpublished note from

1887, Nietzsche associates Tolstoy with "Russian pessimism,"[6] and in 1888 mocks Tolstoy's admiration for the "goodness" of "his muzhiks."[7]

Nevertheless, there are striking and important similarities between Nietzsche and Tolstoy. Some are stylistic: often each is uncompromising in his pronouncements, for instance, and each uses caustic irony to great effect. Each has left to posterity masterpieces of literary style and psychological acumen. Each expresses an unfortunate disdain for women. Especially important is each thinker's diagnosis of the prevailing spirit of European Christianity as an inauthentic perversion and reversal of Jesus's true teaching, and the nearly identical way in which each characterizes that original teaching. Considering Nietzsche's and Tolstoy's retrieval of what they take to be authentic Christianity will shed light on what may be some surprising substantive similarities between the two thinkers, and also will provide a hint of what a non-nihilistic religion might be like.

The Church as Corrupt Inversion of Jesus's Message

Dogmatic, unconditional assertions of "Yes and No" constitute distasteful assaults on "men and things," Nietzsche suggests, whereas learning the "art of nuances" is the "best gain of life."[8] Thus Nietzsche does not shrink from praising Christianity. What "we have to thank them for is inestimable," he writes, and "who could be rich enough in gratitude not to be impoverished in view of all that the 'spiritual men' of Christianity, for example, have so far done for Europe!"[9] Perhaps in a passage such as this Nietzsche has in mind the great architectural and artistic achievements of Christendom. Already in 1872 Nietzsche praises the "ineffably sublime and sacred music of Palestrina," a music that, unlike the more decadent pre–Wagnerian opera, is still capable of "devotion."[10] In 1888 he praises Bach and Handel, Christians both, as rare "Germans of the strong race."[11] Nietzsche recognizes the important roles religions such as Christianity play in consoling those who suffer and helping those who are psychologically and physiologically strong to practice self-discipline, a practice indispensable for "educating and ennobling a race."[12]

Yet, in general, Nietzsche's thinking, from beginning to end, is devoted to exposing and combating what he regards as the calamitous influence Christianity has had on world culture:

> I raise against the Christian church the most terrible of all accusations that any accuser ever uttered[...]. The Christian church has left nothing untouched by its corruption; it has turned every value into an un-value, every truth into a lie, every integrity into a vileness of the soul.[...] I call Christianity the one great curse, the one great innermost corruption, the one great instinct for revenge.[...] I call it the one immortal blemish of mankind.[13]

In the rhetorical fireworks of his enduring battle against the nihilistic Christian morality that, in its hostility to the body, and in its orientation towards a transcendent "beyond" "invented in order to devaluate the only world there is[...]," celebrates "antinature itself," an intriguing feature of Nietzsche's thought often is obscured.[14] His hostility towards Christianity, Christians, and Christian values does not extend to Jesus himself. In fact, in 1878, Nietzsche wrote that Jesus was the "noblest human being."[15] It seems that the title of Nietzsche's book *The Antichrist* all too often is thought to refer either to Nietzsche himself or to the "man of the future [...] this Antichrist and antinihilist" envisioned in his reflections on the "overman."[16] Yet the content of the book makes clear that the eponymous antichrist is not Nietzsche, but is actually the Christian church. There has been but "*one* Christian," he asserts, "and he died on the cross."[17] Since the crucifixion, those who have called themselves Christians have been herd-like conformists, resentful weaklings who preach love and compassion all the while hoping for the opportunity to exact revenge and gain power. Such people are hypocrites incapable of or uninterested in living the kind of life Jesus prescribed for them. Indeed, the church "was constructed" out of the very opposite of Jesus's own teaching: "Mankind lies on its knees before the opposite of that which was the origin, the meaning, the *right* of the evangel[...]."[18] As he puts the point elsewhere, "The church is precisely that against which Jesus preached[...]," for the founder of the church, Paul, "re-erected on a grand scale precisely that which Christ had annulled through his way of living."[19] Nietzsche's indictment of Christianity will not extend to the teaching of Jesus himself.

In the next section I shall clarify what precisely Nietzsche and Tolstoy judge the substantive content of Jesus's message to be as well as the way in which that message came to be distorted in Christianity. Here, the point is that Tolstoy shares Nietzsche's view that church Christianity constitutes a reversal of Jesus's own teaching. The goal of any church, Tolstoy writes, is to "conceal the real meaning of Christ's teaching and to replace it by their own, which lays no obligation on them [...] and what is the chief consideration, justifies the existence of priests supported at the people's expense."[20] Thus:

> Strange as it may seem, the churches as churches have always been, and cannot but be, institutions not only alien in spirit to Christ's teaching, but even directly antagonistic to it [... With] good reason is the history of the Church the history of the greatest cruelties and horrors. The churches as churches, as bodies which assert their own infallibility, are institutions opposed to Christianity.[21]

Tolstoy claims that the nature of a church ("not of something fantastic which we would wish it to be, but of what it is and has been in reality") is a body of people who claim the prerogative of "complete and sole possession of the truth."²² If a church is in essence dogmatic, then it must be in tension with Jesus's true teaching, which, he argues, recognizes human finitude and fallibility. The authentic Christian consciousness recognizes its own perpetual inadequacy, and involves a perpetual striving to ever more adequately understand and embody Jesus's teaching. In other words, better than resting satisfied that one is sufficiently virtuous (even if one's conduct already is quite admirable), is the attitude of admitting to one's own inadequacy and resolutely committing to unceasing efforts to be ever more virtuous.²³ Tolstoy argues that blessedness is nothing but a constant, dynamic progress towards the realization of Jesus's lesson, whereas the churches betray such consciousness through a dogmatic stasis grounded in theological hubris. As Nietzsche puts the same point, Christianity has perverted the original teaching by focusing on "dogmas instead of a way of life. Utter indifference to dogmas, cults, priests, church, theology is [authentically] Christian."²⁴ Tolstoy further criticizes the church for its complicity with and theological buttressing of military and state power. Particularly galling is the way in which clerical involvement in the administering of military oaths encourages naïve young men to think it permissible to subordinate their duties as human beings, such as the unconditional duty to refrain from killing, to what they are deluded into thinking of as the more important duties of soldiers. The institution of the church, Tolstoy tells us, is "blasphemous and demoralizing."²⁵

In fact, Tolstoy claims that one contributing cause of what he understands to be the modern corruption of art is to be found in its being harnessed by the church, which uses art to better obscure Jesus's true message. He thinks that all art has the capacity to bring together or unite people. Those appreciating a work of art through that appreciation empathetically share impressions, ideas, and feelings with the artist as well as with each other. But inauthentic art unites some people together within a community in such a way that "makes that very union a cause of separation between these united people and others[...]. Such is all patriotic art, with its anthems, poems, and monuments; such is all Church art, i.e., the art of certain cults, with their images, statues, processions, and other local ceremonies."²⁶ Church art reinforces rather than diminishes the differences among different communities, thus all too often exacerbating or creating hostility. Such enmity, of course, is exactly the opposite of the goal of authentic Christian life, namely, the "establishment of the greatest possible union between all living beings."²⁷ The best art, on the other hand, should subvert factionalism by being universal, possessed of the capacity to speak to and unite all of humanity. What is more, the churches, which are only "called Christian," employ art to augment some of their own most pernicious effects. The ways in which church "superstitions are supported and produced by the poetry of prayers, hymns, painting, by the sculpture of images and of statues, by singing, by organs, by music, by architecture[...]," contribute to a kind of "ecclesiastical intoxication" that frustrates the goal of general enlightenment and hinders the recognition of Jesus's true teaching.[28] Tolstoy's point seems to be that the aesthetic richness of a person's experience in church will inspire feelings such as wonder, majesty, and elevation. These feelings constitute an appearance of spiritual growth or moral uplift and therefore make one feel as if one is being appropriately religious, yet finally distract one from remembering that the whole point of religion (as of life) is to cultivate within oneself an ever deeper love for others and to pursue those good works required of us by such love. Again, Nietzsche concurs. He says, "Christians have never put into practice the acts Jesus prescribed for them[...]. The Buddhist acts differently from the non-Buddhist; the Christian acts as all the world does and possesses a Christianity of ceremonies and moods."[29]

Authentic Christianity as Practice Not Faith

For Nietzsche and Tolstoy, wherein lies authentic Christianity? What do they take Jesus's real teaching to have been? Each thinks that the essence of Jesus's teaching lies in the sermon on the mountain, and most especially in the injunction, "Resist not evil."[30] It is this message that is ignored and perverted by the existing churches.

Nietzsche claims that Jesus

> died as he had lived, as he had taught—*not* to "redeem men" but to show how one must live. This practice is his legacy to mankind: his behavior before the judges [...] his behavior on the *cross*. He does not resist, he does not defend his right [...] *Not* to resist, *not* to be angry, not to hold responsible — but to resist not even the evil one — to *love* him.[31]

He lived as he did, and died as he did, in order to demonstrate to us that "neither by deeds nor in your heart should you resist him who harms you. [...] You should be angry with no one, you should show contempt to no one. Give alms in secret. You should not want to become rich," and that the best life "consists of love and humility; in a fullness of heart that does not exclude even the lowliest; in a formal repudiation of maintaining one's rights, of self-defense, of victory in the sense of personal triumph; in faith in blessedness here on earth[...]."[32] What is more, the primitive Christian message is the "abolition of the state," for it "forbids oaths, war service, courts of justice, self-defense and the defense of any kind of community, [and] the distinction between fellow countrymen and foreigners[...]."[33] Nietzsche understands the heart of Jesus's teaching to be the lesson of universal love and total, anarchic pacifism.

Tolstoy, of course, concurs. The moral journey of the character Pierre Bezukhov, in *War and Peace*, culminates in a famous expression of such universal love. After meeting in a camp for prisoners of war that "unfathomable, round, and eternal embodiment of the spirit of simplicity and truth," Platon Karataev, Pierre comes to recognize the enduring and "unshakeable" beauty of his "previously destroyed world."[34] This insight leads to his "happy insanity" after the war, which "consisted in the fact that he did not wait, as before, for personal reasons, which he called people's merits, in order to love them, but love overflowed his heart, and, loving people without reason, he discovered the unquestionable reasons for which it was worth loving them."[35] Similarly, the character Iván Ilych finds redemption in the honest and undissimulated love of his son, in pity, and in unconditional forgiveness even of those who had shown him no compassion as he succumbed to his agonizing illness. Such love enables him to conquer death.[36]

The unquestioning and universal love Pierre and Iván discover precludes the possibility of any violence. The "essential positions of true Christianity" include the idea of the "immediate relationship of each man to the Father, the consequent brotherhood and equality of all men, and the substitution of humility and love in place of every kind of violence[...]."[37] We are called to feel reverence for the "dignity of every man and for the life of every animal" and ought to learn to be "ashamed of luxury, of violence, of revenge[...]."[38] The core of Jesus's teaching lies in the "principles" of "equality and fraternity," "suppression of national distinctions," "community of property, [and] non-resistance of evil by force."[39] Indeed, Tolstoy recognizes the irony of the clerical preoccupation with the command against fornication, which is taken to be absolute and the occasion for incessant admonishment, while, at the same, when it comes to the command of non-resistance, "all church preachers recognize cases in which that command can be broken," and in fact go so far as to administer the military oath.[40] In the church's sanctioning the existence of an institution designed to engage in violent conflict, of course, what Tolstoy takes to be the truth of authentic Christianity is reversed and perverted. What is more, Tolstoy holds that governments are inherently coercive. Because power finally is always supported by violence or the threat of violence (evident, Tolstoy notes, in punishment for crimes, enforcement of rent and tax collection, mandatory military service, and violent suppression of civil disobedience), the state by its very existence always leads to and even magnifies exactly the sort of oppression and violence it was originally created to shield people from. The church's association with governments is an entanglement fundamentally at odds with Jesus's requirement of universal love.[41]

The universal love and non-hierarchical brotherhood exemplified in Jesus's teaching is not merely a matter of belief, however. It is both an affective disposition and a practice or way of life. Indeed, Nietzsche and Tolstoy each thinks it is *within or as such a life* that Jesus taught that blessedness is to be found, and each thinks that the emphasis on faith in (inauthentic) Christianity arises primarily as compensation for the inability of Christians to live in this way. As Nietzsche puts it, Jesus's moral message does not "formulate itself: it *lives*, it resists all formulas."[42] Instead, his "glad tidings" constituted a "genuine evangelical practice," such that

> it is not a "faith" that distinguishes the [authentic] Christian: the Christian *acts*, he is distinguished by acting *differently*: by not resisting, either in words or in his heart, those who treat him ill [...] the life of the Redeemer was nothing other than *this* practice — nor was his death anything else. He no longer required any formulas, any rites for his intercourse with God [... He] knows that it is only in the practice of this life that one feels "divine," "blessed" [...] the "kingdom of heaven" is a state of the heart — not something that is to come "above the earth" or "after death."[43]

According to Nietzsche, it was the inability of Christians, especially early Christians such as Paul, to practice the rigorous non-violent brotherly love exemplified in Jesus's life and death, that led them to focus instead on faith, in particular, in redemption through faith in the resurrection, as well as on the whole apparatus of ritual and metaphysical dogma. Jesus inspired what Nietzsche takes to be an anarchic peace movement oriented towards a particular kind of earthly existence. But, he says, this message was succeeded immediately by Paul, a "genius in hatred" in whom was "embodied the opposite type" to Jesus.[44] As Paul was unable to practice the sort of life Jesus lived, and as he needed to compete for adherents with contemporary mystery cults that satisfied a widespread need for violent sacrifice, he refocused the new religion away from exhortations to practice a life of non-resistance, and towards a "blood-drinking" "God on the cross," a new faith "in a miraculous transformation," and the hope for eternal life.[45] Thus Jesus's discrediting of the need for a priesthood to mediate between human and God is transformed into a "new ruling order and a church," and Jesus's doctrine of universal love and non-violence is "reversed by Paul into a pagan mystery doctrine, which finally learns to treat with the entire state organization — and wages war, condemns, tortures, swears, hates."[46] Once rejecting the "blessedness" of the way of life Jesus taught, meaning needed to be found elsewhere, and the church turned to "faith in unbelievable things, in the ceremonial of prayers, worship, feasts, etc." and towards faith "in some sort of miraculous subtraction of sins, accomplished not through man but through Christ's deed."[47]

Nietzsche's de-emphasis of dogma, ritual, and belief in the supernatural as key elements of an authentic Christianity is echoed in Tolstoy. Referring to Luke 17: 20–1, Tolstoy too argues that the "kingdom of God" is to be found precisely within the earthly experience of a certain kind of life, a life oriented by the internal goal of cultivating within oneself the greatest possible love (even towards those who hate one) and the external, practical goal of facilitating the greatest possible union and harmony among living creatures. Jesus taught what it is that "man must do to save himself, i.e., how best to live the life he has come into[...]."[48] Blessedness or salvation is nothing but the life of unconditional and universal love. Jesus's message of universal brotherhood, non-violence, and mutual service was distorted, however, first, as the wealthy classes realized that a Christian life negated "the privileges on which they lived[...]." As does Nietzsche, Tolstoy points to weakness as the cause for the failure to appropriate Jesus's message: not "being strong enough to accept true Christianity, men of these rich, governing classes [...] were left without any religion, with but the external forms of one, which they supported as being profitable and even necessary for themselves, since these forms screened a teaching which justified those privileges which they made use of."[49] Instead of acknowledging universal brotherhood, the church developed a doctrine more amenable to the justification of social hierarchies, erecting a "heavenly hierarchy" and "having introduced the worship of Christ, of the Virgin, of angels, of apostles, of saints, and of martyrs [...] it made blind faith in the Church and its ordinances the essential point of its teaching."[50] Second, as individuals devised idiosyncratic and distorted interpretations of Jesus's message, they needed to sanction these interpretations and their own authoritative capacity to disclose the truth; they did so by referring to "supernatural occurrences" and the "miraculous manner of [their] transmission" as proof (and as proof one would not be permitted to question) of those interpretations. Indeed

> the less the [authentic] doctrine was understood, the more obscure it appeared and the more necessary were external proofs of its truth. The proposition that we ought not to do unto others as we would not they should do unto us, did not need to be proved by miracles and needed no exercise of faith, because this proposition is in itself convincing and in harmony with man's mind and nature; but the proposition that Christ was God had to be proved by miracles completely beyond our comprehension.[51]

Thus Tolstoy, as does Nietzsche, claims that the church theology and ritual arise out of the failure to appropriate authentically the praxis that Jesus himself exemplified for us. The life of authentic piety, such as that embodied in by Tolstoy's character Platon Karataev, includes no theological sophistication, elaborate church rituals, or concern with abstract metaphysical questions or otherworldly arrangements; instead, Karataev speaks in often mutually contradictory clichés (somehow all nevertheless correct), prays his simple folk prayers, is kind to horses and dogs, and "joyfully" "loved and lived lovingly with everything that life brought his way, especially other people[...]."[52]

Nietzsche and Tolstoy each claim that the church's turn away from the requirements of universal brotherhood and non-violence leads to a dark and troubling conception of God. As Nietzsche says that Paul introduced into Christianity a "blood-drinking" God who would only forgive the sins of humanity through receiving a sacrificial payment, Tolstoy argues that the true notion of God as love is inconsistent with the theological view of God as "wicked and senseless" insofar as he "cursed the human race and devoted his own Son to sacrifice, and a part of mankind to eternal torment[...]. The man who believes [...] in a Christ coming again in glory to judge and to punish the quick and the dead, cannot believe in the Christ who bade us turn the left cheek, judge not, forgive those that wrong us, and love our enemies."[53] Nietzsche suggests that with the rise of a putative Christian state even the military comes to be regarded as a Christian institution, and God becomes chief of staff.[54] Most importantly, however, the failure to appropriate and focus on Jesus's example leads to an undue preoccupation with ritual and superstition that threatens to obviate the requirement that we strive resolutely to live in a loving way. Tolstoy claims, then, that if a "man can be saved by redemption, by sacraments, and by prayer, then he does not need good works. The Sermon on the Mount, or the Creed. One cannot believe in both. And Churchmen have chosen the latter."[55]

Nietzsche and Tolstoy: Towards Convergence

Here it is worth noting one of the most striking features of Nietzsche's discussion of authentic Christianity. His attitude towards what he understands to be Jesus's stance is far less hostile than is his attitude towards Christianity. In fact, at times Nietzsche endorses ideas quite similar to those he attributes to Jesus. He writes, "The best way of beginning each day well is to think on awakening whether one cannot this day give pleasure to at any rate *one* person. If this could count as a substitute for the religious practice of prayer, then this substitution would be to the benefit of one's fellow men."[56] Nietzsche frequently praises the virtue of sympathy, and his alter-ego Zarathustra praises kindness and mercy.[57] Similar to Tolstoy's indictment of church hypocrisy, Zarathustra is suspicious of the motivations of moralizers who are effusive about justice, people in whom "the impulse to punish is powerful," for "when they call themselves the good and the just, do not forget that they would be Pharisees, if only they had — power."[58] On the other hand, whereas justice often is not what it pretends to be, Nietzsche lauds the "self-overcoming" of justice, which takes the "beautiful name" of mercy, and "it goes without saying that mercy remains the privilege of the most powerful man[...]."[59] Nietzsche is deeply suspicious too of the state, which he thinks promotes conformity, suppresses individuality with threats of punishment, and encourages the pursuit of power through the base and undignified pursuit of money, whereas true power is to be found rather in independence and creativity of spirit. And criticizing the state's maintenance of standing armies, which he believes only increases international distrust and to be a primary cause of warfare, he recommends rejecting reliance on the military as means both of self-defense and conquest. He anticipates a time when a "people, distinguished by wars and victories" will "exclaim of its own free will, 'We break the sword,' and will smash its entire military establishment[...]. Rendering oneself unarmed when one had been the best-armed, out of a height of feeling — that is the means to real peace[...]."[60] Tolstoy endorses exactly the same point about the geopolitical dangers of standing armies and the consequences of their elimination.[61]

Of course Nietzsche's great, enduring opponent is what he thinks of as resentment, or the spirit of revenge. For him, the danger in Christianity is not that it celebrates kindness, but that its commitments to kindness, goodness, and love are really masks, concealing a festering resentment and the desire for revenge. Significantly, Nietzsche suggests that Jesus himself, unlike Christians in general, was not motivated by resentment. While coiled at the heart of the consciousness and values of Christianity, revenge is the most "unevangelical" feeling, and Jesus was in fact "superior" to any "feeling of *ressentiment*."[62] Nietzsche's denunciation of resentment seems little different from Tolstoy's affirmation of non-resistance. What is more, what Nietzsche and Tolstoy each take to be Jesus's own emphasis on blessedness as a particular kind of life "here on earth," blessedness as the earthly practice of loving kindness, helps avoid Nietzsche's critique of Christianity as life-negating in its emphases on ascetic bodily mortification and sacrificing in this world in the hope of achieving the eternal and transcendent. That blessedness and the kingdom of God are to be achieved here in earthly life by engaging in certain kinds of practices, as Tolstoy and Nietzsche each understand Jesus to have taught, is a message not at all foreign to Zarathustra's (and Nietzsche's own) call to remain faithful to the earth rather than squandering our efforts on a fictitious transcendent "beyond." It may be worth remarking too that, whereas, in his non-fiction works, Tolstoy's treatment of those whom he judges to be morally inadequate frequently is utterly disdainful, in his fiction matters often are different. In *War and Peace* especially, nearly all the diverse characters (except perhaps Napoleon Bonaparte), are treated with compassionate understanding. The ordinary and the momentous, family life and political maneuvering, battle and carousing, the natural world and the world of the salon, romantic love and intellectual searching, the projects of peasants and nobility, French and Russians, all are represented as important parts of a whole both beautiful and important. The character Natasha Rostov, after collapsing into despair and alienation following her guilt over her betrayal of her fiancée Nikolai Bolkonsky, her grief over his later death, and her horrified resignation from life after facing up to the inevitability of death, experiences something akin to an "electric shock" when her mother's need for her becomes clear. Natasha's unconditional love for her mother as her mother's grief nearly pushes her into insanity becomes a "summons to life" to her mother, and her mother's need for her "called Natasha to life[...]. She thought her life was over. But suddenly her love for her mother showed her that the essence of life — love — was still alive in her. Love awoke, and life awoke."[63] Natasha's affirmation of life, and the connection between that affirmation and love, is almost certainly an expression of Tolstoy's own stance. In Tolstoy's literary celebration of all of life is a hint of Nietzsche's Dionysian notion of *amor fati*, the idea that one ought to affirm existence in its entirety, even those dimensions of existence conventionally (from a human, all too human point of view) condemned as evil or tragic.[64]

Thus there is great overlap between Tolstoyan Christianity and Nietzsche's own position. Of course, one must not go too far towards assimilating their respective stances, and the question dividing Nietzsche and Tolstoy finally may be that of the precise sorts of "earthly practices" in which one is to engage. In spite of his preference for mercy and kindness, Nietzsche does not endorse Jesus's message, as Tolstoy does. Nietzsche teaches, as he puts it, not the neighbor but the friend. Tolstoy could not endorse Nietzsche's admiration for ancient pagan Greece and Rome. Nietzsche praises contest, most especially contests of ideas and systems of value, but even if he gestures towards the elimination of the military in order to facilitate global peace, he also is quite sensitive to the benefits flowing from warfare. (To take just one of many examples, Nietzsche thinks that religious wars indicate and work towards the cultivation of an admirable respect for abstract concepts.) Tolstoy thinks that Christ's lessons are the truth and the way to achieving blessedness. Zarathustra says he does not want disciples; Nietzsche does not think that there is but a single way to health and authentic living, but celebrates the clearing of a multiplicity of possible paths. He hopes that his writing will provoke people to shake off their unreflective conformity, become individuals, and create new systems of value. Whereas Tolstoy affirms the importance of universal equality and hopes for a classless society, Nietzsche argues for the importance of an order of rank and diagnoses the desire for equality as decadent. He does not admire the meek and the weak, or simple peasants, but celebrates those elevated in creativity, intellect, and strength of will. Indeed, even Nietzsche's ideas are not suited for everyone: as he tells us, a genuine philosopher believes that "'My judgment is *my* judgment': no one else is easily entitled to it[...]. In the end it must be as it is and always has been: great things remain for the great, abysses for the profound, nuances and shudders for the refined, all that is rare for the rare—"[65] And at the very least, it is unclear whether Nietzsche's project of revaluing all values entails merely the rejection of those value systems prevailing in the Western world since Plato, or whether, on the other hand, it is tantamount to the rejection of morality altogether.

But whereas Jesus's way is not precisely Nietzsche's, as it is Tolstoy's, for Nietzsche it nevertheless is a way both noble and legitimate. The way of universal love and non-resistance to evil does not succumb to the major criticisms he levels at Christianity: it does not affirm the herd-like conformity encouraged by church and state, it does not through superstition turn away from the world and towards a fictitious transcendent afterworld, it is not grounded in resentment, and its transcendence of any need or desire to take revenge presupposes admirable strength. We may have here a clue pointing the way to what, for a thinker such as Nietzsche, an authentic religion would be. Certainly it could not consist in a dogmatism that would encourage conformity. Even more importantly, it would need to remain "faithful" to the earth in what Nietzsche characterizes as a Dionysian celebration and embrace of embodiment and all of existence, and its values would need to be expressions of strength sufficient to overcome any resentful desire for revenge or retribution. If any religion could be consistent with these conditions, and perhaps that of Jesus as Nietzsche and Tolstoy retrieve it comes close, then it may well be the case that Nietzsche is not as implacably hostile to all religion as it sometimes appears. Indeed, Nietzsche admires the "religiosity of the ancient Greeks" for the "enormous abundance of gratitude it exudes: it is a very noble type of man that confronts nature and life in this way."[66] For someone today who is troubled by the many ways in which the churches historically have been complicit in vast hypocrisies and horrific violence, who finds compelling Nietzsche's critique of the religious distrust of the body and earthly life as life-denying, and who rejects belief in "unbelievable things" and "supernatural occurrences," but who nevertheless seeks the kind of existential orientation religion can provide, perhaps Nietzsche's and Tolstoy's reflections on authentic Christian practice might provide the signpost towards a more "noble" way.

Notes

1. Nietzsche, *EH*, p.789. All references to Nietzsche are given as section numbers, except those to *Thus Spoke Zarathustra* and *Ecce Homo*.
2. Quoted in Riser, pp. 284–5.

3. Tolstoy, WA, pp. 160-1.
4. Ibid., pp. 161-2. Later he refers to Nietzsche again, lamenting the "cult of the superior person (overman-ism)" (Tolstoy, WA, p.166). In a short essay from 1902 entitled "What Is Religion, and Wherein Lies Its Essence?," Tolstoy refers to Nietzsche as "semi-sane," and to his "puerile efforts at originality" (WR, p.319). Tolstoy understands Nietzsche to be urging us to live as we please, "paying no attention to the lives of others," and regards the "extraordinary success" of Nietzsche's "ravings" as symptomatic of the "terrible state of stupefaction and bestiality to which our Christian humanity has descended" (WR, p. 320). The majority of educated people, Tolstoy says, have rejected the ascetic self-renunciation and universal love that are so important for virtue, and therefore "gladly welcome a doctrine of egoism and cruelty" that can be used to justify the "system of founding one's own happiness" upon the misery of others, which is "the system in which they live" (WR, p.321).
5. Nietzsche, A, 7, cf. Nietzsche, GM, III, 26.
6. Nietzsche, WTP, 82.
7. Ibid., 434. Riser elaborates some the differences between Nietzsche and Tolstoy more richly in "Modes of Dissent: Nietzsche and Tolstoy."
8. Nietzsche, BGE, 31.
9. Ibid., 62.
10. Nietzsche, BT, 19. His admiration for Palestrina continues into 1888, as evident in *The Case of Wagner*.
11. Nietzsche, EH, p.707.
12. Nietzsche, BGE, 61.
13. Nietzsche, A, 62.
14. Nietzsche, EH, p. 790, p. 788.
15. Nietzsche, HH, 475. Jesus's nobility is reaffirmed in *Zarathustra*. There, in the section entitled "On Free Death," Zarathustra suggests that had he lived long enough to mature, Jesus would have learned to love the earth and laughter—as does Zarathustra himself—for "noble enough was he to recant" (Nietzsche, Z, p.185). Riser misinterprets Nietzsche's reference in the *Antichrist* to Jesus as an "idiot" as indicative of contempt. Given both his interest in Dostoevsky and the context— in fact, just two sections later Nietzsche draws a parallel between the world of the gospels and the world of the Russian novel in which childlike idiocy plays a central role—it is much more likely that by this term he had in mind something more akin to the character Prince Myshkin, Dostoevsky's Christ-like holy fool (cf. Nietzsche, A, 29, 31).
16. Nietzsche, GM, II, 24.
17. Nietzsche, A, 39.
18. Ibid., 36.
19. Nietzsche, WTP, 168, 167.
20. Tolstoy, KG, p.79.
21. Ibid., p.68.
22. Ibid., p. 62.
23. Tolstoy says, "The greater or less blessedness of a man depends, according to this doctrine, not on the degree of perfection to which he has attained, but on the greater or less swiftness with which he is pursuing it. The progress toward perfection of the publican Zaccheus, of the woman that was a sinner, of the robber on the cross, is a greater state of blessedness, according to this doctrine, than the stationary righteousness of the Pharisee. The lost sheep is dearer than ninety-nine that were not lost. [...] Such progress aims] toward establishing more and more firmly an ever greater love within oneself [...]" (Tolstoy, KG, pp. 51-2).
24. Nietzsche, WTP, 159.
25. Tolstoy, KG, p.317, cf. Acts 5.29.
26. Tolstoy, WA, pp. 144-5.
27. Tolstoy, KG, p.368.
28. Tolstoy, WA, p. 165, p.162, cf. Tolstoy, KG, pp.82-3. Nietzsche too is interested in the ways in which religious practices anesthetize, intoxicate, and hypnotize. See, for instance, Nietzsche, GM, III, sections 15-20.
29. Nietzsche, WTP, 191.
30. The Revised Standard Version of the Bible has the passage as "But I say to you, Do not resist one who is evil" (Matthew 5.39). The passage in New American Bible is rendered "But I say to you,

offer no resistance to one who is evil." Nietzsche writes: "'resist not evil' — the most profound word of the gospel, their key in a certain sense[...]" (Nietzsche, *A*, 29).
  31. Nietzsche, *A*, 35. Jesus of course enjoins us not merely to love the neighbor, but to "love your enemies and pray for those who persecute you" (Matthew 5.44).
  32. Nietzsche, *WTP*, 163,169.
  33. Ibid., 207.
  34. Tolstoy, *WP*, p. 974, p. 972.
  35. Ibid., p.1124.
  36. Tolstoy, *DII*, especially pp. 301–2.
  37. Tolstoy, *WA*, p.47.
  38. Ibid., p.186.
  39. Tolstoy, *KG*, p.112, p.113.
  40. Ibid., p. 36.
  41. Tolstoy writes, "Only from the time that the heads of government assumed an external and nominal Christianity, men began to invent all the impossible, cunningly devised theories by means of which Christianity can be reconciled with government. But no honest and serious-minded man of our day can help seeing the incompatibility of true Christianity — the doctrine of meekness, forgiveness of injuries, and love — with government, with its pomp, acts of violence, executions, and wars" (Tolstoy, *KG*, p.237, cf. "Letter," pp. 192–6, and Nietzsche, *WTP*, 167). In this connection, one may think of so called just war theory, which arose in a Christian context (especially in Augustine's response to primitive Christian pacifism), and intends to enumerate conditions under which warfare is not only morally justified, but is morally obligatory. Tolstoy holds that someone who believes in the moral legitimacy of warfare "cannot believe in the brotherhood of all men" (*KG*, p. 76).
  42. Nietzsche, *A*, 32.
  43. Ibid., 33–4, cf. 35, and Nietzsche, *WTP*, 170 and 212: Authentic "Christianity is a *way of life*, not a system of beliefs. It tells us how to act, not what we ought to believe."
  41. Nietzsche, *A*, 42.
  45. Nietzsche, *WTP*, 167, cf. 196. The claim to eternal life constitutes another sort of reversal Jesus's teaching, which, according to both Nietzsche and Tolstoy, in its resistance to selfishness amounts to a de-emphasis of the person. As Nietzsche puts the point, what could count as a more "exaggerated inflation" of the person than the idea of "eternal personal survival" (Nietzsche, *WTP*, 166, cf. Tolstoy, *KG*, p. 100)?
  46. Nietzsche, *WTP*, 167.
  47. Ibid., 169, 170, cf. 212.
  48. Tolstoy, "Letter," p. 196.
  49. Tolstoy, *WA*, p.50.
  50. Ibid., pp. 47–8, cf. Tolstoy, "Letter," p.194.
  51. Tolstoy, *KG*, pp. 53–4. In his contribution to this volume, Tim H. Blessing explores Thomas Jefferson's theological commitments, which turn out to be very similar to Tolstoy's. Just as Tolstoy held that the truth of Christ's message of universal brotherhood is immediately evident, Jefferson held that Christ's message was "plain" to "every understanding," and, as such, was insufficiently obscure to warrant the existence and maintenance of a priestly caste. Thus the "Christian priesthood," Jefferson wrote, "saw in the mysticisms of Plato, materials with which they might build up an artificial system which might ... admit everlasting controversy, give employment to their order, and introduce it to profit, power, and pre-eminence" (as quoted in Blessing, "Revolution by Other Means: Jefferson, the Jefferson Bible, and Jesus"). Jefferson too thought that the Christian churches perverted Jesus's teaching for the purposes of power and wealth. As did Nietzsche two generations later, Jefferson laid the blame for church corruption on Paul's doorstep.
  52. Tolstoy, *WP*, p.973.
  53. Tolstoy, *KG*, pp.75–6. Nietzsche names the idea of the "God on the cross" as "gruesome" and cruel (Nietzsche, *BGE*, 46, 55). And he remarks that the Christian conception of a god whose love is conditional upon being loved and worshiped — "What? A love encapsulated in if-clauses attributed to an almighty god?" — is unworthy of any god worthy of devotion. Any worthy god must have majesty enough to have "mastered the feelings of honor and vindictiveness" and that the Christian god has not is "sufficient critique of the whole of Christianity" (*GS*, 141). It is worth noting that the medieval thinker Peter Abelard anticipates Nietzsche's and Tolstoy's arguments.

Nietzsche and Tolstoy on Authentic Christianity (LUCHT) 77

Abelard believed that a theology focused on the expiatory dimension of the crucifixion is too easily tied to violence. The meaning of the crucifixion lies not in Jesus's being a sacrifice that would pay a debt to satisfy God's offended honor and thus alter God's attitude towards humanity, but rather in the example of love and non-resistance Jesus in facing death set for us. Authentic Christianity is focused on emulating a way of living, and God is not justice but love. Because of God's infinite mercy and love, there is no hereditary sin, all of humanity is always already redeemed, and the crucifixion is a reminder to us that in a life lived according to love and compassion is the life most responsive to God. Abelard's anti-feudal ideas were seen as a threat to the church, and his works were condemned as heretical. See James Carroll's discussion of Abelard as offering a theological alternative (sadly ignored) to the church's doctrinal anti–Semitism (Carroll, ch. 29). There are also striking similarities between stance taken by Nietzsche and Tolstoy and their contemporary Oscar Wilde's interpretation of Christ's message. Wilde claims that Jesus taught that wealth and private property were obstacles to the pursuit of a more important inner perfection, that he was indifferent to society and the state, and that he enjoined upon his followers the path of non-violence, non-resistance, and non-revenge. However, Wilde departs from Tolstoy, at least, in attributing to the true Christian the path of spiritual growth through self-torture and the worship of pain. Tolstoy thinks that a Christ-like life instead would be joyful. See Wilde, especially pp. 1024–5, pp. 1041–2.

54. Nietzsche, *WTP*, 211.
55. Tolstoy, *KG*, p.75.
56. Nietzsche, *HH*, 589. See also Nietzsche, *HH*, 129: "There is not enough love and goodness in the world for us to be permitted to give any of it away to imaginary things," a statement recalling Tolstoy's view that a person believing in "salvation through faith in the redemption or the sacraments, cannot devote all his powers to realizing Christ's moral teaching in his life" (Tolstoy, *KG*, p.76).
57. See, for instance, Nietzsche, *BGE*, 284, and Nietzsche, *Z*, "On Those Who Are Sublime": Let "your kindness be your final self-conquest./Of all evil I deem you capable: therefore I want the good from you." Nietzsche thinks that motivating commitment to the values of Christianity all too often is the desire for revenge, a desire arising out of weakness and the extinction of which he very much hopes for: "I do not like your cold justice; and out of the eyes of your judges there always looks the executioner and his cold steel. Tell me, where is that justice which is love with open eyes? Would that you might invent for me the love that bears not only all punishment but all guilt! Would that you might invent for me the justice that acquits everyone, except him that judges!" (Nietzsche, *Z*, "On the Adder's Bite"). See also Nietzsche, *Z*, "On Tarantulas," where humanity's deliverance from revenge is the "bridge to the highest hope, and a rainbow after long storms."
58. Nietzsche, *Z*, p.212.
59. Nietzsche, *GM*, II, 10.
60. Nietzsche, *WS*, 284, Nietzsche's emphasis deleted. Nietzsche takes nationalism to be a kind of neurosis, again like Tolstoy, and despises "European particularism," hoping instead for a task "great enough to *unite* nations again" (Nietzsche, *EH*, p.777). For a sustained discussion of the state, see Nietzsche, *Z*, "On the New Idol."
61. Tolstoy, *KG*, pp.123–4.
62. Nietzsche, *A*, 40. Richard Bernstein offers a striking argument that whereas Nietzsche's critique of priestly slave morality includes a move towards transcending a particular interpretation of good and evil, he nevertheless never rejects the sense or intelligibility of the very notion of evil. Nietzsche believes certain phenomena to be evil indeed, especially the psychological drive of resentment. See Bernstein, ch. 4.
63. Tolstoy, *WP*, pp. 1078–80.
64. Shestov links Nietzsche's *amor fati* to Matthew 5:45, and suggests that in surpassing ordinary moral conventions to celebrate the "fullness and infinite variety of real life," Nietzsche ascends to the sort of height of moral sensibility expressed in the gospels (Shestov, pp. 131–3, p.140). Shestov claims that Tolstoy too had succeeded in appropriating this attitude in *War and Peace*, a book in which "whoever lives, no matter how he lives—even if it be in an immoral or trivial or crude fashion—did not at all provoke Tolstoy's indignation," and in which Tolstoy sought to "acquit all men" (Shestov, p.60, p.138). Tolstoy could not sustain this sort of (Dionysian) elevation after *War and Peace*, and later is reduced to a moralistic judging of Anna in *Anna Karenina*. Shestov focuses primarily on what he takes to be another major similarity connecting Tolstoy and Nietzsche, namely,

each thinker's life-long engagement with the idea that God is the good, and the biographical experiences that inflected those engagements.
65. Nietzsche, *BGE*, 43.
66. Ibid., 49.

Works Cited

Bernstein, Richard J. *Radical Evil: A Philosophical Interrogation*. Malden, MA: Polity Press, 2002.
Carroll, James. *Constantine's Sword: The Church and the Jews*. New York: Houghton Mifflin, 2001.
Nietzsche, Friedrich. *The Antichrist*. *The Portable Nietzsche*. Ed. and trans. Walter Kaufmann. New York: Penguin, 1982.
———. *Beyond Good and Evil*. *Basic Writings of Nietzsche*. New York: The Modern Library, 1992.
———. *The Birth of Tragedy*. *Basic Writings of Nietzsche*. New York: The Modern Library, 1992.
———. *Ecce Homo*. *Basic Writings of Nietzsche*. New York: The Modern Library, 1992.
———. *The Gay Science*. Trans. Walter Kaufmann. New York: Vintage, 1974.
———. *Human, All Too Human: A Book for Free Spirits*. Trans. R.J. Hollingdale. New York: Cambridge University Pres, 1986.
———. *On the Genealogy of Morals*. *Basic Writings of Nietzsche*. New York: The Modern Library, 1992.
———. *Thus Spoke Zarathustra*. *The Portable Nietzsche*. Ed. and trans. Walter Kaufmann. New York: Penguin, 1982.
———. *The Wanderer and His Shadow*. *Human, All Too Human: A Book for Free Spirits*. Trans. R.J. Hollingdale. New York: Cambridge University Pres, 1986.
———. *The Will to Power*. Trans. Walter Kaufmann and R.J. Hollingdale. Ed. Walter Kaufmann. New York: Vintage, 1968.
Riser, John. "Modes of Dissent: Nietzsche and Tolstoy." *History of Philosophy Quarterly* 23 (2006): 277–294.
Shestov, Lev. "The Good in the Teaching of Tolstoy and Nietzsche: Philosophy and Preaching." *Dostoevsky, Tolstoy and Nietzsche*. Trans. Bernhard Martin. Athens: Ohio University Press, 1969.
Tolstoy, Leo. "The Death of Ivan Ilych." *Great Short Works of Leo Tolstoy*. Trans. Louise and Aylmer Maude. Intro. John Bayley. New York: Perennial Classics, 2004.
———. *The Kingdom of God Is Within You: Christianity Not as a Mystic Religion But as a New Theory of Life*. Trans. Constance Garnett. Lincoln: University of Nebraska Press, 1984.
———. "Letter to a Non-Commissioned Officer." *A Peace Reader: Essential Readings on War, Justice, Non-Violence, and World Order*. Ed. Joseph J. Fahey and Richard Armstrong. New York: Paulist Press, 1992.
———. *War and Peace*. Trans. Richard Pevear and Larissa Volokhonsky. New York: Vintage Classics, 2007.
———. *What Is Art?* Trans. Aylmer Maude. Intro. Marc Lucht. New York: Barnes and Noble, 2005.
———. "What Is Religion, and Wherein Lies its Essence?" *Essays and Letters*. Trans. Aylmer Maude. New York: Funk and Wagnalls, 1904.
Wilde, Oscar. "The Soul of Man Under Socialism." *The Works of Oscar Wilde*. Cambridge, England: Blitz Editions, 1990.

Amnesty for the Devil

GERALD S. VIGNA

So how do we treat our evildoers?

William Munny, "out of Missouri," killed women and children. He had settled into an impoverished life as a pig farmer raising his two motherless children when an opportunity arose for some quick cash to resuscitate his failing farm. A young prostitute in another state had mocked the small size of a john and he vengefully cut her face and scarred her for life. The women of that house put a price on the head of the aggressor and his friend. Would Will be interested?

Readers who have seen Clint Eastwood's masterful *Unforgiven* will remember that his character moves from hapless and somewhat impotent widower — Morgan Freeman's Ned Logan asks him if he just uses his hand nowadays — to cold-blooded assassin, then to vengeful friend of the murdered Ned, who has been whipped to death by Gene Hackman's vicious sheriff, Little Bill Daggett. Munny then returns to the role of a loving father who moves his children to San Francisco where "he prospered in dry goods." What are we to make of this man, once a killer, who marries and settles, reverts to evil, and then becomes a good man once again? It is not a new question. Eastwood may have explored the issue on a non-transcendent humanistic plane, but philosophers and other bearers of wisdom traditions have long wondered how it is we pay for our mistakes after we are gone. This paper will explore how one of the most brilliant minds of the early church, Origen of Alexandria, addressed the question in what scholars of early Christian thought call the first systematic theology, *On First Principles*. This essay, however, is no simple exercise in Christian antiquarianism. Origen put forward a God so loving that his eschatology could allow only for the salvation of all, even that greatest of evildoers, Satan.

Influenced by Plato's thinking, including his idea of the reincarnation of souls, Origen proposed the redemption of the demons in *On First Principles* and implied that even Satan could be redeemed. While the somewhat inchoate Christianity of speculative and Greek Alexandria could absorb such thinking at the beginning of the third century, the more legalistic and Roman world of late fourth century Latin Christianity could not. The Origenistic Controversy was a bitter one, and its final outcome was the loss of Origen's contribution in the West. As is so often the case in religious history, however, the story did not end there. Origen's idea of eternal, total restoration by God, *apokatastasis*, was reexamined by the twentieth-century Roman Catholic theologian, Hans Urs von Balthasar, who asked if we could hope that all might be saved. A look back at the evils of the twentieth century and forward to the new awareness of religious diversity in the twenty-first raises two questions anew: what must one believe to be saved, and how much evil will God forgive? The answers, now as then, frame the issues that themselves shape political and legal action. This essay will examine *On First Principles* and late antique Christianity's objections to it. After a review of von Balthasar I will take up the second of the questions, the punishment for sins, and show how the insistence on a God who damns has affected U.S. ideas of crime and punishment. Is there something to be gained in reclaiming *apokatastasis* in some form?

The First Christian Systematic Theology

Origen was born in Alexandria around 185. His father, Leonidas, was a devout Christian who lost his life to martyrdom — a fate that would have been the young Origen's had his mother not hidden his clothes.[1] He supported himself and his family by teaching in the catechetical school at Alexandria and was its headmaster when only 18. His strict asceticism earned him the epithet *Adamantius*, and in his youth his desire to maintain spiritual discipline led him to misread a passage in Matthew and make of himself a "eunuch for the kingdom of heaven" (*New American Bible*, Matt. 19.12). His reputation as scholar and thinker was peerless, and Christianity owes him the debt of serious biblical textual criticism through his *Hexapla*, a six-column work in which Origen laid side-by-side two Hebrew and four Greek versions of the Old Testament in an attempt to discern the best reading. A victim of the Roman Emperor Decius's persecution, Origen died in 253, having been tortured before being released from prison and never recovering from his injuries.

Between 220 and 230, Origen wrote *On First Principles*. At the outset, he states his intention to affirm those doctrines held by the Church, but to speculate on those not settled. The apostles taught necessary doctrines clearly and plainly, and those have been handed down in an unbroken succession. An example is the doctrine that there exists one God who created the world *ex nihilo* and is the God of both testaments. The apostles left other doctrines incomplete, however, so that the diligent may pursue wisdom. So the soul exists, has free will, and will be rewarded or punished after death, but the exact manner of its origin—and, by implication, the exact manner of its fate—is not a resolved matter. Also, the Church teaches the existence of the devil and his angels, but not the reason for their fall, and although the beginning and the end of this world are taught, the question of worlds before and after this one is not resolved (Origen 1–6; I.i.1–7). Origen's objective is to create an argument against Gnostic predestination. The first move in that argument is to insist on a single creative being who is revealed in both the Old and New Testaments since the Gnostics argued for two different gods; the second, a defense of free will. From the issues Origen puts in play, one can easily see him putting together the case that both devils and humans can choose heaven or hell, and they may get more than one chance to get it right.

Origen has apostolic tradition in defense of the first proposition and so offers no extended argument. The free will argument is intricate and is developed in four steps in Books I and II of *On First Principles*. He begins with a claim for the free will of all rational beings, spiritual and human. He then suggests the salvation of all at the final consummation. Next he addresses specifically the fall of the angels and finishes with a final defense of free will.

To prove his first claim, Origen insists on the freedom of the will in counterpoint to unnamed opponents (read: the Gnostics) who hold that some rational creatures are either good or evil in essence and not by the faculty of free choice. He demonstrates his point both logically and scripturally. In a clever rhetorical twist, the premise of the case is stated at the conclusion and then used to demonstrate a prior question. The logical argument is as follows. Origen asks whether the various evil angels and demons fell from grace because of their essence or by their own free will. By choice, it must be maintained, since to ascribe their fall to their essence would be to find God, who is goodness itself, the cause of evil. Origen had demonstrated that the Trinity, God, Christ, and Spirit, were good in essence earlier (27–28; I.ii.13). Consequently, the demons must have fallen by their own free will: a departure as rational creatures from the advice and purposes of reason. If so, then those beings in positions of authority over other beings, the angels, with whom Origen had begun this line of reasoning (the prior question), hold their places "not by some privilege of creation but as the reward of merit." Origen then suggests the potential amnesty of Satan: "We must believe this to be true even of the devil himself" (44–45; I.v.2). Origen's scriptural argument is no less intriguing (47–49; I.v.4). He interprets two passages, the first from Ezekiel and the other from Isaiah, to make his case. Ezekiel's second prophecy concerning the Prince of Tyre (Ezek. 28.11-19) speaks not only of the Prince's fallen state, but uses language, such as the reference to his being placed among the Cherubim (Ezek. 28.14), that to Origen can refer only to a spiritual being and not a human being. Origen then goes to Isaiah's famous prophecy of the fall of the morning star, a reference to the king of Babylon in the eighth century B.C.E., but to Origen clearly the devil, an insight confirmed by Christ himself (Luke 10.18). Thus the argument from scripture affirms the conclusion drawn by reason:

> All this shows that no one is stainless by essence or by nature, nor is anyone polluted essentially. Consequently it lies with us and with our own actions whether we are to be blessed and holy, or whether through sloth and negligence we are to turn away from blessedness into wickedness and loss; the final result of which is, that when too much progress, if I may use the word, has been made in wickedness, a man may descend to such a state (if any shall come to so great a pitch of negligence) as to be changed into what is called an opposing power [50–51; I.v.5].

The next step is to discuss the final consummation. Origen is clear that there will be punishment for sins, but he reads Paul's First Letter to the Corinthians as a biblical promise for the salvation of all. Paul made an extensive argument about the resurrection of the body and the final consummation in I Corinthians 15. He argued that all will be made subject to Christ and all Christ's enemies will be put under his feet, including death. For Origen subjection means salvation in reference to the saved, and so it must mean that for the wicked also, since the end is like the beginning, and in the beginning before rational beings made choices that resulted in their descent into lower forms, they were with God (52–56; I.vi.1-2). He goes on to assert the corrective effect of divine punishment and the consequence that souls rise or descend from one type of created being to another depending on what they have done. Paul's language concerning the transformation of creation means not its destruction but the final state of blessedness for all.

Origen then takes up the question of angels. The well-known archangels, Raphael, Gabriel, and Michael, were given their tasks of healing, supervising wars, and listening to humanity's prayers, respectively, because of the merit they earned before this world's creation (66–68; I.viii.1). Again Origen drives home the point that all rational creatures, whether spirits or not, are not only in their current state because of free will but move from one condition to another by the same faculty. And again his unnamed opponents seem to be Gnostics when he condemns as "silly and impious fables" the theory that two separate creators made beings of different spiritual natures (68–69; I.viii.2). Some background will clarify this dispute. In the late second century, Irenaeus in his writings against the Gnostics claimed their anthropology postulated three human natures. The pneumatics (spiritual) would achieve salvation in the true heaven with the true hidden God revealed by the Christ of the New Testament. The psychics (mid-level) could have a type of salvation. The choice (fleshly) would be damned (Irenaeus 326; I. vii.v). The argument was predestinarian, as Origen complains. Even if there is only one human nature, a logical dilemma remains. How is it that all rational creatures can have unfettered free will and also not remain forever in rebellion against God? Does God's promise that all will be subjected to Christ — who will then deliver everything to God, "so that God may be all in all" (1Cor. 15.28) — not compromise the argument for free will in a way different from the argument for fixed essences? The story of the Exodus repeatedly says that God hardened Pharaoh's heart. In other words, even if one grants the premise that there are no fixed good and evil natures among angels, demons, and human beings, the story of the Exodus repeatedly states that Pharaoh relented in his enslavement of the Hebrews, only to have God harden his heart and cause a change of mind back to the original state of affairs. What genuine choice can there be if God is manipulating the allegedly free will?[2] Having demonstrated that rational beings have free will, Origen's defense of humanity's freedom must now advance from refuting the assertion of multiple human natures to claiming that God's will does not override the free will of rational creatures.

Origen begins this discussion by noticing the great diversity among all living creatures (76–78; II.i.1–2). This variety in itself speaks to his theory of souls. Further, this multiplicity produces a harmony, a concord that leads some souls to help those in need and even some to put obstacles before those who are making progress. All this occurs because "God ... in providing for the salvation of his entire creation ... has so ordered everything so that each spirit or soul ... should not be compelled by force against its free choice to any action except that to which the motions of its own mind lead it" (77; II.i.2). Note here the driving force behind Origen's theology. The one and only God, maker of the world from nothing and revealed in both the Old and New Testaments, possesses a providence so loving that the very multiplicity of beings seen and unseen is carefully orchestrated to ensure total redemption of God's creation without compromising the absolute freedom of any. But what of Pharaoh? Does Scripture contravene Origen's argument? He reports the heretics' use of this text: "Pharaoh, they say, having a lost nature, is in consequence hardened by God, who has mercy on the spiritual men but hardens the earthly" (169; III.i.8). Origen has refuted this Gnostic anthropology of fixed human natures. He anticipates, however, the second predestinarian objection, that God's will supersedes human freedom, and counters by writing that God's action is like the rain, and as rain brings forth fruit or weeds, so God's work brings forth good or evil according to the will and disposition of the recipient. Whether fruit or thorns, one can indeed say that the rain brought them forth (172–174; III.i.10). Free will is not compromised, but God will also keep the promise of total restoration. When Origen returns to the eschaton (final consummation) later in Book III, he closes with "For to the Almighty nothing is impossible, nor is anything beyond the reach of cure by its maker" (251; III.vi.5). This is Origen's God, the physician who will not let the disease of sin win and who, consequently, will heal even Beelzebub.

Origen was driven by a passion to see all creation returned to its blessed state and united once again with God. He believed these matters not yet settled by Church teaching and so put forward his suggestions as to what might be the case. His other concerns, consequent to his belief in a God whose plan was to be "all in all" at the end time, were to demonstrate the certainty of free will and the lack of contradiction between it and the sure plan of an almighty God. In addition, this God was the only God. There were not two, one of whom made lesser creatures doomed in their very essence. His thesis of complete restoration, *apokatastasis*, was controversial in Origen's time, again around 300, and most bitterly around 400, and it is to this last controversy we now turn.

The Origenistic Controversy and Its Aftermath

Rufinus and Jerome were known for their great friendship and for their mutual admiration of Origen. Much of Jerome's work was the translation of Origen's commentaries on scripture. Origen's allegorical method and attention to the text greatly impressed both men. Yet toward the end of the fourth century, a fanatical heresy-hunter would stir up controversy over the theology of *apokatastasis* so virulently and so completely throughout the ancient Church that these two great friends would become bitter enemies, undermining each other before bishops and insulting each other in polemical *ad hominem* apologia.[3]

Epiphanius of Salamis was no manifestation of the generosity of God. Born around 315, he founded a monastery at age 20 after a visit with the monks of Egypt. He shortly was made bishop of Cyprus (Quasten 3: 384). He disdained metaphysical speculation and saw the defense of orthodox teachings as his mission. His two greatest works, the *Ancoratus* and the *Panarion*, are actually heresiologies (catalogues of false belief). His zeal led him to Jerusalem, where in 392 in the Church of the Holy Sepulcher he condemned Origen before Bishop John of Jerusalem and a full house, many of whom, like John, were ardent admirers of the Alexandrian thinker. Epiphanius's targets were the Egyptian monks who held Origen in high regard. Other suspects were Didymus the Blind and Evagrius Ponticus. Epiphanius then excited a monk named Atarbius for the anti–Origenist cause in 393. Atarbius brought a band of monks to the separate monasteries of Jerome and Rufinus in Bethlehem and Jerusalem, respectively. Jerome, for reasons modern scholars still only guess at, immediately complied with the request to condemn Origen. Rufinus did not, and the relationship between two old friends disintegrated as Jerome increasingly fostered the anti–Origenist cause. By the mid-390s the hostilities between the two, exacerbated by many factors including Epiphanius's intention to have Rufinus roundly condemned as a heretic, were implacable. By 400, despite a brief truce, Jerome and Rufinus had begun a series of ferocious apologies against each other.[4] For the purposes of this essay, however, it is not the apologies but two translations that matter. Rufinus had not only convinced himself of Origen's orthodoxy, he further believed that his works had been doctored by heretics. He therefore began a Latin translation of *On First Principles* intended to excise these unorthodox interpolations in 397. Upon learning this, Jerome fired back with a more literal translation over the winter of 398–399. Finally, a council at Alexandria in 400 condemned Origen with particular reference to *On First Principles*. The story ends about 150 years later when the Fifth Ecumenical Council at Constantinople in 553 issued a set of anathemas against Origen. His theory of *apokatastasis* had now been damned by the Church Universal, and although Rufinus softened the emphasis on the salvation of Satan at every turn in his translation, the testimony of Jerome and other evidence make it certain: Origen granted amnesty to the devil. Origen suffered a fate often visited on controversial theologians: his Greek was lost. *On First Principles* survives in Rufinus's Latin, a translation that Jerome's diatribes demonstrate to be nearly disingenuous at critical points. Greek fragments survive from the fifteen anathemas pronounced against Origen at Constantinople, a fourth-century compendium of his works by Basil and Gregory Nazianzus titled the *Philocalia*, and a few other sources. Meanwhile Augustine's careful argument in favor of eternal punishment articulated in his *City of God*, which I will take up later, won not only the day but the Western centuries until the Renaissance and Radical Reformation.

Augustine's favor among the Protestant Reformers combined with their legalistic theory of Atonement further strengthened the belief in eternal punishment.[5] Origen nonetheless benefitted from the Renaissance's interest in retrieving ancient texts, and the great student of classics, Erasmus, began to write favorably of him. He also found favor with a few of the Anabaptist reformers as well as with a seventeenth-century British thinker, George Rust (Patrides 475–478). Along with these ideas came a revitalization of the concept of the eventual salvation of all human beings, which was known in Protestant circles as universalism. Among Roman Catholics *apokatastasis* gained no foothold. However, Catholic theologian Hans Urs von Balthasar asked the question "Dare we hope that all men be saved?" in a book of that title. Balthasar offers no amnesty to the devil. God's redemptive act is intended for humanity, not this fiercely evil power (143–147). Yet Balthasar still holds out hope for humanity and finds in scripture at least the warrant for believers to hope that God may eventually save all human beings, even as *apokatastasis* must be rejected. His aspiration for the salvation of all humanity arises from those texts that espouse such hope, but they must be balanced against the bible's threats of condemnation. Nonetheless, there is sufficient warrant for agnosticism toward the doctrine of humanity's damnation so that one may trust "that the light of divine love will ultimately be able to penetrate every human darkness and refusal" (178). In his final chapter, Balthasar moves from universalistic hope permitted the Christian to a Christian obligation to hope in the name of neighbor-love. He closes with a long passage from Edith Stein's *World and Person: A Contribution to Christian Truth Seeking*, from which I repeat: "Faith in the unboundedness of divine love and grace also justifies *hope for the universality of redemption*, although through the possibility of resistance to grace that remains open in principle, the *possibility* of eternal damnation also persists" (220; emphasis in original).[6]

Redeeming Evil: Two Examples in Literature and Film

What has all this to do with controversial theological themes in literature and the arts? I have brought forward a Christian idea that will not go away however much criticized. As Balthasar contends, that is because the Christian hope that God's redemption will leave no one behind is a fire banked deep in the hearth of Christian love. From the mid-twentieth century I will examine the reflections of a popular Christian writer, C. S. Lewis, in *The Great Divorce*. I will then turn to a great film with no explicit theological argument, *Unforgiven*. My look at Clint Eastwood's masterpiece will set us up to examine some ideas in the U.S. criminal justice system that arise from Christian arguments that wrongdoers must be punished severely.

C.S. Lewis wrote *The Great Divorce* in response to William Blake's *The Marriage of Heaven and Hell*. Blake had argued for the natural oneness of heaven and hell. He blamed religion for ruining that union, writing that priesthood originated in a desire to exploit the plurality of all existence until "men forgot that all deities reside in the human breast" (20–21). Humanity needed to free itself to see things as they are. Blake's most famous quote, "If the doors of perception were cleansed, everything would appear to man as it is, infinite" (26), captures his mystical thought, as do the book's last words: "For everything that lives is holy" (47). Lewis rejected Blake's thesis, not because he feared that all might be saved but because he thought salvation could not come to all unless sinners corrected their course. Between heaven and hell, good and evil, one must recognize not a marriage but a great divorce: "Evil can be undone, but it cannot 'develop' into good" (*The Great Divorce* 466).

The Great Divorce is set somewhere after this life but before judgments stand for all eternity. At the end, the reader discovers that the narrator, Lewis himself, has had a vision in a dream. The conceit allows Lewis to review all sorts of human behaviors, as he also does in *The Screwtape Letters*, and to praise or blame them as he judges right. Those on the right path are the "Solid People." Others are shades. Some characters merit comment for my purposes. There is Len, Jack's murderer. The Big Ghost recognizes him and is surprised to know that he and Jack have reconciled. That is not all. Len's more serious sin, to the Big Ghost's disbelief, is his murdering the Big Ghost in his heart for years. He is here to make up for it. The Big Ghost grows angry. He had done things with an arch sense of responsibility all his life, and now he insists on a justice commensurate with his efforts, his "rights." Len gently tells him he does not understand and asks that he follow along. But the Big Ghost demands those rights with a triumphant "I'd rather be damned that go along with you" (482). Here is the first of Lewis's emphases on the divinely given freedom of the will, a point he will make at the end of the book when he explicitly addresses universalism.

In addition to the refusal to leave the land of shadows (Hell) for Heaven because of a false sense of justice, as the Big Ghost exemplifies, the willful misdirection of love can also keep one from salvation. The illustration now is the mother who cannot, actually *will* not, recover from the loss of her son. After all, she argues, a mother's love "is the highest and holiest feeling in human nature" (519). Not so, argues the Bright Spirit Reginald who had been this ghost Pam's brother. Human parental love is right when it is subordinated to the love of God. As Reginald points out, Pam's instinctive mother-love is no different from the beasts (tigresses, actually). But Pam will have none of it: "I don't believe in a God who keeps mother and son apart. I believe in a God of love.... I hate your religion and I hate and despise your God. I believe in a God of love" (520).

In addition to telling stories to demonstrate the need to reform one's understanding of how things really are, Lewis creates a conversation with the Scottish theologian whom he considered his greatest influence, George MacDonald. Lewis gushes over MacDonald at this point and quite sincerely praises him for his book, *Phantastes*, which Lewis writes began his long return to Christianity when he was sixteen. MacDonald continues to elaborate the theme that salvation may be granted after death. If that grey town from which Lewis's journey began and which the two men now regard from a distance, is left behind, it is Purgatory; if not, the souls there have chosen to stay and it is Hell. The suffering is purgative if one willingly reforms. It is damning if one responds like Pam or the Big Ghost. The latter choice is made by souls' insistence on focusing on themselves (which is what both Pam and the Big Ghost have done) so that they will say misguidedly "at least they have been true to themselves" (503). Hell is not a physical place of eternal fire. It is a state of mind because "every shutting up of the creature within the dungeon of its own mind — is, in the end, Hell" (504). MacDonald then quotes *Paradise Lost* as the best description of damned souls. They say, "Better to reign in Hell than serve in Heaven." The picture is not bleak, however: "No soul that seriously and constantly desires joy will ever miss it" (506). Lewis has reconstructed MacDonald to give him a belief like Lewis's own. The actual MacDonald was a universalist, however, and toward the end of the book, Lewis questions him. MacDonald's extensive answer again emphasizes humanity's free will, the characteristic that most resembles God. Both predestination and universalism contradict the idea of free will. Although they cannot be true, it is true that with a rightly directed will, anyone can be saved. So Lewis and his mentor both argue for the possibility of each human being's salvation, but it is not unconditional.

It would seem from *The Great Divorce*'s final comments that Lewis rejects *apokatastasis*. He certainly rejects its modern British descendent, universalism. Yet he may do so reluctantly. Why else have shades review their lives *post mortem* encouraged throughout by Solid People to see things differently? The key to the gates of heaven is a free will that neither stubbornly insists on its own prerogatives like the Big Ghost, nor turns its love inward like Pam. What Lewis will not compromise is human freedom. His case is that there may be many chances to get it right, but not a God who will in any way force a happy ending.[7] Lewis argued the point more forcefully a few years earlier in *The Problem of Pain*.

In his discussion of Hell in *The Problem of Pain*, Lewis refers several times to the refusal of some human beings to be saved, writing, "Some will not be redeemed" (620).[8] Lewis readily admits that he has denied a long-believed divine attribute:

> Finally, it is objected that the loss of a single soul means the defeat of omnipotence. And so it does. In creating beings with free will, omnipotence from the outset submits to the possibility of such a defeat. What you call defeat I call miracle: for to make things which are not Itself, and thus to become, in a sense,

capable of being resisted by its own handiwork, is the most astonishing and unimaginable of all the feats we attribute to the Deity [626].

Lewis somewhat lightly rejects the doctrine of God's power. Why did he not reclaim Origen? Certainly Pharaoh remains problematic in any scriptural discussion of free will. Origen knew the tension between holding that an almighty will and power desired the salvation of all and insisting that creatures were made in that Being's image and, therefore, were entirely free. It might be said that Origen advanced a theory of double causation. He lived with ambiguity and resolved it as best he could. Lewis instead apparently saw an either-or choice between universalism and free will. Yet he did not envision a vengeful God and took no pleasure in his conclusion. Referring to Hell, Lewis writes, "There is no doctrine which I would more willingly remove from Christianity than this, if it lay in my power" (620). His defense of the doctrine of hell is not vindictive but one of loving concern for his fellow human beings. He closes *The Problem of Pain* by telling readers to be attentive not to the damnation of our enemies but ourselves: "This chapter is not about your wife or son, nor about Nero or Judas Iscariot; it is about you and me" (627).

Clint Eastwood's gripping *Unforgiven* is also about you and me. What would we do to ensure that our children will eat? Would that passion rekindle our cold-blooded murderous ways, if only for a moment, to regain financial equilibrium for them and us? How many times can we descend in the depravity of contract killing compounded by an alcohol-fueled slaughter, an act of indiscriminate vengeance in memory of a beloved friend, and hope not to be lost eternally? Sara Anson Vaux, citing Mikail Baktin, writes that ambiguity marks a great narrative and praises Eastwood for the ambiguity of this movie (73). Vaux's analysis focuses on Eastwood's rejection of violence as a means to justice. I want to look at the ascent and descent of Eastwood's character, William Munny, within the context of what has been discussed in this essay.[9]

William Munny is the recipient of a salvific grace. Her name is Claudia Feathers and she is his deceased wife. He says to the Schofield Kid, who recruits him into the murder plot, "I ain't like that no more kid." He goes on to say that Claudia changed him; he does not drink anymore either. As Vaux comments, Munny has had a conversion and he now practices a virtue ethic (64–65). Munny's virtue is strong but the moral hazard in which he finds himself is stronger. To return to contract killing or to let his children starve is a stark choice. He takes the job, but vows not to descend into the evildoer who once killed women and children. Relearning old skills is not easy, however, and at first Munny cannot even mount his horse, falling to the ground to the embarrassment of his son and daughter. As he, Ned Logan, and the

Kid ride north to Wyoming, he maintains his virtue and refuses Ned's bottle. And the more the Kid pushes him for details of his past life, the more his responses are words like "I don't recollect." Things soon change, however. Ned Logan cannot return to the life of a mercenary killer. Will has to shoot one of the marks with Ned's prized Spencer rifle. The Kid's attempt to legitimate the killing with an appeal to just deserts is met by Will's laconic "We all have it comin', Kid."

The opposite of virtue is vice and it too comes by habit. Will's descent, motivated by adversity as was his original decision, continues. He does not drink whiskey until he is told of Ned's death. The Kid shortly afterward recognizes what Will has become. After the next shooting, in which the Kid has shot an unarmed and helpless man sitting on an outhouse john, he tells Munny, "I'm not like you, Will." The Kid rides off with the reward money and instructions from Will to see that Ned's widow gets Ned's share.

William Munny is again the solitary killer he once was. He returns to the Greeley Saloon where Ned's corpse has been desecrated by Little Bill's sign warning off hired killers. His first shot kills the unarmed saloon owner. After the ensuing bloodbath, he threatens to kill anyone who takes a shot at him as he leaves the saloon — and their wives, too. He swears a vengeful return if he discovers that Ned's body has not been properly buried. As Origen might have speculated, William Munny has again descended by choice to the demonic. As Balthasar might have suggested in his discussion of Satan, William Munny has so thoroughly cut off relationship with anyone that he is, in a sense, an un-person (145–147). We no longer see the human being watchful of his children and of his wife's grave. We see only murderous rage. The movie ends with a scrolling epilogue that not only tells us that Munny once again returned to his family responsibilities, but also that he succeeded at them. We also learn that Claudia's mother could not understand why her daughter married him. We know why, however. The assaulted prostitute, Delilah, has a grace-filled conversation with Will. She was already dehumanized in her work, an object of pleasure treated brutally for insulting a customer. Now scarred, she has lost her standing even as a prostitute. As the saloon owner and pimp, Skinny Dubois, complains to Little Bill, no man will want to pay for her now. But Munny does not see that, even as he refuses to humiliate her again by accepting her offer of a "free one." Her scars are external; his internal. They both have scars, but she retains her dignity in Will's eyes. In a scene reminiscent of Jesus's forgiveness of the adulteress condemned to be stoned (John 8. 1–11), Will returns Delilah to a noble state: "You're a beautiful woman." Prostitution is not Delilah's road to dignity; knowing her intrinsic worth is. A virtuous spark remained in Will — a reason to hope that even this man would be saved.

It is clear that Eastwood, in Sara Vaux's words, "asks again and again, when, if ever, we need to kill; it [*Unforgiven*] insists that as flawed human beings we can and must be redeemed by love" (72). Lewis, in contrast, defends retributive punishment in *The Problem of Pain* (604–605). Writing that the suffering of bad men appeals to the universally human instinct for justice, Lewis rejects deterrence and rehabilitation as logical reasons for punishment. Pain serves to eject the wrongdoer from his illusion with a dose of reality. Pain is God's megaphone, God's way of shouting to get our attention, and as such "it plants the flag of truth within the fortress of a rebel soul" (605). In this view, William Munny should have been hanged not once but twice. We are given no reason why he escaped apprehension in Missouri and managed to establish a farmstead in Kansas, nor are we apprised of how he managed to reach San Francisco and become a successful businessman. Except for Little Bill's small-town tyranny in Big Whiskey, law enforcement is absent in *Unforgiven*.

How do we treat our evildoers? *Unforgiven* (1992, Warner Bros.), directed by and starring Clint Eastwood, raises questions about the possibility of redeeming William Munny, a killer of women and children, in the spirit of Universalism and Origen of Alexandria's idea of *apokatastasis*.

To this point, this essay has examined the thought of theologians ancient and modern and of an essayist and a filmmaker. Only one, Lewis, addressed crime and punishment, and he did so abstractly and briefly. Theological doctrines should have ethical application, however, especially those that claim to understand God's intentions toward wrongdoers. This discussion now should take up the enforcement of criminal justice. That conversation begins with an examination of the dominant idea of divine punishment in Western Christianity.

The Augustinian Purpose of God's Punishment

After the Origenistic Controversy, the Latin West reemphasized the doctrine of the eternal punishment of evildoers, both human and demonic, that it had long held. At the beginning of the third century, the man considered the father of Latin theology, Tertullian, had made the point in several writings. He enjoined the issue extensively in his *Apology*. Toward the end of that work, Tertullian criticized the Pythagorean theory of the transmigration of souls and sarcastically dismissed it with the remark that, if true, we must all become vegetarians under pain of digesting a former relative (53; xlviii). His more serious turn was to state "the profane ... shall be consigned to the punishment of everlasting fire" (54; xlviii). Tertullian set the tone for Latin Christianity and his intellectual descendent, Augustine, elaborated on God's eternal judgment in the penultimate book of *The City of God*. This is an important passage for our purposes since Augustine explicitly mentions Origen's theory.

In the midst of the Origenistic Controversy, Augustine had written his friend Jerome and asked him to continue to translate Greek biblical commentaries, especially Origen's, into Latin. Later, Augustine also asked Jerome to list specifically what errors he found in Origen's thinking (Kelly, *Jerome*, pp. 217–220). In Book XXI of *The City of God*, finished in 426, Augustine lists eight objections to the doctrine that God plans eternal punishment for sinners. These are the punishments are merely purgative, no human will be punished eternally, the intercession of the saints shall prevent damnation at the Last Judgment, heretics are preserved from damnation if they have once been baptized and partake of the Eucharist, those baptized as Catholics are similarly protected, Catholics who remain Catholic unto death will not be damned despite sinful lives, a life comingled with sins and almsgiving will not be damned, and the punishment of the devil and wicked persons is not eternal (463–478; XXI.13–27). Augustine carefully refutes all these suggestions in a comprehensive series of arguments. These mistaken notions come from "tender-hearted" Christians who propose that no humans will be punished eternally. Origen was softer still, he contends, since he argued for the deliverance of the devil (466; XXI; xvii). Augustine points to three mistakes in Origen's argument (468–469; XXI; xxiii).[10] The first is theological.

Origen's theory jeopardizes the possibility of eternal blessedness if saints can rise and fall from one incarnation to another. The second is biblical. Scripture speaks of everlasting fire, most notably in Matthew's parable of the sheep and the goats at the Last Judgment (Matt. 22.31–46).[11] Last, the idea of happiness everlasting but punishment that is merely temporal is both unscriptural and illogical. In Matthew's parable the clarity of the Judge's (Christ's) decree cannot be mistaken, for he says "eternal fire" and "eternal blessedness."

Moreover, beatitude and damnation are correlative: if heaven is eternal, so is hell. With Augustine's multifaceted attack on the idea that divine punishment is merely corrective and not eternal, the door to *apokatastasis* in the West was not only closed, it was nailed shut.[12] As Balthasar points out, Augustine's Matthean argument is a tipping point in that "Augustine interprets the relevant texts in such a way as to show that he plainly and simply *knows* about the outcome of divine judgment" (65; emphasis in original). As he also suggests, we do the greatest Latin theologian an injustice to paint him so cruelly, for he also was a man of love, manifested as a concern for the souls of Christians who in their enthusiasm over their salvation might think a dissolute life no threat to eternity with God (71).

U. S. Criminal Justice and Harsh Sentences

America worries about law and order. It worries about crime on the streets. For a few decades now, one of the growth industries in this country and fastest-rising items in state budgets has been the construction of prisons. The phenomenon owes its existence in part to Christian ideas of reward and punishment, indebted, as I have pointed out, to Augustine's theology. Protestant theologian T. Richard Snyder explored the Christian influence on our politics of retribution in *The Protestant Ethic and the Spirit of Punishment*. Snyder's is a work of theological analysis followed by a constructive proposal to foster restorative punishment in a society he finds to have gone too far in the direction of payback. His thesis can be buttressed by a scientific study that suggests that certain Christian doctrines may lead believers more readily into harsh ideas of retributive punishment in criminal justice. Sociologist Harold G. Grasmick, assisted by three colleagues, surveyed 330 people in a southwestern city to test the hypothesis "that individuals affiliated with fundamentalist Protestant denominations will score higher on a measure of support for the retributive doctrine than individuals with other religious affiliation or no affiliation" (27). With Likert-scale questions that asked about the appropriateness of the *lex talionis* as a sentencing guideline and similar sentiments, Grasmick *et al.* demonstrated their hypothesis. I do not intend to single out a particular population of Christians with either this study or Snyder's book, however. I want to look at the content of these beliefs and follow Snyder's recommendations for an alternative philosophy of punishment. Consequently, although Snyder focuses on the Protestant tradition in America, the attitudes he criticizes can be seen throughout American Christianity, and I intend no criticism of Protestant thought alone. Moreover, as Snyder contends, the argument applies to American culture and its contempt for those convicted of crimes.

Snyder writes out of lived Christian experience. Raised a fundamentalist and a graduate of Philadelphia Bible Institute, now Cairn University, he had taught prisoners at Sing Sing for nearly twenty years before writing his book. He sees two problems with American Protestant theology: its emphasis on the thorough corruption of humanity through Original Sin and the emphasis on redemption in individualistic terms. Combined, these emphases lead to an evaluation of criminals and other marginalized as justly deprived of certain human goods. They also help shape a societal response to crime that focuses on the individual and is insufficiently attentive to other causes. He writes, "It is incumbent upon us to discover other ways of thinking about God and God's grace that might provide a foundation for a more humane response to crime" (15). He sees these possibilities as those things broadly named restorative justice. Snyder does not mention *apokatastasis* or universalism. His tack is different but his moral impulse the same.

Snyder works with three doctrines central to Christian faith, Covenant, Trinity, and Incarnation. Snyder uses Jacob's wrestling with the angel as his example of covenant (112–117). This illustration is important to him for two reasons. First, Jacob is "a liar, a schemer, and a thief." Second, Jacob does not let go of the angel (God?) until he blesses Jacob. These show that even criminals have rights under covenant and that covenant requires mutual accountability. Most important, Jacob does not have this experience until he first makes amends with his brother Esau, whom he cheated out of his birthright. The relevance of the story arises because Snyder had earlier placed restorative justice in the role of reconciling parties while repairing injuries done. It brings together victims, offenders, and communities. Consequently, there is a correspondence between restorative justice and covenant. Second, Incarnation implies that one can meet God Incarnate (Christ) in the face of those on the margins (120). Snyder tells of his own experience of "the presence of God" in the incarcerated with whom he has worked. Ironically, although Snyder does not mention Matthew's parable, it is the foundational text in the doctrine of seeing the face of Christ in another, especially the poor, sick, and imprisoned. When both the blessed sheep and the damned goats are assigned their everlasting fates, they ask, "Lord, when did we see you?" Augustine used the text to prove eternal damnation; Christians have often used it as a mandate for social justice and in Snyder's case restorative justice in the penal system. Last, the Christian doctrine of the Trinity, although illogical, is born of the Church's experience and teaches that God is intimately relational. Thus, the doctrine of Trinity does not demand that Christians merely recognize the intrinsic relationship between the individual and her fellow human beings—it requires that relationship to be spiritually intimate, that is, to hear the "sighs" of the most wanton. Snyder follows this theological excursus with a detailed outline for restorative justice in the U.S. prison system that I do not report here. More important for my purposes is his final call for a conversion first in the churches and then throughout U.S. culture that moves both "from the spirit of punishment to the spirit of healing" (155–157).

The Instantiation of an Idea and Its Consequences

With Snyder my essay has moved from a theological controversy to a political and social issue. The study by Grasmick *et al.* cited earlier attributed the preference for retributive punishment to a tendency to interpret scripture literally (32–33). Snyder argued that the doctrine was present throughout Protestantism. The doctrine, however, has its origin in Augustine and, therefore, influences all of American Christianity. As both authors conclude, their findings have consequences for the fabric of future U.S. society. Grasmick *et al.* simply warn that undoing the retributive movement is difficult; Snyder offers an alternative. If Origen were alive today and teaching prominently, would he be considered tender-hearted if he tried to apply his theories to our prison system? Would his supporters bowdlerize his works as did Rufinus? Would we heartily approve of Augustine? What can we glean from our contemporaries Eastwood and Lewis?

I look for a clue in the life experiences of these men, but find little help. Origen saw his father murdered by the power of the state when just a boy, but Augustine saw the sack of Rome by Alaric and the horrible pillaging and rape that followed. It spurred him to write the *City of God*. Lewis was in the military and was wounded in the trench warfare of World War I. Eastwood had the hardscrabble childhood of a poor family in the depression. All saw suffering and their judgments differ. Having discussed film and literature, I turn to music for a final word. Iris Dement is a country singer who often writes her own hymns. Alternately beautiful, profound, and wry, she takes up the matter of the end-time in "Let the Mystery Be" on her 1992 CD *Infamous Angel*. Having reviewed the options offered by religions (Christian and otherwise, but mostly Christian), she opts to "let the mystery be." I am convinced that the country's move toward increasingly severe retributive punishment over the last few decades is bad policy and by no means the only Christian alternative. Experiments in restorative justice continue to occur and should be fostered.

As for eternity, I, too, will let the mystery be.

Notes

1. There are many good scholarly biographies of Origen. All depend on Eusebius of Caesarea's *Ecclesiastical History*, Book VI, as does this account.

2. Indeed, I assign the story of the Exodus to my students in the 100-level introduction to theology and some inevitably object to God's behavior in this tale. As one student put it rather angrily, "Pharaoh didn't have a choice."
3. The story is engagingly told over several chapters by J.N.D. Kelly. The following summary depends on Kelly's excellent work.
4. English translations of the apologies and other relevant writings are available in *Theodoret, Jerome, Gennadius, Rufinus* (405–568).
5. The course of this idea in Western Christianity is the subject of Patrides's article.
6. Balthasar titles this chapter "The Obligation to Hope for All."
7. Jerry L. Walls wrestles with the same ambiguity in Lewis (255, 258–263). He rightly concludes, "Lewis's picture, however, is of a God of love who does everything he can to save all persons, short of overriding their freedom" (262).
8. See also pp. 622, 626–627.
9. I am captivated by Eastwood's films because of the moral ambiguity of his heroes. His is no simplistic morality.
10. Balthasar provides an excellent and useful comparison of the two (47–72).
11. Balthasar points to the importance of the parable of the sheep and the goats (Matt. 25. 31–46) to the argument for the eternality of hell from the second century on (49–50).
12. Balthasar tries to reopen that door by quoting a French theologian, Andre Manaranche, in a footnote that bears repeating. "The limitation of the great Saint Augustine is found at that point where he throws sacred history out of balance by centering it on Adam instead of Christ.... How does Augustine know that there are men who are damned? ... Augustine ... has damned the whole world in Adam. He is no better informed than Origen, who puts no one in there" (72).

Works Cited

Augustine. *The City of God.* Trans. Marcus Dods. 1871. *The Nicene and Post-Nicene Fathers.* Vol. III. *St. Augustin's City of God and Christian Doctrine, City of God.* Ed. Philip Schaff. Grand Rapids: Eerdmans, 1973. 463–478. Print.
Balthasar, Hans Urs von. *Dare We Hope That All Men Be Saved?* 1986. Trans. David Kipp and Luther Krauth. San Francisco: Ignatius Press, 1988. Print.
Blake, William. *The Marriage of Heaven and Hell.* Boston: John W. Luce, 1906. Web. 18 Jan. 2012.
Dement, Iris. "Let the Mystery Be." *Infamous Angel.* Warner Bros., 1992. CD.
Eusebius of Caesarea. *Ecclesiastical History.* Trans. J. E. L. Oulton. 1932. Vol. 2. Cambridge: Harvard University Press, 1973. Print.
Grasmick, Harold G., Elizabeth Davenport, Mitchell B. Chamlin, and Robert J. Bursik, Jr. "Protestant Fundamentalism and the Retributive Doctrine of Punishment." *Criminology* 30.1 (1992): 21–45. Print.
Irenaeus. *Against Heresies. The Ante-Nicene Fathers.* Vol. I. Eds. Alexander Roberts and James Donaldson. Grand Rapids: Eerdmans, 1973. 309–567. Print.
Kelly, J. N. D. *Jerome: His Life, Writings, and Controversies.* New York: Harper & Row, 1975. Print.
Lewis, C. S. *The Great Divorce.* 1946. *The Complete C. S. Lewis Signature Classics.* New York: HarperCollins, 2002. 463–541. Print.
_____. *The Problem of Pain.* 1940. *The Complete C. S. Lewis Signature Classics.* New York: HarperCollins, 2002. 543–646. Print.
The New American Bible. New York: Catholic Book Publishing Company, 1992.
Origen. *On First Principles.* Trans. G.W. Butterworth. Gloucester, MA: Peter Smith, 1973. Print.
Patrides, C. A. "The Salvation of Satan." *Journal of the History of Ideas*, Vol. 28, No. 4 (Oct.-Dec. 1968), pp. 467–478. Web. 8 Aug. 2011.
Quasten, Johannes. *Patrology. Vol 3: The Golden Age of Greek Patristic Literature.* Utrecht: Spectrum, 1966. Print.
Snyder, T. Richard. *The Protestant Ethic and the Spirit of Punishment.* Grand Rapids: Eerdmans, 2001. Print.

Tertullian. *Apology*. Trans. S. Thewall. *The Ante-Nicene Fathers*. Vol. III. *Latin Christianity: Its Founder, Tertullian*. Eds. Alexander Roberts and James Donaldson. Grand Rapids: Eerdmans, 1973. 17–55. Print.
Theodoret, Jerome, Gennadius, Rufinus. Trans. W.H. Fremantle. 1892. *The Nicene and Post-Nicene Fathers, Second Series*. Vol. 3. Eds. Philip Schaff and Henry Wace. Grand Rapids: Eerdmans, 1975. Print.
Unforgiven. Dir. Clint Eastwood. Perf. Clint Eastwood, Morgan Freeman, Gene Hackman. Malpaso Productions, 1992. Film.
Vaux, Sara Anson. *The Ethical Vision of Clint Eastwood*. Grand Rapids: Eerdmans, 2012. Print.
Walls, Jerry L. "The Great Divorce." *The Cambridge Companion to C.S. Lewis*. Eds. Robert MacSwain and Michael Ward. Cambridge: Cambridge University Press, 2010. Print.

Lamb Unslain: Nonhuman Animals and Shelley's Panentheism

RUTH VANITA

This essay examines Percy Bysshe Shelley's poetical rewriting of some animal symbols that are central to Christian theology and literature, especially the lamb and the snake.[1] I suggest that through this rewriting, Shelley adumbrates an alternative theology based on what one may term Romantic panentheism, drawing on Hindu sources among others.

Shelley's view of the universe not as the creation of one God but rather as animated by universal spirit is perhaps the most important dimension of his thinking that distinguishes him from socialist-leaning materialists. Robert Southey recounted how, when he met Shelley in 1812, and told the younger man that he was not an atheist but a pantheist, Shelley, who had not heard the word, "seemed much pleased at discovering what he really was."[2] Shelley's discontent with the exclusiveness of mainstream Christian theology had led him to embrace atheism in a reactive gesture; Henry Salt perceptively remarks, "it was not the presence but the absence of spirituality [in the Anglican Church] that made Shelley an unbeliever."[3]

As Ellsworth Barnard points out, although Shelley considered "religion as a historical fact ... largely a series of perversions and abuses," he was deeply involved with the question of human connections with invisible forces in the universe.[4] Senior Romantic poets had begun to develop a theology, most notably Wordsworth through Deistic ideas of universal oneness in such poems as *Tintern Abbey*, and Coleridge in his radical re-visioning of snakes as ineffably beautiful stimuli to love in *The Rime of the Ancient Mariner*. Shelley takes these theological suggestions much further, both critiquing and demystifying established Judeo-Christian notions of salvific sacrifice, and also evolving a vision of spirituality that hinges on nonviolence.

In a 1960 essay, John Holloway argued that "leading attitudes and feelings of earlier times ... have in many cases entirely disappeared from the modern mind ... [but] the ideas and attitudes and emotions which the Romantic movement minted ... have now penetrated down into every corner of modern life and modern awareness ... have descended to ubiquitous banality."[5] While it is true that many of Shelley's concerns, such as republicanism, women's rights, and freedom of speech, have become commonplace in the modern West, other aspects of his thinking (such as his arguments against killing for food and his advocacy of releasing snakes and insects rather than killing them) remain marginal and are often still viewed as embarrassing eccentricities.

Recent examinations of Shelley's politics and his relationship to India tend to focus on imperialism and colonialism, failing to even mention his vegetarianism or his concern with the lives of animals.[6] In this respect, they follow earlier studies which approached him as a political radical or a proto-Marxist.[7] Remarkably, even Harrington-Austin, who integrates Shelley's indebtedness to Hindu thought into her analysis of his attitudes to colonialism, ignores his deep commitment to respect for nonhuman life.[8] The couple of scholars who focus on the issue of animal life constitute the exception that proves the rule in Shelley studies.[9] At first, it seems puzzling that major studies of Shelley as poet and thinker, and even studies of his religion either reduce to a footnote or a sentence his preoccupation with the shared condition of human and nonhuman creatures, or ignore it altogether.[10] But this is consistent with the modern world's emphasis on human equality and human rights which has developed on the basis of a Cartesian divide between human and nonhuman creatures. The medieval and Renaissance idea of the great chain of being gives animals a place as lesser beings, while Descartes reduces them to machines that do not feel pain and that exist not to manifest God's glory but solely to serve human purposes. The English Romantics were critical of this as of many aspects of Cartesian thinking.

Modern academics' generally dismissive, even contemptuous, attitude towards vegetarianism reproduces the dominant views of Shelley's time; thus, Meena Alexander, noting Shelley's central influence on Gandhi's vegetarian doctrine, writes: "If this were all, one might have let it drop, writing off Gandhi's pleasure in Shelley as part of the eccentricity of a vegetarian vision, its meatless quest fit fulfillment of an ideality that flees the bodily realm."[11] In this odd formulation, an opposition to killing nonhuman bodies is framed as a desire to flee the bodily realm, and nonviolence to animals is viewed as eccentric, as distinct from nonviolence to humans, which is laudable.

Likewise, the consistent neglect of the influence of Hindu thought on

Shelley has continued for over a century, and through the ups and downs of many critical approaches, which is suggestive of the Christian underpinnings of even non-Christian writers' thinking. Thus, a rare essay on Shelley's vegetarianism nowhere mentions Hindu thought, treating the practice as a product of individual psychopathology rather than of a philosophy with an intellectual genealogy.[12]

For that genealogy, one has to return to Keith Thomas's monumental work, which demonstrates that eighteenth-century England saw a rapid spread of sentiments against cruelty to animals, and a shift away from a purely anthropocentric view of nonhuman life.[13] Some of these sentiments derived from older traditions, such as Greek and Christian debates on vegetarianism, and early as well as medieval traditions, such as the Manichean and the Franciscan. Despite the new sentiment against cruelty, vegetarianism continued throughout the nineteenth century to be viewed as highly eccentric if not completely mad. The late Victorian anti-imperialist and vegetarian movements that Leela Gandhi examines remained marginal in British society.[14]

In a rare exception that proves the rule, John Drew, in *India and the Romantic Imagination*, demonstrates that Hindu philosophy had much to do with Shelley's laying aside his gun and turning vegetarian in 1812.[15] Hindu ideas of the oneness of all life, mirrored in the worship of cows, snakes, monkeys, rats, elephants, peacocks and swans, as deities and in association with deities, and Hindu symbols of oneness, such as Krishna the divine cowherd, were introduced into eighteenth-century England via translations such as Charles Wilkins' widely discussed and reviewed *Bhagavad Gita* (1785). Other such translations were Wilkins' *Hitopadesha* (1787), and William Jones' *Shakuntala* (1789) and *Gita Govinda* (1792). Raymond Schwab, in his pathbreaking book *The Oriental Renaissance*, demonstrates the tremendous impact these translations had on the European literary scene, especially on Romantic writers.[16]

In his excellent though neglected study of Shelley and Hindu thought, S. R. Swaminathan presents perhaps the only extensive analysis of Shelley's 1812 reading of Edward Moor's *Hindu Pantheon* (1810), and the influence of Hindu iconography on the poet's animal symbols.[17] The 300 illustrations in Moor's book abound in vividly rendered images of animals, both lifelike and symbolic, as companions to anthropomorphic Gods as well as Gods themselves, agents as well as subjects.[18]

At the time Shelley ordered Moor's book, he had just been expelled from Oxford in 1811, and was "feverishly reading religious, metaphysical, and scientific writers, and formulating his own philosophy of life."[19] In 1812 too, Swaminathan points out, Shelley was converted to vegetarianism by his friend

Frank Newton, who had himself been converted while living in India. Newton was the author of a book entitled *Return to Nature or Defence of Vegetable Regimen*, wherein he propounds the same ideas that Shelley later does, with regard to flesh-eating as the cause of both physical and mental disease.[20] This was in keeping with trends of the time; as Kenyon Jones notes, "Pythagorean" and "Brahmin" were the two most common epithets for vegetarians in England during the Romantic period.[21]

Hinduism has been aptly described as panentheistic (God both in and beyond the universe) rather than pantheistic (God in and coterminous with the universe); Shelley's argument for nonhuman life as an indicator of the universe being an animate entity inclines in the same direction:

> I think that the leaf of a tree, the meanest insect on which we trample are themselves arguments much more conclusive than any which can be adduced that some vast intellect animates Infinity.[22]

It is in his poetry, not his prose, that Shelley most powerfully evolves visions of loving oneness that counter the Bible's powerful visions of good versus evil as embodied in sacrificial animals versus death-dealing animals. As Christianity's central animal symbol, the lamb is simultaneously the human soul (iconically, the lamb in the savior-shepherd's arms) and the salvific innocence of the divine turned human (Christ as Lamb of God).[23] The divorce of the literal from the symbolic in the former equation rests, however, upon a terrifying if sentimentalized paradox. The shepherd-sheep relationship that is centrally and more or less continuously celebrated in European literature and art derives from the Greco-Roman pastoral, but its symbolism is strongly reinforced by Judeo-Christian allegory, such as that expressed in Psalm 23. However, the glorification of the shepherd's tender care of sheep and lambs masks a reality rarely dwelt upon — that of the slaughter for which the animals are destined. This duality is made possible by the second equation — Christ as the lamb who was willingly led to the slaughter and opened not his mouth.

The symbolic valence of the divine lamb masks the real-life suffering of innumerable lambs and sheep who are unwillingly led to slaughter and whose cries go unheard. The icon of the crucifixion evokes compassion for the human victim, entirely displacing the animal victims whose deaths are rarely made visible in painting or poetry. The validation of Christ's self-sacrifice as necessary, desirable, and divinely ordained silences questions regarding the much more common slaughter of animals for the table.

Eighteenth-century literature and poetry, because of its Augustan self-image, was particularly rich in glorification of the shepherd-sheep relationship, and late eighteenth-century literature's sentimental cult of pet animals, although focused on dogs and cats, also extended to other creatures, as in the considerable body of anti-hunting literature. Farm animals, however, do not receive much attention; some eighteenth-century writers notice the paradox of the lamb only to advise the reader not to be troubled by it. Thus, in Pope's *An Essay on Man*, the lamb who "licks the hand just raised to shed his blood," like "the poor Indian" who expects his "faithful dog" to accompany him to heaven, is an object lesson to the reader not to question the fate that God has ordained.[24] Romantic writers begin to highlight this paradox. Blake, working in an antinomian tradition, displaces the crucified Christ by a joyful human Jesus, and replaces God's forgiveness with human forgiveness ("And throughout all Eternity, I forgive you, you forgive me"). In "The Lamb," the child perceives the lamb not as a victim meant for sacrifice but as a companion in a cosmic play that unifies animal, human, and divine:

> He is called by thy name
> ...He became a little child.
> I a child, and thou a lamb,
> We are called by his name.[25]

Blake's thinking grows more uneasy, however, when in "Auguries of Innocence" he considers the lamb being slaughtered and attributes forgiveness to it:

> The lamb misus'd breeds Public Strife
> And yet forgives the Butcher's knife.[26]

Dorothy Wordsworth instructs a child to distinguish between love for living creatures and liking for those killed for the table; however, she does not reprehend the latter:

> Say not you *love* a roasted fowl
> But you may love a screaming owl.[27]

William Wordsworth, in "The Pet Lamb," dramatizes the irony of the loving owner's inability to understand the mountain lamb's unhappiness; since she gives it food and water, she expects it to be content, but it yearns for freedom. Keats, in a brief vignette in "Ode on a Grecian Urn," visualizes the pathos of the "heifer lowing at the skies" as she is led to the altar.

The contradiction was perhaps sharpest in the work of William Cowper, most of whose poems plead eloquently against bloodshed. He reluctantly allows killing for food to be permissible for fallen man whom he describes as "carnivorous ... through sin,"[28] but denounces hunting, the "Detested sport/That owes its pleasures to another's pain."[29]

Yet, Cowper's Christian hymns almost revel in the paradox when they glorify bloodshed and connect it with the idea of pleasure:

> Comfortable thoughts arise
> From the bleeding sacrifice[30]

and

> There is a fountain filled with blood
> Drawn from Emmanuel's veins.[31]

The logic of the hymns (in contrast to that of the more "secular" poems) is that God considers one kind of life less valuable than another — the ram's than Isaac's, the foreign enemy's than the chosen one's:

> This Abraham found: he raised the knife;
> God saw, and said, "Forbear!
> Yon ram shall yield his meaner life;
> Behold the victim there."
>
> Once David seem'd Saul's certain prey;
> But hark! The foe's at hand;
> Saul turns his arms another way,
> To save the invaded land.[32]

These equations do not come easily to Cowper, however; he struggles with them, and even the use of such a term as "his meaner life" indicates an awareness of the ram's life having some value, which one does not find in most representations of the story, including the Biblical one. Cowper's image of the bloodless millennium when sheep are finally freed from fear derives directly from the image of blood sacrifice:

> The lion, and the libbard, and the bear
> Graze with the fearless flocks...
> All creatures worship man, and all mankind
> One Lord, One Father...
> One song employs all nations, and all cry,
> "Worthy the Lamb, for he was slain for us!"[33]

Cowper's poems betray deep disturbance around these paradoxes; in an 1819 rebuttal of *The Quarterly Review*'s attack on Shelley's *Revolt of Islam*, Leigh Hunt suggested that the contradiction between Church dogma, especially the idea of Hell, and Cowper's own notions of a compassionate "Supreme Goodness" had driven him mad, and made of him a human sacrifice, "like a child on the altar of Moloch."[34]

It was left to Shelley, however, to expose the assumptions on which the paradox rests. With his curiously literal as well as myth-making imagination, he at one stroke divests the lamb of its mystified status, when he focuses sharply on the act of a man killing an animal whose innocence consists not (like Blake's lamb) of forgiveness but of harmlessness (the literal meaning of "innocent") and incomprehension:

> ...no longer now
> He slays the lamb that looks him in the face.[35]

Shelley's notion of a bloodless world, unlike Cowper's, rests not on blood sacrifice but on the abstention from such sacrifice. In *The Revolt of Islam*, Shelley suggests that the first innocent blood that was shed in *Genesis* was not that of Abel but that of the sheep that Abel sacrificed. Elsewhere, he refers to this kind of bloodshed as "original and universal sin,"[36] and in his essay on vegetarianism, he interprets the forbidden fruit as a diet of flesh which brings both cruelty and suffering in its wake. This reading suggests that by killing other animals, humans disobey divine natural law and perpetrate a universal sin, creating a contaminated social order that rests on a sea of blood.

Purification from this sin, in Shelley's view, requires not being washed in blood but rather ceasing to deal in blood:

> Never again may blood of bird or beast
> Stain with its venomous stream a human feast
> To the pure skies in accusation streaming...[37]

This recalls God's asking Cain, "What hast thou done? The voice of thy brother's blood crieth unto me from the ground" (*KJV*, *Genesis* 4: 10), and also recalls the first death in *Genesis*, that of unnamed animals whose skins God makes into coats for Adam and Eve (*Genesis* 3: 21).

Shelley rewrites the first murder of brother by brother, because for him a human's brother need not be human. The opening invocation of *Alastor*, for instance, stresses the kinship of human and nonhuman in a way reminiscent of religions like Hinduism and Jainism which see the same spirit as animating human and nonhuman beings that may be reborn in either form:

> Earth, ocean, air, beloved brotherhood!...
> If no bright bird, insect or gentle beast
> I consciously have injured, but still loved
> And cherished these my kindred...[38]

Figuring lion and lamb as both literal and emblematic, Shelley presents nonviolence as an indispensable precondition for human freedom and equality:

> ... no longer now
> He slays the beast that sports around his dwelling
> And horribly devours its mangled flesh,
> Or drinks its vital blood...
> All things are void of terror; man has lost

> His desolating privilege, and stands
> An equal amidst equals....³⁹

Here, Cowper's millennial vision of animals worshiping man (built into his imperialist notion of all nations worshiping one God) is replaced by the idea of all creatures as equal, and of God as animating spirit.

The notion of humans enjoying the status of an equal with nonhuman animals reverses many centuries of Christian theology which had read the *Genesis* notion of "dominion" as legitimizing what Shelley powerfully terms a "desolating privilege" (although a minority of Christian theologians had indeed read "dominion" to mean kingship based on protection, not destruction, of subjects). By emphasizing the necessity to end terror in a nonselective manner ("all things"), Shelley addresses the contradiction at the heart of Isaiah's vision of the wolf lying down with the lamb.

The Jewish prophets' ideal of nonviolence ("They shall not hurt nor destroy in all my holy mountain," *KJV*, *Isaiah*, 11:9) was undercut by their calls for bloodshed — both the blood of animals at the altar and the blood of idolaters. This contradiction remains even in Jesus of the Gospels' more radically nonviolent teachings, because although he forbids humans to violently punish other humans, he expands the idea of humans suffering eternal, divinely inflicted violence in Hell. This theological paradox lies at the heart of much Christian legitimization of violence; such legitimization depends not so much on hypocrisy or failure to live up to doctrine as on doctrine itself.

Shelley repeatedly points to the history of Europe as an illustration of the contradiction, drawing on Spinoza, Hume, and Paine for his account of "the extermination of infidels, the mutual persecution of hostile sects; the midnight massacres, and slow burning of thousands," and the killing of "eleven millions of men, women and children" on religious pretexts.[40]

As an artist sensitive to the effects of symbols on the imagination, he critiques the iconic glorification of torture and bloodshed in European art. In an 1818 letter written in Italy, he comments on Guido's paintings:

> There was a J[esus] C[hrist] Crucified by the same, very fine. One gets tired indeed whatever may be the conception & execution of it of seeing that monotonous & agonized form forever exhibited in one prescriptive attitude of torture — but the Maddalena clinging to the cross with the look of passive & gentle despair ... & the figure of St. John, with his looks uplifted in passionate compassion ... of the contemplation of this one never would be weary.[41]

In his poetry, Shelley builds word-pictures of human-nonhuman relations that counter mainstream Christian depictions. In *The Revolt of Islam*, both serpent and eagle are complex symbols, drawing on iconography found in Moor's *Hindu Pantheon*.[42] For his re-conception of the serpent, Shelley draws on Greek, Egyptian and Hindu notions of snakes, which may be, among other things, symbols of wisdom, healing and immortality. In Hinduism, cobras (Nagas) are worshiped as royal forces; the snake also symbolizes destructive forces controlled by devotion, as in the figure of Hindu preserver God Vishnu who stands on a thousand-headed snake with hoods open over his head, and the figure of the God Shiva, who has snakes coiled around his neck and upper arms. As John Drew writes, "in *The Revolt of Islam* as in Indian mythology ... the magical cycle of creation within which we exist is ultimately reduced (or expanded) to an archetypal pattern, or mythic triad, of male, female and snake."[43]

In a "fragment of a romance," entitled "The Assassins," written in 1814 and left incomplete, Shelley imagines a Utopian egalitarian society of early followers of Jesus isolated in a valley away from the reach of the Church. The characters have Islamic names, and the fragment ends with an Edenic picture of two children, Maimuna and Abdullah, playing with their favorite snake near a river:

> The girl sang to it, and it leaped into her bosom and she crossed her fair hands over it, as if to cherish it there. Then the boy answered with a song, and it glided from beneath her hands and crept towards him.[44]

This little vignette rewrites the Adam and Eve story. Now the snake is protected and loved by the innocent human female and male. The girl's crossed hands recall the crucifix but they protect the serpent whom the crucifix is intended to destroy. The scene enacts a utopian transfiguration through love, one of Shelley's central themes, as stated by Asia in *Prometheus Unbound*:

> Common as light is love,
> And its familiar voice wearies not ever.
> Like the wide heaven, the all-sustaining air,
> It makes the reptile equal to the God.[45]

Here, Shelley carries further the redemptive moment in *The Rime of the Ancient Mariner*. In *The Rime*, when the mariner realizes that the water snakes are neither good nor evil but are "happy living things" and, therefore, unutterably beautiful, his love for them heals him. In Asia's statement, however, it is not only human beings who feel love and are transfigured by it; all creatures feel and respond to love, and this mutual current of love renders all equal.

Like Gandhi, whose interlocutors pushed him to examine his tenets of nonviolence, asking him how he would deal with venomous snakes, rabid dogs or poisonous insects, Shelley thinks about the practicalities of his utopianism. In *The Sensitive Plant*, the exquisite images of insects ("the plumed insects swift and free,/Like golden boats on a sunny sea"[46]) are not merely decorative but illuminate a relationship between human and nonhuman, demonstrated when the young woman has to preserve her garden from creatures that would destroy it:

> And all killing insects and gnawing worms,
> And things of obscene and unlovely forms,
> She bore, in a basket of Indian woof,
> Into the rough woods far aloof,—
> In a basket, of grasses and wild-flowers full,
> The freshest her gentle hands could pull
> For the poor banished insects, whose intent,
> Although they did ill, was innocent.[47]

The basket "of Indian woof" is significant, suggesting that the idea of preserving insects rather than exterminating them comes from India. Many traditional Hindus and Jains avoid killing snakes, rats, mice and insects, although they may convey them outside their homes to wilderness areas. For instance, Gandhi kept a basket at his Wardha ashram for poisonous snakes who entered the premises. They were released into the nearby forests.

Shelley's images slide constantly between the literal and the symbolic, fusing the two planes of meaning in a way that disconcerted some readers. For instance, an 1821 review of *Adonais* in *The Literary Gazette* quoted as an example of "incomprehensible folly"[48] the lines "And the green lizard, and the golden snake/Like unimprisoned flames, out of their trance awake."[49] This image goes beyond reversal; drawing on antiquity's view of time as cyclical, it suggests the renewal of the world through fertility ("green") and prosperity ("gold"). The snake shedding its old skin is an ancient image of rejuvenation that Shelley is fond of: "The earth doth like a snake renew/Her winter weeds outworn."[50] The reviewer, however, could make neither head nor tail of it.

Reviewers, berating what they saw as Shelley's blasphemous atheism, often termed him a worm (which can also mean "snake"). Thus an unsigned review of *Queen Mab* in *The Literary Gazette* proclaims:

> And what substitute have we for piety, good-will to man, religion, and a God? The answer of this incarnate driveller is, a "Spirit of Nature!" ... Miserable worm! Pity pleads for thee; and contempt, disgust and horror are tempered by compassion for thy wretched infirmity of mind.[51]

The word "worm," used for human beings as distinct from God, and for the devil as opposed to God, derives from Christian discourse. Cowper refers to himself as a "feeble worm," to the devil as a "loathsome worm," and to the abstract idea of "the serpent Error" as "poisonous, black, insinuating worms" twined "round human hearts."[52]

Shelley's pet-name amongst his intimates was "Serpent" or "Snake," and he identified with that creature, for instance, his poem, "To Edward Williams" begins with a reference to himself, "The serpent is shut out from Paradise," and proceeds to describe paradise as the company of his friends.[53] Similarly, his "Sonnet to Byron" concludes, "the worm beneath the sod/May lift itself in homage of the god."[54] Here, worm and God are friends; Shelley assumes towards his friend the attitude of humility he refuses to an authoritarian God. This deification of the human would for orthodox Christians constitutes idolatry and blasphemy. In *Julian and Maddalo: A Conversation*, Maddalo (Byron) playfully accuses Julian (Shelley, named after the pagan apostate Emperor) of being "Among Christ's flock a perilous infidel/A wolf for the meek lambs..."[55]

A third strategy Shelley employs is that of changing the conventional values attached to certain animals. Thus, pigs, "the swinish multitude," become the victimized masses in his verse drama *Oedipus Tyrranus* or *Swellfoot the Tyrant*; significantly, Shelley got the idea for this play from a herd of pigs he saw put up for sale at a fair in Italy, that is, pigs destined for slaughter.[56] Orwell would later rewrite the image as dystopian, but Shelley was among the first to politicize pigs.

Likewise, dogs (especially hunting dogs), so celebrated in English literature, generally get a bad press in Shelley, who follows Shakespeare in this regard. He figures British society (symbolized by the dog) as built on slavery and violence:

> I met Murder on the way
> He had a mask like Castlereagh–
> Very smooth he looked, yet grim;
> Seven bloodhounds followed him;
> ...For one by one, and two by two,
> He tossed them human hearts to chew."[57]

On the occasion of Shelley's centenary, in 1892, Henry S. Salt, eminent socialist reformer, believer in nonviolence, campaigner for animal rights, and friend and associate of M.K. Gandhi, wrote, in one of his books on Shelley:

> He did not, like our modern school of sentimentalists, prate of men's benevolent feelings towards the objects of their gluttony, and preach peace under conditions where peace does not exist, but boldly and consistently arraigned the prime cause of animal suffering...[58]

M.K. Gandhi, who more than once referred to and quoted Shelley, also stressed the inalienable importance of nonviolence to nonhuman animals from nonviolence between humans. In a 1932 letter to Salt, he writes:

> May I say in all humility that one rarely finds people outside India recognizing non-human beings as fellow beings. Millennium will have come when mankind generally recognizes and acts up to this grand truth.[59]

Gandhi also repeatedly emphasizes that this truth acts through poetic symbols. Cultural attitudes towards nonhuman life reveal themselves perhaps most startlingly and ubiquitously in the unexamined symbols that appear in literature and art, for example, in book-titles like *Chicken Soup for the Soul* and *Sacred Cows Make the Best Burgers*, the latter neatly fusing contempt for animals and for Hindus. For Gandhi, the cow was a symbol, which "means the entire sub-human world.... The appeal of the lower order of creation is all the more forcible because it is dumb."[60]

Written in a culture that was aggressively monotheistic and violently imperialist, at a time when Europe was not only trying to colonize but also to Christianize the world, Shelley's symbols counter the bias that sets up individual, race or species as enemy to that which appears alien. His emphasis on the oneness of all things ("The One remains, the many change and pass...") is close to that of the *Bhagavad-Gita*, which, in Wilkins' translation, evokes animals both as symbols and as real beings in much the way Shelley does, to focus on the equal divinity of all:

> The learned behold him alike in the reverend Brahman perfected in knowledge, in the ox and in the elephant; in the dog and in him who eateth of the flesh of dogs. Those whose minds are fixed on this equality, gain eternity even in this world.[61]

Invisible spirit taking visible and fleshly forms, human and non-human, is one of Shelley's most common tropes, as when Demogorgon at the end of "Prometheus Unbound," invokes

> Ye elemental Genii, who have homes
> From man's high mind even to the central stone
> Of sullen lead; from heaven's star-fretted domes
> To the dull weed some sea-worm battens on...
> Spirits, whose homes are flesh: ye beasts and birds,
> Ye worms, and fish; ye living leaves and buds; ...
> Man, who wert once a despot and a slave...[62]

Like many Hindus, too, Shelley posits individual Gods or divinities as manifestations of one mother Goddess, simultaneously suggesting that all living things are manifestations of the divine:

> Sacred Goddess, Mother Earth,
> Thou from whose immortal bosom

> God, and men, and beasts have birth,
> Leaf and blade, and bud and blossom[63]

Perhaps Shelley's most powerful adumbration of this theology occurs in "Adonais," where not all forms are equally animate, because some forms are more amenable to spirit than others:

> ...the one Spirit's plastic stress
> Sweeps through the dull dense world, compelling there,
> All new successions to the forms they wear;
> Torturing th' unwilling dross that checks its flight
> To its own likeness, as each mass may bear;
> And bursting in its beauty and its might
> From trees and beasts and men into the Heaven's light.[64]

These aspects of Shelley's thought have left their imprint not so much on the critical record as on the creative heritage, from Wilde to Forster and Woolf to Mary Oliver.[65] E. M. Forster, whose work, like that of Virginia Woolf, is heavily influenced by Shelley's, evokes the utopian moment of Shri Krishna's birth celebrations in a temple, in *A Passage to India*, in terms very similar to Shelley's, with every form in the universe becoming irradiated:

> All sorrow was annihilated, not only for Indians, but for foreigners, birds, caves, railways, and the stars; all became joy, all laughter; there had never been disease nor doubt, misunderstanding, cruelty, fear.[66]

This literary continuity in the Western canon continues to counter mainstream contempt for cows and cow-worshipers, for non-human life and for those who view it as participating in divinity.

Notes

1. This is an updated version of an essay that first appeared in *Yearly Review*, the journal of the Department of English, Delhi University, in December 1992.
2. Robert Southey, extract from letter to John E. Reade, 12 June 1838, *Shelley: The Critical Heritage*, ed. James E. Barcus (London: Routledge, 1975).
3. Henry Salt, *Shelley's Principles: Has Time Refuted or Confirmed Them, A Retrospect and Forecast* (London: W. Reeves, 1892), 35.
4. Ellsworth Barnard, *Shelley's Religion* (Minneapolis: University of Minnesota Press, 1937), 3.
5. John Holloway, "Shelley's Achievement in Perspective" (1960) in *Shelley: Shorter Poems and Lyrics, A Casebook*, ed. Patrick Swinden (London: Macmillan, 1976), 134–35.
6. See, for example, Nigel Leask, *British Romantic Writers and the East: Anxieties of Empire* (Cambridge: Cambridge University Press, 1992), and the essays in *The New Shelley: Later Twentieth-Century Views*, ed. G. Kim Blank (New York: St Martin's Press, 1991).
7. Daniel J. MacDonald, *The Radicalism of Shelley and Its Sources* (1912; New York: Phaeton Press, 1970); Gerald McNeice, *Shelley and the Revolutionary Idea* (Cambridge: Cambridge University Press, 1969); Paul Foot, *Red Shelley* (London: Sidgwick, 1980); Michael Henry Scrivener, *Radical Shelley: The Philosophical Anarchism and Utopian Thought of Percy Bysshe Shelley* (Princeton: Princeton University Press, 1982).

8. Eleanor J. Harrington-Austin, *Shelley and the Development of English Imperialism: British India and England* (Lewiston, NY: Edwin Mellen, 1999).
9. Christine Kenyon Jones, *Kindred Brutes: Animals in Romantic-Period Writing* (Aldershot: Ashgate, 2001), and Timothy Molton, *Shelley and the Revolution in Taste: The Body and the Natural World* (Cambridge: Cambridge University Press, 1994).
10. See, for example, Ellsworth Barnard, *Shelley's Religion;* A.M.D. Hughes, *The Theology of Shelley* (Folcroft, PA: Folcroft Press, 1938).
11. Meena Alexander, "Shelley's India: Territory and Text, Some Problems of Decolonization," in *Shelley: Poet and Legislator of the World*, ed. Betty T. Bennett and Stuart Curran (Baltimore: Johns Hopkins University Press, 1996), 169–78; 173. In this same anthology, Marilyn Butler, "Shelley and the Empire in the East" (158–68), mentions Shelley's vegetarianism in passing, but considers his animals, including the lamb looking his murderer in the face, "decorative" (165).
12. Lisbeth Chapin, "Science and Spirit: Shelley's Vegetarian Essays and the Body as Utopian State," in *A Brighter Morn: The Shelley Circle's Utopian Project*, ed. Darby Lewes (Lanham, MD: Lexington, 2003), 123–42.
13. Keith Thomas, *Man and the Natural World: A History of the Modern Sensibility* (New York: Viking, 1983).
14. Leela Gandhi, *Affective Communities: Anticolonial Thought, Fin-de-Siecle Radicalism, and the Politics of Friendship* (Durham: Duke University Press, 2006).
15. John Drew, *India and the Romantic Imagination* (New Delhi: Oxford University Press, 1987).
16. Raymond Schwab, *The Oriental Renaissance: Europe's Rediscovery of India and the East 1680–1880* (Paris, 1950; English translation New York: Oxford University Press, 1984).
17. S.R. Swaminathan, *Vedanta and Shelley* (Salzburg: University of Salzburg, 1997). More recent books and essays on Shelley fail to cite Swaminathan.
18. See Edward Moor, *Hindu Gods and Goddesses: 300 Illustrations from "The Hindu Pantheon"* (New York: Dover, 2006).
19. Editor's Introduction to "A Refutation of Deism," in *Shelley's Prose: The Trumpet of a Prophecy*, ed. David Lee Clark (Albuquerque: University of New Mexico Press, 1966), 118.
20. Swaminathan, *Vedanta and Shelley*, 26–27.
21. Kenyon Jones, *Kindred Brutes*, 110, note 6.
22. Letter to T.J. Hogg, 3 January 1811, *The Letters of Percy Bysshe Shelley*, ed. Frederick L. Jones (Oxford: Oxford University Press, 1964), vol. I, 35.
23. Swaminathan considers some of Shelley's animal symbols, such as eagle and serpent, but not the lamb.
24. John Butt, ed., *The Poems of Alexander Pope: A One-Volume Edition of the Twickenham Text* (London: Methuen,1963), 507–08.
25. "The Lamb," lines 13; 16–18, *Blake: Complete Writings*, ed. Geoffrey Keynes (London: Oxford University Press, 1974), 115.
26. "Auguries of Innocence," lines 23–24, *Blake: Complete Writings*, ed. Keynes, 431. Peter L. Thorslev comments briefly on these contradictions, *Romantic Contraries: Freedom versus Destiny* (New Haven: Yale University Press, 1984), 121.
27. Dorothy Wordsworth, "Loving and Liking: Irregular Verses Addressed to a Child," *Yarrow Revisited and Other Poems by William Wordsworth* (London: Longman, Rees et al., 1835), 265.
28. "The Task," *The Poetical Works of William Cowper*, ed. J.M. Ross (Edinburgh: William P. Nimmo, 1864), 131.
29. Ross, ed., *Poetical Works of William Cowper*, 175.
30. Hymn no. viii, "Lord, I will Praise Thee," *Poetical Works of William Cowper*, ed. Ross, 273.
31. Hymn no. xv, "Praise for the Fountain Opened," *Poetical Works of William Cowper*, ed. Ross, 269.
32. Hymn no. ii, "Jehovah-Jireh, The Lord will Provide," *Poetical Works of William Cowper*, ed. Ross, 269.
33. "The Task," *Poetical Works of William Cowper*, ed. Ross, 138.
34. Leigh Hunt, "*The Quarterly Review* and *The Revolt of Islam*," *The Examiner*, Sept.-Oct. 1819, in *Shelley: The Critical Heritage*, ed. Barcus, 138.
35. *Queen Mab*, part viii, lines 211–12, *Shelley: Poetical Works*, ed. Thomas Hutchinson and G.M. Matthews (London: Oxford University Press, 1970), 795.
36. "A Vindication of Natural Diet," *Shelley's Prose*, ed. Clark, 86.

37. *The Revolt of Islam*, Canto V, lines 2245–47, *Shelley: Poetical Works*, ed. Hutchinson and Matthews, 92.
38. "Alastor or The Spirit of Solitude," lines 1, 13–15, *Shelley: Poetical Works*, ed. Hutchinson and Matthews, 15.
39. "The Daemon of the World," Part II, lines 443–46; 458–60, *Shelley: Poetical Works*, ed. Hutchinson and Matthews, 10.
40. "A Refutation of Deism," *Shelley's Prose*, ed. Clark, 124–25.
41. Letter to Thomas Love Peacock, 9 November 1818, from Bologna, *The Letters*, Vol. II, 50.
42. Swaminathan, *Vedanta and Shelley*, 32.
43. Drew, *India and the Romantic Imagination*, 267.
44. "The Assassins," *Shelley's Prose*, ed. Clark, 154.
45. *Prometheus Unbound*, II.v. 40–44, *Shelley: Poetical Works*, ed. Hutchinson and Matthews, 241.
46. *The Sensitive Plant*, Part First, 82–83, *Shelley: Poetical Works*, ed. Hutchinson and Matthews, 591.
47. *The Sensitive Plant*, Part Second, 41–48, *Shelley: Poetical Works*, ed. Hutchinson and Matthews, 592.
48. Unsigned review, *The Literary Gazette and Journal of Belles Letters*, 8 December 1821, in *Shelley: The Critical Heritage*, ed. Barcus, 300.
49. "Adonais," XVIII, 161–62, *Shelley: Poetical Works*, ed. ed. Hutchinson and Matthews, 435.
50. "Hellas," 1062–63, *Shelley: Poetical Works*, ed. Hutchinson and Matthews, 477.
51. Unsigned review, *The Literary Gazette and Journal of Belles Letters*, 19 May 1821, in *Shelley: The Critical Heritage*, ed. Barcus, 78.
52. See, for example, Hymn V, line 17, Hymn LI, *passim*, and "The Progress of Error," lines 4–8, *Poetical Works of William Cowper*, ed. Ross, 271; 298; 18.
53. Hutchinson and Matthews, eds., *Shelley: Poetical Works*, 644.
54. Hutchinson and Matthews, eds., *Shelley: Poetical Works*, 658.
55. "Julian and Maddalo," lines 116–17, *Shelley: Poetical Works*, ed. Hutchinson and Matthews, 192.
56. "Note on Oedipus Tyrranus," by Mrs. Shelley, *Shelley: Poetical Works*, ed. Hutchinson and Matthews, 140.
57. "The Mask of Anarchy," lines 5–8; 11–12, *Shelley: Poetical Works*, ed. Hutchinson and Matthews, 338.
58. Salt, *Shelley's Principles*, 56–57.
59. Letter to Henry S. Salt, 28 October 1932, *The Collected Works of Mahatma Gandhi* (Ahmedabad: Navajivan Trust, 1972), LI, 309.
60. "Hinduism," in *Young India*, 6 October 1921, in *The Collected Works*, XXI (1966), 248.
61. Charles Wilkins, trans., *The Bhagvat-Geeta or Dialogues of Kreeshna and Arjoon in Eighteen Lectures with Notes* (London: Nourse, 1785), 59.
62. "Prometheus Unbound," IV: 539–42; 544–45; 549, *Shelley: Poetical Works*, ed. Hutchinson and Matthews, 267.
63. "Song of Proserpine," *Shelley: Poetical Works*, ed. Hutchinson and Matthews, 612.
64. "Adonais," XLIII, *Shelley: Poetical Works*, ed. Hutchinson and Matthews, 441.
65. Forster took the title for his novel *The Longest Journey* from Shelley's "Epipsychidion"; for the influence of Shelley, especially his "Rosalind and Helen" on Forster's *Howards End*, and his "The Question" on Woolf's *The Waves*, see Ruth Vanita, *Sappho and the Virgin Mary: Same-Sex Love and the English Literary Imagination* (New York: Columbia University Press, 1996), 146–47, 207; 210–11.
66. E.M. Forster, *A Passage to India* (1924; Delhi: Dorling Kindersley, 2006), 257.

Works Cited

Alexander, Meena. "Shelley's India: Territory and Text, Some Problems of Decolonization," in *Shelley: Poet and Legislator of the World*, ed. Betty T. Bennett and Stuart Curran. Baltimore: Johns Hopkins University Press, 1996. 169–78.
Barcus, James E., ed. *Shelley: The Critical Heritage*. London: Routledge, 1975.
Barnard, Ellsworth. *Shelley's Religion*. Minneapolis: University of Minnesota Press, 1937.

Blank, G. Kim, ed. *The New Shelley: Later Twentieth-Century Views*. New York: St Martin's Press, 1991.
Butler, Marilyn. "Shelley and the Empire in the East," in *Shelley: Poet and Legislator of the World*, ed. Betty T. Bennett and Stuart Curran. Baltimore: Johns Hopkins University Press, 1996. 158–68.
Butt, John, ed. *The Poems of Alexander Pope: A One-Volume Edition of the Twickenham Text*. London: Methuen,1963.
Chapin, Lisbeth. "Science and Spirit: Shelley's Vegetarian Essays and the Body as Utopian State," in *A Brighter Morn: The Shelley Circle's Utopian Project*, ed. Darby Lewes. Lanham, MD: Lexington, 2003. 123–42.
Clark, David Lee, ed. *Shelley's Prose: The Trumpet of a Prophecy*. Albuquerque: University of New Mexico Press, 1966.
Drew, John. *India and the Romantic Imagination*. New Delhi: Oxford University Press, 1987.
Foot, Paul. *Red Shelley*. London: Sidgwick, 1980.
Forster, E.M. *A Passage to India*. 1924. Delhi: Dorling Kindersley, 2006.
Gandhi, Leela. *Affective Communities: Anticolonial Thought, Fin-de-Siecle Radicalism, and the Politics of Friendship*. Durham: Duke University Press, 2006.
Gandhi, M. K. *The Collected Works of Mahatma Gandhi*. Ahmedabad: Navajivan Trust, 1972.
Harrington-Austin, Eleanor J. *Shelley and the Development of English Imperialism: British India and England*. Lewiston, NY: Edwin Mellen, 1999.
Holloway, John. "Shelley's Achievement in Perspective" (1960) in *Shelley: Shorter Poems and Lyrics, A Casebook*, ed. Patrick Swinden. London: Macmillan, 1976.
Hutchinson, Thomas, and G. M. Matthews, eds. *Shelley: Poetical Works*. London: Oxford University Press, 1970.
Jones, Frederick L., ed. *The Letters of Percy Bysshe Shelley*. Oxford: Oxford University Press, 1964.
Kenyon Jones, Christine. *Kindred Brutes: Animals in Romantic-Period Writing*. Aldershot: Ashgate, 2001.
Keynes, Geoffrey, ed. *Blake: Complete Writings*. London: Oxford University Press, 1974.
Leask, Nigel. *British Romantic Writers and the East: Anxieties of Empire*. Cambridge: Cambridge University Press, 1992.
MacDonald, Daniel J. *The Radicalism of Shelley and Its Sources*. 1912. New York: Phaeton Press, 1970.
McNeice, Gerald. *Shelley and the Revolutionary Idea*. Cambridge: Cambridge University Press, 1969.
Molton, Timothy. *Shelley and the Revolution in Taste: The Body and the Natural World*. Cambridge: Cambridge University Press, 1994.
Moor, Edward. *Hindu Gods and Goddesses: 300 Illustrations from "The Hindu Pantheon."* New York: Dover, 2006.
Ross, J.M., ed. *The Poetical Works of William Cowper*. Edinburgh: William P. Nimmo, 1864.
Salt, Henry. *Shelley's Principles: Has Time Refuted or Confirmed Them, A Retrospect and Forecast*. London: W. Reeves, 1892.
Schwab, Raymond. *The Oriental Renaissance: Europe's Rediscovery of India and the East 1680–1880*. Paris, 1950. English translation New York: Oxford University Press, 1984.
Scrivener, Michael Henry. *Radical Shelley: The Philosophical Anarchism and Utopian Thought of Percy Bysshe Shelley*. Princeton: Princeton University Press, 1982.
Swaminathan, S.R. *Vedanta and Shelley*. Salzburg: University of Salzburg, 1997.
Thomas, Keith. *Man and the Natural World: A History of the Modern Sensibility*. New York: Viking, 1983.
Thorslev, Peter L., ed. *Romantic Contraries: Freedom versus Destiny*. New Haven: Yale University Press, 1984.
Vanita, Ruth. *Sappho and the Virgin Mary: Same-Sex Love and the English Literary Imagination*. New York: Columbia University Press, 1996.
Wilkins, Charles, *The Bhagvat-Geeta or Dialogues of Kreeshna and Arjoon in Eighteen Lectures with Notes*. London: Nourse, 1785.
Wordsworth, William. *Yarrow Revisited and Other Poems*. London: Longman, Rees et al., 1835.

Shaw's Subversion of Biblical Language

GUSTAVO A. RODRÍGUEZ MARTÍN

Bernard Shaw was born to be a heretic. To say the least, his religious ideas were bound to be unusual: he was raised–formally–in the faith of the Church of England, which in Ireland was tantamount to being labeled "Protestant." His father was a dipsomaniac whose regard for the Bible was, in his own words, that it was "the damndest parcel of lies ever written" (Pearson, 12). In addition, although Shaw's mother was too stern to share his husband's peculiar vein of humor against the Scripture, she indulged in a morally censorable–certainly not very Christian–*ménage à trois* with her singing teacher, George Vandeleur Lee. The family line contains other early influences that seem to have shaped Shaw's impression about the effects of religion on people. For example, his mother's brother (Uncle Walter) was reputed for having a sense of humor that "though barbarous in his blasphemous indecency, was Scriptural and Shakespearean in the elaboration and fantasy of its literary expression" (*Sixteen Self Sketches*, henceforth *SSS*, 15). Shaw himself seems to give his uncle's religious flippancy some credit in his subsequent attitude, given that "his efforts were controlled, deliberate, fastidiously chosen and worded. But they were all the more effective in destroying all my incalculated childish reverence for the verbiage of religion, for its legends and personification and parables" (Pearson, 27). His father's brother, Uncle Barney, was (together with Shaw's own father, George) the paragon of the family anticlimactic sense of comedy: not because he was intentionally funny, but because he shifted from "a largely fuddled life until he was past fifty ... full of smoking and drinking" to his betrothal to a lady of "distinguished social position and great piety." After this sudden and unexpected change in behavior and status, "the fantastic imagery of the Bible so gained on [Shaw's] uncle" that his sudden ascetic fit made him lose his mind to the point of committing suicide (Holroyd, 3). In all, "mockery of death and mockery of religion were appropriately set against the background of Mrs. Shaw's music, and punctuated by Mr. Shaw's drunken sprees" (Ohman, 75).

In view of all the above biographical data, it is hardly surprising that Bernard Shaw became methodically critical towards religion (especially Christianity) throughout his entire life. After an early phase in which agnosticism succeeded atheism in an attempt to reject "the old tribal idol called Jehovah" openly (*SSS*, 74), Shaw's reflections upon Christianity and its sources gave way to a broad religious eclecticism. He analyzed and, to a greater or lesser extent, entertained certain views he borrowed from many different "denominations." At different stages in his life, he called himself an atheist, a secularist, a Catholic, a vitalist, an evolutionist, and so on, sometimes simultaneously. Regardless of this mesmerizing chaos, Shaw never overlooked the importance that religion had for people's lives, and his own. Therefore, his critical views were only Shaw's peculiar way of aiming at the realization of God's will and of true belief, as proven by his search of a common religion for the British Empire and for the future of humankind. Of course, his irreverent attitude made him gain a hearing, as well as many detractors who could not see beyond the clouds of smoke of Shavian discourse. This everlasting state of affairs is best illustrated by the following anecdote (Elliot, 269–70): when asked, "Are you a Christian?" by a clergyman who had been listening to one of his speeches, Shaw responded, "Yes, but I often feel very lonely."

In stylistic terms, Shaw's critical stance towards religion heavily relied on his inexhaustible capacity for storing information on the most disparate topics, whose discourses also permeate his plays. Bernard Shaw was one of the most learned men of his generation–given his longevity, one should say his generations.[1] Despite leaving school at fifteen, his devotion to reading enabled him to accrue a vast scholarship on issues that many people had not even heard of at the time. That was part of Shaw's attitude towards life: his "hunger for knowledge was unappeasable. For more restful souls his trips abroad would have been tasks" (Pearson, 141). Not surprisingly, one of the areas of culture that Shaw was most keen on was religion. Not only did he have an ample command of biblical studies,[2] but he also reflected on the religious and otherwise spiritual dimensions of humankind.

In this essay I will state the fundamental religious values that shaped Shaw's spiritual beliefs, especially those on which Shaw was contrary to traditional religious convention. These controversial items of faith gained him a hearing as a polemicist who would systematically go against the universally acknowledged conventions of Victorian times.[3] I will then go on to gauge the importance of these unorthodox aspects in conforming Shaw's religiosity, both as a man and as a playwright. These ideas will be illustrated with some examples from his plays, as well as from other supplementary materials, including his prefaces and other essays. These literary materials will facilitate the appraisal of how these ideas made their way into Shaw's dramatic art and, consequently, will allow us to come closer to the literary and stylistic (i.e., fictional) dimension of Shavian religion.

Perhaps the primary source of discontent for Shaw with traditional religion was the literal interpretation of the Bible.[4] Already in his childhood he "gave up the inculcated belief that the Bible was the literally inspired and dictated word of an omniscient and infallible anthropomorphic god" (*SSS*, 25–6), mainly because some of the events recorded therein were hard to reconcile with Shaw's common sense. Biblical literality was discarded on more scientific grounds when the theory of evolution made the pre–Darwininan age "be regarded as a Dark Age in which men still believed that the book of Genesis was a standard scientific treatise" (*Complete Prefaces*, henceforth *CP*, 501). The disregard for the literal interpretation of the Bible was undoubtedly also linked to the unintelligible quality of some of its passages. Indeed, "Biblical idioms, figures of speech, and words, even when translated into English, have unfamiliar meanings" (Brake, 22), which is the vernacular equivalent of Shaw's "it will not do to read the gospels with a mind furnished only for the reception of, say, a biography of Goethe. You will not make sense of them" (*CP*, 550). This disparagement of the literal interpretation of the Bible grew stronger in view of the moral implications that it had for Christians, despite the plain evidence that "the word morality, if we met it in the Bible, would surprise us as much as the word telephone or motor car" (*CP*, 138). This is probably why Shaw was much fonder of the Gospel of John than of the Synoptic ones, especially because the former raises the question of whether we really understand the message of God's will, one of Shaw's crucial conceptions, as we shall see. This particular theological divergence in John's Gospel poses an intriguing intellectual challenge, as Smith (1044) points out:

> If a fundamental question in the synoptic tradition is how one should understand and respond to God's will as expressed in the law, the fundamental question of the Fourth Gospel is whether one will understand and respond to Jesus as the definitive expression of God's will or revelation.

From the point of view of the didacticism in his plays, Shaw was aware that he had to initiate the promotion of his revolutionary ideas by attacking biblical language rather than religious institutions, because "our religious ideas and beliefs are largely fed and nourished by the gospels. Even regarding the life and teachings of Jesus we entirely depend on the so-called history presented in the four narratives" (Pathak, 76). In his irreverent–though strictly logical–contempt for the traditional reading of the Bible, Shaw often resorts in his plays to the exploitation *ad absurdum* of biblical idiom, which reveals itself as an adroit technique for pinpointing the blatant misinterpretation of certain biblical passages.

The phrases of Scripture that Shaw manipulates most often are those of metaphoric nature, since they allow the audience to posit different interpretations for biblical discourse–whether literal or figurative–if the right cues are provided. Einsohn (110), for example, acknowledges the metaphor-based, multidimensional semantic potential underlying biblical discourse:

> Words cannot fully encompass the absolute, the cosmic process that creates and supports life, but metaphors provide simulacra that approximate this extralinguistic reality. In brief, metaphors inaugurate semantically. Out of an initial cognitive impertinence, at the heart of metaphoric predication, comes new meaning, an expansive, innovative pertinence that posits Jesus as an archetype of the ineffable, eminently worthy of emulation. In a mysterious way, it is not we who use language to constitute the world. It is language — "the Word made flesh" — that constitutes us.

One of the most far-reaching examples of this kind in the plays of Bernard Shaw is the manipulation of the biblical phrase "turn the other cheek,"[5] which is completely disfigured in *Androcles and the Lion*, both in its physical and moral sense. From a strictly physical point of view, "turn the other cheek" no longer refers to submitting meekly to aggression by offering the other cheek to strike on. In the mouth of Lentulus, a young Roman who jeers at the Christian slaves, the phrase becomes a subtle insinuation, some sort of pick-up line to try on the beautiful Christian Lavinia. It particularly refers to the alternative offering of both cheeks when kissing as a gesture of salutation[6]:

> LENTULUS [*indicating Lavinia, who is still looking towards the arches after the captain*]. That woman's got a figure. [*He walks past her, staring at her invitingly, but she is preoccupied and is not conscious of him*]. **Do you turn the other cheek when they kiss you?**
> LAVINIA (starting) What?
> LENTULUS. **Do you turn the other cheek when they kiss you,** fascinating Christian?
> LAVINIA. Dont be foolish. (To Metellus, who has remained on her right, so that she is between them) Please dont let your friend behave like a cad before the soldiers. How are they to respect and obey patricians if they see them behaving like street boys? (Sharply to Lentulus) Pull yourself together, man. Hold your head up. Keep the corners of your mouth firm; and treat me respectfully. What do you take me for?

It must be said that, in Shavian terms, this sort of linguistic manipulation is one of the most irreverent ones, given the scarcity of any type of innuendo in Shaw's plays.

But it is the moral and philosophical side of the phrase that is disfigured the most, because the author is able to isolate an ethical contradiction in it: If one turns the other cheek out of fear, it is a nonsensical action for a Christian. If, on the contrary, one finds it comforting to suffocate anger, then the best you can do is strike others so that they can also sublimate their faith through martyrdom and penitence. The following scene exacerbates this paradoxical argument by assigning the role of the patient Christian to the massive Ferrovius, and that of the pagan who strikes to Lentulus:

> LENTULUS. Haw! Good! [*Indicating the kneeling Ferrovius*]. Is this one of the turn-the-other-cheek gentlemen, Centurion?
> CENTURION. Yes, sir. Lucky for you too, sir, if you want to take any liberties with him.
> LENTULUS [*to Ferrovius*] You turn the other cheek when youre struck, I'm told.
> FERROVIUS [*slowly turning his great eyes on him*] Yes, by the grace of God, I do, NOW.
> LENTULUS. Not that youre a coward, of course; but out of pure piety.
> FERROVIUS. I fear God more than man; at least I try to.
> LENTULUS. Lets see. [*He strikes him on the cheek*] [...]
> FERROVIUS [*with the calm of a steam hammer*] I have not always been faithful. **The first man who struck me as you have just struck me** was a stronger man than you: he hit me harder than I expected. I was tempted and fell; and it was then that I first tasted bitter shame. I never had a happy moment after that until I had knelt and asked his forgiveness by his bedside in the hospital. [*Putting his hands on Lentulus's shoulders with paternal weight*]. But now I have learnt to resist with a strength that is not my own. I am not ashamed now, nor angry.
> LENTULUS (uneasily) Er — good evening. [*He tries to move away*].
> FERROVIUS [*gripping his shoulders*] Oh, do not harden your heart, young man. Come: try for yourself whether our way is not better than yours. **I will now strike you on one cheek; and you will turn the other** and learn how much better you will feel than if you gave way to the promptings of anger. [...]
> LENTULUS. Let me go. Your religion forbids you to **strike** me.
> FERROVIUS. **On the contrary, it commands me to strike you. How can you turn the other cheek, if you are not first struck on the one cheek?**
> LENTULUS [*almost in tears*] But I'm convinced already that what you said is quite right. I apologize for **striking** you.

The manipulation of this biblical passage is Shaw's denunciation of the traditional reading of several passages of the Gospels in which Jesus does not respond to violence. The clear understanding that the conduct of Jesus cannot systematically be a role model for humans is the basis of Shaw's heresy:

Whether you accept his [Jesus's] belief in his divinity as fully as Simon Peter did, or reject it as a delusion which led him to submit to torture and sacrifice his life without resistance in the conviction that he would presently rise again in glory, you are equally bound to admit that, far from behaving like a coward or a sheep, he showed considerable physical fortitude in going through a cruel ordeal against which he could have defended himself as effectually as he cleared the moneychangers out of the temple. "Gentle Jesus, meek and mild" is a snivelling modern invention, with no warrant in the gospels [*CP*: 549].

Another undisputable characteristic of the Shavian creed is its intense disdain for sectarian, orthodox religions. He rejects everything resembling a dogma, both in the sphere of religion and in that of science, which were the two sides of his Creative Evolution. Baker (236) readily underscores Shaw's dual skepticism:

> Shaw's scientific religion strikes many as neither scientific nor religious because it is based on the logical denial of the most cherished dogmas of each belief system. He found his faith by rejecting two great orthodoxies and embracing what remained.

Shaw always rejects the faith of any established Church as a means to attain perfect communion with God, free from redundant middlemen. This feature is also prominent in Shaw's total heroine, the mystic and ascetic Joan, whose martyrdom is foreshadowed because she has never "in all her utterances said one word of the Church.... It is always God and herself." Nevertheless, as usual with the paradox-prone Shaw, his anti-sectarian discourse usually takes the form of the most dogmatic sermon. This stylistic peculiarity is substantial enough to define Shaw's approach to religious ideas, as Smith (xxiii) points out in his introduction to the *Religious Speeches of Bernard Shaw* (henceforth *RS*):

> A section from almost any of his religious speeches could be placed in a sermon in almost any church without violating the sermon's context; yet there is no doubt that his utterances are truly heretical.

This principle represented an obvious distress to a great part of Shaw's audience, whose religious values were based on the assumption that there was only one true religion which meant salvation, all the rest leading to damnation. Thus The Elder goes over this disheartening conception in a play fittingly entitled *Too True to Be Good*:

> "What must I do to be saved?" Nothing can save us from a perpetual headlong fall into a bottomless abyss but a solid footing of dogma; and we no sooner agree to that than we find that the only trustworthy dogma is that there is no dogma.

The eradication of dogmatism is one of the most important steps in the development of the Shavian religion, since it represents the foundation of his universal faith. As a consequence, Shaw is obliged to be critical towards all religious denominations and their respective dogmas by means of a spiritual relativism that is mostly superficial — it cannot be forgotten that Shaw intended to spread *his* religion. That is the case of Burge's opinion on the code of belief of the Church of England in *Back to Methuselah*:

> BURGE. Nonsense! That notion about the Church being unprogressive is one of those shibboleths that our party must drop. The Church is all right essentially. Get rid of the establishment; get rid of the bishops; get rid of the candlesticks; get rid of the 39 articles; and the Church of England is just as good as any other Church; and I dont care who hears me say so.

If one is to single out one Christian dogma that Shaw was particularly reluctant about, that is atonement. As he argued in the preface to *Androcles and the Lion*, there are two main characteristics that made it an antireligious concept. First, it is simply a very convenient notion that made Christianity terribly popular on the grounds that a single redeemer for all sins is a handy mechanism (*CP*, 553):

> Nothing easier, nothing cheaper. The yoke is easy, the burden light. All you have to do when the redeemer is once found (or invented by the imagination) is to believe in the efficacy of the transaction, and you are saved. The rams and goats cease to bleed; the altars which ask for expensive gifts and continually renewed sacrifices are torn down; and the Church of the single redeemer and the single atonement rises on the ruins of the old temples, and becomes a single Church of the Christ.

At the same time, the ethical foundation of atonement is naturally disgraceful for a man like Shaw who aimed at fulfilling the Life Force, thus providing his own push towards perfection. In this sense, the rejection of atonement is the ultimate sign of self-realization (*CP*, 598):

> Consequently, even if it were mentally possible for all of us to believe in the Atonement, we should have to cry off it, as we evidently have a right to do. Every man to whom salvation is offered has an inalienable natural right to say "No, thank you: I prefer to retain my full moral responsibility: it is not good for me to be able to load a scapegoat with my sins: I should be less careful how I committed them if I knew they would cost me nothing."

The obvious flaws that Shaw perceives in the theory of atonement could easily beget injustice in the process of salvation (or damnation) in the afterlife. That is what Don Juan tries to explain to the Old Woman (Doña Ana, one of Don Juan's former conquests) in the second scene of the third act of *Man and Superman*[7]:

THE OLD WOMAN. But I have sincerely repented; I have confessed.
DON JUAN. How much?
THE OLD WOMAN. More sins than I really committed. I loved confession.
DON JUAN. Ah, that is perhaps as bad as confessing too little. At all events, Senora, whether by oversight or intention, you are certainly damned, like myself; and there is nothing for it now but to make the best of it.
THE OLD WOMAN [*indignantly*] Oh! and I might have been so much wickeder! All my good deeds wasted! It is unjust.
DON JUAN. No: you were fully and clearly warned. For your bad deeds, vicarious atonement, mercy without justice. For your good deeds, justice without mercy. We have many good people here.

One can easily imagine that these words must have been a shock for audiences. If the difference between heaven and hell, good and evil, salvation and damnation, is only a matter of insignificant details, the whole religious system of values, which is based on the rightfulness of repayment for one's good deeds, automatically crumbles down.

Notwithstanding Shaw's rejection of dogmas in religion, what his works lack in theological orthodoxy, they make up for in structural ritualism, hence the detailed layout of his most religion-laden plays, given that "the performance in the theatre is the celebration in miniature of the mysterious working of the Life Force, in which the spectators participate as surely as the actors. In a word, it is ritual" (Smith, 203). For instance, one can draw several structural parallelisms between the most formal Christian ceremony (the Catholic mass) and Shaw's *Saint Joan*. Among others, there is the prayer over the gifts (hens lay eggs only when Joan is granted an interview with the Dauphin); also Joan's death is a conspicuous sacrifice, a dramatic sacrificing of the "daughter of God" for the salvation of her people. Finally, the forgiveness scene in which all the main characters kneel before Joan depicts the Catholic sacrament of penance.[8] This is all evidence supporting Shaw's idea of the magical properties of art (Kennedy, 50). And, of course, things like these made people spread rumors as to whether, like his friend G.K. Chesterton, Shaw would be received into the Catholic Church in his late years, to which he retorted that there was not "room in Rome for two Popes!" (Elliot, 272).

On the broader plane of religious denomination, "mysticism" is perhaps the most popular epithet to label Shaw's beliefs. In fact, he acknowledged his mystical ideas on several occasions, to the extent of stating: "As for my own position, I am and always have been, a mystic" (*RS*, 33). In this, he claims to follow the teachings of Jesus himself, since "He did not mean to establish a church. He meant practically he was one of the prophets. What he was dealing with was mysticism" (*RS*, 79). What mysticism really means for Shaw is that religion cannot be detached from the earthly issues of the population. As a result, his other intellectual and philosophical interests had to be intertwined with his religious ideas.

> In calling himself a mystic, Shaw was emphasizing what he regarded as the heart of his belief, the part that was beyond reason. But hearts do not live by themselves; they need bones and muscle and digestive systems and all sorts of less poetic support systems. The mystical part of Shaw's religion is its reason for existing; it is life and hope and purpose, but it must not be mere wishful thinking or a cowardly evasion of reality. It is an easy matter to develop a creed that is only a projection of the heart's desire, a castle in the air without foundation; it is a different chore to build such a faith on a solid basis of fact and to use it as a guide for living in a real and heartbreakingly imperfect world [Baker, 14].

Therefore, despite the deep theoretical implications that Shaw's religious ideas have had for men of letters and philosophers alike, Shaw is mostly concerned with the quotidian implications of religion for people's lives (emphasis added):

> Shaw like an anatomist scientifically scrutinises the Bible with special investigations on the life and message of Jesus Christ, and critically examines the **practical effectiveness** of his teachings [Pathak, 75].

This is a simple consequence of Shaw's knack for mixing socialism and theology (Berst, "Some Necessary Repairs," 77). In fact, it is not at all uncommon for Shaw's "holy characters" to keep a very practical attitude regarding ordinary matters such as their bodily needs.[9] The beginning of Act II in *Buoyant Billions* epitomizes the attitude of those characters that are theoretically mystical or ascetic, and yet firmly seize whatever the world has to offer. On a lonely island, SHE is a "holy woman"—idolized by the indigenous savages who bring food and drink to her doorstep every day because they believe she has supernatural powers.

> THE NATIVE. Yes, sir. And you no speak holy woman. Speak to her forbidden. She speak with great spirits only. Very strong magics. Put spell on you. Fetch gaters and rattlers with magic tunes on her pipe. Very unlucky speak to her. Very lucky bring her gifts.

However, the way SHE treats visitors is far removed from the ideal of hospitality and amiability that asceticism often suggests. Not at all inconsistently, her vocabulary contains certain hints of capitalist theory ("private property," "business"):

> SHE. Now then. This clearance is private property. Whats your business?
> HE. No business, dear lady. Treat me as a passing tramp.
> SHE. Well, pass double quick. This isnt a doss house.
> HE. No; but in this lonely place the arrival of any stranger must be a godsend. Besides, I am hungry and thirsty.
> SHE. Most tramps are. Get out.

In addition, the "holy woman" acts selfishly by denying his guest some food at first. As SHE later explains, it is the duty of a "holy lady" to take care of the material before tackling the spiritual.

> HE. Yes, holy lady; but what about your conscience? A hungry man asks you for food. Dare you throw him to the gaters and rattlers? How will that appear in the great day of reckoning?
> SHE. Neither you nor I will matter much when that day comes, if it ever does. But you can eat my lunch to shut your mouth.
> HE. Oh, thanks!
> SHE. You need not look round for a tumbler and a knife and fork. Drink from the calabash: eat from your fingers.
> HE. The simple life, eh? [*He attacks the meal*].
> SHE. No. In the simple life you ring for the servants. Everything is done for you; and you learn nothing.
> HE. And here you wait until that kindly native comes and feeds you, like Elijah's ravens. What do you learn from that?
> SHE. You learn what nice people natives are. But you begin by trying to feed yourself and build your own shack. I have been through all that, and learnt what a helpless creature a civilized woman is.

In a strict sense, the only religious "sect" to which Shaw ever claimed to belong was that of Creative Evolution. This somewhat nebulous religious group claims that there is a driving force inside every individual ("The Life Force" or *Élan Vital*) that drives organisms towards ever greater complexity and perfection.[10] In the end, humans are nothing but the implements through which God's will is done because, as Shaw puts it:

> I believe God, in the popular acceptance of the word, to be completely powerless. I do not believe that God has any hands or brain of our kind. What I know he has, or rather is, is will. But will is useless without hands and brain [*RS*, 6].[11]

This is one of the most crucial ideas to understand Shaw the philosopher (and the playwright), since Creative Evolution implies the eradication of the mechanical determinism of science and the animism of vitalists. He needs to believe the world is bound to go in the right direction, yet his beliefs are anchored in the hard facts of everyday life, much like in the case of his mysticism. Ohman (123) sees in this a synthesis of the sublime out of the ordinary:

> Around him he sees women endowed with a mating instinct much more convincing than the lip service of the Victorians to sexual propriety. He finds artists imaging life in original and superior ways. He discovers social prophets (Jesus or Joan of Arc, for example) voicing doctrine for which there is no parentage in their milieu, hundreds or thousands of years before the average mind is ready to receive it. Such anomalies seem to him inexplicable by the ordinary laws of history, so he takes them as evidence of an extramaterial force.

Some of Shaw's characters experience the same sudden realization. They understand that the apparent futility of human endeavor is not such, because we are an essential part of a higher plan to fulfill the will of the Life Force. This is the definitely optimistic side of Shaw's beliefs, which greatly differ from his unconstructive pose as an agitator and reformer. Conrad, Lubin, and Burge, despite their disparate backgrounds, seem to share the same idea in Part II of *Back to Methuselah*:

> CONRAD. It's no use arguing about it. It is now absolutely certain that the political and social problems raised by our civilization cannot be solved by mere human mushrooms who decay and die when they are just beginning to have a glimmer of the wisdom and knowledge needed for their own government.
> LUBIN. Quite an interesting idea, Doctor. Extravagant. Fantastic. But quite interesting. When I was young I used to feel my human limitations very acutely.
> BURGE. God knows I have often felt that I could not go on if it had not been for the sense that I was only an instrument in the hands of a Power above us.
> CONRAD. I'm glad you both agree with us, and with one another.

The two politicians (Burge and Lubin) are consulting Conrad (a biologist), who claims that Creative Evolution will produce humans able to live 300 years by sheer force of will. It is not coincidental that these two characters discard the idea because of its impracticality, since there is no magic formula for longevity, but they have to rely on the strenuous effort of superior men who are willing to rise to the occasion. Franklyn, Conrad's brother, states this idea with persuasive precision:

> FRANKLYN. Do not mistake mere idle fancies for the tremendous miracle-working force of Will nerved to creation by a conviction of Necessity. I tell you men capable of such willing, and realizing its necessity, will do it reluctantly, under inner compulsion, as all great efforts are made. They will hide what they are doing from themselves: they will take care not to know what they are doing. They will live three hundred years, not because they would like to, but because the soul deep down in them will know that they must, if the world is to be saved.

It is worth considering how distant these ideas of God's will and the Life Force are from the submissive and passive "Thy will be done" of the Lord's Prayer. Humankind is a vehicle for God's will, but they have a will of their own.

Shaw's unconventional religious ideas are not limited to philosophical discussion in his most argumentative plays. Another obvious vessel for heretical language in Shaw's plays is name symbolism. A wide range of characters are named after biblical characters, while others bear the name of theological concepts. Needless to say, it is not the mere mention of these names that adds up to the general stylistic effect of the plays, but the paradoxical features of the characters on whom the names are bestowed, especially when compared to their homonymous alter-egos. The dramatic implementation of such powerful symbolism is possible because the expectations of the reader/audience vary when characters called Adam, Eve or Cain are on stage.

Take, for instance, Boanerges in *The Apple Cart*. The name was borrowed from the appellative that Jesus chose for his disciples John and James,[12] meaning "the sons of thunder," because of their impetuous and impulsive nature.[13] In the Bible, their zeal is particularly aimed at defending Jesus and attacking those who do not follow his teachings. Shaw's Boanerges also exhibits this violent behavior, to the extent that even the King's secretaries call him a "bull-roarer." However, his individualistic views on politics and lack of comradeship make him a conceited rowdy minister who prides in being a "self-made man." What is more, the spiritual dimension of this character ends with his symbolic name. From the start we are presented with a man that is visually associated with soviet communism (he enters the stage "dressed in a Russian blouse and peaked cap, which he keeps on"), and his convenient philosophical materialism is blatantly exposed in his first conversation with the king, early in the play:

> BOANERGES. A soul, eh? You kings still believe in that, I suppose.
> MAGNUS. I find the word convenient: it is short and familiar. But **if you dislike being called a soul, let us say that you are animate matter** as distinguished from inanimate.
> BOANERGES [*not quite liking this*] **I think I'd rather you called me a soul**, you know, if you must call me anything at all. I know I have too much matter about me: the doctor says I ought to knock off a stone or two; but there's something more to me than beef. Call it a soul if you like; only not in a superstitious sense, if you understand me.

Despite the appropriateness of the name Boanerges, according to the self-assertive way in which the character behaves, it is clear that the religious dimension of its meaning is significantly far from true in the case of Bill Boanerges. In all, the paradoxical aspect of this particular symbolic name reveals itself as a useful framing device for the entire play, since the Shavian character echoes the biblical disciples in a deliberately distorted manner.

Other characters bear names, surnames or appellatives reflecting theological concepts, such as Paradise, Eudoxia (from the Greek for "good doctrine") or Domesday ("Doomsday"). Perhaps the character whose theological name is most closely connected to her role in the play is Epifania Fitzfassen, from *The Millionariess*. Epifania[14] is a version of the Greek word-loan for "manifestation" (i.e., "epiphany"), which is used in religious texts to denote the manifestation of the power of God.[15] In this respect, for example, one can mention the use of the Greek word ἐπιφάνεια (appearing) in the New Testament to refer to the second coming of Christ from heaven to earth. By

In Shaw's *The Millionairess* (1960, Dimitri De Grunwald Production, publicity shot courtesy Fox Lorber), Dr. Kabir (Peter Sellers) and Epifania (Sophia Loren) fall in love despite their religious differences, embodying the religious communion between different creeds that Shaw advocated for. From the 1960 film adaptation directed by Anthony Asquith.

extension, epiphany has come to mean any sudden realization of the essence of something that may have been previously neglected. Epifania Fitzfassen[16] is a superb dramatic example of the importance of epiphanies, both in religion and in other aspects of life. First, when she falls in love with an Egyptian doctor, she has a first-hand experience of the hard conditions that laborers have to endure, because she must keep herself for six months with thirty-five shillings as her only asset if she is to marry him. That is the first "epiphany" she experiences:

> EPIFANIA. My pulse will never change: this is the love I crave for. I will marry you. Mr Sagamore: see about a special licence the moment you have got rid of Alastair.
> THE DOCTOR. It is not possible. We are bound by our vows.
> EPIFANIA. Well, have I not passed your mother's test? You shall have an accoun-

tant's certificate. I learned in the first half hour of my search for employment that the living wage for a single woman is five shillings a week. Before the end of the week I had made enough to support me for a hundred years. I did it honestly and legitimately. I explained the way in which it was done.

In addition, the man she has fallen in love with is a Muslim, and she quickly realizes (in a fit of Shavian relativism) that all religions are the same when it comes to practical matters. This second "epiphany" is consistent with the religious and philosophical principles that have been described so far:

EPIFANIA. I have to take the world as I find it.
THE DOCTOR. The wrath of Allah shall overtake those who leave the world no better than they found it.
EPIFANIA. I think Allah loves those who make money.
SAGAMORE. All the evidence is that way, certainly.

The previous example leads to a necessary final remark about Shaw's heretical opinions. Most often he is content to find fault in the Christian faith as a sort of touchstone for his "Religion of the Future." Sometimes, however, he looks up to other religions as a source for more reasonable forms of faith. Shaw's interest in non-Christian sources proves his ingrained determination to find a true religious faith that can serve mankind spiritually, and yet provide guidance through life's earthly tribulations. In the previous example, we have already seen the (Muslim) Egyptian doctor, only one of the many "pagan" characters that can be found in Shaw's plays, the opinions of whom often cast a helpful light on the deficiencies of Christianity and of Victorian morals in general. Another character that must be highlighted in this section is Sir Jafna (*On the Rocks*), whose monologue is a denunciation of the bigotry with which oriental perspectives were treated, and the narrow-mindedness of the insular Britons:

SIR JAFNA [*finding his tongue*] I am despised. I am called nigger by this dirty faced barbarian whose forefathers were naked savages worshipping acorns and mistletoe in the woods whilst my people were spreading the highest enlightenment yet reached by the human race from the temples of Brahma the thousandfold who is all the gods in one. This primitive savage dares to accuse me of imitating him: me, with the blood in my veins of conquerors who have swept through continents vaster than a million dogholes like this island of yours. They founded a civilization compared to which your little kingdom is no better than a concentration camp. What you have of religion came from the east; yet no Hindu, no Parsee, no Jain, would stoop to its crudities. Is there a mirror here? Look at your faces and look at the faces of my people in Ceylon, the cradle of the human race...

On some occasions the several advantages that can be adopted from those other religions are spoken out for by Christian characters, even if in a futuristic scenario, as is the case in *Back to Methuselah*:

> THE ELDERLY GENTLEMAN [*diplomatically interrupting his scandalized son-in-law*] There can be no doubt, I am afraid, that by clinging too long to the obsolete features of the old pseudo-Christian Churches we allowed the Mahometans to get ahead of us at a very critical period of the development of the Eastern world. When the Mahometan Reformation took place, it left its followers with the enormous advantage of having the only established religion in the world in whose articles of faith any intelligent and educated person could believe.

There are times, nevertheless, when a direct defense of alien beliefs, such as Hinduism, is not only part of a religious argument, but the basis of a spiritual change for one of the characters. Thus recounts Keegan his experience with a dying "Hindoo" in *John Bull's Other Island*:

> KEEGAN [*blandly*]. That is not quite what occurred. [*He collects himself for a serious utterance: they attend involuntarily*]. I heard that a black man was dying, and that the people were afraid to go near him. When I went to the place I found an elderly Hindoo, who told me one of those tales of unmerited misfortune, of cruel ill luck, of relentless persecution by destiny, which sometimes wither the commonplaces of consolation on the lips of a priest. But this man did not complain of his misfortunes. They were brought upon him, he said, by sins committed in a former existence. Then, without a word of comfort from me, he died with a clear-eyed resignation that my most earnest exhortations have rarely produced in a Christian, and left me sitting there by his bedside with the mystery of this world suddenly revealed to me.

In the previous examples, Shaw makes use of his characters to praise what he believes are two positive characteristics of Muslims and Hindi; i.e. sensible articles of faith and unbreakable resignation, respectively. It is relevant to remind the reader of the deficiencies that Shaw found in certain elements of the Christian doctrine, especially in the dogma of atonement. On the one hand, he complains that it is a nonsensical belief that is only accepted because of its convenience, hence the admiration for Muslim common sense. On the other, it deprives people of their natural accountability for their actions (sins), hence Shaw's commendation of the attitude of the Hindu, who can bear to be punished for actions committed in a former existence.

Notwithstanding Shaw's inbuilt critical attitude, it is also true that the passage from *John Bull's Other Island* indirectly portrays a recreation of the biblical "Parable of the Good Samaritan."[17] Although the Shavian Samaritan is not successful in that the Hindoo dies in the end, there is also a silver lining to the fact that fruitful contact between religions results in enormous improvement for spiritual understanding.[18]

In view of the interpretation offered above, some tentative conclusions can be drawn regarding Shaw's religious ideas. First, it almost goes without saying that Shaw gave religion a tremendous importance in both his dramatic and non-dramatic writings. His speeches, essays and prefaces encompass the bulk of his philosophical views on the subject, yet his plays exemplify in fiction the shocking and paradoxical dimension of his impious ideas. It must be borne in mind that, although many of Shaw's religious ideas–as expressed in his plays–are no longer shocking for contemporary audiences, the uproar his every word provoked and the response of critics and the censorship are very telling of the type of religious controversy he stirred. Furthermore, his religious unorthodoxy carried a synergic effect. For example, after he argued in a public lecture in 1909 that people admired and followed Jesus because they had a feeling that "a man who could raise people from the dead might possibly on sufficient provocation reverse the operation" (Shaw, *RS*, 22), the very same year censors were eager to ban *The Shewing-up of Blanco Posnet*, despite being "a story of conversion, told with sincerity and depth of conviction" (Henderson, 400).

Despite the fact that his religious thoughts range from the unorthodox to the completely heretical, they were all aimed at the foundation of the one "true" religion. Shaw did not agree with any of the established religious ideas that existed in Victorian Britain. For example, he despised the discrimination of people on religious grounds, and he was consistently against any form of sectarianism. Furthermore, he believed that the very theory underlying the salvation of souls and life after death was unbelievable and unethical because it would not give people full responsibility for their acts. That is why he basically endorsed Creative Evolution, a form of mysticism in which God's will works through the actions and thoughts of humans. One is even tempted to say that certain megalomaniac aspects of Shaw's life and legacy are clearly at ease with a religion that envisions the permanent communion between the men and their maker.

Shaw's lack of agreement with the established religious ideals of his lifetime has philosophical roots, but it also bears stylistic fruit. In its most apparent manifestation, Shaw likes to distort biblical phrases, names and concepts in the text of his plays. This literary device is a direct way to stage his irreverent attitude towards conventional religiosity. On a subtler plane, the disfigurement of religious imagery brings about a conceptual shift that calls for an extensive logical debate. This stylistic strategy is fittingly used most often in Shaw's Discussion Plays as well as in his well-known religious plays.

In conclusion, whatever the viewpoint from which one looks at Shaw's works, the commonplace perception of the atheist, strictly rational playwright falls down flat like the walls of Jericho. Shaw was a religious man, no less than he was a religious writer. He only happened to be a little ahead of his time, which explains his popular quip: "Christianity might be a good thing if anyone ever tried it."

Notes

1. To gauge what Shaw's 96 years of age represented at the time, it suffices to say that the average life expectancy at birth for the population of the British Isles was estimated around 40 in the 1850s (Floud, 291; Hollis, 92). Even if the outrageous infant death rate is eliminated from the equation, it is worthy of note that midlife was said to start a little after 30, as many newspapers and magazines pointed out (Heath, 6).

2. Despite his zeal for learning (*Religious Speeches*, 103), "Shaw's Bible scholarship was sometimes faulty."

3. To assess the meaning of Shaw's ideas in his own lifetime, it is worth reminding the reader that "religion has probably never seemed so important, to so many people, as in Victorian England. It was part of every area of life, subsuming the political, educational, professional, social, familial" (Dennis and Skilton, 77). Exaggerated as this quotation may seem, most of the social, political, scientific and philosophical debates in Victorian England had a religious controversy behind them (consider, for example, Darwinism, socialism, agnosticism as opposed to atheism, or women's rights).

4. It is hardly surprising that Shaw should use the Bible as a source for his religious criticism. The Bible had much in common with other prominent institutions of his time (the British Empire, monarchy, democracy, Shakespeare's canonical status, and the like) that Shaw also critiqued. As Prickett (xi) puts it: "The Bible is the basic book of our civilization. It holds a unique and exclusive status not merely in terms of the religious history of the western world but also in literary history and even in what might be called our collective cultural psyche."

5. See Matthew 5:39 and Luke 6:39.

6. Emphasis has been added in all the extracts from Shaw's plays, highlighting the most relevant phrases.

7 *Don Juan in Hell*, sometimes played separately.

8. See Wetmore, *Catholic Theatre and Drama*, for further connections between drama and the Catholic faith.

9. Shaw is known for not displaying carnal encounters in his plays. In other words, he "avoids getting thick about love" (Berst, 112). Therefore, the bodily functions that these characters pivot around for the most part are eating, drinking and resting.

10. Shaw sees obvious evidence that the human race finds itself in a state of constant amelioration, and he expresses his view in his usual shocking words: "Just think about yourselves, ladies and gentlemen. I do not want to be uncomplimentary, but can you conceive God deliberately creating you if he could have created anything better?" (Shaw, *Religious Speeches*, 17).

11. The metaphor is particularly adept, given Shaw's denial of an anthropomorphic God. As usual, this idea was expressed in a particularly orthodox way to convey quite an unorthodox message in the preface to *Back to Methuselah*: "St John might say that 'God is spirit' as pointedly as he pleased; our Sovereign Lady Elizabeth might ratify the Article again and again; serious divines might feel as deeply as they could that a God with body, parts, and passions could be nothing but an anthropomorphic idol: no matter: people at large could not conceive a God who was not anthropomorphic: they stood by the Old Testament legends of a God whose parts had been seen by one of the patriarchs, and finally set up as against the Church a God who, far from being without body, parts, or passions, was composed of nothing else, and of very evil passions too" (*CP*, 518).

12. According to *Fausset's Bible Dictionary* (1878), Boanerges is "the Aramaic name given to James and John by Jesus. Hebrew *beney regesh*; Their fiery zeal appears in (Luke 9:54) their desiring the Lord's permission that they should command fire from heaven (like Elias) to consume the Samaritans who would not receive Him, 'because His face was as though He would go to Jerusalem.' Also in (Mark 9:38) their forbidding one casting out demons in Christ's name, because he followed not with them. Compare also their ambition for the highest place in Christ's kingdom, next Himself (Mark 9:35–41). Grace subsequently corrected this zeal without knowledge, making

James the willing martyr (Acts 12) and John the apostle of gentleness and love. Still the old zeal against perverters of the truth as it is in Jesus appears in 2 John 1:10–11; 3 John 1:10."
13. See Mark 3:17.
14. One finds it difficult not to mention Shaw's apology for a phonetic alphabet, given the spelling of the /f/ sound in Epifania's name. The importance of phonetics and spelling cannot be undermined, as they found their way into Shaw's will, where a generous allowance was set aside to publish his plays using his own forty-letter phonetic alphabet. Shaw's views on the advantages of "ootomatik speling" have been edited under the title *On Language* (1965).
15. It is also relevant to bring up that the word epiphany has particular connotations in literary terms, stemming from Joyce's *Portrait of the Artist as a Young Man*, in which "sudden spiritual manifestations," whether trite or transcendental, are epiphanies to be recorded by the man of letters. For more information on Shaw's reading of Joyce, see Holroyd (598–600).
16. Epifania states her full name as Epifania Ognisanti ("all saints") di Parerga, which enhances the plausibility of religious symbolism in it.
17. Luke, 10:25–37.
18. Furthermore, a fraternal religious entente must avoid ill-meant superstition, lest we mistake a good Samaritan for the Devil, as Larry does just before Keegan recounts the tranquil death of the Hindoo: "LARRY. I am informed that when the devil came for the black heathen, he took off your head and turned it three times round before putting it on again; and that your head's been turned ever since."

Works Cited and Consulted

Baker, Stuart E. *Shaw's Remarkable Religion: A Faith That Fits the Facts.* Gainesville: University Press of Florida, 2002.
Berst, Charles A. *Bernard Shaw and the Art of Drama.* Chicago: University of Illinois Press, 1973.
———. "'Some Necessary Repairs to Religion': Resurrecting an Early Shavian 'Sermon.'" *SHAW* 1 (1981): 77–98.
Brake, Donald L. *A Visual History of the English Bible.* Grand Rapids: Baker, 2008.
Dennis, Barbara, and David Skilton, eds. *Reform and Intellectual Debate in Victorian England.* Beckenham: Croom Helm, 1987.
Einsohn, Howard I. "Ideology, Utopia, and Faith: Shaw, Ricoeur, and the Passion for the Possible." *SHAW* 15 (1995): 105–121.
Elliot, Vivian, ed. *Dear Mr Shaw: Selections from Bernard Shaw's Postbag.* London: Bloomsbury, 1987.
Floud, Roderick. *The Cambridge Economic History of Modern Britain*, Vol. II. Cambridge: Cambridge University Press 2004.
Heath, Kay. *Aging by the Book: The Emergence of Midlife in Victorian Britain.* Albany: State University of New York Press, 2009.
Henderson, Archibald. *George Bernard Shaw: His Life and Works, a Critical Biography.* Cincinnati: Steward & Kidd, 1911.
Hollis, Daniel W. *The History of Ireland.* Westport, CT: Greenwood Press, 2001.
Holroyd, Michael. *Bernard Shaw: The One Volume Definitive Edition.* New York: Random House, 1997.
Kennedy, Andrew. *Six Dramatists in Search of a Language.* Cambridge: Cambridge University Press, 1975.
Moody Smith, D. "John." In *Harper's Bible Commentary*, ed. James L. Mays. San Francisco: Harper & Row, 1044–1076.
Ohman, Richard M. *Bernard Shaw: The Style and the Man.* Middleton, CT: Wesleyan University Press, 1962.
Pathak, Dayananda. *George Bernard Shaw: His Religion and Values.* Delhi: Mittal Publications, 1985.
Pearson, Hesketh. *Bernard Shaw: A Biography.* London: Macdonald and Jane's, 1975.
Pricket, Stephen. Introduction to *The Bible: Authorized King James Version.* Eds. Robert Carroll and Stephen Prickett. Oxford: Oxford University Press, 1997, xi–xlvi.

Shaw, Bernard. *The Complete Prefaces of Bernard Shaw*. London: Paul Hamlyn, 1965.
_____. *George Bernard Shaw on Language*. Ed. Abraham Tauber. London: Peter Owen, 1965.
_____. *The Religious Speeches of Bernard Shaw*. Ed. Warren Sylvester. University Park: Pennsylvania State University Press, 1963.
_____. *Sixteen Self Sketches*. London: Constable, 1949.
Smith, Joseph P. *The Unrepentant Pilgrim*. London: Gollancz, 1966.
Wetmore, Kevin J., ed. *Catholic Theatre and Drama. Critical Essays*. Jefferson, NC: McFarland, 2010.

Song of Myself: Teaching Whitman's New Bible Today

TRACY FLOREANI

The head is more than churches or bibles or creeds.
— Walt Whitman, *Song of Myself*, line 528

I've been teaching American literature at small, Midwestern, church-affiliated liberal arts colleges for about a dozen years, and most of my students were raised in Protestant/evangelical communities. Inevitably, when I teach the 19th-century Transcendentalists, they get intrigued. By the time we get to Whitman's *Song of Myself*, they're ready to convert. Sure, there are the holdouts, the students who find his writing too disorganized and too "hippie" in its sentiments. His form is admittedly confusing, not at all like the closed-form poems they have studied earlier, and at first some have trouble processing a sixty-page poem that looks like a mixture of "*Bhagavad Gita* and the *New York Tribune.*"[1] And all those inexplicable ellipses in the 1855 version! Other students are less dismissive but seem only temporarily captivated, in the Transcendentalist moment for a small portion of the semester, posting quotes from Thoreau and Whitman on their Facebook pages for a few weeks. Some stick with it, though, seeking out the longer works of Emerson by day, talking half-drunken Transcendentalist philosophy under the trees late into the night after the bars have closed. I have even had, on one occasion, a student raise her hand in class and declare, "I want to convert to Transcendentalism." Alas, though some may be ready to convert, there is nothing to convert to — at least not in the way of formal joining of an organized religion and a place to perform the conversion ceremony. (Well, actually there *is* a place, perhaps on a patch of clover right outside the classroom building, but there's no recognizable building like the churches of their families.) What is it about Transcendentalism, and Whitman in particular, that appeals so strongly to college-age students in the midst of many new intellectual explorations, any one of which could affect their real lives outside of the classroom?

The appeal is not too surprising, given that Whitman referred to *Leaves of Grass* as a "New Bible."[2] Yet, oddly enough, relatively little scholarship from the past twenty years explores the religious or spiritual elements of his most famous work. Perhaps the super-saturated Transcendentalist work is so infused with spirituality that one need not explicate it further. Still, students new to the poem cannot truly understand what Whitman preaches without understanding the spiritual underpinnings of his work. What I describe in this essay is certainly not unique to my experiences of teaching Whitman's most famous poem, though I don't know that I've ever seen anyone formally discuss the "religious conversion" phenomenon. After more than a decade of teaching the poem in American literature survey courses — and witnessing this phenomenon repeatedly — I have some thoughts as to why the conversion desire occurs. Simply put, Whitman's pluralist approach to human experience as divine experience opens doors to a D.I.Y. approach to spirituality and belief that is nonjudgmental, firmly grounded in American cultural ideals, and centered on the familiar self as a resource for moral guidance.

While I often ease my students into Whitman's writing style and worldview through some of the shorter, topical poems (such as the Civil War poems from *Drum-Taps*), the one piece of scripture that pushes them to the point of conversion and the one text that seems to fulfill their new spiritual needs is *Song of Myself*. As those who teach Whitman know, the poem isn't always an instant hit. However, the unfamiliar and seemingly disorganized form that some students first see in Whitman's work (compared to, say, Tennyson's poems) immediately clears up with an "Oh. Okay," when I lay a Whitman passage next to a passage from Ecclesiastes. While this mimicry of biblical text in such a "sexy" poem might seem blasphemous to some very devout students, they never say so. Instead, the similarity codifies a respect for scriptural writing on the poet's part and provides a rhetorical gateway into the poem. This also helps them see a double familiarity in the language of the poem, its tone at times very much informed by the lofty cadence of scripture, but also distinctly American and somewhat casual in voice.

While Christians who pull biblical lines out of context and ignore the more disagreeable parts of the Bible may be labeled hypocrites, I have no qualms about encouraging students to pull individual lines or passages from Whitman's poem. In fact, there is no "out of context" in *Song of Myself*'s mostly non sequitur-filled structure, so there is no possibility of hypocrisy. If they can't see the whole at first, I encourage them to isolate a line or passage they like — for reasons they are not required to explain — and simply read it aloud. They are encouraged to wallow in the beauty of one line without having to understand the logic of the whole for a while. Perhaps this approach to textual analysis is familiar to them, as well, as it may be how they were taught to approach other religious texts at a young age.

Not only do I encourage students to lift lines out of context, I support their love of lines that oppose one another in sentiment. Should new followers of Whitman feel somehow hypocritical in thought or action, they need only turn to the famous lines "Do I contradict myself?/Very well then ... I contradict myself; I am large ... I contain multitudes."[3] Instead of all that doctrinal contradiction written by multiple recorders of Holy texts in an ancient society nothing like ours, we find a spirituality that, like modern American society, provides for a natural pluralism (even debate) within one's own body and mind. And again, the individual gets to decide the right and the wrong of the moment, because the "I" (whether Whitman's or his reader's) is in charge in this religion:

> There will soon be no more priests. Their work is done. [...] A new order shall arise and they shall be the priests of man, and every man shall be his own priest. The churches built under their umbrage shall be the churches of men and women. Through the divinity of themselves shall the kosmos and the new breed of poets be interpreters of men and women and of all events and things. They shall find their inspiration in real objects today, symptoms of the past and future.... They shall not deign to defend immortality or God or the perfection of things or liberty or the exquisite beauty and reality of the soul. They shall arise in America and be responded to from the remainder of the earth.[4]

These lines offer the reader the power to be the priest of the self. Rather than being expected to abide by a series of rules for living, individuals are trusted to find the right and the good on their own — and are given some rhetorically passionate instructions for how to do so. As George Sixbey notes, Whitman saw in the poet the power to re-create God in his own image. This is both a Romantic notion of the poet's privileged position in accessing the divine and translating it for others, as well as a purely democratic belief that if humans are made in the image of God, God is also made in the image of humans: "Taking myself the exact dimensions of Jehovah and laying them away."[5]

The above passage also echoes the important democratic theme throughout the poem, Whitman's implicit argument that only through American democracy — as conceived and in-the-making in the young nation — may real equality be realized, and this equality is requisite to the understanding of the divine in all living beings.[6] In such an affirmation lies both an appeal to the notions of patriotic equality students are taught in public schools as well as to a sense of American exceptionalism still persistent in our culture. Moreover, the passage above proclaims that the best priests in our culture will be English majors! "[T]he new breed of poets be interpreters of men and women and of all events and things," as another line in isolation, may bolster my English majors who seem to have no idea *why* they are English majors.

If the youthful soul is already moving away from a Christian upbringing after taking a World Religions course, as I have seen happen many times (even in myself as a nineteen-year-old looking for independence from a Catholic upbringing), *Song* offers additional comfort, advice, and justification. When a young Anglo Protestant is torn between whether Buddhism or Sufism seems like the new spiritual path to follow, well, guess what: Whitman says you can have it all, "enclosing all worship ancient and modern, and all between ancient and modern," organized and primal simultaneously:

> Making a fetish of the first rock or stump ... powwowing with sticks in the circle of obis,
> Helping the lama or brahmin as he trims the lamps of the idols,
> Dancing yet through the streets in a phallic procession ... rapt and austere in the woods, a gymnophyst,
> Drinking mead from the skull-cup ... to shasta and vedas admirant ... minding the koran,
> Walking the teokallis, spotted with gore from the stone and knife — beating the serpent-skin drum,
> Accepting the gospels, accepting him that was crucified, knowing assuredly that he is divine,
> To the mass kneeling — to the puritan's prayer rising — sitting patiently in a pew...[7]

While Emerson seems to find all organized religion (even Unitarianism) too limiting to one's own moral seeking — to the extent that he seems at times to be a moral relativist — Whitman embraces it all, insisting that through experimenting with a variety of spiritual practices we find ourselves in connection to all of the divine. Some students do warm to Emerson, of course, but many find him perhaps too fatherly, too absolute, too focused on the individual as intellectual sovereign and, therefore, in some ways very much alone. In Thoreau, they find something to admire, but most find his experiment at Walden Pond such a specific, ascetic experience that they don't see room for themselves in it. In Whitman, one finds Emerson's ideal nonconformist *being* a nonconformist (as with Thoreau), and doing so in a more socially aware way that reaches out to others and affirms their faiths and identities. For Whitman, the entire world is Walden, and in that expansive approach students seem to find their own potential Waldens more easily.

This reaching out extends, then, to seeing the divine in all living beings, including those the official institutions of Whitman's day did not recognize as human, such as slaves of African descent and Native Americans.[8] The persona of the poem, however, goes beyond recognition to an extension of the Golden Rule, to a connection with the Other we are often incapable of making ourselves enact without an inspirational shove. In his argument for the divine-as-realized via democracy, Whitman creates a speaker who makes an example of himself connecting to the divine in everyone he encounters: "All these I feel or am./ I am the hounded slave ... I wince at the bite of the dogs."[9] The poet knows that Jesus Christ is divine, because, through the connected "oversoul" of Transcendentalism, "I am the man ... I suffered ... I was there"; "That I could look with a separate look on my own crucifixion and bloody crowning!"[10] For Whitman, the poet and the slave are as divine as Jesus, the president as divine as a prostitute or a farmer, and real democracy requires not that we judge others' performance within a narrow interpretation of scripture, as our puritanical cultural roots have influenced many to do, but that we (like the historical Jesus) declare allegiance to criminals and whores:

> I will not have a single person slighted or left way,
> The keptwoman and sponger and thief are hereby invited ... the heavy-lipped slave is invited ... the venerealee is invited,
> There shall be no difference between them and the rest.[11]

David Reynolds describes the first edition of *Leaves of Grass* as "a utopian document, suggesting that boundaries of section, class, and race that had become glaringly visible in America's political arena could be imaginatively dissolved by affirmation of the cross-fertilization of its various cultural arenas." Whitman reminds us what real (utopian) democracy can be when he "speak[s] the password primeval.... I give the sign of democracy;/By God! I will accept nothing which all cannot have their counterpart of on the same terms"; he reminds us, too, that the enactment of democracy requires empathy: "I do not ask the wounded person how he feels.... I myself become the wounded person."[12] Like any religion or ethical system, we see in these examples how Whitman's poem reminds us to try to be our best selves, and to take those best selves out into our contemporary society.

And guess what: our best selves can be sexually active! With whomever we want! Know why? That's right, all connection to other living beings is essentially divine. This seems like an especially welcome — but also confusing — revelation to those students who have been immersed in the contemporary culture of abstinence-only sex education, or who have come to college still wearing their purity rings.[13] Just as the "I" of the poem puts himself inside the consciousness of the slave, he does so with the opposite sex, physically putting himself inside of another man's experience with his new bride, to "tighten her all night to my thighs and lips," but also, in the very next line, inside the grief of a widow, "My voice is the wife's voice, the screech by the rail of the stairs,/They fetch my man's body up dripping and drowned." He literally transitions his sexuality to the necessary moment. Consequently, if all human experience is an expression of the divine, then it need not be strictly heterosexual, as affirmed in the well-known passage that hints at fellatio as divine experience beyond judgment and sin:

> I mind how we lay in June, such a transparent summer morning;
> You settled your head athwart my hips and gently turned over upon me,
> And parted the shirt from my bosom-bone, and plunged your tongue to my barestript heart,
> And reached till you felt my beard, and reached till you held my feet.
> Swiftly arose and spread around me the peace and joy and knowledge that pass all the art and argument of the earth;
> And I know that the hand of God is the elderhand of my own.[14]

To express connection to others with the body is not the work of the devil; in fact, in Whitman's theology, "wickedness is most likely the absence of freedom and health in the soul."[15] I have known gay students who encounter this poem in those formative college years as they attempt to get beyond the rejection of parents, churches, or counselors who have tried to "cure" them of their homosexuality. Instead, Whitman offers validation of all experiences: "Seeing, hearing and feeling are miracles, and each part and tag of me is a miracle./ Divine am I inside and out, and I make holy whatever I touch or am touched from;/ The scent of these arm-pits is aroma finer than prayer."[16]

Even if you don't have anyone to make out with, nature is there for you, and awareness of the body within nature is divine, too:

> You sea! I resign myself to you also.... I guess what you mean,
> I behold from the beach your crooked inviting fingers,
> I believe you refuse to go back without feeling of me;
> We must have a turn together.... I undress ... hurry me out of sight of the land,
> Cushion me soft ... rock me in billowy drowse,
> Dash me with amorous wet ... I can repay you.

Ultimately, he asks that we tune into sensory experiences and see those as sacred in themselves. For Whitman, the minutiae of human existence are divine and worthy of our attentions; even in our most navel-gazing moments we can tune into the holy: "not objecting to special revelations ... considering a curl of smoke or a hair on the back of my hand as curious as any revelation."[17]

For every trial belief system or lifestyle at an age of strong convictions

Song of Myself (FLOREANI) 139

on social issues, the pluralist poem offers something.¹⁸ For the animal rights activist:

> I think I could turn and live awhile with the animals...
> [...]
> They do now sweat and whine about their condition,
> They do not lie awake in the dark and weep for their sins,
> They do not make me sick discussing their duty to God,
> Not one is dissatisfied ... not one is demented with the mania of owning things,
> Not one kneels to another nor to his kind that lived a thousand years ago [...]¹⁹

There are passages that speak to the environmentalists, the budding feminists, the maybe-probably agnostics, the newly signed-up up or just-out soldiers getting their heads around the realities of war. I even had one country boy student who started out thinking of Whitman as a leftist "hippie," then discovered several passages describing hunting (again, Whitman himself occupying the body of the hunter) in non-judgmental ways. This student found a way into the poem, and enlightened me to passages I had never really noticed before. When students find these specific passages and highlight them in class, I learn with them — with literature as the religious text that brings us together.

For those who are experiencing their first losses, deaths of family members or friends their own age, but who are finding little comfort in organized religion or the traditional notion of heaven as an actual place, Whitman offers this well known passage:

> All goes onward and outward ... and nothing collapses,
> And to die is different from what any one supposed, and luckier.
> Has any one supposed it lucky to be born?
> I hasten to inform him or her it is just as lucky to die, and I know it.

In his idealized conception of the universal fabric, we are all immortal, always-present in the "kosmos" in some form or another, and death is simply part of the divine experience of life. Like Whitman himself, we can be "under your boot souls," always present to those who are tuned-in to the all-connected divinity in all living things; likewise, our loved ones can be present to us in the grass, "the beautiful uncut hair of graves." When one works to perceive pain as simply a part of a divine life — rather than a test upon an individual or family by a specific God — one realizes that, simply, "Agonies are one of my changes of garments."²⁰

While I do not often ask my students to connect their own beliefs and experiences with what we read, *Song of Myself* seems to require that we do so in order to make sense of it. As Lawrence Buell describes it:

In plain language, Whitman seems to be saying that his poem, more than most, depends for its meaningfulness upon our participation. This is true, and not merely of this one lyric, but of all of Whitman's poetry. It requires us to take part in two main ways. First, the reader must respond sensuously: smell the scents; feel the fingers tighter than vines, and the breezes; hear the gushes from the throats of birds; taste the frost-mellowed berries; and behold all. This is not as easy to do as it may seem. The sensuous appeal of poetry is made via the intellect and is too often weakened in the process; it is one thing to recognize the technique of synesthesia used here, another thing to participate in it."[21]

Our job as teachers, then, is to become facilitators of synesthesia.

Similarly, John B. Mason writes that "[f]or Whitman the suggestiveness of the poem exists to prompt readers to construct the very poem they are reading. This was a radical and ambitious conception of poetry in the mid-nineteenth century, and it presents a challenge yet today for those first reading and studying Whitman's poems."[22] Yet the poem's invitation to participate in the creation of its meaning makes it also exciting, for in creating the poem's meaning — in developing one's own interpretation of its spiritual and theological teachings, in particular — students have the power to use it as a guide toward a self-created, liberating religion. Both the search for meaning in the poem and the meaning of life are challenging, and the allegorical work of interpreting the poem may provide real comfort — or at least the pleasure found in attempting to solve a puzzle: "Let up again to feel the puzzle of puzzles, And that we call Being."[23]

Facilitating synesthesia isn't always easy, and some students resist the invitation to loaf with Whitman much longer than others, often because they find him arrogant. Even after days of working with the text, a student might contend, "He talks about himself a lot," or "He acts like we have to see everything the way he does and agree with him." True, in isolation a line like "Accepting the rough deific sketches to fill out better in myself ... bestowing them freely on each man and woman I see" might seem a rather grandiose notion of the self's power to view the world as a god and "bestow" worth on others. Likewise, the size of the poem — the need to express these ideas at such *thorough* length — might seem rather egotistical. Often, though, students have lost focus by the end of the poem and miss the lines where Whitman reminds us that he's dragging us along through his vision of the world to help us find our own visions. He admits, "I know perfectly well my own egotism." We synesthesia facilitators have to remind students that the "I" isn't just Whitman; we need to occupy the "I" and accept as our own the creed, "I resist anything better than my own diversity,/ And breathe the air and leave plenty after me,/ And am not stuck up, and am in my place."[24]

Every time I teach *Song of Myself* and ask students to pick out lines they want to read aloud, without fail someone will pick this passage:

And I call to mankind, Be not curious about God
For I who am curious about each am not curious about God,
No array of terms can say how much I am at peace about God and about Death.
I hear and behold God in every object, yet I understand God not in the least.
Nor do I understand who there can be more wonderful than myself.[25]

The slog through the sixty-page poem may be hard going for some students, but this line's persistence as one that stands out to them speaks the poem's spiritual force for many. The line can fit with their own religious views, already in place; it can express a wavering of faith; it definitely expresses a very American faith in the individual self; it contains contradictions that may exist in their own minds. In any case, it's comforting to find a secular text that assures us "our rendezvous is fitly appointed.... God will be there and wait till we come."[26] Even if we have to invent who or what God is ourselves.

Notes

1. Paul Zweig, *Walt Whitman: The Making of the Poet* (New York: Basic Books, 1984), 8.
2. Ibid., 12–13.
3. *Walt Whitman, The Complete Poems* (New York: Penguin, 2004), 1314–16. All citations of line numbers are from the first version of *Song* (1855) in the Penguin edition.
4. Prologue to the 1855 edition, *Walt Whitman, The Complete Poems* (New York: Penguin, 2004), 760.
5. George L. Sixbey, "'Chanting the Square Deific'—A Study in Whitman's Religion," *American Literature* 9.2 (1937): 171–95, [173–74], JSTOR, 19 March 2012.
6. See also Thomas Parkinson, "'When Lilacs in the Door-Yard Bloom'd' and the American Civil Religion," *The Southern Review* 19.1 (1983): 1–16; and Jared Hickman, "The Theology of Democracy," *The New England Quarterly* 81.2 (2008): 177–217.
7. Whitman, 1097–1103.
8. In retrospect, Whitman's championing of westward expansion and the doctrine of Manifest Destiny is now very much in conflict with a respect for the Mexican and Indian natives of the West, as many contemporary critics of Manifest Destiny have effectively argued. In his idealism at the time, Whitman saw expansion less as an encroachment on tribal lands than as a necessary means of spreading democracy, and, therefore, divine equality.
9. Whitman, 833–34.
10. Ibid., 827; 960.
11. Ibid., 374–76.
12. David S. Reynolds, *Whitman's America: A Cultural Biography* (New York: Vintage, 1996), 309; *Whitman*, 507–08; 841.
13. For discussions of modern purity culture, see Jessica Valenti, *The Purity Myth: How America's Obsession with Virginity Is Hurting Young Women* (New York: Seal Press, 2009), as well as its documentary film adaptation by Media Education Foundation, 2011.
14. Whitman, 816–17, 78–83.
15. Qtd. in Sixbey, 185–86. Nineteenth-century disciples believed that following Whitman "might become an organized religion, possibly rivaling Christianity" explainable by the "crisis of faith" in late 19th-century American culture (9). Whitman's work also "fit perfectly with the pro-

gressive optimism common among nineteenth-century spiritual seekers, the notion that earlier religions had been rough sketches for a fully realized democratic spirituality that was manifested equally in every man and woman and expressed in the inspired verse of a modern poet-prophet" (Michael Roberton, *Worshipping Walt: The Whitman Disciples* [Princeton: Princeton University Press, 2008], 11).

16. *Whitman*, 525–27. The connection between the body as sacred and the concept of an idealized democracy is nicely and succinctly articulated in the American Experience documentary *Walt Whitman*, dir. Mark Zwonitzer, WGBH (2008).

17. *Whitman*, 451–56; 1034.

18. "Cognitively, the ability to think abstractly opens the way to critical assessment of [adolescents'] own ideas and ideas of others. Superego processes may be altered in response to new configurations of experience. The increased capacity to test assumptions and construct theories supports the idealistic thrust toward social change (Colarusso 1992)." Alice M. Graham, "Identity in Middle and Late Adolescence," *Human Development and Faith: Life-Cycle Stages of Body, Mind, and Soul*, ed. Felicity B. Kelcourse (St. Louis: Chalice, 2004), 223–235.

19. *Whitman*, 684–87.

20. Ibid, 120–23; 101; 840.

21. Lawrence Buell, "Transcendentalist Catalogue Rhetoric: Vision Versus Form," *American Literature* 40.3 (1968): 325–39; 327.

22. James B. Mason, "The Poet-Reader Relationship in 'Song of Myself,'" *Approaches to Teaching Whitman's Leaves of Grass*, ed. Donald D. Kummings (New York: MLA, 1990), 41.

23. *Whitman*, 609–10.

24. Ibid.,1031; "Not I, nor any one else can travel that road for you,/You must travel it yourself," 1208–09; 1079; 347–49.

25. Ibid., 1271–75.

26. Ibid.,1197

Works Cited

American Experience: Walt Whitman, dir. Mark Zwonitzer, WGBH, 2008.
Buell, Lawrence. "Transcendentalist Catalogue Rhetoric: Vision Versus Form." *American Literature* 40.3 (1968): 325–39.
Graham, Alice M. "Identity in Middle and Late Adolescence." *Human Development and Faith: Life-Cycle Stages of Body, Mind, and Soul*, ed. Felicity B. Kelcourse. St. Louis: Chalice, 2004.
Hickman, Jared. "The Theology of Democracy." *The New England Quarterly* 81.2 (2008): 177–217.
Mason, James B. "The Poet-Reader Relationship in 'Song of Myself.'" *Approaches to Teaching Whitman's Leaves of Grass*, ed. Donald D. Kummings. New York: MLA, 1990, 41.
Parkinson, Thomas. "'When Lilacs in the Door-Yard Bloom'd' and the American Civil Religion." *The Southern Review* 19.1 (1983): 1–16.
Reynolds, David S. *Whitman's America: A Cultural Biography*. New York: Vintage, 1996.
Roberton, Michael. *Worshipping Walt: The Whitman Disciples*. Princeton: Princeton University Press, 2008.
Sixbey, George L. "'Chanting the Square Deific'—A Study in Whitman's Religion." *American Literature* 9.2 (1937): 171–95.
Valenti, Jessica. *The Purity Myth: How America's Obsession with Virginity Is Hurting Young Women*. New York: Seal Press, 2009.
Whitman, Walt. *Walt Whitman, The Complete Poems*. New York: Penguin, 2004.
Zweig, Paul. *Walt Whitman: The Making of the Poet*. New York: Basic Books, 1984.

Part II. Angels and Demons Among Us: The Politics and Economics of Heaven and Hell in Popular Culture

The Gospel According to Comic Strips: On Peanuts and The Far Side[1]

Eric Michael Mazur

> *God is dead! God remains dead! And we have killed him! ... Is not the magnitude of this deed too great for us? Shall we not ourselves have to become Gods, merely to seem worthy of it?* —Friedrich Nietzsche, The Gay Science, Book 3, §125

According to the *Oxford English Dictionary* (2nd edition, 1989), the word "gospel" has its roots in Old English, and is the result of blending the two words for "good" and "story." Traditional Christian doctrine teaches that there is only one "good story," and that "good story" is a true story—*the* true story, as in the "gospel truth"—contained in the narratives related by Matthew, Mark, Luke, and John, about Jesus of Nazareth, "the way, the truth, and the life" through whom one may come to the Father (John 14:6). But what happens when the Truth becomes a truth? Is that still a good story?

This essay examines changes in late twentieth-century American religion by tracking the transformation of the Gospel into a gospel—or rather, quite a few gospels—in popular culture, charting the movement of the religious impulse from traditional institutional religious expression into diffuse, non-traditional, non-institutional settings.

Come the Revolution

By the last third of the twentieth century, argued *Time* religion editor John Elson (1966), Nietzsche was no longer the "prophet" of only those few "skeptics for whom unbelief [was] the test of wisdom." Instead, the questions Nietzsche asked — or more accurately, the position he averred — seemed much more pressing to a new generation of theologians — Christians and Jews — who were pondering not only the nature of the Divine, but also the Divine Presence's very existence.

These "death of God" theologians, as they were known, created such a stir that by the spring of 1966, their concerns had made it to the cover of *Time* magazine. But the topic was of interest to more than just academics and theologians. According to *New York Times* writer William Grimes (2009), the April 1966 "Is God Dead?" issue of *Time* that carried Elson's comments "caused an uproar, equaled only by John Lennon's offhand remark, published in a magazine for teenagers a few months later, that the Beatles were more popular than Jesus."[2] This first issue in *Time* history without a cover photograph or illustration — bearing only the infamous central question in "giant blood-red letters" — was the best selling one off the newsstands for the publication since the 1940s, and attracted the highest number of readers' letters the magazine had seen up to that time. As Grimes rightly points out, this issue of *Time* "remains a signpost of the 1960s, testimony to the wrenching social changes transforming the United States."[3]

But to borrow from humorist Mark Twain, reports of God's demise were greatly exaggerated; nowhere in his article did Elson say that God was actually dead.[4] The article that was at the center of the furor — the one around which this particular issue of *Time* was built — was rather innocently (and somewhat academically) titled "Theology Toward a Hidden God," and focused less on a God that had died (or been killed) than on one that had become less relevant in the lives of contemporary Americans. Reflecting (more than the issue's cover) post-Holocaust, non-Nietzschean trends in American theology, the article grappled with a world (or rather, an English-speaking American world) in which many seemed to live life without God — in which God was hidden from them (or by them) — in what Protestant theologian Harvey Cox (1965) called the "secular city." Argued Gabriel Vahanian, one of the early voices in the movement (1967, 4), "there was a Christian era" in which "culture corresponded with its theology," but currently "the world has been deprived of its sacramental significance; human existence has lost its transcendental dimension," and the language did not "necessarily entail or presuppose communion." Jewish philosopher Eugene Borowitz (1967, 93) agreed, noting that "Western culture and society are no longer Christian," and the citizens of the modern world were, "in all the effective levels of their lives, non-religious." "Modern man," he argued, "is secular and happily so." Rather than from Twain, maybe the best line for the "death-of God" theologians was to be borrowed from 1960s American folk singer Phil Ochs: God wasn't dead, he was just missing in action (Ochs 1989, from the liner notes).

And yet, if the reaction to the *Time* cover is any indication, far from God's death (or removal) being a preoccupation among American believers, the 1960s were halcyon days for thinking about God in the English-speaking world. The Second Vatican Council ("Vatican II," 1962–1965) and the 1968 Medellin Conference (which the Vatican opposed) brought greater public attention to American Catholic theology, ritual, and practice, while the work of the Rev. Martin Luther King, Jr., and evangelist Billy Graham brought greater attention to Protestant spirituality and religious interpretation, and beyond. If the publication of a book is any indication of the public's interest in its contents, then there is also a more mundane data set that suggests great spiritual activity during this period; according to the Library of Congress, in the 150 years from 1815 to 1965, 152 different versions of the canonical gospels were published, an annual average of just over one gospel per year (1.01), but in the 47 years from 1965 through September 2011 (during which time there were 98 copies of the same gospels published), the annual average doubled (2.09).[5]

Not counted among those gospels, but often credited with being on the vanguard of the 1960s revolution of religion and culture, was a small volume of a slightly different sort, written by a Presbyterian minister, suggesting that contrary to the "death-of-God" theologians, God and God's message could actually be found among the most mundane of sources.[6] Just before *Time* magazine posed its provocative question, Robert Short published *The Gospel According to Peanuts*, exploring the Christianity of the cartoon strip of the same name. Written "with the blessing of Peanuts creator Charles Schulz," the work became a bestseller, and despite the observation from noted American church historian Martin Marty that "[a] lot of people were nervous about this idea of mixing popular culture and the Bible," the volume eventually sold more than 10 million copies globally and has been translated into eleven different languages (Sanders 2009).[7]

The volume's introduction was written by Nathan Scott, one of the founders of the field of religion and literature populated by scholars who, beginning in the mid-1950s, promoted the examination of literature through a theological lens. According to Jeffrey Mahan (2007, 48–49), Scott's "germinal work drew our attention to the relationships between religion and art," making him the perfect person to be associated with Short's work "which used Charles Shultz' [sic] Peanuts cartoons to invite a popular audience to reflect theologically."[8]

146 Part II. Angels and Demons Among Us

Charlie Brown (left) speaks with Linus van Pelt in the snow. *A Charlie Brown Christmas* (Warner Bros.) has aired every Christmas since its prime-time television premiere in 1965. Based on Charles M. Schulz's *Peanuts* comic strips, the cartoon has a notable religious message. Robert Short's *The Gospel According to Peanuts* was published the same year.

As a subject for Short's theological analysis, Schulz's work was an obvious choice. Schulz was a religious man—"a reasonable Midwestern student of the Bible" (Van Biema 1999)—and a member of the Church of God, where he taught Sunday school and "would occasionally deliver the Sunday sermon" (Boxer 2000). In an interview he had once described his "philosophy of life" by quoting a passage from the Gospel of Luke (17:2): "It were better for him that a millstone were hanged about his neck, and he cast into the sea, than that he should offend one of these little ones" (Boxer 2000).

Schulz was credited for taking the comic strip genre "to a new level, intellectually and spiritually" (Ahrens 1997). His characters were identified as "tiny contemplatives" who were "the embodiment of childlike faith" (Ahrens 1997) yet who "exist after the fall of man from the Garden of Eden," and who therefore portray childhood in all of its "Augustinian corruptness" (Berger 1976, 299). Snoopy in particular was identified as "a commentator from a mock-pulpit, calling man to see his errors and return to the straight and narrow path" (Berger 1976, 301), demonstrating to all, noted one scholar, that "ultimately we are all free to create ourselves as we wish, no matter what our status on the Great Chain of Being might be. We can all be authentic if only we will have to courage to be what we can be" (Berger 1976, 303; emphasis deleted). This same scholar saw the strip as "little homilies and morality plays to help us maintain our righteousness," and marveled at how Schulz was able to disguise an "ethical element in his work so beautifully that we seldom see it" (Berger 1976, 301). As theologian, Short was able to demonstrate that Schulz was "delivering parables for our time" (Burns 1985, 33); the religious elements of the strip, "written as moral instruction by artist Charles Schulz, were analyzed as scriptural literature" (Ahrens 1997). Concluded Short's editor David Dobson, Short "really invented the study of religion through popular culture" (Sanders 2009).

But the gospel according to Short — and the lesson of locating the Truth in the mundane of everyday life — was less a cause of a revolution than a by-product of it.

The Revolution

Somewhere between Protestant theologian H. Richard Niebuhr's 1951 analysis of the five relationships of Christ to culture ("Christ and culture," "the Christ of culture," "Christ above culture," "Christ and culture in paradox," "Christ the transformer of culture") and religion scholars Bruce Forbes and Jeffrey Mahan's 2000 related analysis of religion to popular culture ("religion in popular culture," "popular culture in religion," "popular culture as religion," and "religion and popular culture in dialogue") lies the revolution of which Short's *Gospel* is but an artifact.

As the "death-of-God" theologians rightly observed — and as Niebuhr's construction unabashedly reveals — in the English-speaking world there had indeed been a Christian culture, or at least (in public) the façade of a Christian culture. Even in early American history — despite arguments from such historians as Jonathan Butler (1990) and Nathan Hatch (1989) that the populace was diverse, not particularly observant, and not traditionally pious — the public institutions (laws, public rhetoric, judicial pronouncements) were decidedly synchronized with a general yet recognizable form of Christianity (Handy 1984). Even as late as the second half of the nineteenth century, the most powerful perceived public threat was not that good American citizens (meaning white European Protestants) would become non-Protestant, but that those beyond the reach of "civilization" (everyone else) would be impossible to assimilate into American culture.[9]

A series of highly important religio-demographic turns during the nineteenth century—the so-called "Second Great Awakening" and the concomitant increase in Protestant denominationalism (1810s-1830s), increased Catholic and Jewish immigration (1840s and 1880s, respectively), and the fracturing of a great portion of Protestantism along "modernist"/"fundamentalist" lines (1890s-1900s)—meant that by World War I the façade was starting significantly to weaken (see Handy 1991). What has come to be called the "second disestablishment"—the beginning of the end of a public Protestant cultural monopoly—became more evident as more Catholic, Jews, and even non-mainstream Protestants began to play an increasingly public role in American society.

This weakening in the public sphere of a Protestant cultural monopoly coincided with—facilitated, actually (see Mazur 1999)—a strengthening in the authority of the federal government, enabling a utilitarian and politically expedient expansion in the notion of religious pluralism that better corresponded to the kind of religio-demographic diversity identified by historians of 19th century American religion. From the 1940s through the 1960s, the Supreme Court's interpretation of the First Amendment's "free exercise" clause expanded exponentially, leaving behind the arrogance of such 19th century dicta as the ruling identifying Mormon religious practices as "odious" (*Reynolds v. United States*, 1878), or the United States as a Christian nation (*Church of the Holy Trinity v. United States*, 1892), and admitting that citizens might not only believe that which they could not prove (*United States v. Ballard*, 1944), but might also be required to act on those beliefs (*Sherbert v. Verner*, 1963)—a very non-traditional view for a majority Protestant Court that had traditionally privileged faith over works in its conceptualization of religion (Hammond et al. 2004, especially chapters 3 and 4). The Court's interpretation of the First Amendment's "no establishment" clause followed a similar path, and increasingly the state's historic intimacy with institutional Protestantism was dismantled in the name of "benevolent neutrality." A nation dominated numerically, culturally, and politically by various (but, by and large, mainstream) Protestant denominations since the British colonial period had, by the time of Catholic Senator John Kennedy's election as President in 1960, entered what American religious historian Sydney Ahlstrom (1972) would call its "Post-Puritan" period.

By the time the American public was asked "Is God dead" or read Short's *Gospel According to Peanuts*, it was in the midst of what Robert Wuthnow (1988) called the "restructuring of American religion" (from denominational to ideological foundations) and what Phillip Hammond (1992) labeled the "third disestablishment" (the liberation of the individual believer from an inherited religious identity). The rise of the post–World War II "baby boomer" generation (those born between 1948 and 1963), their perception of the failure of traditional cultural institutions (government, religion) to adequately provide meaning — or worse, to endorse the wrong meaning — and the introduction of alternative meaning systems (which, as a result of the *Immigration Act of 1965*, included non-Western forms of religiosity), meant that religious institutions increasingly were on the defensive in American society, competing with each other and with new entrants into the market for the attention and loyalty of the up-and-coming generation. The new religious "consumers" — identified by Wade Clark Roof (1993) as a "generation of seekers" — increasingly identified themselves as "spiritual" (as opposed to — not in addition to — religious), and sought to express what once had been considered traditional religious energy in a variety of self-designated outlets.

One fear of the de-institutionalization of spirituality was that, as Borowitz (1967, 92) noted pejoratively, "theology threaten[ed] to become popular!" A new fear arose that the temptations of the modern world would lead Americans to be less religious, by which was meant less Protestant. Notes Stephen Warner (1993, 1046–1047), this fear was "rooted in a paradigm that conceived religion, like politics, to be a property of the whole society" wherein the separation of church and state — and the concomitant dilemma of expanded religious diversity — presented two options: religion as increasingly general so as to remain communal, or increasingly privatized and thus increasingly socially inconsequential. In either case, the fear was that the diminishment of the public role of a very specific religious identity (namely mainstream denominational Protestant Christianity) would lead to a secularized American public, a fear perceived by the "death-of-God" theologians as already taking place. In his analysis of the movement, sociologist and rabbi Will Herberg (1966a, 771) concluded that the death-of-God theologians' argument was that "whatever meaning and relevance God may once have had, He has now lost this meaning and relevance for modern man." He noted that modern man "may abandon Christian faith, and lose his Christian consciousness: but that only means that the spiritual void will be filled with a legion of modern idolatries, some of them almost too weird to describe" (Herberg 1966b, 840).

Some of the "legion of modern idolatries" were not quite as weird as Herberg feared, but were, to be sure, less than traditional in the Euro-American Protestant world. From the end of the 1960s into the 1970s, transformative works were being published in African American liberation theology (James Cone's *Black Theology and Black Power*, 1969), Latin American liberation theology (Gustavo Gutiérrez's *A Theology of Liberation: History, Politics, and Salvation*, 1973), feminist theology (Mary Daly's *Beyond God the Father*, 1973), and Neo-Pagan theology (Starhawk's *The Spiral Dance*, 1979). Works in eco- and gay theology would soon follow.

Transformations in Culture and the Explosion of "Gospels"

In a market-driven, competitive religious environment it is the "consumer" who—albeit influenced by the available choices—drives the development of alternatives by making "rational [or mostly rational] choices" according to her needs and desires. Stephen Warner (1993, 1057) argues that "what is important about religious markets ... is not so much the diversity of alternatives available to consumers as the incentive for suppliers to meet consumers' needs"; as the "competition" between worldviews increased, so did the "market" for materials to meet the consumer demand. In the religious economy of the United States, this included those seeking historically traditional religious products as well as those seeking non-traditional, increasingly "spiritual" products (see Mazur and McCarthy 2010).

The proof is in the publishing. As described earlier, the rate of publishing the canonical gospels doubled after 1964; so too did the rate of publishing the non-canonical gospels[10] and other biblically related gospels.[11] But the number of "gospels" published that were "popular"—that is, not canonical gospels, not those writings traditionally recognized as among the non-canonical gospels, and not biblically related interpretations of gospels—increased from six between 1815 and 1964 (or an average of 0.04 per year) to 79 between 1965 and 2011 (or an average of 1.68 per year)—an increase of nearly 1,217 percent.[12] Since 1954 the publisher that originally produced Short's *Gospel*, John Knox Press—now merged with Westminster and officially affiliated with the Presbyterian movement in the United States—has produced 21 "gospels" (not counting three leader's guides), 19 of which (over 90 percent) are "popular" gospels (according to the Beatles, Disney, Bob [Zimmerman] Dylan, Hollywood, Harry Potter, science fiction, the Simpsons, Bruce Springsteen, *Star Wars*, J.R.R. Tolkien, *Twilight*, U2, Oprah Winfrey, etc.) that, like Short's ur-*Gospel*, investigate Christian themes, ideas, and lessons.[13] Since 1965 (when Short's *Gospel* was first released), the Press has published nearly a quarter (24 percent) of the popular "gospel" volumes available, and since its merger with Westminster (and particularly after the 2000 reissue of Short's *Gospel* and the launch of an entire "gospel according to" series), it has published no new canonical gospels, at least none with a title beginning with the phrase "the gospel according to."[14]

A similar pattern can be found in film. According to the Internet Movie Database (IMDb.com)—a standard resource for information related to movie production in the English-speaking world (if not globally)—of the fifteen English-language films that have been distributed in theaters (or gone directly to video) and have used the phrase "gospel according to" in their primary title, none were produced before 1965, and none have been based on a canonical gospel. The closest candidates are the 1964 film *The Gospel According to St. Matthew* (directed by Pier Paolo Pasolini) — which was originally released in Italy (*Il vangelo secondo Matteo*) — and the 1973 film *Godspell* (directed by David Greene), which nearly makes the list but was only subtitled *A Musical Based on the Gospel According to St. Matthew*. The remaining films include documentaries, comedies, and one drama; two portray the careers of gospel singers (and are accordingly titled *Gospel According to ...* rather than *The Gospel According to...*). As of early October 2011, two more "gospels" — a comedy and a documentary — were scheduled to be released in 2012.

But, argues Bible scholar Frank Burns (1985, 33–34), "the comic strip is the preeminent form of popular humor in America in the twentieth century," and Schulz's *Peanuts* (1950–2000) was not the only one to express some form of religiosity. Indeed, continues Burns, "[m]any major cartoon strips rely heavily on allusions to the Bible." Bil Keane's *The Family Circus* (1960-present) has occasionally presented religious images, symbols, and ideas, similar to *Peanuts* "in a sentimental, child's-eye mode" (Van Biema 1999) but with a heavier treacle coating.[15] Johnny Hart's *B.C.* (1958–2007) expressed views that some considered "hard-core gospel" (Van Biema 1999) or "unabashedly evangelistic" (Weingarten 1999), but did so only around Christian holidays, and only beginning in 1989 when, after prolonged exposure to religious programming during the installation of his home's satellite dish (in biblically named Nineveh, New York), he had a born-again experience and became a biblical literalist (Weingarten 1999). As a result of his desire to express this newfound religiosity in his strips, Hart on occasion had strips pulled from publication by newspaper editors who anticipated a strong negative public reaction to what some readers of differing religious perspectives might consider offensive (Price 2001).

But Schulz apparently never touched the third rail of cartooning. *Peanuts* "contains the most frequent and most consistent references to the Bible" — including Linus's reading from the Gospel of Luke at the conclusion of *A Charlie Brown Christmas* (TV, 1965) — and also was "the most consistent in presenting an affirmative view of life" (Burns 1985, 33), but strenuously avoided anything that might have been considered too sectarian. Lindsey and Heeren (1992, 74–75) conclude in their study of over 65,000 "entertainment" cartoons published in the *Los Angeles Times* during the late 1970s and early 1980s that "[t]he total exclusion of the latter two elements of the Trinity [Son and Holy Spirit] suggests that cartoonists wish to avoid touching matters of theological detail or sectarian differences," possibly because they are both "more sacred and potentially more controversial as divine personages." Use of the Bible, they note, "permits a kind of shorthand communication between author and audience" that is fragile, and at great risk if exposed to too much specificity. As they conclude — likely more presciently than they may have realized — "Generic Christianity is preferred."

While historians may argue that "generic" Christianity has been at the heart of American culture for most of its history, its scriptures have until recently avoided exploitation for mass marketing in the (visual) artistic world.[16] But "[j]ust as the wise and witty sayings of the popular culture of Solomon's kingdom found their way into the Bible as the collection called Proverbs," concludes Burns (1985, 39), "the Bible has now contributed to the humorous elements of American popular culture." Within the past twenty years there has been a significant increase in the number of comic Bibles published — Bibles depicted as comic (or graphic) art (see Meskin 2007, 372–373). Not illustrated Bibles, which have been published since the 1950s and are designed for use with children, these more recent publications (Siku's *The Manga Bible*, 2008; Doug Mauss's *The Action Bible*, 2010, etc.) fit the more traditional (if contested) definition of "sequential art" that depend on images (rather than words) to sustain the narrative (see Meskin 2007). Their appearance in recent years may be due to an increased receptivity on the part of the reading (or purchasing) public to engage sacred materials that are more — rather than less — ambiguous.

This ambiguity is amplified in a cartoon not only because of the diminished role of text, but because of the multiple interpretations available for the images. Scholar of religion and the arts. S. Brent Plate (2002, 57–58) has pointed out that "[i]mages are dangerous, out of control, linked to passions rather than reason, linked to the body rather than the mind, linked to the earthly rather than the heavenly"; those who have opposed them ("iconoclasts") have done so for fear they could "incite religious devotion in ways not fully controllable and conformable to the institution of the church." But, ironically, it may be the *lack of image*— what Greg Hayman and Henry John Pratt (quoted in Meskin 2007, 371) call "the gutter" (the "perceptible space" between each picture)— that in cartoons is most subversive.[17] These empty spaces encourage readers to deviate from orthodoxy and fill the gaps with their own imagination. In a culture where religious identity is more a matter of personal choice than ascription or coercion, the simple (and often overlooked) act of "filling in the blanks"— between cartoon frames as between other activities—can assume religious significance.

In 2008, Robert Short published *The Parables of Dr. Seuss* (a *Gospel According to Dr. Seuss* having already been published), but this time "without the cooperation of creator Theodore Seuss Geisel's widow" (Sanders 2009). According to Short's editor David Dobson, his real goal was to write a book that focused on Bill Watterson's popular strip *Calvin & Hobbes*, but Watterson refused to grant permission to use his materials.[18] Said Dobson after Short's death, "he was heartbroken about it" (Sanders 2009).

On *The Far Side* of the Revolution

It is probably fair to say that, by the 1980s, the revolution had been waged. Evangelicals and conservative Christians had been "rediscovered" by the secular media, and were organizing behind various public figures, including Ronald Reagan, while an ironically labeled group ("Nones") — as in the response to "What is your religious preference?" — appeared with greater frequency in polling data illuminating American religious identities. A 2009 issue of *Newsweek* served as the journalistic bookend for the 1966 *Time* issue; the cover — using only words, formed in the shape of a cross — proclaimed "The Decline and Fall of Christian America." But this time, it was the article rather than the issue cover that bore the bad news; its headline declared "The End of Christian America" (Meacham 2009).

Robert Short's desire to explore *Calvin & Hobbes* for theological depth therefore was way off the mark — the real gospel truth for the era could best be found in Gary Larson's *The Far Side*, a single-frame cartoon published regularly from early 1980 until its abrupt end in 1994. During those fourteen years, *The Far Side* was one of the most popular cartoons in the United States. By 1988, Larson had published twelve *Far Side* collections, selling more than eleven million copies (Weiner 1988, 276). In combined licensing (mugs, cards, and particularly calendars), the franchise made over $3 million annually, putting the artist "in the top ten of cartoon-related sales," behind *Peanuts*, but ahead of Garry Trudeau's *Doonesbury* (Weiner 1988, 276).

In many ways, Larson was the polar opposite of Schulz. Both felt a sense of fulfillment from their work. Schulz's friend Lynn Johnston, the creator of the cartoon strip *For Better or For Worse*, commented after his death that it was "'amazing that he dies just before his last strip is published.' Such an ending, she said, was 'as if he had written it that way,'" a point confirmed by Schulz's wife Jeannie, who noted that he had "done everything he wanted" (Boxer 2000). Larson, who abruptly quit drawing *The Far Side* in 1994, recently saw "every cartoon he ever syndicated" republished in a "giant, two-volume hardcover boxed set" of over 1,200 pages. "It's just a very cool thing for a cartoonist to have," commented Larson. "It's my death book. I can die now" (Stein 2003). But Schulz was immediately and easily identified as an illustrator for children, while Larson encountered some difficulty from "family newspapers" that "sometimes wouldn't run his gallows humor" (Stein 2003). While Schulz saw himself (and was described by others) as a cartoonist and as a religious person, Larson admitted that he wasn't really "into cartoons"

(Stein 2003); instead, he was identified as "the unofficial cartoonist laureate of the scientific community" (Miller 1989), the "madcap sage of the biological sciences" by biologist Edward O. Wilson (Gilmour 2010) and, by Harvard scientist Stephen Jay Gould (1988), as "our national humorist of natural history." His work has been displayed (in a show titled "The Far Side of Science") at the museum of the California Academy of Science (in San Francisco), the Smithsonian Institution (in Washington, D.C.), the Los Angeles County Museum of Natural History, and the American Museum of Natural History (in New York). Larson's "surreal, pothead-meets-scientist take on humans' overestimation of their species," concludes one journalist, "made cartoons cool" (Stein 2003).

Originally titled *Nature's Way* (Higdon 1994, 49), *The Far Side*'s penchant for science is easily misinterpreted as an anti-religious trope rather than as a reflection of the culture and the time in which it was created. Michael Gilmour (2010), who suggests that "the extent of ... biblical and religious-themed content in Larson's work might surprise casual readers," posits the power of Larson's humor on "unanticipated turns of phrase and shifts away from the usual rhythms of religious narrative," and concludes that his "religious-themed cartoons are playful, not theological statements with any agenda attached." Citing Steve Martin's foreword in *The Complete Far Side*—which lampoons religious scholarship and theological inquiry—Gilmour writes (with tongue in cheek): "Clearly, we need more theological analysis of *The Far Side*. (Or is it less?)"

The correct answer is "more," but only if the study of *The Far Side* is not theological, but historical and contextual. David Higdon (1994, 54–55), using broader religious terminology, argues that Larson's regular use of the filmic version of the Frankenstein narrative serves as a form of "authorizing myth" for *The Far Side*. Analyzing fourteen volumes of collected *Far Side* cartoons that were published between 1982 and 1992, Higdon identifies 139 panels that "have clear intertextual ties with particular films, and some 27 cartoons comment on the act of watching films" (49). Based on two quotes from Larson concerning his approach to drawing ("I don't resort to current events or other stimuli. I don't read or watch TV to get ideas. My work is basically sitting down at the drawing table and getting silly" and "A strange juxtaposing of things takes place that I don't understand. It just happens"). Higdon concludes that "Larson has adopted the role of Frankenstein the creator, the power capable of generating an alternative world to our own and, by his own admission, Larson stands in awe of this power..." (54, internal referenced omitted).

Higdon takes Larson at his word, and thereby fails to locate him or his use of the Frankenstein narrative within the context of contemporary issues in American religion that may not have been on TV, but certainly would have been in the atmosphere enough to have an impact.[19] In one particularly pointed passage, Higdon describes a specific Larson cartoon (published on September 11, 1987; see Larson 2003, ii:88) in which a young Frankenstein is "remaining after class one day to write repeatedly on the chalkboard as punishment, 'I will not play in God's domain'" (51). Of course, Frankenstein *had* been playing in "God's domain" by creating life, the very point of the subtitle of Mary Shelley's 1818 novel (*The Modern Prometheus*). Prometheus not only gave humans the gift of fire, but (in some versions of the legend) is also credited with their creation. Frankenstein is being punished because he *has* played in God's domain. But in a culture where the traditional Christian God no longer enjoys a monopoly, he is (a) God — or at least could be. Despite Higdon's assertion, Larson has not only provided evidence of an interest in the Frankenstein narrative, or more broadly in film or science, but has (maybe unknowingly) reflected the religious and theological ethos of his own time.

To measure this reflection, one need only survey the vast collection of Larson cartoons (Gilmour [2010] calls them "Lartoons") published from 1980 to 1994. Of the 4,337 panels in the collection, 233 (or just under 5.5 percent) address religion in some way.[20] By comparison, Lindsey and Heeren's 1992 study of religion in newspaper comics identified 365 (or just over 0.5 percent) that addressed religion in some way.[21] Not only is Larson's work eleven times more "religious" than the *Los Angeles Times* sample, it is also religious in a particular way. There is no doubt that images drawn from Christianity can be found in relative abundance; 58 percent of the panels contain images from the Old and New Testaments, extra-biblical figures like Santa Claus, Crusaders, and figures praying or teaching "Bible" lessons, and one "Jesus fish." The remaining 42 percent of the panels do not. Like the United States, there is extraordinary diversity within this non–Christian 42 percent, with representation from various religious traditions (Buddhism, Confucianism, Greco-Roman and Norse religions, Hinduism, Islam, native traditions, Scientology, Spiritualism, Voodoo, and Wicca) and the world of spirits and the "undead" (genies, skeletons, ghosts, mummies, and zombies). Excluding representations of God, Old Testament images (Eden, Noah, Moses, Samson, and Jonah) outnumber New Testament images (Jesus and the Magi), 9 percent to 1 percent.

The context of the images suggests an abandonment of the traditional "generic Christianity" found in the older generation of cartoonists like Schultz and Keane — who was reported to have been fond of Larson's work (see Myers 2011) — in favor of a broader notion of "spirituality" common in late 20th century American culture (see Wuthnow 1998). Representations of Hell (over 23 percent) outnumber all other religious panels, ahead of representations of native religious traditions (nearly 12 percent), and ghosts (nearly 8 percent). Dogs, chickens, and slugs pray, cows preach their religion door-to-door, and the "Jesus fish" on the rear bumper of a flying saucer has three "googly" eyes. Larson's irreverence—"Anything that's set up to be very serious has comic potential when it all comes unraveled" (Miller 1989)—seems to be a perfect match for an era populated by those who were disillusioned by the perceived weakness of social institutions like religion and yet empowered to find their own paths in the variety of options available to them.

Conclusions

"I am become death," J. Robert Oppenheimer recalled thinking as the first atomic fireball lit the sky over New Mexico in the summer of 1945, "the destroyer of worlds." Oppenheimer, often called the "father of the atomic bomb" for his role in the Manhattan Project during World War II, was able to quote Lord Krishna because of a life-long fascination with the Bhagavad-Gita, a foundational Hindu text. Born into a Jewish family that was heavily involved in Felix Adler's Society for Ethical Culture, he had early in his life begun a search for a deeper sense of the mystical, the transcendent—a "more profound approach" (Hijiya 2000, 129).

In many ways, Oppenheimer well represents the changes that took place in American culture in the second half of the twentieth century; it is telling that, while he may have actually thought these words from the Bhagavad-Gita at the exact moment of the atomic blast, he is on record no earlier than 1965 as having done so (Hijiya 2000, 123). What happened in those intervening twenty years?

The *Oxford English Dictionary* locates the roots of the word "heresy" in the Greek word for "choice," and by the late 1960s there was a growing list of choices throughout the American religious landscape. Will Herberg (1966c, 884) noted that "for heresy to mean anything, there must be orthodoxy, a firm and self-confident orthodoxy, as there is not today..." But maybe that was the heresy—that after so many centuries of Euro-Christian cultural dominance, individual Americans were increasingly moving to the music of their own god's creation. Jesuit theologian John Courtney Murray—who had been so influential in assisting the participants at the Second Vatican Council to take a more ecumenical approach to non-Catholics—identified the period's unbelief not as refusal to believe in God, or even to question or doubt the existence of nature of the Divine, but as "the atheism of distraction," in which people were "just too damn busy to worry about God at all" (Elson 1966, 82). Nobel Prize winner and Holocaust survivor Elie Wiesel (1986) came to the same conclusion when he suggested that "the opposite of faith is not heresy, it's indifference."

But they aren't indifferent, really. They may be disinterested in religious institutions, but they are happily pursuing their own religious knowledge in what Robert Bellah and associates (1985) label "Sheilaism" (named for one of the many people interviewed for their study). Newspapers have been replaced by the Internet, and Snoopy, the "commentator from a mock-pulpit, calling man to see his errors and return to the straight and narrow path" (Berger 1976, 301), has been replaced in the public's imagination by Brian Griffin, the pseudo-urbane alcoholic atheist dog on the animated television show *Family Guy* (Fox, 1999-present). "In its suspicion and rejection of singular meta-narratives," writes Mike Grimshaw (2010, 153), "postmodern spirituality turns toward a salvific, redemptive use of pop culture — often against traditional religion and its claims and institutions. Spirituality is therefore a commodity of possibilities for individuals to make use of as they can." Thus "the death of God," he continues, "is the creation of hope and new possibility, not the end of meaning." Lindsey and Heeren's argument about cartoons (1992,76) is equally valid for the broader world of "gospel" proliferation: "religion as a spiritual framework and moral compass still appears to be significant, but it may not be religion in the same forms it has had in centuries past."

Amen.

Notes

1. The working title of this essay was "The Gospel According to *The Gospel According to*...: From the Near Death of God to the Far Side of the Baby Boom." I would like to thank Nichelle Mack and Arianne Avery at the Henry Clay Hofheimer II Library for their assistance securing materials. Research support was graciously provided by the Batten Professor Fund at Virginia Wesleyan College; thanks to Midge Zimmerman for not laughing when I requested *The Complete Far Side* for my "research." Special thanks to longtime collaborator Kate McCarthy, who once paid me the highest compliment possible to a sociologist by saying I had a "tin ear" for theology.

2. Originally published in the March 4, 1966, edition of the *London Evening Standard* — one full month before this particular issue of *Time* hit the stands — the interview conducted by Beatles' friend Maureen Cleave was propelled into the limelight when it was republished in August 1966 in *Datebook*, an American fan magazine (see Spangler n.d.).

3. In 2008, the *Los Angeles Times* identified the *Time* issue as one of the "Magazine Covers that Shook the World" ("Magazine Covers" 2008), the oldest of those so identified.

4. Contrary to Elton John, neither did the *New York Times*.

5. Search was conducted on September 21, 2011, using the Library of Congress online database (http://catalog.loc.gov). Statistics are based on a title search ("Title Begins: gospel according") and was structured to mirror the title of Short's *Gospel According to the Peanuts* (see note 14, below).

6. Religion scholar Jeffrey Mahan (2007, 49) identifies it as one of two "precursors to the wider scholarly conversation about religion and popular culture."

7. One reviewer concluded that, while Short's volume was worth reading, he had found "just too much" in the cartoon, and was not actually "exegeting the gospel according to Peanuts" (Hakes 1965).

8. The introduction to the first Italian edition was written by novelist and professor of semiotics Umberto Eco (Boxer 2000).

9. See Mazur (1999) for an account of efforts to "Americanize" Native Americans.

10. Between 1815 and 1964, three gospels according to the Hebrews were published; between 1965 and 2011, 11 gospels according to Thomas (3), Philip (1), Judas (2), Mary (4), and Barnabbas (1) were published, an increase of 267 percent.

11. Between 1815 and 1964, 13 gospels according to Paul (3), Jesus (3), Moses (3), and one each according to James, Isaiah, Revelation, and "scripture" were published; between 1965 and 2011, 34 different gospels were published, according to Paul (6), Jesus (7), Job (2), Genesis (2), as "sermons" (5), and one each according to Abraham, angels, apostles, Aurelius, Barabbas, Elijah/Elisha, Esther, Isaac/Jacob, Jonah, Moses, Pilate, and Rome, an increase of 162 percent.

12. A quick check of titles starting with "The Tao of" (and "The Dao of") and "Zen and the Art of" produced similar patterns. According to the Library of Congress online database, no titles starting with either of the phrases was published before 1956, and between 1956 and 1973, only four volumes using the phrase "the Tao of" were published (a publishing average of 0.235 per year); three of those were English translations of ancient Taoist texts. The pattern following the 1974 publication of Robert Pirsig's *Zen and the Art of Motorcycle Maintenance* and the 1975 publication of Fritjof Capra's *The Tao of Physics* parallels the 1965 publication of Short's *Gospel*; between 1974 and October 28, 2011 (when the search was conducted), 280 titles using one of the two phrases were published, an average of 7.37 per year. (Thanks to colleague Paul Rasor for suggesting this comparison.)

13. While most of the titles produced by Westminster John Knox have kept to a religious (if broad and general) mission, competing titles have not. A good number of them — gospels according to [comedian Sacha Baron Cohen's character] Ali G., the Harvard Business School, the *New York Times*, Ayn Rand, and Casey Stengel, to name a few — are primarily monographs espousing the "truth" revealed in (or according to) the central subject.

14. Audio and video recordings, fiction (novels and dramas), duplications, and "leader's guides" were omitted. The search strategy automatically eliminated volumes whose subtitle included the desired phrase (including *The Dude Abides: The Gospel According to the Coen Brothers*, by Cathleen Falsani, 2009, Zondervan) and titles not of a parallel construction (including Robert Short's *The Gospel from Outer Space*, 1983, HarperCollins). A few titles available for purchase (on Amazon.com) had no record on the Library of Congress database (including James Geiger's *The Gospel According to Relativity*, 2005, Xulon Press). The observation that none of the automatically omitted titles was published before 1965 is intriguing but possibly coincidental. Alternative search strategies yielded the following: "Title Begins: gospel of" (891 records); "Title Begins: gospel" (4,185 records); "Title Keyword: gospel" (10,000+ records); "Title Keyword: gospel, of" (8,033 records); "Title Keyword: gospel, according" (966 records); "Keyword: gospel" (10,000+ records); "Keyword: gospel, of" (10,000+ records); "Keyword: gospel, according" (1,056 records).

15. Bil Keane died on November 9, 2011, as this essay was being written. According to his obituary (Myers 2011), his son Jeff had taken over the strip's production in recent years.

16. The history of Protestantism is the history of Bible publication for mass markets, and there has been a recent effort within the Bible-publishing world to produce "niche" Bibles for specific markets ("New Adventures" 2008). It is curious to note that graphic Bibles came to prominence after the decline of the topically unrelated but ironically named "Tijuana Bibles" of the 1920s–1950s (see Heller 2004).

17. In a close parallel, there is a rabbinic interpretation that suggests that, since the Torah cannot be fully understood by humanity, those engaged in Talmudic interpretation must read not only the letters on the page, but the white spaces between them, too.

18. According to the licensing representative for *Calvin & Hobbes* distributor Andrews McMeel Universal, the strip "has never done any official licensing"; the various popular images of Calvin — kneeling in prayer or urinating on corporate logos — are both (equal) violations of copyright law (personal communication, October 26, 2011).

19. A review of *The Complete Far Side* reveals a number of panels directly related to news of the day.

20. Evaluations of this sort are inherently subjective, and are offered here merely to illustrate a point. Panels were judged based on references to specific religions (Buddhism, Hinduism, etc.), religious figures (deities, mythic/scriptural figures, clergy, etc.), religious symbols, images, or references (heaven, hell, Eden, crucifixion, etc.), religious acts (prayer), religious teachings (repentance), and the paranormal (ghosts, zombies, mummies, etc.). The number of panels quoted is Larson's own admission — no independent count was made. Spread over two volumes on over 1,300 pages — most with three or four panels per page — the count seems reliable.

21. The 365 cartoons identified by Lindsey and Heeren were distributed according to the following categories: "ministering religion" (22.5 percent); "death and afterlife" (19.7 percent); "reli-

gion and the world of adults" (17 percent); "religion and the world of children" (15.6 percent); "prayer" (9.3 percent); "deity" (8.8 percent); and "biblical texts and contexts" (7.1 percent).

Works Cited

Ahlstrom, Sydney E. 1972. *A Religious History of the American People*. New Haven: Yale University Press.
Ahrens, Frank. 1997. "The Gospel According to 'Calvin and Hobbes.'" *Washington Post* (March 15): D9.
Bellah, Robert N., Richard Madsen, William M. Sullivan, Ann Swidler, and Steven M. Tipton. 1985. *Habits of the Heart: Individualism and Commitment in American Life*. Berkeley: University of California Press.
Berger, Arthur Asa. 1976. "Peanuts: The Americanization of Augustine." In *Humor in America: An Anthology*, ed. Enid Veron, 298–304. New York: Harcourt Brace Jovanovich.
Borowitz, Eugene B. 1967. "God-is-Dead Theology." In *The Meaning of the Death of God: Protestant, Jewish and Catholic Scholars Explore Atheistic Theology*, ed. Bernard Murchland, 92–107. New York: Random House.
Boxer, Sarah. 2000. "Charles M. Schulz, 'Peanuts' Creator, Dies at 77." *New York Times* (February 14): 1.
Burns, G. Frank. 1985. "The Bible in American Popular Humor." In *The Bible and Popular Culture in America*, ed. Allene Stuart Phy, 25–39. Philadelphia: Fortress Press.
Butler, Jonathan. 1990. *Awash in a Sea of Faith: Christianizing the American People*. Cambridge: Harvard University Press.
Cox, Harvey. 1965. *The Secular City: Secularization and Urbanization in Theological Perspective*. New York: Macmillan.
Elson, John T. 1966. "Theology Toward a Hidden God." *Time* (April 8): 82–87.
Fiske, Edward B. 1968. "'God is Dead' Doctrine Losing Ground to 'Theology of Hope.'" *New York Times* (March 24): 1.
Forbes, Bruce David, and Jeffrey H. Mahan, eds. 2000. *Religion and Popular Culture in America*. Berkeley: University of California Press.
Gilmour, Michael J. 2010. "The Far Side of Religion: Notes on the Prophet Gary Larson." *Direction: A Mennonite Brethren Forum* 39, 2 (Fall): 189–203. Accessed online: www.directionjournal.org/article/?1601 (accessed November 6, 2011).
Gould, Stephen Jay. 1988. "Foreword." In *The Far Side Gallery 3*, Gary Larson, 9–12. Kansas City: Andrews McMeel.
Grimes, William. 2009. "John T. Elson, Editor Who Asked 'Is God Dead?' at Time Dies at 78." *New York Times* (September 18): 1.
Grimshaw, Mike. 2010. "On *Preacher* (Or, the Death of God in Pictures)." In *Graven Images: Religion in Comic Books and Graphic Novels*, ed. A. David Lewis and Christine Hoff Kraemer, 149–165. New York: Continuum.
Hakes, J Edward. 1965. "*The Gospel According to Peanuts*, by Robert L. Short" [book review]. *Bulletin of the Evangelical Theological Society* 8, 3 (Summer): 118.
Hammond, Phillip E. 1992. *Religion and Personal Autonomy: The Third Disestablishment in America*. Columbia: University of South Carolina Press.
Hammond, Phillip E., David W. Machacek, and Eric Michael Mazur. 2004. *Religion on Trial: How Supreme Court Trends Threaten Freedom of Conscience in America*. Walnut Creek, CA: AltaMira.
Handy, Robert T. 1984. *A Christian America: Protestant Dreams and Historical Realities*, 2d ed. New York: Oxford University Press.
Handy, Robert T. 1991. *Undermined Establishment: Church-State Relations in America 1880–1920*. Princeton, N.J.: Princeton University Press.
Hatch, Nathan O. 1989. *The Democratization of American Christianity*. New Haven: Yale University Press.
Heller, Steven. 2004. "Strip Tease." *Print* (July/August): 106–109.
Herberg, Will. 1966a. "The 'Death of God' Theology—I: The Philosophy Behind It." *National Review* 18 (August 9): 771, 779.

Herberg, Will. 1966b. "The 'Death of God' Theology—II: Secularization and the Collapse of Meaning." *National Review* 18 (August 23): 839–840.
Herberg, Will. 1966c. "The Death of God Theology—III: What is Wrong with It?" *National Review* 18 (September 6): 884–885.
Higdon, David Leon. 1994. "Frankenstein as Founding Myth in Gary Larson's The Far Side." *Journal of Popular Culture* 28, 1 (Summer): 49–60.
Hijiya, James A. 2000. "The Gita of J. Robert Oppenheimer." *Proceedings of the American Philosophical Society* 144, 2 (June): 123–167.
Larson, Gary. 2003. *The Complete Far Side: 1980–1994*, 2 vols. Kansas City: Andrews McMeel.
Lindsey, Donald B., and John Heeren. 1992. "Where the Sacred Meets the Profane: Religion in the Comic Pages." *Review of Religious Research* 34, 1 (September): 63–77.
"Magazine Covers That Shook the World." 2008. *Los Angeles Times* [n.d.]: www.latimes.com/entertainment/news/la-et-10magazinecovers14-july14-pg,0,5472017.photogallery (accessed October 21, 2011).
Mahan, Jeffrey H. 2007. "Reflections on the Past and Future of the Study of Religion and Popular Culture." In *Between Sacred and Profane: Researching Religion and Popular Culture*, ed. Gordon Lynch, 47–62. New York: Palgrave Macmillan.
Mazur, Eric Michael. 1999. *The Americanization of Religious Minorities: Confronting the Constitutional Order*. Baltimore: Johns Hopkins University Press.
Mazur, Eric Michael, and Kate McCarthy. 2010. *God in the Details: American Religion in Popular Culture*, 2d ed. New York: Routledge.
Meacham, Jon. 2009. "The End of Christian America." *Newsweek* (April 13): 34–38.
Meskin, Aaron. 2007. "Defining Comics?" *The Journal of Aesthetics and Art Criticism* 65, 4 (Autumn): 369–379.
Miller, Thomas R. 1989. "The Far Side of Science." *Natural History* 5 (May): 78.
Myers, Amanda Lee. 2011. "'Family Circus' Creator Bil Keane Dies at 89." Associated Press (November 9): Entertainment News.
"New Adventures in Niche Bible Publishing." 2008. *Christian Century* 125, 23 (November 18): 16.
Niebuhr, H. Richard. 1951. *Christ and Culture*. New York: Harper and Row.
Nietzsche, Friedrich. 1887. *The Gay Science*. 1974. Trans. Walter Kaufmann. New York: Random House.
Ochs, Phil. 1989. *The Broadside Tapes 1*. Washington, D.C.: Smithsonian/Folkways Records.
Plate, S. Brent, ed. 2002. *Religion, Art, & Visual Culture: A Cross-Cultural Reader*. New York: Palgrave.
Price, Joyce Howard. 2001. "Easter 'B.C.' Sparks Controversy Among Jews." *Washington Times* (April 12): A2.
Roof, Wade Clark. 1993. *A Generation of Seekers: The Spiritual Journeys of the Baby Boom Generation*. San Francisco: Harper San Francisco.
Sanders, Jacob Quinn. 2009. "Theologian of Peanuts, Robert Short, 76, Dies." (Little Rock) *Arkansas Democrat-Gazette* (July 9): 11.
Short, Robert L. 1965. *The Gospel According to Peanuts*. Richmond: John Knox Press.
Short, Robert L. 2008. *The Parables of Dr. Seuss*. Louisville: Westminster John Knox Press.
Spangler, Jay. [n.d.] "John Lennon Interview: London Evening Standard, 'More Popular Than Jesus' 3/4/1966." *The Beatles Ultimate Experience*. www.beatlesinterviews.org/db1966.0304-beatles-john-lennon-were-more-popular-than-jesus-now-maureen-cleave.html (accessed October 21, 2011).
Stein, Joel. 2003. "Life Beyond The Far Side." *Time* (October 6): 71.
Vahanian, Gabriel. 1967. "Beyond the Death of God." In *The Meaning of the Death of God: Protestant, Jewish and Catholic Scholars Explore Atheistic Theology*, ed. Bernard Murchland, 3–12. New York: Random House.
Van Biema, David. 1999. "Preach it, Caveman!" *Time* (April 4): 51.
Warner, R. Stephen. 1993. "Work in Progress Toward a New Paradigm for the Sociological Study of Religion in the United States." *American Journal of Sociology* 98, 5 (March): 1044–1093.
Weiner, Steve. 1988. "Funny Money." *Forbes* 142, 12 (December 12): 272, 276.

Weingarten, Gene. 1999. "God, That's Funny; Or Is It?" *Washington Post* (April 4): F01.
Wiesel, Elie. 1986. "One Must Not Forget." *U.S. News & World Report* (27 October): 68.
Wuthnow, Robert. 1988. *The Restructuring of American Religion: Society and Faith Since World War II*. Princeton, N.J.: Princeton University Press.
Wuthnow, Robert. 1998. *After Heaven: Spirituality in America Since the 1950s*. Berkeley: University of California Press.

Religious Discourse in Lost
and Battlestar Galactica

VAL NOLAN

The television series *Lost* (2004–2010) and *Battlestar Galactica* (2004–2009) provide two recent examples of mainstream pop-cultural success stories to which the interrogation of religious certainties are an integral, arguably essential element. While these shows hooked audiences with immediately engaging premises (respectively attractive-actors-do-*Survivor*-as-scripted-hour-long and aircraft-carrier-in-space-does-War-on-Terror), both also questioned received religious teachings from an early stage. Though largely spurned by fans, this sustained investigation of religion as a practice and as a social construction — an investigation often mediated through the dichotomy between science and faith — became very much a central subject matter of the shows' final seasons. Both *Lost* and *BSG* manipulated the symbolic language of Judeo-Christian religions to posit idiosyncratic portraits of the cyclical conflicts humanity must move beyond if it is to achieve genuine transcendence. While the theological inquiry proffered was often received and rejected without consideration for what the writers were trying to articulate, *Lost* and *BSG* had profound messages to communicate about life, belief, community, and the dangerous tendency of religion to divide humanity into ideological factions rather than to unite people into truly accepting societies. As such, thoughtful viewers must ask themselves what is the purpose behind *Lost* and *BSG*'s use of heretical notions such as apathetic deities, resurrections that are not, and the deliberate collision of contemporary belief systems with archaic or esoteric forms of worship?

At first glance, contemporary television science fiction seems very far removed from the realm of theological inquiry. Traditionally such material has been lighter in tone than its literary antecedents, eschewing sustained consideration of religion and its effects on individuals and societies. Obvious exceptions include shows such as *Babylon 5* (1993–1998) and *Star Trek: Deep Space Nine* (1993–1999), but, as with *Lost* and *BSG*, these favoured a serialized narrative style that allowed for a long-term, *in situ* focus on social and theological themes generally outside the remit of episodic television sci-fi. *Lost* and *BSG* built upon the success of such precedents, transcending the niche genre audiences of the 1990s and achieving genuine mass appeal with atypical material. For better or worse, these shows number among the most discussed television series of the twenty-first century thus far.

Lost, set on a mysterious island which seems to exist outside space and time as we generally perceive them, was created by J. J. Abrams, Damon Lindelof, and Jeffrey Lieber, but produced and masterminded throughout most of its run by Lindelof and Carlton Cuse, who together contributed many of the most important scripts. Trading heavily on mystique and misdirection, the most philosophically resonant moments of *Lost* were those which dramatized the contemporary disconnect between the certainties of science and the convictions of religion. While this discourse was packaged within sensationalist science-fictional elements such as time travel, magnetic anomalies, global conspiracies, and so on, the show's real strength lay in how its characters personified the demarcation between knowledge and belief, or — to use the show's own parlance — between science and faith in the form of main protagonists Jack Shepherd and John Locke. In particular, Locke's assertion that the show's disparate characters were brought to the island for a reason serves as the starting point for an interrogation of "faith" which was continually refined as *Lost* progressed: What does it mean to have belief? What obligations are incumbent upon those who believe? Is it possible to reconcile provable knowledge of the physical world with belief in transcendent reality?

These same questions were asked by *Battlestar Galactica*, a self-consciously gritty reimagining of the kitsch 1970s series by the same name. The modern *Battlestar Galactica* follows the crew of the titular spacecraft in their defense of a rag-tag fleet, human survivors of a nuclear holocaust on the Twelve Colonies of Man. This new version of the show was developed by Ronald D. Moore, who also produced and wrote for *Deep Space Nine* throughout much of its run. Moore served as executive producer on *BSG* along with David Eick, and together they constructed an intricate universe which took its lead from the original series but which was simultaneously rooted in contemporary concerns about religious fundamentalism, terrorist sleeper cells, and the fragility of civil liberties. Issues of theology are woven into the basic premise of the show, with the polytheistic humans pursued by the Cylons, a monotheistic adversary responsible for the holocaust and humanity's onetime robotic slaves who have evolved into flesh and blood "machines." Both sides boast figures that blur the divide between the rational and the religious, chief among which is Dr. Gaius Baltar, a deeply flawed scientist who is manipulated by the Cylons into allowing them access to the Colonial defence network and so, in many ways, is accountable for the destruction of the human race. Baltar's journey from atheist lab-coat through cynical politician and cult-leader to, in the final episode, true believer in the saving power of spirituality is one of the more remarkable and engaging transformation in recent popular culture.

A hybrid series, *BSG* subsumes its theological inquiry beneath a veneer of straightforward military sci-fi in the same way *Lost* conceals the full scope of its intentions within a succession of mysteries and narratological trickery (for instance, the bait-and-switch whereby flashbacks became flashforwards). While both shows display the genre hallmark of complex mythologies—which in this context refers to their elaborate back-stories—they also insist on a religious subtext antithetical to the science of science-fiction. The protagonists of both are in search of an ultimate or seemingly unobtainable reality: for the characters of *Lost* it is a way to escape the mysterious island on which they have been stranded; for those of *Battlestar Galactica* it is Earth, safe haven from their Cylon pursuers and the mythical homeworld of the Thirteenth Tribe of Humanity. More often than not, these characters all discover the essence of their being in the course of these journeys, a strong thematic similarity of *Lost* and *BSG*'s final seasons. Likewise, both series are successful in tapping into that most potent aspect of science fiction, its ability to represent the present in allegorical form. *Lost* and *BSG* are inseparable from the post–9/11 context in which they were created. The linkages may be more apparent in the case of *BSG*—essentially a drama about the ambiguities of life in wartime which just happens to be set in space—however it is possible to discern one common message from both it and from *Lost*: religion is bad, spirituality is good.

God, in the universes of *Battlestar Galactica* and *Lost*, does not exist as typically imagined in popular culture. While organized religion tends to function along recognizable lines, the object of such worship is closer to a force of nature than to the stereotypical bearded man in the sky. Both *Lost* and *BSG* exhibit a profound skepticism with regard to the veneration of God-like figures and/or pantheons composed of such deities, depicted as being largely indifferent to the fate of those who pray to them. This lack of interest in mortal affairs comes through not just in the obvert religious material but also in the prevalence of absent or problematic fathers throughout both shows.

Jacob on *Lost* is one such figure. The ageless and seemingly omnipotent protector of the Island, Jacob may as well be God as far as many of the Island natives are concerned.[1] Certainly he controls the destiny of all those on the Island — even many of those around the world — and is able to grant seemingly divine gifts such as immortality. Though "He," as the character is frequently referred to, remains unseen until the final episode of season five, his influence, like that of any deity, is felt through the actions of followers, the mysterious Others who menace *Lost*'s protagonists throughout the show's early years. The absent father par excellence, he is later shown in flashback to have visited many of the main characters in their youth. Yet, despite his powers and abilities, the character's first on-screen appearance in "The Incident" (written by Lindelof and Cuse) depicts him as a false god, one who is unable to prevent his own dethronement once directly challenged by an acolyte. He is, in the end, murdered by a mere mortal who has grown frustrated with his inaccessibility and with his issuing of orders and doctrinal edicts from on high.[2]

With Jacob's demise, the Island succumbs to a period of lawlessness and chaos while its inhabitants struggle with a lack of guidance and the malevolent, opportunistic activities of Jacob's opposite, the Man in Black. This spiritual anarchy constitutes the on-island plotline of *Lost*'s final season and so runs concurrently with what is known as the "flash-sideways universe." The flash-sideways universe derives its confusing, subsequently *inaccurate* designation from misdirection on the part of the show's writers. Whereas the previous seasons had used both flashbacks and flashforwards to divulge crucial segments of *Lost*'s mythology, season six portrayed what at first appeared to be a parallel universe (seemingly created by interference with the established timeline during the season five finale). This unusual narrative device seemed to present the story of what might have happened had the protagonists' plane not crashed on the island. However, in the show's final episode ("The End," written by Lindelof and Cuse), *Lost*'s "flash-sideways universe" is revealed to be the ultimate flash-*forward*, a kind of waiting room for the afterlife created so that the characters might find each other again before they finally move on together.[3]

The flash-sideways universe is the most obvious of the show's religious elements and the one which is least vulnerable to accusations of window dressing. Simply put, while iconic and ritualistic elements of religious symbolism appear frequently in *Lost*, the story of the characters on their way to the afterlife represents the writers' most successful integration of the theological into the show's narrative. It is essential to the ending of the series and, moreover, constitutes the clearest statement of *Lost*'s central thesis: the importance of community and how individual lives — or deaths — are defined by

"We've been waiting for you": In one of the final scenes of *Lost*'s finale, "The End," the souls of the main characters are joyously reunited in a timeless "waiting room" for the afterlife. This "is the place that you, that you *all* made together so that you could find one another," Jack Shepherd is told by the spirit of his father. "The most important part of your life was the time that you spent with these people. That's why all of you are here. Nobody does it alone, Jack. You needed all of them and they needed you." Left to right: Matthew Fox as Jack Shepherd, Terry O'Quinn as John Locke, Cynthia Watros as Libby Smith, Daniel Dae Kim as Jin-Soo Kwon, Evangeline Lilly as Kate Austen, Jorge Garcia as Hugo "Hurley" Reyes, and Josh Holloway as James "Sawyer" Ford.

our relationships with those around us. Live together, die alone is not simply the survivalist mantra of main character Jack Shepherd, but a central tenet of the series as a whole.[4] The waiting room is explained to Jack (and so to the audience) by the spirit of his father, the perfectly named Christian Shepherd who—as an absent father finally come to make amends—guides the souls of the survivors into the next world. Though the characters have, in many cases, died alone, this temporary existence is a place their souls constructed so that they could find each other again. This is, Christian says, because the most important part of their lives was the time that they spent together. None of them found fulfillment in isolation. None of them succeeded alone.[5]

Of course, given the widespread confusion over the meaning of "The End," it should be clearly stated here: the characters of *Lost* are not in purgatory throughout the series. Events that occurred on the Island, however remarkable, inexplicable or strange they were, actually occurred in the world of the series. Everything that happened on the island actually happened, Christian explains.[6] That said, events occurring in the flash-sideways universe do constitute a state of being with purgatorial characteristics. While the survivors and the other characters all died at different points, their souls congregate in this space outside of time so that they can come to terms with their lives and all move on together. While the true nature of the flash-sideways universe is unambiguously defined by Christian, misunderstandings did occur, being particularly apparent in online discussions where the immediate responses to "The End" ranged from dissatisfaction to outright anger. The finale, said one commentator, "was a lame duck, such a shame they abandoned most of the interesting threads: time travel, physics, [and] the wheel under the Island" while another review—headlined "The *Lost* finale was incredibly dumb"— rejected "The End" as "two-and-a-half hours of slow-motion bullshittery."[7] Continuing online hostility towards the finale is occasionally inflamed by the profound misreadings of the show propagated by mainstream commentators and cultural critics. Take, for instance, this interview which fantasy novelist George R.R. Martin gave to *Time* in 2011:

> Having been a veteran of not only writing for but watching *Twilight Zone*, it was about the second episode of *Lost* I said, "Oh, they're all dead." They're all dead. That's what it would be in a half-hour Rod Sterling *Twilight Zone*, in 1958. And [*Lost*'s writers] took what? How many seasons to get to the point where they were all dead?[8]

Though there can be no doubt that Martin is wrong, the comments of such a widely read and influential author perpetuate the inaccuracies associated with *Lost*'s conclusion, serving as tacit approval of fan backlash against the religious elements of the show's mythology and, beyond "'The End,'" the wider incorporation of spiritual themes into genre television.[9] Furthermore, his dismissal negates the purpose of "The End" and of the show's final series in a more general sense: to deliver closure for, on one hand, the characters' relationship to each other and, on the other, the viewer's relationship to them. Achieving both aims, "The End" provides a beautiful, emotionally resonant conclusion to the series, one which requires the kind of contemplation which is increasingly lacking in this digital age of instantaneous reaction and online discussion. Would the spiritual elements of "The End" have been better understood if the audience had allowed themselves time to absorb the message of the series? More than likely yes, for *Lost* was always more about its characters than its mysteries, a line Lindelof and Cuse stuck to despite it being little comfort to fans of the show's puzzle-box aspects. Viewers who valued the science-fictional elements of *Lost* rejected the spiritual content of "The End" as anathema to the atheistic tendencies of a genre where technology almost inevitably trumps theology. This group, core members of the show's audience, was particularly vocal in disparaging "The End" as weak mysticism or even a wholesale cop-out.

For many, such griping constituted a form of active resistance against the spiritual message of *Lost*'s finale: the implication that — in fiction as in real life — some things will never be explained and that adherence to teaching or doctrines which promise such enlightenment will inevitably let you down. In "The End," Christian Shepherd emphasizes this by holding forth from a multi-domination house of worship, a building of superficially Christian architecture but one which is adorned with the symbols of many major religions: the Islamic Star and Crescent, the Star of David, the Hindi Aum, the Christian Cross, the Buddhist Dharmacakra, and the Taoist Yin/Yang. Their appearance together serves as a leveller, denying the primacy of any single system of belief and underlining how both *Lost* and *BSG* employed religious symbolism to demonstrate the divisive aspects of ideology. Religion — propagated mainly by individuals — is portrayed as a fractious distraction from the kind of genuine healing necessary in the aftermath of tragedy, a spiritual undertaking which requires true communities to succeed. That the final moments of *Lost* play out in the absence of dialogue only reinforces this; the characters have found each other again, rejoicing in each other's company before Christian opens the church doors and ushers in their next existence. Though much derided, the white light through which the protagonists progress into the afterlife is akin to the "God" of *Battlestar Galactica*, typically defined as a force of nature rather than a distinct entity.[10] Both transcendent powers are unknowable and that is the point. From the perspective of the viewer, the critic, or the online blogger, attempts to understand where *Lost*'s survivors are going or what is manipulating the fates of *BSG*'s protagonists are not just unsuccessful but counter-productive, marring the emotional, contemplative content of the shows with a reductive search for answers that sadly typifies one of sci-fi fandom's most negative characteristics.

Indeed, the final season of *Battlestar Galactica* provides a case in point, with the spiritual content inherent in the ending of that series being just as, if not more controversially received than the conclusion of *Lost*. Echoing that show's emphasis on light and dark, good and evil, *BSG* advances two diametrically opposed theological constructions: the robotic Cylons's Abrahamic belief in one true God versus the polytheistic Human faith which espouses worship of a pantheon closely resembling the real-world Greek deities. Reinforcing its thematic connection with the post–9/11 War on Terror, the conflict between the Cylon and Human is depicted as a clash of civilizations, one in which powerful political grievances are expressed through a violent discourse of disparate religious philosophies. In particular, the Cylons claim divine inspiration and endorsement for their genocidal attack on the human race which begins the series and so, on an immediate level, *BSG* speaks readily to the twenty-first century American fear of religious extremists with nuclear ambitions. What separates the show from similarly themed television series (say *24*) is not that it eschews conservative or reactionary tendencies—*BSG*'s engagement with these topics is one of its strengths—but instead that it makes a concerted effort to understand the role of religion in provoking those responses in the first place. Again and again, the argument proposed by the series is that arbitrary religious division manifests always as destructive, disastrous conflict.

It is no accident that in the final episode of the series, "Daybreak" (written by Moore), the survival of Human and Cylon alike is contingent on finding a way to work in cooperation with each other, to look past the differences of ritual and rite so that they might—tellingly—begin to construct a new world together. Like *Lost*, the show espouses a philosophy of spiritual growth through community-building rather than through organized religious institutions or instruction. Religion is depicted as actively retarding the spiritual growth of the Human and Cylon races, trapping their opposing doctrines in an endless spiral of hatred and holocaust. God, though the entity eschews that title, sends his agents, described as angels, amongst the mortals but he never appears in person to any of the characters.[11] Whereas *Lost*'s Jacob, for his many flaws, at least presented himself in the form of a man, the God of *BSG* is best characterized as a brutal and mechanical force. Despite sending investigative figures or guides to manipulate the variables, this entity's behavior is closer to a computer incessantly running variations on a simulation than it is to any traditional notion of a supreme being.

As a result, the betterment of humanity on *BSG* is the business of humanity alone. For a stirring summation of how this is so, one must turn to Gaius Baltar in "Daybreak," with the philosophical implication of what he says being equally applicable to the theological position of *Lost* as well as *BSG*. God, claims Baltar, is an undeniable force at work in the universe and one which has been witnessed by many of the characters. Trying to understand its motivation is a meaningless exercise and, worse, one which has led Human and Cylon into an endless cycle of good and evil, war, destruction, and escape. The only rational thing to do, the only way to break the cycles on which the fictional history of the *BSG* universe are predicated, is to replace terror of divine judgment with a willingness to live in hope.[12] It is a speech which highlights how religion, throughout both series, is a source of fear, a paradigm of human behavior which inhibits true spiritual growth and retards hope. Baltar himself is a prime example of how this message is expressed not in a moralistic fashion, but more subtly, through the evolution of character from skeptical scientist to a man who, for all his self-described unconscionable crimes, has come to understand the power and the value of redemption. Through his transformation he finds a measure of salvation, though this is something which the universe only offers once he chooses to accept his fate and not to fight it anymore.[13]

What then is Baltar's fate? It is certainly less belief than it is predestination. He is to ensure the safety of the first mixed-race, Human-Cylon child, something he accomplishes with the assistance of his once and future Cylon lover, Number Six. Originally, the attractive Number Six seduced Baltar and used him to compromise the Human defence systems on the eve of the holocaust. Subsequently she is resurrected in a new but identical form — as machines, Cylons do not die they "download" into a replacement body — while Baltar is haunted by a representation of her whom no one else can see. The demeanor of this apparition, described as "Head Six," differentiates her from the various physical appearances of other Sixes throughout the series. From the initial episodes of *BSG*, the Head Six character is noticeably more aggressive than the original Six, particularly in her instance that God has a plan for Baltar, in fact a plan for everything and everyone.[14] There is an intentional sense of ambiguity in how the series portrays Head Six, the possibilities raised including Baltar having been brainwashed, having had a chip implanted in his brain, or simply having experienced a mental breakdown due to his involvement in the destruction of the human race. The truth of the matter is actually far stranger, with Head Six eventually transpiring to be a messenger from a higher, though not necessarily divine power.[15]

While she, unlike the ghosts and sundry supernatural apparitions of *Lost*, is capable of interacting with the material realm when called to, Head Six's role in the narrative is primarily as a guide for Baltar's personal and spiritual development. Steered by this entity, Baltar makes the leap from denial of the inexplicable to a cynical understanding of the role played by faith in society at large when he runs for president at the end of season two.[16] His linkage of religion and politics reveals more than just his developed talent for opportunism (and, later, his remarkable sense of self-preservation), it also echoes the relationship between declared faith and electoral success in the United States.[17] Playing to said galleries, Baltar manages to win the election but his resulting administration — a cornerstone of the show's barbed commentary on US policy in Iraq — proves to be a disaster for what remains of the human race. President Baltar is eventually tried for collaborating with the enemy, and, though he is unexpectedly acquitted due to a lack of solid evidence, he soon discovers that no one will grant him sanctuary except for a human cult which has adopted the Cylon system of belief. Finding himself in a situation where he has to preach for his upkeep, Baltar delivers a series of sermons on

"The Last Supper." Playing up the religious subtext of the series, the Sci-Fi Channel released this promotional image for the fourth and final season of *Battlestar Galactica* along with explanatory comments by producer and writer Ronald D. Moore. Mirroring the composition of Leonardo's famous painting, the pose and position of each *BSG* character hinted at developments in the final episodes of the show. Note how Baltar looks to Head Six for guidance and how Kara Trace is embraced by only Samuel Anders after her resurrection. From left to right: Mary McDonnell as President Laura Roslin, Tricia Helfer as Natalie Faust, Michael Hogan as Col. Saul Tigh, Jamie Bamber as Cpt. Lee Adama, James Callis as Dr. Gaius Baltar, Tricia Helfer as Head Six, Katee Sackhoff as Cpt. Kara Thrace, Michael Trucco as Ens. Samuel Anders, Aaron Douglas as Chief Galen Tyrol, Grace Park as Lt. Sharon Agathon, Tahmoh Penikett as Cpt. Karl Agathon, Edward James Olmos as Admiral William Adama.

how the Human Gods cannot be blamed aiding the survivors of the Cylon Holocaust because they simply do not exist.[18] Instead of embracing the established religion, Baltar backs the theology of humanity's enemy, a belief in one true God.

Though he cites the remarkable turnaround in his own fortunes as evidence of supernatural interest in his existence, Baltar's turn to "God" is problematic and is not an expression of his true convictions. In actuality, Baltar does not believe; his limited prospects in the aftermath of his trial (along with his sexual needs and his previous knowledge of religion as a powerful instrument of control) lead him to see this group of scorned human monotheists as his only viable option for survival. While he affirms their belief in public, his private comments describing himself as a king of fools and doomed to live his life in a loony bin are much more telling.[19] His cult is essentially a cult of personality which he maintains by regurgitating the comments of Head Six rather than via any genuine spiritual insight of his own. It is only when he separates himself from existing religious paradigms and moves beyond clichéd conceptions of divinity that he is truly open to the revelation of another force which occurs in "Daybreak." Once he experiences the enormity and the indifference of God, the disparate religious beliefs of the Human and Cylon factions pale into insignificance. God has no interest in helping them and, as such, the metaphorical promised land — the rich continents of a new world — can be reached only when Human and Cylon put aside their ideological differences and work together, when they believe in themselves and what they can accomplish as a unified community.[20]

As with the final season of *Lost*, it takes the collapse of the existing belief systems to motivate such an epiphany. Just like the death of Jacob led to a period of social and spiritual disorder for the inhabitants of the Island, the Human characters of *Battlestar Galactica* endue a catastrophic breakdown, a protracted period of hopelessness and despair once they reach Earth in the middle of the final season. The home of the Thirteenth Tribe, described in their sacred scrolls as a safe haven, is actually a dead world ruined by a nuclear war two millennia earlier. What's more, remains recovered from the rubble show that the Thirteenth Tribe were not even Human, they were Cylons who — like Number Six and her cohort — had evolved to emulate their creators. The Thirteenth Tribe went on to create their own artificial life, machines which inevitably rose up and annihilated them. The shock of these revelations pushes the Human fleet to civil war. It is the nadir of their exodus from the Twelve Colonies, and, having placed all their hopes in religious teachings rather than attempting to reaffirm their individual and community spirituality, the characters find they have nothing to fall back upon.

The fact that *BSG*'s pilot miniseries was titled "Night" and the finale "Daybreak" has a further effect on how we judge the journeys of the show's characters at this junction. In essence, the four seasons of *BSG* constitute a single dark night of the soul, the loneliness, desolation, and desperation of the last human beings in existence; a permanent state of spiritual crisis during which their religion and its theological foundations are challenged to the point where they lose all experiential value, life devolving into a more or less literal existential wandering in the void. The civil uprising and military mutiny depicted in "The Oath" (written by Mark Verheiden) and "Blood on the Scales" (written by Michael Angeli) results from a society which has lost its way, not just literally — for after they have found Earth they have nowhere else to go — but also spiritually. Long reliant on appeals to their Gods, the characters discover that they have been abandoned and have nothing to believe in anymore. Again, these final season developments underline how deeply rooted the theologies of *BSG* and *Lost* are in the post–9/11 mindset, one in which belief in human authority and in God has been fatally undermined. The question asked by both shows as they move towards their conclusions is neither "What do we do now that man has killed God?" nor "Where is the safe homeland promised by the Gods?' but essentially 'How can we continue to believe in God when he has allowed so many to die on American soil?"

In the case of *BSG*, this religious anxiety builds to a head in the final season with many of the characters expressing a belief that their Gods have abandoned them.[21] Tied to this is the manner in which the show's main characters all come close to losing themselves and their sense of purpose in the course of their journey, an aspect of the series which give *Battlestar Galactica* its reputation as one of the most relentlessly dark television shows of recent years. Nonetheless, *BSG*'s dark night does provide at least a semblance of a blessing in disguise. The human race becomes more virtuous as they emerge from their trials; or at the very least they become less materialistic, abandoning their technology in the closing hour of the series and opting instead to return to basics on a newly discovered planet, a veritable Garden of Eden which they christen Earth as it represents both the true end of their journey and also an end — be it temporary or not, "Daybreak" leaves that open — to the cycle of violence between mankind and its creations.

In fact, by the end of the series, the most important difference between Human and Cylon has been eliminated by the destruction of the Cylon "Resurrection Hub." Death has become permanent for all Cylons and it has an astonishing, unexpected consequence: it has given each moment of life its own significance; it is a violent realization, but with the end of resurrection many Cylons begin to understand that, for the existence to have any value, it must be an existence with an end. Mortality, a human flaw they have previously sought to overcome, is revealed as crucial to their growth as individuals and as a society.[22] The effect is the same for the characters of *Lost*, meeting again on the way to the afterlife. The limbo space of the final season is not just a What-If predicated on an alternate history, it is an opportunity for them to process deep-rooted and destructive personal issues, a chance to come to terms with the true value of their lives.

Moreover, just as Christian Shepherd ushers those characters into the hereafter, the final journey of *Battlestar Galactica*'s protagonists is orchestrated by the character of Kara Thrace, callsign Starbuck. A pilot who is apparently killed in action during season three, Starbuck returns from the dead to guide the fleet to Earth in the course of season four.[23] After her mortal remains are discovered amongst the ruins of that world, Starbuck is proclaimed an angel by Baltar, and through what seems like divine intervention she leads the fleet to a new planet, a new Earth, which they can finally call home. When her work is done, Starbuck simply vanishes into thin air. This last development generated considerable fan outrage about the intrusion of mysticism into the archly atheistic realm of science fiction, something which, as primarily an online phenomenon, continues to this day and so echoes the manner in which the ending of *Lost* was received in many quarters.

With that in mind, it is perhaps no surprise that the *Lost*-bashing George RR Martin would also have a go at the *BSG* finale:

> *Battlestar Galactica* ends with "God Did It." Looks like somebody skipped Writing 101, when you learn that a *deus ex machina* is a crappy way to end a story [....] Yeah, yeah, sometimes the journey is its own reward. I certainly enjoyed much of the journey with *BSG* [...] but damn it, doesn't anybody know how to write an ending anymore? Writing 101, kids. Adam and Eve, God Did It, It Was All a Dream? I've seen Clarion students left stunned and bleeding for turning in stories with those endings.[24]

Again though, Martin's comments are erroneous. God might well have done "it," but God had been doing it all along and, as with *Lost*, the clues had been there from the earliest episodes. Head Six's ongoing religious dialogue with Baltar is only the most up-front aspect of a spirituality which was central to the series from the pilot miniseries and from the initial stories of season one; at no point did it become less important to either the characters or to the writers. What's more, the ending of *Battlestar Galactica* cannot rightly even be considered a *deus ex machina*; "Daybreak" was not the sudden and abrupt solution of a seemingly inextricable problem by the contrived and unexpected appearance of a heretofore unseen character, ability, or object. Though off-screen, God had been part of the series from the very beginning, and any analysis which denies this is predicated upon a fundamentally flawed understanding of the series in its entirety.[25]

Contrast Martin's claims with what an actual *deus ex machina* might have looked like, one of Ronald D. Moore's abandoned concepts for the season one finale:

> [Baltar] comes into a room and he hears music and it's a recognizable Earth tune to the audience and to him. It was Jimi Hendrix was playing, actually, and he goes, "God, I recognize that." And then somebody's voice says, "You recognize that?" And he says, "Yes." And he turns and it's Dirk Benedict [star of the original *BSG*]. And Dirk Benedict says, "Hi. I'm God." And you just cut. We just cut out on that[....] That was gonna be the end of that whole storyline and the episode.[26]

While such a development would have comprised an all-too ridiculous wink at the audience, the fact that it was considered and discounted illustrates a valuable point: those involved in the writing and running of *Battlestar Galactica* were, from an early point, concerned not simply with the theological underpinnings of their story but with an appropriate integration of such material into their ongoing narrative. Much like *Lost*'s Christian Shepherd or the mentions of Jacob dropped throughout that series, God was a mysterious presence on *BSG* as far back as the pilot. That the creative minds behind the series consistently resisted the inclusion of a *deus ex machina* is evidenced by Moore's comment above and by the careful manner in which Starbuck's arc was prepared and executed.

In many ways, Starbuck's story is more meticulously planned then that of Gaius Baltar, the clues to her death, "resurrection," and special purpose as saviour of humanity having been introduced as far back as the start of season two. It is her destiny to lead humanity to its end, though despite the ominous nature of such a prophecy, the resurrected Starbuck—reborn as another of God's messengers—rallies Humanity and Cylon alike to the completion of their long journey.[27] Yet her function is not simply to act as guide; she, again like Christian Shepherd, brings together a community heretofore shattered by the arbitrary divisions of religion. In a clear statement on 9/11's divisive effect on the early twenty-first century world, *Battlestar Galactica* eventually shows both sides of its destructive, religiously motivated conflict to have more in common than they ever dared admit. Human and Cylon work together to construct a new society which, in the finale's pointed flashforward of an astonishing 150,000 years, eventually develops into our twenty-first century civilization. "Daybreak," with its epilogue of contemporary robotic achievements, suggests that this society is on the verge of the same technological leaps which led to the creation of the Cylons, and so is poised to begin the cycle of violence once again. Some may see this ending as pessimistic; however, the epilogue is ambiguous, offering at least the possibility that the society created by the merger of Humans and Cylons will be able to avoid the mistakes of the past.

Such ambiguity is essential, for had *BSG* offered a concrete statement on the future of the hybrid civilization it would have been a cheat on the part of the show and a negation of how, in a metafictional touch, the series concludes in the era which inspired its narrative of holy war. The endless, biblical wandering of the human fleet which precedes "Daybreak" (or, for that matter, the aimlessness of the survivors throughout large stretches of *Lost*) speaks to a widely felt lack of direction in the years after 9/11. The focus on large-scale goals and threats such as the War on Terror, and how these were pursued at the expense of individual and community spiritual development is something which informs both narratives. Consider the manner in which the mythologies of both shows focus on continuous cycles of violence, or the implication of the rebuke to the life-and-death mission of *Lost*'s protagonists by long-term background characters Rose and Bernard in "The Incident." Characters who have, by the end of season five, stood by and endured more than their share of epic conflicts and melodramatic last stands, Rose and Bernard have been threatened with death so many times that they have lost their fear of it. They are jaded by the struggle between good and evil; they have opted out of it entirely, choosing to be happy with what they have instead of partaking in the insistent vacillation between the various factions—read little religions— which continue to inhibit the spiritual development of the main protagonists.[28] In this way Rose and Bernard provide a model for the eventual fate of all the characters in the show's waiting room for the afterlife as well as for the characters of *Battlestar Galactica*. In both cases, communities are continually broken down to the extent that they eventually rebel against conventional religious doctrine or systems of belief, striking out at the absent father figures of both narratives.

Paraphrasing, of all things, the opening of the filmic *Peter Pan*, the oft-repeated religious mantra of both Human and Cylons is "all of this has happened before, and all of this will happen again."[29] Thematically, *BSG*'s mutiny episodes represent another instance of humanity trying to overthrow its deities (in this case their political and military leaders) before they themselves are overthrown in turn by their creations. The cyclical nature ascribed to the universe here serves as a key component of the human theology on *BSG*, with characters told many times that belief in their Gods equates with a belief in a cycle of time and predestination in which they are all fulfilling role which occur again and again throughout eternity.[30] The implication here is clear: religious belief retards the ability of individuals and societies to transcend petty grievances and achieve true peace, prosperity, or happiness. It is a message which is mirrored by the question of eternal recurrence debated by *Lost*'s Jacob and the Man in Black. The latter argues for a cycle of corruption and devastation which always ends the same way; the former believes that all destruction is merely progress and that the story only ends once.[31]

Given that *Lost* and *BSG* are narrative texts, stories carefully constructed with—insofar as episodic television allows—clear beginnings, middles, and ends, it is no surprise that the finales of both depict their characters successfully breaking out of their respective cycles. "The End" and "Daybreak" are both aspirational conclusions which portray their protagonists moving on literally and figuratively. In doing so, *Lost* and *Battlestar Galactica* both end in a fashion entirely consistent with the marked prevalence of theological themes and religious allegory throughout their runs. Both series challenged viewers in an uncommon fashion, demanding an unusually high level of involvement from their audience and, as a result, arming fans with the double-edged sword of fierce loyalty and a misguided sense of ownership with regard to the properties. This loyalty was cemented as every new twist of *Lost* and *Battlestar Galactica*'s plots confounded audience expectation anew. However, such investment on the part of viewers turned ugly when both shows actively pursued directions antithetical to fan reaction.

While the theological underpinnings of both *Lost* and *BSG* are more coherent than generally perceived by fan and critic alike, the manner in which this material was received is troubling. Though the shows offered intelligent, allegorical discussion of personal spirituality and belief in a contemporary world racked by fundamentalism and religiously motivated conflict, it is clear that audiences—particularly the shows' vocal internet followings—did not like what they saw in the mirror of their television screens. Though a component of this was the rejection of so-called mysticism by science fiction fans, the fashion in which viewers rounded on the finale of *Lost* in particular betrays a deeper discomfort amongst mainstream viewers forced to confront the ugly potential of religion to divide rather than to unify. Charlie Brooker, writing in *The Guardian*, dismissed the final scene in the church as "a pretentious building society advert."[32] Another commentator deemed "The End" to be "the worst ending Hollywood has ever done," an extreme position though one which continues to be widely expressed online.[33] The *BSG* finale fared little better, *Salon* deeming it to be "40 minutes of speeches about lessons learned and the need to 'break the cycle,' the naiveté of which did indeed feel like a break—from the knowing, worldly stoicism that made *Battlestar Galactica* so refreshing to begin with."[34] Another more extreme review, adopting the vernacular of the show itself, accused Ron Moore of succumbing to "superstitious mumbo jumbo" and having "finally got to douse us in his pro-God, anti-society, anti-technology philosophy":

> Why the frak does Baltar have an imaginary friend? Answer: It's God! Why isn't Starbuck dead and what the frak is she? Answer: Oh it's God! Why did the Cylons destroy the colonies? Oh it's God! How are the Humans going to find a home? Oh it's God! Every remaining question was answered tonight and the answer to every question was: Oh it's God.[35]

If anything, reception of "The End" and "Daybreak" demonstrates that the defining characteristic of *Lost* and *Battlestar Galactica*—their attempts to open a unique dialogue with popular entertainment audiences through deployment of idiosyncratic theological material—is also their Achilles' Heel. In the years since they wrapped, the reception of both shows has been dogged by confusion over their meaning and outright dismissal of their moral messages. As a result, it seems unlikely that we will see such a sustained investigation of the theological in popular science fiction television any time in the near future. All of this may have happened before, yes, but will it ever happen again?

Part II. Angels and Demons Among Us

Notes

1. "The Incident, Part II," *Lost*, Damon Lindelof and Carlton Cuse, 13 May 2009.
2. "The End," *Lost*, Damon Lindelof and Carlton Cuse, ABC, 23 May 2010.
3. "White Rabbit," *Lost*, Christian Taylor, ABC, 20 October 2004.
4. "The End," *Lost*, Damon Lindelof and Carlton Cuse, ABC, 23 May 2010.
5. "The End," *Lost*, Damon Lindelof and Carlton Cuse, ABC, 23 May 2010.
6. Steve Busfield and Richard Vine, "A *Lost* embrace," *Guardian* (London), 25 May 2010, p.12; Max Read, "The *Lost* finale was incredibly dumb," *Gawker*, 23 May 2010. http://gawker.com/5545877/, accessed 10 November 2011.
7. James Poniewozik, "GRRM Interview Part 3: Twilight Zone and Lost," *Tuned In Blog*, *Time.com*, 19 April 2011, http://tunedin.blogs.time.com/2011/04/19/grrm-interview-part-3-the-twilight-zone-and-lost/, accessed 15 August 2011.
8. In fact it appears that Martin saw what he wanted to see, having stated in April 2009 that "if it turns out that They Were Dead All Along I'm really going to be pissed." George R.R. Martin, "Writing 101," http://grrm.livejournal.com/82239.html, 5 April 2009, accessed 20 August 2011.
9. "Daybreak, Part II," *Battlestar Galactica*, Ronald D. Moore, Sci-Fi Channel, 20 March 2009.
10. "Daybreak, Part II," *Battlestar Galactica*, Ronald D. Moore, Sci-Fi Channel, 20 March 2009.
11. "Daybreak, Part II," *Battlestar Galactica*, Ronald D. Moore, Sci-Fi Channel, 20 March 2009.
12. "The Road Less Travelled," *Battlestar Galactica*, Mark Verheiden, Sci-Fi Channel, 2 May 2008.
13. "33," *Battlestar Galactica*, Ronald D. Moore, Sci-Fi Channel, 14 January 2005.
14. "Daybreak, Part II," *Battlestar Galactica*, Ronald D. Moore, Sci-Fi Channel, 20 March 2009.
15. "Tigh Me Up, Tigh Me Down," *Battlestar Galactica*, Jeff Vlaming, Sci-Fi Channel, 4 March 2005.
16. "Lay Down Your Burdens, Part I," *Battlestar Galactica*, Ronald D. Moore, Sci Fi Channel, 3 March 2006.
17. "The Road Less Travelled," *Battlestar Galactica*, Mark Verheiden, Sci-Fi Channel, 2 May 2008.
18. "Escape Velocity," *Battlestar Galactica*, Jane Espenson, Sci-Fi Channel, 25 April 2008.
19. "He That Believeth In Me," *Battlestar Galactica*, Bradley Thompson and David Weddle, Sci-Fi Channel. 4 April 2008.
20. "33," *Battlestar Galactica*, Ronald D. Moore, Sci-Fi Channel, 14 January 2005; "Daybreak, Part II." *Battlestar Galactica*, Ronald D. Moore, Sci-Fi Channel, 20 March 2009.
21. "Faith," *Battlestar Galactica*, Kevin Fahey, Sci-Fi Channel, 9 May 2008.
22. "Guess What's Coming to Dinner?" *Battlestar Galactica*, Michael Angeli, Sci-Fi Channel, 16 May 2008.
23. "Crossroads, Part II," *Battlestar Galactica*, Mark Verheiden, Sci-Fi Channel, 25 March 2007.
24. George R.R. Martin, "Writing 101," http://grrm.livejournal.com/82239.html, 5 April 2009, accessed 20 August 2011.
25. "Daybreak, Part II," *Battlestar Galactica*, Ronald D. Moore, Sci-Fi Channel, 20 March 2009.
26. Ronald D. Moore, "Podcast for Kobol's Last Gleaming, Part II," http://en.battlestarwiki.org/wiki/Podcast:Kobol%27s_Last_Gleaming%2C_Part_II, accessed 23 August 2011.
27. "Razor," *Battlestar Galactica*, Michael Taylor, Sci-Fi Channel, 24 November 2007; "Daybreak, Part II," *Battlestar Galactica*, Ronald D. Moore, Sci-Fi Channel. 20 March 2009.
28. "The Incident, Part I," *Lost*. Damon Lindelof and Carlton Cuse, ABC, 13 May 2009.
29. "Flesh and Bone," *Battlestar Galactica*, Toni Graphia, Sci-Fi Channel, 25 February 2005.
30. "Kobol's Last Gleaming," *Battlestar Galactica*. Ronald D. Moore. Sci-Fi Channel. 1 April 2005.
31. "The Incident, Part II," *Lost*. Damon Lindelof and Carlton Cuse, ABC, 13 May 2009.
32. Charlie Brooker, "Charlie Brooker's Screen Burn: *Lost* and *24*," *Guardian* (London), 29 May 2010, "The Guide," p.52.
33. "tmaster" commentating on the *LA Times* article "Of love 'Lost,'" 25 May 2010, http://www.latimes.com/entertainment/news/tv/la-et-lost-review-20100524,0,289843.story, accessed 10 November 2011.
34. Laura Miller, "Goodbye, Calactica," *Salon*, 21 March 2009, http://www.salon.com/2009/03/21/battlestar_galactica_2/, accessed 10 November 2011.
35. Josh Tyler, "Why The Battlestar Galactica finale is a huge cop-out and why it doesn't matter,

Cinemablend, 20 March 2009, http://www.cinemablend.com/television/Why-The-Battlestar-Galactica-Finale-Is-A-Huge-Copout-And-It-Doesn-t-Matter-16337.html, accessed 10 November 2011.

Works Cited

Battlestar Galactica. Prod. Ronald D. Moore and David Eick. Perf. Edward James Olmos, Mary McDonnell, Katee Sackhoff. SyFy Channel. 2004–2009.
Brooker, Charlie. "Charlie Brooker's Screen Burn: *Lost* and *24*." *Guardian* (London), 29 May 2010. "The Guide," p.52.
Busfield, Steve, and Richard Vine. "A *Lost* embrace." *Guardian* (London), 25 May 2010, p.12.
Lost. Prod. J.J. Abrams and Damon Lindelof. Perf. Matthew Fox, Naveen Andrews, Evangeline Lilly, Terry O'Quinn. Buena Vista Television/ABC. 2004–2010.
Martin, George R.R. "Writing 101." http://grrm.livejournal.com/82239.html, 5 April 2009. Accessed 20 August 2011.
Miller, Laura. "Goodbye, Galactica." *Salon*, 21 March 2009, http://www.salon.com/2009/03/21/battlestar_galactica_2/, accessed 10 November 2011.
Poniewozik, James. "GRRM Interview Part 3: Twilight Zone and Lost." "Tuned In Blog," *Time.com*, 19 April 2011, http://tunedin.blogs.time.com/2011/04/19/grrm-interview-part-3-the-twilight-zone-and-lost/, accessed 15 August 2011.
Read, Max. "The *Lost* finale was incredibly dumb." *Gawker*, 23 May 2010, http://gawker.com/5545877/, accessed 10 November 2011.
Tyler, Josh. "Why The *Battlestar Galactica* finale is a huge cop-out and why it doesn't matter." *Cinemablend*, 20 March 2009, http://www.cinemablend.com/television/Why-The-Battlestar-Galactica-Finale-Is-A-Huge-Copout-And-It-Doesn-t-Matter-16337.html, accessed 10 November 2011.

The Radical Theology of Krzysztof Kieślowski's Decalogue

Matthew Yde

In his classic work of Christian apologetics, *Mere Christianity*, C.S. Lewis suggests that for the sake of linguistic clarity we apply the word "Christian" only to "one who accepts the common doctrines of Christianity" and not to those who, though they may exemplify the "spirit of Christ," do not accept or are unsure about those same doctrines. To those who accept the doctrines of Christian faith yet lead dishonest and selfish lives we must simply say that they are "bad Christians."[1] This is sensible enough, yet increasingly problematic. We live in a world where hollow professions of faith by public figures reverberate in the media incessantly. Pundits are continually asking politicians seeking office "How important is prayer in your life?" and "How important is your faith?" Not surprisingly, the politicians most committed to making the rich richer and enacting policies detrimental to the most vulnerable in our society are the most emphatic and the most voluble in their protestations of Christian faith. And the pundits play along, taking them at their word and never mentioning the obvious fact that it is Mammon, and not the God of Christianity, that has their allegiance.

Yet it seems to me that the gospels are quite clear about what it means to be a Christian, if by Christian we mean a follower of Jesus Christ. The fine points of Christian doctrine developed over centuries, yet Jesus (or the evangelists' depiction of Jesus in their gospels) is perfectly clear about what constitutes a righteous life in the eyes of God. Asked which commandment was the most important, Jesus replied, "YOU SHALT LOVE THE LORD THY GOD WITH ALL THY HEART, WITH ALL THY SOUL, AND WITH ALL

THY MIND. This is the first and great commandment. And the second is like unto it, THOU SHALT LOVE THY NEIGHBOR AS THYSELF."[2] Yet it was a "born again Christian" who presided over the most executions in our country's history while governor of Texas, and as president launched two devastating wars against weak countries that posed no threat to the United States, while cutting taxes for the rich and gutting social programs for the poor wherever he could get away with it.

Unlike George W. Bush, Polish filmmaker Krzysztof Kieślowski does not claim to be a Christian. In fact he is notoriously vague and enigmatic when questioned about his religious views. Yet any survey of his work will not fail to impress the sensitive viewer with how deep a faith, and specifically a Christian faith, is at work in many of his films, for instance his *Three Colors Trilogy* and his ten hour film *The Decalogue*. With all due respect to C.S. Lewis, to my mind Kieślowski is a Christian and George W. Bush is not, and in the following essay I hope to show why by briefly examining his 1988 masterpiece *The Decalogue*.

The Decalogue consists of ten individual films just under an hour in length, each based on one of the Ten Commandments. While each of the ten films can stand independently, together they form an integral whole and are meant to be seen in succession over a short time. All of them take place in and around Warsaw in the last years of Polish Communism, and most of them are set in the same dreary apartment complex, which in the earlier episodes resembles a kind of cosmic or post-apocalyptic wasteland. Kieślowski shows how the Ten Commandments are not an anachronism, but are relevant still; we see them complicated as they are given concrete reality in the messy lives of Kieślowski's characters. Yet beyond each individual commandment stands Christ's greater commandment to love one another, the only way, ultimately, to fulfill the law of God. Most of the emphasis is on the second part of Jesus's admonition quoted above, for while "God" as an abstract noun might be difficult for some people to love, the noun "neighbor" is perfectly intelligible to all. And in case there is any confusion, Jesus makes his meaning unambiguously clear in the Gospel of Luke[3]; our neighbor is every single human being, even our enemies (how radical this commandment is becomes strikingly apparent when we realize that in a twenty-first century context the two characters in the parable of the Good Samaritan might be a Palestinian and an Israeli). Therefore most, but not all, of the emphasis in *The Decalogue* is on loving your neighbor, which is only another way of loving God. As the great Christian theologian Karl Barth puts it: "The decision lies in our answer to the question—Do we, in the unknowable *neighbor*, apprehend and love the Unknown God? Do we, in the complete Otherness of *the other*—in whom the whole riddle of existence is summed up in such a manner as to require its solution in an action on our part—hear the voice of the One?"[4] In fact it might be said that Kieślowski is a Christian existentialist, for his emphasis is on how his characters answer the question posed by Barth, the critical choices they make at every moment as free human beings.

That said, *Decalogue One* is about our fundamental relation to God himself. As well it might be since it is based on the first Commandment (in the Roman Catholic version of the Decalogue): "I *am* the LORD thy God ... thou shalt have no other gods before me. Thou shalt not make unto thee any graven image.... Thou shalt not bow down thyself to them, nor serve them." *Decalogue One* involves three central characters: an atheist father, his ten-year-old son, and the father's sister and boy's aunt, a devout Catholic. As mentioned, the *Decalogue* films can stand independently, as each film introduces a new set of characters and a new story line; nonetheless there is a thematic progression to the series (moving from judgment to reconciliation) and there is one character who appears in all but the last of the *Decalogue* films. He usually appears at significant moments, never speaks, and is only on screen for a few seconds; yet he is vitally important to Kieślowski's overall metaphysical vision. The character clearly represents an aspect of divinity incarnated, or *Shekhinah*—a visible manifestation of divine presence (for convenience I will usually refer to this character as "the angel"). The first character we see in *Decalogue One*, and thus in *The Decalogue*, is this nameless figure sitting pensively before a fire by a frozen lake. (This lake is of central significance: symbolically, thematically, and to the plot itself.) Alone by the shore of the frozen lake and huddled before a fire, he invokes homelessness, profound separation, and thus I am reminded, among other things, of Jesus's identification with the sick, the hungry, the naked, the imprisoned, the stranger—the "least of these" in Matthew 25.

Decalogue One opens with a long slow God's-eye panning of the surface of the frozen lake, the camera finally coming to a stop on this mysterious figure. It is a cold, grey, ominous day. All the while the haunting otherworldly flute music of Zbigniew Preisner is heard. The scene then shifts to a woman walking at night, crying; she stops before a television in a store window staring at a pre-recorded scene of children running. The camera freezes on the happy face of a boy in the center of the group of children, Pavel, who will come to be the center of the story which is about to unfold. Then back to the man by the lake, wiping away a tear. This prologue, which is subsequent to the action we are about to see, comes to an end as the camera sweeps up a tall apartment building (we only seen the texture of the grey granite at first and do not know what we are seeing); we hear the flutter of birds' wings, and finally one pigeon is on a window ledge with the boy, Pavel, staring in wonder. The contrast between the mysterious frozen lake and the television screen sets up the thematic tension. Later the aunt will tell her nephew that at a young age the boy's father came to believe that everything could be measured. God, associated with the deep mystery at the center of the universe and, in his judgmental aspect, symbolized here by the frozen lake, has been forgotten.

The heart of this first episode is Pavel, a precocious child who early in the film encounters a stray neighborhood dog lying dead on the cold ground. He is disturbed and asks his father to explain death to him. The father feebly remarks that death occurs when the heart stops pumping blood to the brain. Unsatisfied the child then asks about the soul; the father remarks that there is no such thing as a soul; it is simply a fabrication meant to console. His aunt does a better job answering his questions, demonstrating the answer to the most difficult question of all. When Pavel asks about God she hugs the boy, telling him that God is where love is. It is the choices we make and the actions which ensue from them — especially actions directed empathically toward other persons— that are most important to Kieślowski, and which demonstrate our commitment to God and to his creation.

The father is a Professor of Linguistics whose god is scientific measurement. He seems to believe in the infallibility of computers and in a class lecture even ascribes the possibility of choice, selection, even "aesthetic preference" to a properly programmed computer. In this first film the computer is an idol that, for the father at least (and for our technocratic political, intellectual, and business classes) has usurped the place of God. The professor, whose name is Krzysztof, had told his students that for him a computer can almost have its own personality, and in this film computers are strangely anthropomorphized, inevitably bringing to mind Hal from Kubrick's *2001*. When Pavel wants to go skating his father tells him to ask the computer; he tells his son to find out the ground temperature of the three previous days and then see what the computer's response is regarding whether the ice will be strong enough to hold someone of his son's weight. The computer assures him that the ice will be safe to skate on; the ice breaks and Pavel is drowned.

When the distraught father returns home from the lake after the death of his child he walks slowly towards the computer, mysteriously on and glowing from its place in the room, its screen reading in English: "I am ready." He leaves, as if in recoil, going to a large cathedral under construction, conspicuous throughout this first film. Candles envelope a large picture of Virgin and Child; in anger he overturns the altar and wax falls like tears from the eye of the Virgin. He puts his hand into the basin of holy water, finds a sphere of ice and applies it to his feverish forehead. The camera lingers on this for a moment before cutting to a close up of his beautiful son running in slow motion on a television screen; the camera freezes, starts, freezes again, and the first part of *Decalogue* comes to a close. This is a powerful opening into this investigation of the relevance of the Ten Commandments in our contemporary world, and a number of themes and clues have been given to us.

First, in *Decalogue Eight* one of the central characters says that "no ideal, nothing, is more important than the life of a child." In *Decalogue Five* a young girl of twelve is killed through the carelessness of others. And in *Decalogue One*, as we just saw, one of the last images before the final image of the young boy's face, so full of the future he won't have, is the prescient Mother of the incarnate God weeping for her own child's cruel death at the hands of institutional power as well as for the grieving father and his own lost child. Children represent New Life; they are the most vulnerable; and they are the most dependent on the responsible care of adults. There is something especially sacred about children: they are creative, open, trusting, and full of wonder. If it is true that to enter heaven we must become like little children, then it must be one of the gravest of sins to be the cause of a child's harm. *Decalogue Seven* revolves around the commandment "Thou shalt not steal," and opens with the off screen diegetic sound of a child screaming: haunting, plaintive, unidentifiable at first, the screaming continues for four full minutes before the camera finally settles on a child having a nightmare. In desperation a middle-aged woman shakes the child violently, saying as she wakes, "Are you dreaming of the wolves again? I've told you there are no wolves." But we soon understand that there are wolves indeed, as little Ania is caught in the middle of a tense struggle for her possession. Born to a sixteen year old mother, Majka, she has been raised by her grandmother, Eva. Now, six years later, Majka wants the child back. But Eva has legal possession of Ania and Majka is forced to kidnap her own child. We see how Kieślowski and his co-writer Krzysztof Piesiewicz masterfully complicate the commandments: who is the thief here? Did the grandmother steal the child from her biological mother or does Majka steal the child from Eva, the child's primary caregiver for the first six years of her life?

While it is perhaps not clear who is committing the theft, it is clear that the child is the real loser here, as both women are possessive rather than loving. In that sense they are both thieves, stealing the child's future. As the grandmother finally stops Ania's crying the camera lingers on Ania's haunted face — it is a stunning picture: we see in the child's dilated eyes and catatonic stare a ruined life, a lost soul, a doomed future. Kieślowski's brilliant work with actors and his many fascinating close-ups of his actors' faces has to be seen to be appreciated, but it is a wonder to me how he managed to capture such a haunted look in this little girl's face. Despite the selfishness of both the women, our sympathy should extend to the biological mother Majka as well as to the child. For Majka was a child once too; and it is clear that her own mother does not love her, blaming Majka's birth for her own subsequent

Model Valentine Dusot (Irene Jacob) is photographed for a chewing gum ad campaign in Kieślowski's *Three Colors: Red* (1994, MKZ Productions). The camera's eye is like the audience's, voyeuristically enjoying Dusot's beauty. Voyeurism is a recurring theme in Kieślowski's films. In *Red*, a misanthropic judge eavesdrops on the phone calls of his neighbors to confirm to himself that humanity is doomed, while in *Decalogue*, a jealous husband spies on his adulterous wife. Kieślowski draws a distinction between those who stand in judgment of others, ogle them, and try to possess them, while he urges us to be more God-like and to look upon our neighbors with mercy and forgiveness — to respect their autonomy and privacy and to love them despite their flaws.

incapacity to have more children. While the credits show that the actor Artur Barcis who plays the angel appears in this film just as he does in all the previous ones, I am unable to discern his presence even after repeated viewings. The possessiveness of the two women, their stealing of the little girl's future, seems to banish divinity from the environment. As Lloyd Baugh puts it in an essay whose thesis is similar to my own, "Where there is no love ... divine Providence, the power of Grace, represented by this mysterious figure is unable to function."[5]

While the theme of children and the need to care for them is central to *The Decalogue*, it is possible to extend this view metaphorically. We are all children to God, and he never falters in his watching over us. We are frequently tempted to judge negatively, but only because we are unable to watch incessantly and therefore to really know our brothers and sisters. We feel sympathy for Majka, but only because Kieślowski has revealed enough of her circumstances to awaken our compassion. We feel less sympathy for Eva, but that is, perhaps, because we know less about her. Many of the characters in *The Decalogue* invite a similar negative response at first, until Kieślowski reveals more of their situation. In this way Kieślowski has involved us concretely in one of the themes of the film (we might call it positive voyeurism). As we watch the film we come slowly to understand the characters, and thus like God — the ultimate watcher and knower — come to love and care for them, and this love covers over a multitude of sins.[6]

Another theme found in *Decalogue One*, which recurs throughout the series, is the journey which leads to the moment of choice, and the choice itself, the choice of faith. It is always somewhat risky to read into an author's characters evidence of the author's own private life, but *Decalogue* is a deeply personal film and it is impossible not to conjecture on the nature of Kieślowski's own faith as represented by certain characters, especially as Kieślowski himself has said, "I turn the camera on myself in all my films."[7] The name of the father in *Decalogue One* is Krzysztof, the actual name of both Kieślowski and his writing partner Krzysztof Piesiewicz. As the first film of the series, this character's movement away from "idol worship" and toward acknowledgement of the divine is telling. Krzysztof is a man of science, an intellectual; he is completely at home in the secular world, yet as his sister says to Pavel, "we should not rule God out for him entirely." He is a good father, a very sympathetic character, and he seems to possess at least some doubt about the infallibility of his god, as he checks the ice himself even after the computer assures him that it will be safe to skate on. It is significant that the cathedral seen in the film is under construction, a work in progress; and Krzysztof's entering the site of worship and applying holy water to his forehead tells us that the construction of this holy site will continue in his own life. One of the most stunning images in the whole film is a long lingering shot of a huge magnificent cross which covers one of the walls of the cathedral; Kieślowski holds the shot for a long time, signifying the mystery of the sacrifice that brings Life, even as the sacrifice of his own son will bring Krzysztof to spiritual life.

In *Decalogue Two* another man of science, this time a doctor, is asked if he believes in God. He says that he has a God, "but there's only enough of him for me." When asked, then, if this is a private God, he responds that it is. In *Decalogue Eight* a professor of philosophy says that she tries to help her students "discover themselves," to find the good that exists in every human being. When asked who evaluates, she answers, "He who is in all of us." But "I never found God" in any of your books, her questioner remarks. The professor — whose name Zofia means wisdom — responds that she does not use the word God or go to church, yet nonetheless she "knows." A choice must be made, she says, whether to leave God behind or to accept him — even if one never uses the word God or worships in any orthodox or customary way, that existential choice will make a profound difference in the life of the one who chooses as well as in the lives of those he or she comes into significant contact with. The alternative to choosing God is choosing emptiness, which she utters with profound distaste, even horror. All of these characters are intellectuals, and the latter two believe without belonging to any church or submitting to any sort of dogma. These characters' actions give evidence of the choice they have made. The doctor is confronted early on with a hostile woman who needs his help; years ago she ran over his dog, and before it is clear that he is going to help her she says that she wishes she had run over him instead. Yet he helps her. Zofia is devoted, in a sense, to a kind of missionary work; she works to bring her students to a sense of The Good in an otherwise bleak and meaningless world. While in a Nazi prison waiting to be executed, the great Lutheran Minister Dietrich Bonhoeffer wrote of a "religionless <u>Christianity</u>." Disgusted with the hypocrisy and ineffectuality of organized religion, he came to feel that Christ might best be served outside the church; and that is the kind of Christianity Kieślowski reveals in his characters.

Kieślowski is not concerned with a vague and general kind of faith that exists on the periphery of his characters' consciousness. He is concerned with moral choices of profound life-changing significance. We have already discussed the doctor in *Decalogue Two*, but more needs to be said about him. Like Krzysztof in the preceding episode this man has suffered a profound loss, losing his family in a World War II bombing raid. In a sense Kieślowski is showing us what the fruits of Krzysztof's choice might be as he moves on with his life after the loss of his child. This doctor is usually seen caring for his plants, his bird or his patients. It is clear what kind of choice he made after his catastrophe; he chose life, and service to his private God, not emptiness and despair. In contrast, the other central character, Dorota, is destructive: we know she ran over his dog two years ago; we see her in her pain attempt to destroy a plant; she smokes incessantly, inadvertently and symbolically setting a pack of matches ablaze as she ashes her cigarette in the matchbox; and she slides a glass of hot coffee across the table just to watch it break on the floor. She is a type of Kieślowski character we will see again, just as we will see another destructive character, Jacek in *Decalogue Five*, slowly bump a rock off a bridge and onto the windshield of a coming car. But Kieślowski is sympathetic with his more destructive characters, recognizing this propensity as both a cause and a consequence of their suffering.

Dorota loves her husband very much; she loves him for the "tranquility and support" he provides, but she is a very passionate woman and loves another man as well, a lover who fulfills her sexually in a way that her husband does not. Her husband is dying; she is pregnant with her lover's child and we learn that this is her only chance to have a baby; but if her husband manages to recover she needs to abort the child. She demands that the doctor tell her if her husband will live or die. To save the child he tells her that her husband will die. She makes him swear, which he can not do truthfully but does anyway. The commandment this episode explores is, "Thou shalt not take the name of the Lord thy God in vain." This is another example of Kieślowski complicating the commandments; the doctor swears that her husband will die even though there is a slight chance he may recover; but he does this to save the child, which as we saw earlier is central to the theme of *The Decalogue*. The crucial scene takes place in her husband's hospital room. The angel, this time a caregiver in the hospital, is present in the room and focused on the intensity of contact of wife to dying husband; with profound emotion she tells her unconscious husband that she loves him, and we know that she has chosen him and will not go away with her lover, although he is waiting for her. She fails to show up for her abortion, her husband miraculously recovers and tells the doctor that he and his wife are going to have a baby. "Do you know what that means?" he asks the doctor. The doctor says that he does, and the film ends. We have moved from judgment and the death of a child in *Decalogue One*, to new life — both the child growing in Dorota's womb and her husband's resurrection — in *Decalogue Two*. This theme continues throughout *The Decalogue*, for instance just before Jacek's execution in *Five* we learn that Piotr and his wife have just had a child.

The choice of honoring marital commitment, and of an enduring love with a partner that is much deeper than erotic attachment, is also the theme of *Decalogue Nine*, "Thou shalt not covet thy neighbor's wife." The husband learns that he is impotent with no chance of recovery; his wife says she does not care, that she loves him and that they will manage. Even so, she has been having an affair — purely physical, with apparently little or no emotional content — and does not tell her husband about it. He discovers the affair, and is actually caught spying on his wife as she tells her lover she cannot continue to see him. (The theme of voyeurism, as we have seen, recurs frequently, and is, indeed, implicit throughout as we are caught up ourselves in the act of voyeurism, continually watching the characters.) A week earlier he had spied on them as well, but that time had seen them making love. After a very emotional scene she convinces him not to leave her. He agrees and they decide to adopt a child (always a sign of new life and possibility in *The Decalogue*). Through a complication in the plot he has reason to believe his wife is seeing her lover again, although she is not. He leaves her a suicide note and drives his bicycle off a broken bridge, the angel riding behind him and then looking on compassionately as he lies on the rocky ground, unconscious. He learns from the nurse in the hospital that his wife is home, she has returned prematurely from her trip; he has the nurse dial his number and place the receiver so he can talk; after hesitating, his distraught wife answers the phone, hearing his voice she says only, "God, you are there." He replies in the words of God in the Pentateuch, "I am." With these words of multiple meaning, *Decalogue Nine* ends.

Kieślowski has said that the commandment that each film is supposed to be about "is really not important,"[8] that some episodes could apply to more than one of the commandments. *Decalogue Nine*, for instance, could easily have been the subject of *Decalogue Six*, "Thou shalt not commit adultery," as could have *Decalogue Three*. And, indeed, this really attests to my thesis that what unites the series is not so much the Old Testament Decalogue as the New Testament commandment to love, which the gospels aver is the fulfillment of "the law and the prophets."[9] *Decalogue Three* also seems to have its provenance in a gospel story, specifically Jesus's healing on the Sabbath Day, and where—to counter the Pharisees' accusation—he asks, "Is it lawful to do good on the sabbath day, or to do evil? to save life, or to kill?"[10] It is Christmas Eve and Eva, abandoned by her husband three years earlier after she had been caught in adultery, is desperate and intends to commit suicide if she remains alone throughout the long night. She concocts a ruse to entice her former lover away from his family. Although not entirely a disinterested act of love, as he used to love Eva and perhaps to some degree still does, it is nonetheless clear that the happily married Janusz would much prefer to spend the holiday at home with his wife and family. Eva is reminiscent of Dorota in her propensity for destruction, and most of the evening consists of the two driving, often recklessly, around the cold barren streets of Warsaw. Janusz's spirit of love and giving is also symbolized by the Santa Claus suit and beard he wears in the opening scene when we first see him coming into the apartment building as Krzysztof from *Decalogue One* is going out; and is manifested not only in the time he gives to the suffering Eva, but also in the way he confronts a cruel guard in the drab "alcoholics' cell" where the two go searching for Eva's, so she says, missing husband. This scene also foreshadows the harrowing scene in the state execution facility in *Decalogue Five*. We see the incarcerated men naked, cruelly being sprayed with cold water by a sadistic guard, when Janusz with righteous indignation comes to their aid. He manages to stay with Eva until 7:00 A.M. and so she is able to go on. Instead of being home with his family celebrating this holiest of Sabbaths, he has done good and saved a life.

Decalogue Six, "Thou shalt not commit adultery," would actually seem to apply less to the commandment than *Two* or *Nine*, as neither of the two central characters is married. This is a powerful piece of storytelling, and indeed it is one of two sections that Kieślowski expanded and released as separate films, this one titled, *A Short Film about Love*. A nineteen-year-old boy named Tomek spends his evenings spying on his neighbor Magda, a promiscuous young artist who lives alone and frequently entertains men in her apartment. Although Tomek used to watch her having sex, he has since stopped; he continues to watch her obsessively with a telescope, but no longer when she is sexually engaged (and, therefore, he has ceased masturbating while he watches as well). As he watched Magda he grew to love her (just as we have grown to love Kieślowski's characters in our own act of watching) and he has suppressed or sublimated the sexual aspect of his love. Tomek's obsession goes beyond just watching; he manages to get a job delivering milk to her apartment early in the morning before he goes to his job at the post office; and he has been putting counterfeit notices in her mailbox so that she will come into the office where he works. When Magda discovers what he is up to she is at first angry, but soon she is more intrigued than upset. Magda confronts him one morning when he is delivering the milk, and Tomek confesses that he does not want to go to bed with her; in fact he wants nothing from her at all. But he does, after a few moments, muster up the courage to ask her to go for ice cream. After she says yes we see him, in a high angle shot from the window, practically dancing as he runs along swerving exuberantly with his milk cart. At this point he crosses the path of the angel. After their date they arrive back at Magda's apartment, Magda telling him that there is no such thing as love. She seduces him and he ejaculates almost immediately after she guides his hands up her thighs: "You see," she says, "that's all there is to love; now go to the bathroom and clean yourself off." After this humiliation Tomek storms out (we see him again from the same high angle shot as before), crosses paths with the angel, again, and once home slits his wrists.

Although the young woman's name is Magda in this version, when it was released as a separate film, expanded by about twenty-five minutes, the character is named Maria Magdalena. This simple name change impels the viewer to see the film as an allegory. If Magda is Mary Magdalene then Tomek must be Jesus Christ, which would explain the "non-sexual" and selfless nature of his love for her. In fact, Baugh believes that Tomek's act of volitional bloodletting should be understood as a sacrifice for Magda just as Jesus sacrificed himself on the cross for the real Mary Magdalene and for all humanity.[11] And indeed, Magda is transformed by the act. The Greek word for "repent" is *metanoeo*, a transformation of the mind, and this is what happens to Magda. The film at this point shifts from Tomek's obsession for Magda to Magda's obsession with Tomek. There are no scenes of Tomek in the hospital and we do not see him again until the very end of the film when Magda returns yet again to the post office to see if he has returned to work. He has returned, and when he tells her that he has got over his habit of peeping on her a look of great disappointment comes over Magda's face, and the movie ends.

It should be noted that there is a third important character in this film, Tomek's landlady, a maternal older woman who resents Magda's intrusion into her surrogate child's life and continually proves unhelpful when Magda seeks information about Tomek after his suicide attempt. There is a subtle Oedipal tension between the lodger and the older woman, which resonates with the theme of *Decalogue Four*. Yet it is unconscious and innocent, and the larger thematic point of the older woman in this film is the maternal love she offers the orphan Tomek; she is the spiritual mother of Tomek — and hence in this triangle can be likened to the other Mary in Jesus's life — and provides much needed love to him. Thus the vital importance of loving and nurturing children is implicit in this film as it is in so many of the other *Decalogue* films as well.

The other part of *The Decalogue* that Kieślowski expanded into its own feature film, *A Short Film about Killing*, is *Decalogue Five*, based on the commandment "Thou shalt not kill." While most of *The Decalogue* films revolve around two central characters, this one dramatizes the eventually intersecting lives of three disparate characters, each equally essential to plot and theme: a taxi driver, an alienated young man, and a recent graduate of law school. The story focuses on the young man's gratuitous and brutal murder of the taxi driver and his own equally brutal institutionalized murder by the state. Unlike more conventional filmmaking Kieślowski skips over the apprehension and trial of the killer, moving from the murder to the murderer's sentencing and execution.

As in the gospels, and in many of the other *Decalogue* films, our sympathy is directed to the troubled young sinner Jacek. We find out toward the end of the film that his favorite sister was run over by a tractor and killed by his friend after the two had been drinking. He has been wandering aimlessly around Warsaw ever since. He is intensely alone, confused, and alienated, and Kieślowski and the actor Miroslaw Baka capture this beautifully in a myriad of ways. His confused psyche is signaled when he asks if it is possible to tell from a photograph if someone is alive or not. While in a café Jacek sees two young girls watching him from the other side of the window; with his spoon he flicks some of his coffee at the window and the girls laugh with pleasure before walking away. This is the only moment in the entire film where we see Jacek smile; but the smile quickly fades as the girls recede, immediately replaced by an expression of the most profound estrangement. Jacek is always seen alone, internally framed or shot separately when he is with someone, and in this scene he is of course divided from the two young girls by the window.

Except for his horrifying murder, which Kieślowski does not mitigate in any way (at almost seven minutes it is supposedly "the longest murder scene in the history of cinema"[12]) the taxi driver is an unsympathetic character. He is selfish and unkind, even sadistic. When a young couple (Dorota and her husband from *Decalogue Two*) anxious to get out of the cold, approach him for a ride he tells them he is busy cleaning his car. While they are waiting he ogles an attractive young woman (girl, really) and then offers her a ride; she refuses and he leaves alone, abandoning the young couple who had been waiting. Later he throws the pearls of his wife's domestic love and care, half a sandwich she had made for him, to a stray dog, and we are put in mind of the aphorism from the Gospel of Matthew, "Do not give dogs what is sacred, do not throw your pearls to pigs, If you do they may trample them under their feet, and then turn and tear you to pieces."[13] Of course, he is torn to pieces, in a sense, as we will see shortly — and in fact the other half of the sandwich is eaten by Jacek after he commits the murder. Chance or fate plays a large roll in the cinema of Kieślowski, and here it must be acknowledged that had the taxi driver extended the simple courtesy of giving the young couple a ride he would not have been killed; the rest of his day would have followed a different pattern and he almost certainly would never have encountered Jacek. In another scene a man is helping an unsteady and certainly inebriated man to the taxi so that he can get home, and just before they get to the car the taxi driver drives off, much to the Good Samaritan's consternation. We also see him gleefully terrify a group of dogs with his horn as they pass before his car. There is always some degree of mystery in the question of why things happen the way they do, but in the metaphysics of this film it seems the taxi driver has fallen under the divine judgment of an angry God. One thing is certain — his selfishness and lack of kindness in some mysterious way leads him to his death.

The third lead character, a lawyer named Piotr, demonstrates charity and active love throughout. After he is unable to prevent the state from exacting its revenge on Jacek, and the prisoner is led away by guards after sentencing, he calls out to the doomed boy from a window, demonstrating compassion and a sense of common humanity by the simple act of calling the boy's name; later Jacek tells him that the gesture moved him to tears. Such actions, Kieślowski seems to suggest, may have the power to prevent such tragedies from happening in the first place; and in fact Kieślowski has acknowledged that one of his motives for making *Decalogue Five* and *A Short Film about Killing* was to express his sense of Poland as a "world where people don't have any pity for each other, a world where they hate each other, a world where they not only don't help but get in each other's way. A world where they repel each other. A world of people living alone."[14] Piotr exemplifies *caritas*, the predominant characteristic of the Jewish rabbi from Nazareth, and the only available means of healing a broken world.

The last part of the film takes place in the prison before the execution, ending with the execution itself. Jacek asks to see Piotr, who comes to him in his cell. He tells the lawyer the sad story of his sister's death, asking him to retrieve and bring to his mother a picture of his sister that he left with a photographer to have enlarged. When the guard asks a second time if the lawyer is done yet, Piotr angrily asserts that he will never say he is done. At the chief's instruction the guard terminates their conversation, calling his men to bring out the prisoner. This scene and the execution itself are profoundly disturbing. Eight guards brusquely manhandle Jacek as they lead him out of his cell; and in a bizarre scene of just a few seconds duration one of the technicians of death draws the rope down with a demonic intensity. While Jacek has a last cigarette the chief seems bored, perhaps impatient to get back to the coffee we saw him enjoying in a previous scene. In a sense this institutional murder is more inhumane than Jacek's, even if the state can assert at least a putative reason for its killing while Jacek's was a desperate act with no apparent motive. Kieślowski indicts a society that remains indifferent to human suffering, and an institution that punishes those who have already suffered more than anyone ever should.

Decalogue Five is an exploration of evil. The area around the apartment complex looks even more like a wasteland then it had in previous episodes; Kieślowski's cinematographer for *Five*, Slawomir Idziak, used pale green filters to create a sickly color tone; there is little vegetation seen, and none at all in the muddy hell where the taxi driver throws his food to the dog. We do not know why the taxi driver is cruel; we only see his callous attitude and his sadistic sense of humor as he drives around the bleak city. Jacek as well wanders around Warsaw indifferent to the cruelty he sees (he walks indifferently away as two boys beat someone in an alley) while adding himself to the harsh cityscape himself with his own cruel behavior (he pushes a young man he thinks is eying him with prurient intent into a urinal). Yet the object we most associate with the taxi driver is a devil's head that hangs from his rear view mirror, the camera slowly zooming in to close range at one point as the demonic icon dangles ominously. The object we associate with Jacek, besides the rope he uses as a murder weapon, is the picture of his sister that he carries around with him. Just before he is taken off to die, he wonders if things might have been different had his sister lived. He is able to love, at least one person, even if she is no longer there for him; and it is this love, and the love shown to him by Piotr, that redeems him.

I had said that the execution is the final scene, but there is one final shot, a sort of coda. In a beautiful meadow by a forest, perhaps where Jacek's sister was killed, we see a bright intensely shining otherworldly light in the distance; the camera holds on it for a number of seconds before slowly panning to Piotr, vehemently decrying over and over, "I abhor it! I abhor it!" And with this mysterious light, and this expression of revolt, *Decalogue Five* ends.

The Decalogue is a dark film, anatomizing a broken world and its broken, suffering occupants with steadfast honesty. Yet it is a film that is unrelenting in its search for transcendence. *Decalogue Five* is surely one of the darkest in a series of dark films, yet the final image we are left with clearly intimates that "the light shines in the darkness, and the darkness has not overcome it."[15] In every episode we get glimpses of this spiritual light, somehow inextinguishable. The doctor in *Two*, having lived through the most destructive war in human history and losing everything he most loved, somehow manages to emerge from his cocoon-like existence, helping and nurturing life where he can. The theme of *Two* is resurrection, most saliently epitomized in the miraculous recovery of the husband, but also in a bee that struggles successfully to emerge from a syrupy glass and a plant that will not die, emerging slowly to an upright position after Dorota attempts to smother it.

The philosophy professor Zophia in *Eight* also lived through the war, and for forty years has felt responsible for the probable death of a Jewish child that she was unable to take in. (She had been tipped off, falsely, that one of her associates was a spy.) Her husband died shortly after the war and her own son has no interest in her anymore, yet she refuses to relinquish her sense of an ultimate scale of values in the world, evident in the profound sense of responsibility she has for her students and the great care with which she manages her own life. *Eight* beautifully shows the reconciliation and growing friendship of Zophia and Elzbieta, the child she could not save, now a grown woman living in America. But Kieślowski never evades the pain and ambiguity of life. In the last ten minutes of the film he introduces another character, the associate mentioned above, who has been unable to similarly recover from the trauma of the war years. The commandment this film explores is "Thou shalt not bear false witness against thy neighbor," and this man, we learn, had been falsely accused of being a Gestapo spy and sent to prison after the war, even as he risked his life to save others as an active member of the Underground. Elzbieta wants to thank him for risking his life to save her, but he is unable to even talk about it. As she finally gives up and leaves, we see him watching her and Zophia through the window as they talk outside, demonstrating their affection through physical contact (a motif in this episode) and a warm attentiveness to one another. Perhaps even to witness such strength and evident spiritual growth (again, the watching and knowing theme) is enough to turn someone in a more hopeful direction. Earlier Zophia had told Elzbieta of her theistic philosophy, and later that same night she had seen Elzbieta (whom she had invited to stay the night with her) praying in her son's bedroom. Film scholar Joseph Kickasola has said that Kieślowski is always searching for "ultimate reality amid the bewildering uncertainties of postmodernity,"[16] and without ever evading life's difficulties or acquiescing to the spiritual nostrums so commonplace in our world, he finds glimmers of transcendence and ultimate reality in the faith, hope, and love of his struggling, conscientious characters.

The Decalogue opens in the cold gray of a bitter winter and moves steadily toward spring, reinforcing the theme of resurrection. *Eight* opens with a close-up of two hands clasped and moving along together on a beautiful spring day, an adult and a child, and the whole episode takes place in a similar setting; for the first time we see foliage and a lake that is not frozen, the wasteland by some miraculous power utterly transformed. Likewise the final two episodes take place in the temperate months, and are also about reconciliation. *Ten*, the last of the series, is the only episode that is clearly a comedy. Two brothers, Artur and Jerzy — the former the lead singer of a punk rock band called City Death and the latter a respectable suburban family man — have not seen each other for two years, and are reunited after the death of their father. The film opens with the bourgeois Jerzy attending one of his bohemian brother's concerts to tell him of their father's passing. As Artur performs during the credit sequence and Jerzy moves closer to the stage trying to get his attention, we hear the words to the City Death song diegetically: "Kill, kill, kill / Screw who you will / Lust and crave / Pervert and deprave / Everyday of the week / Everyday of the week / On Sunday hit mother / Hit father, hit brother / Hit sister, the weakest / And steal from the meekest / 'Cos everything is yours / Yeah, everything's yours." It seems to me these lyrics and this opening sequence provide a number of tactical purposes: It sets the tone for this final episode as comic, and provides an ironic context to a film about the Ten Commandments; but it also demonstrates that the postmodern era has totally subverted the ethos of the Ten Commandments; we live in an age where self-indulgence and personal lawlessness are actually encouraged, usually in the interests of a consumer-based society, which invites speculation on another irony: self-indulgence is encouraged under the stamp of personal liberation while actually enforcing the new status quo of material culture and strengthening the power base of capitalist society's new ruling class. I write this from the perspective of a citizen of the capitalist US, but it should be noted that Kieślowski and his co-writer Krzysztof Piesiewicz wrote their script with the anticipation that it would play to an extra-national audience, and they deliberately muted anything that would single it out as a film specifically about

Poland; and it also worth pointing out that Poland was on the verge of moving to a capitalist society itself when this film was made (and in episode *Four* our eye is continually directed to a huge poster advertising Winston cigarettes on the bedroom wall of the film's teenage heroine Anka). The opening sequence to *Ten*, "Thou shalt not covet thy neighbor's goods," could not be more fitting.

The episode centers on the brothers discovering that their father, whom they were both estranged from, had in his possession a stamp collection worth millions of zloty. (Incidentally, we see the father briefly in episode *Eight*, when he stops by Zophia's apartment to show her a rare pair of stamps.) In fact, we learn that it was his obsession with stamps—his own covetousness—that destroyed his family. Even as the brothers muse on the question of why some people are so concerned with acquiring things, they are unwittingly overcome with covetousness themselves. Before learning of the collection's value Jerzy had given a couple of the stamps to his son, who had then traded them. The humor of the piece is generated by the lengths the brothers will go to get the stamps back, as well as their desire to add another valuable stamp to the collection. In other words, rather than be satisfied with inheriting a valuable collection it merely makes them covetous for more, which is, of course, the nature of greed: the more one gets the more one wants. They add additional security to the apartment and go on a mad chase for the lost series of stamps, while the hilarious culmination of all this has Jerzy agreeing to undergo the removal of a kidney, which he will then trade for a stamp they are desperate to acquire. While the operation is being performed their father's apartment is robbed and they are both, for all their pains, left with nothing at all. After the operation and the discovery of the theft each brother begins to suspect the other. Both brothers are obviously ashamed of their suspicion, and the scene in a cafe where Jerzy confesses his suspicion to a detective is a tour de force of comic acting by Jerzy Stuhr, the actor playing Jerzy; shot close-up, and with a multitude of conflicting emotions registering on his face, Jerzy's shame is palpable. This scene is followed by Artur confessing his identical suspicion to the same detective. Finally they confess their shameful action to one another, and the film ends with laughter and reconciliation.

The Decalogue is a monumental artistic achievement. While each short film is a little masterpiece in itself and may be watched alone, they are held together as a unified work of art by the apartment complex where these characters live, by the brief reappearances its denizens make in later episodes, as well as by the regular appearance of the angel, and the thematic structuring around the Ten Commandments. Kickasola is surely right in viewing the apartment complex as a "universal microcosm," and seeing the fleeting appearances of characters from previous episodes as a reminder of the marvelous unknown stories that are encapsulated in the human beings we see all around us every day.[17] Filmed shortly after the cessation of Martial Law and shortly before the Solidarity Movement and a Polish Pope by the name of John Paul II helped bring an end to Communism, the film resonates more powerfully for leaving the specific political realities of late 1980s Poland out of the picture. And while *The Decalogue* works on multiple levels, it is impossible to deny the profoundly Christian resonances throughout. Each individual film contributes in some way to an affirmation of the greater commandment that is necessary for the fulfillment of them all. And this is one reason the film has so much to say to us today, when it sometimes seems that dark forces—and this need not necessarily imply anything more sinister than the concentrated power of organized greed—have co-opted Christianity and turned it into its opposite. For it is hard to believe that Christianity— the religion of such aphoristic masterpieces as, "Again I tell you, it is easier for a camel to go through the eye of a needle than for a rich man to enter the kingdom of God"[18]— is, with a straight face, claimed as the religion of so many millionaires and billionaires, as well as those who would like to join their ranks; millionaires and billionaires who, incidentally, turn their faces way away from and, therefore, refuse to see and know the suffering many.

Kieślowski's theology is radical, as I announce in the title to this essay, not because he is himself in any way a theological radical, but rather because it resembles in every way the theology of Jesus, which is there for all to read in the gospels. The command to "love your neighbor as yourself," especially when extended to our enemies, is the most radical exhortation ever to issue from the lips of a prophet, and is antithetical in every way to the so-called "Christianity" of the many power brokers and their deluded subjects who are waging an all-out war against the poor and vulnerable that Jesus came to save. If what Jesus is recorded to have said in Matthew 25:31–46 is true, some of those same power brokers—modern day Pharaohs, enslaving their brothers and sisters—may have a very unwelcome surprise waiting for them after their departure from this world.

Notes

1. C.S. Lewis, *Mere Christianity* (New York: Macmillan, 1952) 9–10.
2. Matthew 22:37–40. See also Luke 10:26–28. I am quoting from the King James Version, which unless otherwise noted I will use throughout. The capitals are in the original.
3. Luke 10:29–37.
4. Karl Barth, *The Epistle to the Romans*, trans. Edwyn C. Hoskyns (London: Oxford University Press, 1933) 494. The emphases are Barth's.
5. Lloyd Baugh, "*The Decalogue* Films of Krzysztof Kieślowski: The Essentially Christian World-View of an Atheist," 5. This essay is from a keynote lecture that Baugh delivered in 2006 at a seminar in Barcelona entitled "Ten Years Without Kieślowski, Ten Hours with Kieślowski," and can be found online at http://www.signis.net/IMG/pdf/Kieślowski_Lloyd_Baugh_en.pdf.

6. "Above all, love each other deeply, because love covers over a multitude of sin" (1 Peter 4:8, New International Version).
7. Annette Insdorf, *Double Lives, Second Chances: The Cinema of Krzysztof Kieślowski* (New York: Miramax Books, 1999) 44.
8. Quoted in Insdorf 71.
9. Matthew 22:40.
10. Mark 3:4.
11. Baugh 9.
12. In 1993, anyway, according to "an expert on horror films." *Kieślowski on Kieślowski*, ed. Danusia Stok (London: Faber and Faber, 1993) 162.
13. Matthew 7:6, New International Version.
14. *Kieślowski on Kieślowski* 160.
15 John 1:5, English Standard Version.
16 Joseph G. Kickasola, *The Films of Krzysztof Kieślowski: The Liminal Image* (New York: Continuum, 2004) xii.
17 Kickasola 238.
18 Matthew 19:24, New International Version.

Works Cited

Barth, Karl. *The Epistle to the Romans*. Trans. Edwyn C. Hoskyns. London: Oxford University Press, 1933.
Baugh, Lloyd. "*The Decalogue* Films of Krzysztof Kieślowski: The Essentially Christian WorldView of an Atheist." "Ten Years without Kieślowski, Ten Hours with Kieślowski." Web. Accessed July 27, 2012. http://www.signis.net/IMG/pdf/Kieślowski_Lloyd_Baugh_en.pdf.
The Decalogue. Dir. Krzysztof Kieślowski. Writ. Krzysztof Kieślowski and Krzysztof Piesiewicz. DVD. Facets Home Video. 2003.
Insdorf, Annette. *Double Lives, Second Chances: The Cinema of Krzysztof Kieślowski*. New York: Miramax Books, 1999. 44.
Kickasola, Joseph G. *The Films of Krzysztof Kieślowski: The Liminal Image*. New York: Continuum, 2004. xii.
Kieślowski on Kieślowski. Ed. Danusia Stok. London: Faber and Faber, 1993. 162.
Lewis, C.S. *Mere Christianity*. New York: Macmillan, 1952. 9–10.

Fanaticism and Familicide from Wieland to The Shining

DARA DOWNEY

In an isolated setting in rural America, a close-knit family group finds their claustrophobic relationships disintegrating with alarming rapidity, as preternatural voices push the father of the family closer and closer to a murderous frenzy that, all too inevitably, erupts in the form of a violence that is devastating in its effects and sickeningly intimate in its choice of victims.

Due at least in part to its sheer cultural visibility, this brief description will, for many, immediately evoke *The Shining*, not merely Stephen King's 1977 novel, but also the texts it has directly spawned: Stanley Kubrick's iconic film from 1980 (often voted the scariest film of all time); the more "faithful" 1997 television mini-series directed by Mick Garris; and, arguably most successfully, *The Simpsons*' 1994 parody *The Shinning* (in the Halloween special "Treehouse of Horror V").

What is perhaps less widely recognized, however, is the extent to which the basic plot outlined above pervades and persists within American culture, popular and otherwise; indeed, it can be traced back to before the nineteenth century and forward to the beginning of the twenty-first — with variations, of course, but largely unchanged in its central elements. America is — at least ostensibly — a country founded upon utopian democratic principles, where the family unit was encouraged to supply the gap in authority created by the rejection of monarchical or otherwise tyrannical systems of government.[1] It is, therefore, perhaps unsurprising that a recurrent trope in popular culture should revolve around the anxiety that the family itself might come to mirror a tyrannical state, complete with despotic monarch in the form of the all-powerful father.[2]

What is surprising is the manner in which the texts that have extended and perpetuated this trope — specifically, Charles Brockden Brown's *Wieland; or, the Transformation: An American Tale*, from 1798, one of the earliest American Gothic novels; John Neal's short story "Idiosyncrasies" (1843); King's *The Shining*; and Bill Paxton's film *Frailty* (2002) — repeatedly spectralize this violently patriarchal figure, a move which might appear to function as a means of figuratively reducing and containing his frightening and anti-democratic power. However, it is here that what is arguably the source text — Brown's *Wieland* — becomes most important, particularly its engagement with the tendency in eighteenth-century theology to malign the body in favor of the spirit. In *Wieland*, the first-person narrator, Clara Wieland, becomes increasingly spectralized and invisible to the narrative gaze that she herself wields as she narrates the horrific events that befall her extended family as a result of her brother's religious fanaticism. In the later manifestations of the trope, by contrast, father figures inflict potentially divinely, satanically or otherwise supernaturally inspired violence upon their immediate family groups, and first-person narrators or writer figures are transformed into haunting presences. Here, however, significantly, the narrative positions of murderous authority and spectral author are occupied by the same character.[3] Consequently, they ignore *Wieland*'s critique of an (arguably) essentially Calvinistic but enduring manifestation of the patriarchal gaze, one which seeks to reify both body and soul, and subsequently to destroy the former in order to reveal and release the latter. More troublingly, the power over representation (and from there, as I shall argue, over the destiny of others) and invulnerability that Clara wields is transferred to the very figures whose fatherly tyranny is most antithetical to America's alleged post–Enlightenment ideals, and authority is therefore placed back in the hands of those most determined to recreate monarchical abuses within the context of the nuclear family.

In many ways, *The Shining* — particularly King's novel — serves as the most typical illustrative example of this process. It focuses primarily on the actions and psychological processes of Jack Torrance, a writer of fiction and former alcoholic who functions both as the protagonist and, ultimately, the central human villain of the book. As the book opens, Jack has been fired from his position as a high school English teacher for violently assaulting a student, leaving him all but unable to support his young family and struggling against both the overwhelming urge to drink and crippling writer's block and his tendency to lash out when angry, which results on one occasion in his breaking his son Danny's arm. When he accepts a job as winter caretaker of the isolated mountain-top Overlook Hotel in Colorado, Danny and his

Jack Nicholson as Jack Torrance in Stanley Kubrick's *The Shining* (1980, Warner Bros.): The family man as demonic killer.

wife, Wendy, join him there in an effort to heal the growing rifts between them. Gradually, the supernatural presences that haunt the hotel persuade him that murdering his family will allow him to restore his eroded masculinity. As Jack's sanity crumbles, he's drawn further and further into the bloodsoaked fantasy world that permeates the hotel, becoming increasingly convinced that the murders will gain him a promotion of some kind within the hotel's spectral "management" system. With his position as breadwinner and patriarchal head of the family under threat, violence against those over whom he no longer feels he has sufficient authority presents itself as a means of rectifying the situation.

Beyond this, what links *The Shining* to the other texts I will be discussing in this essay is its conceptualization of human subjectivity and physicality. The catastrophic events of the novel are catalyzed by the presence of Jack's son Danny, who has considerable psychic gifts, mainly in the form of telepathy and precognition. Only once he is dead can the hotel absorb this power, taking Danny's psychic essence into itself to join the host of spirits already trapped there. What is more, Jack's own corporeal status is less than stable throughout the novel. This is first insinuated when Wendy, recalling the events that led up to his dismissal from the teaching post, feels that, following a particularly heavy bout of drinking and an unnerving car accident, "he had been replaced by some unearthly doppelgänger that she would never know or be quite sure of."[4] This figurative evocation of his uncanniness becomes rather more literal at the very end, when he dies in a conflagration that destroys the hotel (due to his neglect of his caretaker duties), and, it is to be assumed, is subsumed into the Overlook's community of malign specters. Kubrick's film goes so far as to render this explicit following his death, his smiling face appears within a group photograph of hotel staff, a monument to his own violent obedience to the hotel's ghostly urgings.[5]

This, as I shall argue, is not merely the once-off invention of a supernatural horror writer, but mirrors the denigration of the body and glorification of the soul that informed much eighteenth- and nineteenth-century Protestant thinking about death and the afterlife. Moreover, these three elements— patriarchal violence, the privileging of the spirit over the body, and the spectralization of writer figures—which are linked only by contiguity in *The Shining*, become inextricably bound up with one another in *Wieland*, "Idiosyncrasies," and *Frailty*. Where Jack is simply a protagonist who writes fiction, the narrative power of the father figures in these texts is further emphasized by the fact that each features a first-person narrator who controls the shape of the storytelling process itself.

A socio-cultural issue, a theological doctrine, and a figurative trope respectively, these textual motifs might seem to be strange bedfellows. In order to explain their rhythmically repetitious appearance together throughout American literature and popular culture over the course of two centuries and more, it is necessary to go back to an early example of American horror fiction—Brown's *Wieland*, a succinct and disturbing work set in the early days of the American Republic—in which the narrator, Clara Wieland, is subjected to one source of emotional trauma after another. When her brother, Theodore Wieland—who has killed the rest of the family and attempted to murder her—kills himself in front of her, she feels that she can take no more of horror or grief, and tells the reader,

> The body of Wieland was removed from my presence, and they supposed that I would follow it; but no, my home is ascertained; here I have taken up my rest, and never will I go hence, till, like Wieland, I am borne to my grave.
> Importunity was tried in vain: they threatened to remove me by violence— nay, violence was used; but my soul prizes too dearly this little roof to endure to be bereaved of it.[...]
> They besought me—they remonstrated—they appealed to every duty that connected me with him that made me, and with my fellow-men—in vain. While I live I will not go hence.
> [...]
> I will eat—I will drink—I will lie down and rise up at your bidding—all I ask

is the choice of my abode.[...] Shortly will I be at peace. This is the spot which I have chosen in which to breathe my last sigh.[6]

The point at which she writes these words, in a letter to unnamed "friends" of which the novel claims to be a transcript, is the crisis of a book that is largely made up of crises, or at least of the succession of one bizarre and unsettling incident after another. For there is much of the bizarre in *Wieland*, from ventriloquism and elaborately engineered deception to spontaneous human combustion, religious fanaticism and the murder-suicide mentioned above. As so eclectic a list of fictional occurrences might suggest, and as critics have insisted almost since it was published, coherence and clarity are not the principles by which the text operates—far from it.[7] The novel spends much time telling us that authority of any kind is a slippery thing; that totalizing interpretations are contingent at best and dangerous at worst; and that effects do not follow automatically from causes, actions, motives, or intentions.[8] Rather, in the imaginative universe it sets up, chaos appears to rule all things, and no character—let alone the reader—is capable of predicting accurately what will be the outcome of his or her words, thoughts, desires or actions.[9] Indeed, attempting to do so repeatedly has disastrous consequences, not only for those directly involved, but also for those connected to them by ties of affection and blood.

What the passage above articulates is an attempt on Clara's part, however abortive, to transform herself into the one fixed or stable point in the whole narrative, effectively to haunt, while still alive, the place where the greatest disaster of her life has occurred. Moreover, this spectralization is in fact the culmination of her effective invisibility and bodilessness throughout the novel, made possible, I would argue, by her position as first-person narrator. This position allows her to complicate and obscure her status as narrative object, both in terms of her physical appearance (of which we know almost nothing) and her character itself—in other words, to employ the narrative gaze in a way that permits her to elude the narrativizing gazes of those around her. This is turn helps her to resist the dangerous operations of authority, and specifically the drive towards pinning her down both visually and epistemologically that consumes the men in her life. Doing so makes it possible for her to escape the very literal violence wreaked by her brother—who believes himself to be performing God's will—upon almost every other living member of their second-generation American family.

What is more, Clara's evasion of the gaze goes hand-in-hand with the novel's sustained critique of the theological rejection of the physical form. It places far more narrative weight than does *The Shining* on the use of this doctrine as a means of legitimating, even advocating, violence against the physical body. By extension, the novel can be read as a critique of untrammeled male power, unlike the later texts discussed here, which, by conflating the spectralized (and, therefore, invulnerable) narrator figure with murderous father figures, covertly uphold the very patriarchal, religiously (or supernaturally) motivated authority that they ostensibly establish as dangerous and frightening.

* * *

Brown's *Wieland* revolves around an almost incestuously close family group who enjoy considerable privileged seclusion on an estate in rural Pennsylvania, and whose interpersonal affections are often depicted explicitly in terms of mutual idolatry, a blasphemous worship of the human, the physical, and the mundane. When, however, the apparent harmony of their domestic arrangements is broken by the intrusion of Francis Carwin, a mysterious, grotesque but erudite and strangely attractive figure with the gift of throwing his voice and mimicking those of others, this idolatry rapidly descends into an appalling and violent iconoclasm on the part of Clara's brother, Theodore. Misunderstandings caused by the misuse of Carwin's gift destroy the security of their relationships, and seem finally to spur Wieland into a religious frenzy of ultimate self-sacrifice that leaves all but the narrator Clara and her brother-in-law dead, though Wieland's murderous rampage could equally be interpreted as the result of either insanity or supernatural interference.

Theodore, at any rate, believes himself to be in direct communication with the divine, and the intimations regarding his idiosyncratic religious convictions give the reader some (but not much) prior warning of what is to come. To a certain extent, the reader is dissuaded from drawing too close an analogy between the sketchily drawn but devastatingly compulsive theological attitudes displayed by Theodore Wieland and those of seventeenth-century New England Puritans.[10] Much space is devoted at the opening of the novel to explaining that he, and his father before him, practice a form of religious rigor which forbids them to follow any creed or doctrine other than that which the elder Wieland has imbibed from a "hasty" but strictly conceived reading of a Camissard tract, through which he then interprets the Bible itself. We are told that, based on his reading, he "allied himself with no sect, because he perfectly agreed with none" (Brown, 11). Nevertheless, the rigidly applied beliefs which seem to lead to the elder Wieland being burnt to death by some demonic or heavenly agent in the little temple he has built himself for solitary prayer, and which lead ultimately to the younger Wieland's slaughter of his family, do seem to be founded upon principles which bear some superficial resemblance to Calvinistic or Puritan thinking in general. They certainly bear a close resemblance to what Barbara Judson cautiously dubs "'Puritan' habits of agonized introspection."[11]

Essentially, these habits become entrenched because an individual who adheres to extreme Calvinistic Protestantism "is called upon to make clear choices in his life but at the same time he is forbidden to regard these acts as self-induced. They are attributed either to the grace of God or else to the temptations of Satan," and the adherent must continually scrutinize his or her thoughts and actions in the hope that it is the former, and the fear that it might be the latter.[12] Consequently, "the Puritan consciousness not only suffered from insecurity but [...] actively cultivated insecurity, being acutely aware that its inner light could prove delusive, its conviction of virtue a symptom of the heart's perversion."[13] Since what is at stake is no less than the future of one's immortal soul, and the status of one's innermost self, vigilance over the self, and over others, who may either be lost to sin or have been awarded honors which one can never attain for oneself, is constant, urgent, and anxiety-driven. Carol Margaret Davidson asserts that the result is "a sense of division that engenders acute anxiety, paranoia and persecution" as the world becomes "an ever-shifting, sign-filled domain of uncertainty where God the Father is unpredictable and an ineluctably mysterious withholder of truth."[14]

At the same time, as *Wieland* highlights grimly, the possibility always remains that the opposite effect may occur — that when an individual becomes convinced that he or she has somehow gained access to this ultimate truth, the result can be enormous arrogance and a sense of supreme authority. Indeed, the entire system encourages individuals to assume simultaneously that they know nothing and everything about themselves. As John Calvin himself put it, because "Simple knowledge may exist in man, as it were shut up," and hidden both from the world at large and from one's own conscious self, the conscience "is set over him as a kind of sentinel to observe and spy out all his secrets, that nothing may remain buried in darkness."[15] The individual is therefore at once utterly ignorant and enjoined to seek to be omniscient, not only about him- or herself but about others in the immediate community. It is this that later Unitarian and Universalist theologians saw as one of the most dangerous elements of Puritanism and creeds like it. Denouncing as a form of madness and melancholy a belief that one has been divinely inspired, spoken to and admitted to the holy presence, Charles Chauncy cautioned that those under the influence of religious enthusiasm are capable of wild and dangerous acts, and are extremely unpredictable. Worse still, they tend to "disregard [...] the Dictates of *reason*," considering their special status to place them "above the force of argument."[16]

As an extension of this, as Michael J. Colacurcio argues, Puritanism was "a sect which reified the private self by advertising its vices most unremittingly[...]."[17] In other words, it elevated the "inside" of the self to such giddy heights of spiritual importance that it sought to bring it "outside," to render the flesh invisible and the soul available for all to see, either in its purity or its depravity. In *Wieland*, the sense of self-importance, of power over both one's own spiritual standing and that of others that this form of Protestantism encourages, causes precisely this erosion of the perceived ontological status of the flesh. Most devastatingly, the juxtaposition of the elevation of the soul and the vilification of the body erupts in the novel as physical violence. In particular, the men in the family seem to have internalized the doctrine that denigrated bodily existence as an unhealthy clinging to the mortal trappings of this world, and as an implicit rejection of the promised glory of the next, an attitude that pervaded Puritan (and generally Protestant) thinking in eighteenth-century America. Drawing upon 2 Corinthians 5:6–8, which states that "while we are at home in the body, we are absent from the Lord,"[18] Robert Bolton, an English Puritan, wrote in 1635 of how we should not forget that

> thy body, when the soule is gone, will be an horrour to all that behold it; a most loathesome and abhorred spectacle. Those that loved it most, cannot now finde in their hearts to looke on't, by reason of the griefly deformedness which death will put upon it. Down it must into a pit of carions and confusion, covered with wormes, not able to wag so much as a little finger, to remoove the vermine that feed and gnaw upon its flesh; and so moulder away into rottennesse and dust[...]. [W]hen the soule departs this life, it carries nothing away with it, but grace, Gods favour, and a good conscience.[19]

That this sentiment was transported largely undamaged across the Atlantic by the Founding Fathers and took firm root in American soil is testified to by John Collins' assertion in 1721, "Death is only sweetened to us as we can look upon it our priviledge; as an out-let from sin and misery, and an in-let to *Glory* both in Holiness and Happiness."[20] Specifically, to leave the world was not merely to abandon a hopelessly godless locale, but to free oneself finally from the "meaningless husk" of a body in which each of us is entombed during our lifetime.[21] Even in the latter half of the nineteenth century, little had changed in terms of such attitudes, apart from an increased emphasis upon the sentimental longing for the dear departed, and the complete absence of any enthusiasm for the gorier aspects of death.[22] As Thomas Baldwin Thayer remarked in the consolatory text, *Over the River*, in 1864,

> the body is the tabernacle, or tent, in which the spirit takes up its abode while on its journey to the promised land; and when this mortal habitation is dissolved, when the *tent* is struck by Death, then the soul is clothed upon with the immortal, and enters into its heavenly *house*, the building of God, where, its pilgrimage ended, it will dwell rejoicingly forevermore!
>
> [...] Here everything is transient, changing, temporary — there everything is permanent, fixed and final.[23]

Essentially, this form of dichotomous thinking, which rigidly divides not only life from death, but eternal soul from decaying, obscuring and imprisoning body, underpins much American early religious belief, and forms the basis for the Wieland patriarchs' attitudes towards those most dear to them. Although it could not be said that the family, whose large farm has been made possible by slave labor and commercial success, spurn material luxuries, it is evident that both men value the rewards of heaven far above earthly ones, and are haunted by a conviction that they should subordinate all mundane objects, passions and even people to their efforts to remain on a positive footing with the celestial realm.

While it is strongly hinted that the spontaneous combustion of the elder Wieland one night while alone in his temple is divine punishment for his refusal to do precisely that — to sacrifice his family's lives in order to prove the worthiness of his own immortal soul — his son is far more willing to put his inherited theological convictions into practice. Indeed, he does so with a zeal and efficiency that is chilling in its assumption that death is preferable to life, even (or rather particularly) for those who he loves unconditionally and upon whose happiness his own is dependent. Systematically killing first his wife Catharine, and then his four children and teenage ward Louisa Conway, before trying to kill Clara, he believes himself to be following the irresistible dictates of a divine voice — the very same, it is intimated, that was heard by his deceased father, and possibly also by a grandfather, who ended his life by throwing himself off a cliff in England in response to what seemed to be the demands of an unseen interlocutor. The very model of Chauncy's dangerous religious enthusiast, both by his actions and his words, Wieland shows himself to be in agreement with the doctrine of despising the flesh. Indeed, he is convinced that he has proven himself to be liberated from any selfish desire to keep his loved ones alive, rather than sacrificing them for the sake of demonstrating his "'faith and [his] obedience'" to the divine, which he has "'burnt with ardour to approve[...]'" (Brown, 151).

In the transcript of his trial that Clara reads during her recovery from the illness into which the horrific experiences plunge her, Wieland recounts hearing what he believes to be the voice of the Almighty commanding him to kill his wife. He rejoices that the opportunity of just such a proof has finally been given to him. When the deed is done, it becomes clear to him (whether through further divine revelation or his own faulty reasoning we are left to guess) that to fail to do the same for the rest of his family would be to fail outright in his demonstration of faith. In the wake of the murders, having been thwarted by Carwin's timely intercession in his efforts to add his sister to the list of his victims, he kills himself, possibly because it seems, briefly, as if Carwin himself is the all-too human origin of the voices he heard. Due to the text's failure — or refusal — to provide clear motivating factors, explanations or psychological insights, however, it remains equally possible to read Theodore's suicide as motivated by his certainty that he will be following his loved ones into the great beyond, thus demonstrating once and for all his carelessness for life — even his own.

When one considers the Calvinist attitude towards not only the body but also visual images more generally, this perilous slippage from belief to violence becomes more than the mere product of a disordered psyche. Using the war against the Pequot tribe and the persecution of the rebellious Puritan Anne Hutchinson as examples, Ann Kibbey asserts that seventeenth- and eighteenth-century America was marked by a "profound synthesis of religion and prejudice in the perception of material shapes." She argues that "the Puritan belief in the necessity and righteousness of deliberate physical harm was deeply indebted to the ideology of Protestant iconoclasm in Renaissance Europe" to the extent that the "violent destruction of artistic images of people developed into a mandate for sacrosanct violence of human beings[...]."[24] This commitment to iconoclasm, as practiced by the Wieland patriarchs, can be seen not only as partaking of this violence against the physical, the visual, and the material, but as implying that to be the object of idolatry is to be placed in mortal danger. In other words, a rejection of the material, and specifically the worship of images created by human hands, has its logical extension in a direct repudiation and destruction of those images, and from there slides all too easily into literal violence against the materiality of the body itself.

What also becomes clear, however, is the extent to which the descriptive act itself, and particularly idolatrous descriptions imputing divinity to human beings, is represented by the novel as a form of conceptual violence. This is made particularly evident through the figure of Henry Pleyel, the brother of Theodore's wife, a "champion of intellectual liberty, [who] rejected all guidance but that of his reason" (23), and whose hyper-rational skepticism is directly opposed to, but as rigid and as stringently applied, as the younger Wieland's religious fanaticism. He too is subjected to censure by the text, harshly critical as it is of attempts to impose artificial order upon the chaotic world it conjures up.[25] Pleyel's advocacy of the accuracy of sensory data, and sensory data alone, leads him to misinterpret the apparently supernatural voices which Carwin produces. The dangerous limitations of Pleyel's devotion to empiricism becomes all too clear when Carwin, delighted to have the opportunity to fool someone of such intellectual stature, mimics Clara's voice, leading her brother-in-law and future husband to believe that she has given herself sexually to the evidently lower-class and potentially criminal stranger. Confronting her, unable to imagine that his senses may have deceived him, he exclaims, "'O wretch!—thus exquisitely fashioned—on whom nature seemed to have exhausted all her graces; with charms so awful and so pure! how art thou fallen! From what height fallen!'" (94).

It is here that the similarity—even the identity—emerges between Pleyel's attitude towards Clara and her brother's, in that both are predicated upon a conviction that she will continue to conform to their carefully constructed mental image of her as a quasi-divine being. Indeed, theirs is merely a slightly more extreme version of a habit that pervades the entire microcosmic community that inhabits the novel. Clara's sister-in-law Catherine, is, Clara tells us, Wieland's "angel." Wieland himself is described by his uncle as delivering his confession with "a tranquility of majesty, which denoted less of humanity than of godhead" (149). Even Clara's servant Judith explicitly admits that she cannot help but "worship" her practically "divine" mistress, who her brother apostrophizes as "'Thou angel whom I was wont to worship!'" (205). Unified and strongly held as these opinions might appear, in every case, the worship of the heavenly in human shape is transformed with little difficulty into a horror of the demonic, in a dichotomy inextricable from Puritan thinking. Both the jury in his trial and Clara herself see Wieland as being possessed by or himself a devil or fiend. Carwin, whose voice and manner initially bewitch and fascinate Clara, is loaded with the same epithets on numerous occasions, and she admits towards the end of the novel to being incapable of ascertaining whether he is "black as hell or bright as angel [...]" (212). Pleyel, however, is troubled by no such inability to decide, and laments that having committed "'so consummate, so frightful a depravity,'" she has fallen prey to a "'ruin so complete—so unheard of'" that there is now a "'cursed stain'" on her previously spotless character (94).

Pleyel's unjust deprecations help to draw attention to the highly problematic, even dangerous nature of the pervasive double trope of election and perdition, divinity and diabolism, particularly when employed as a means of determining or seeking to establish the ontological status or spiritual character of another. Some time after his initial outburst, he tells Clara, "'The image that I once adored existed only in my fancy'" (107), going on to reiterate that previously he had considered her to be an ideal "image," a "'picture which [...] was devoid of imperfection[...]'" (113). As Andrew Scheiber puts it, "implicit in [Pleyel's] description is the idea that her essence is [...] that of an angel, or, more precisely, of an art work. She is in his paradigm [...] an unearthly muse, an inspiration and object of cultural consciousness rather than author or agent."[26] In other words, his representation of her evacuates her of subjectivity, transforming her into a reified image of angelic beauty and virtue that she can only escape, in his imaginative economy, by reversing it and becoming demonic, depraved and irrevocably lost. Moreover, while this is a method of interpretation that saturates the world she inhabits, it finds its most strident and powerful advocates in the men with the greatest power over her life.

It is, after all, in matters of life and death that the Puritan body/ soul binarism most comes into its own. Laura M. Stevens illustrates how Puritanism demands that its devotees

> see death as an emotionally evocative text that should be read for spiritual signs. The Protestant Reformation had introduced the notion that the moment of death was a template, an event offering diagnostic possibilities for enhanced understanding. Protestants scoffed at deathbed conversions, but they remained wary of assuming salvation until the moment of death. A good death, following a good life, offered the best assurance of preservation from a descent into hell.[27]

Consequently, Protestant death in the eighteenth century was seen, not as a loss of life but as a clarification of the inner self and, as Stevens elaborates, functioned again as a convenient means for the deaths of others to be reinterpreted, not as a violent wrenching away from a beloved existence, but as a moment of religious truth and revelation of one's status as elect or reprobate. In other words, death is when our selfhood is most visible to—and definable by—both ourselves and those around us. To some extent, this view of death waned somewhat towards the end of the eighteenth century; with the rise of sentimentalism and the increased importance placed on family bonds, grief at the passing of loved ones took precedence over religious orthodoxy. Poised between two centuries, what *Wieland* illustrates graphically is a horrific juxtaposition of just these two, allegedly opposing strategies for confronting death, by combining in the figure of Wieland an image of paternal love and religiously inspired patriarchal despotism. It is this juxtaposition that leads to Wieland murdering his adored family precisely because his vision of love incorporates the view that the body is merely a hindrance to the spectacle of the spiritual truth of their essential selves.

Paul Lewis argues that "in this distorted re-enactment of the story of Abraham and Isaac, Wieland's victims cease (in the murderer's mind) to be individual people with independent value and become only lambs he brings to the altar."[28] This is particularly evident at the death of his wife, Catharine. In his confession, he describes being overwhelmed by a numinous "'effulgence'" that temporarily blinds him. From out of the dazzling light, he hears a voice and turns to look, but tells the jury, "'It is forbidden to describe what I saw: Words, indeed, would be wanting to the task. The lineaments of that being, whose veil was now lifted, and whose visage beamed upon my sight, no hues of pencil or of language can portray'" (153). The divine is for Wieland all-powerful and sacred precisely because it is unavailable to representational or actual violence, and he himself has no desire whatsoever even to attempt to subject it to epistemological freezing through language. By contrast, however, he lavishes considerable descriptive energy upon the dead body of his wife. As she lies, strangled by him, on Clara's bed, Wieland becomes transfixed by the physical spectacle his violence has made of her. He tells the jury how Catharine's "'eye-balls started from their sockets. Grimness and distortion took place of all that used to bewitch me into transport, and subdue me into reverence.'" His former idol becomes, in death, "'[h]aggard, and pale, and lifeless,'" which he takes as a sign that she has "'ceasedst to contend with [her] destiny'" (157). The use of the word "destiny" is particularly resonant. Now that she has become the "meaningless husk" that contemporary religious thinking declared the body to be, now that the repulsive physicality of life has been made all too evident because the soul no longer animates it, she has achieved her "destiny," simultaneously released to the eternal reward (or punishment) of the hereafter and reduced to the abject horror of livid, lifeless corporeality. Wieland's strict division between body and soul positions him as the proprietor of both, in that he violently brings the former to the end of its earthly existence in order to release the latter.

What is more, precisely because the visual and visible body excites, even demands violence within this Calvinistic framework, while Clara may be continually menaced throughout the novel, Wieland never succeeds in causing her physical harm, and neither does anyone else. Even the murderers who she believes to be hiding in her closet and following her on her solitary midnight walks are only the invention of Carwin's ventriloquism, intended to prevent her from discovering that he has been hanging around the grounds of their house. Clara's ability to survive the disasters that overtake her brother and his family can, I would argue, be traced back to her relative invisibility within the text — an invisibility which figuratively prepares us for her insistence on haunting, ghostlike, her already memory-haunted abode. As first-person narrator, she is herself immune from visualizing representation. She cannot be turned into an "idol" or a graven image reflecting another's conception of her, since the power of representation is literally in her hands, and the narrative gaze is turned outwards, towards others. For much of the start of the novel, she barely even appears to have a self, since the "I" of Clara's narration is all but absorbed into the "we" of the group with which she so strongly identifies. Barring the author's "Advertisement" that precedes her narrative, it is not until half way through Chapter IV that the information that Clara is female is supplied to the reader and her name mentioned, while she only names *herself* "Clara Wieland" in Chapter XII.

To be a narrative object in *Wieland* is to be textually "real" and vulnerable to violence; her position behind the narrative gaze can be seen as mitigating this effect. Pleyel and Wieland attempt to transform her, either into an angel whose bodily form merely obscures her true beauty, or a demon lurking within her "exquisite" but deceptive exterior. For Wieland, therefore, whichever is the case, to destroy that physicality is in no way to harm her. In order to evade the attempts by both men to evacuate her of subjectivity, reifying both body and soul to the point that she becomes a mere function of their representative processes, she disappears into textuality. Becoming the author of her own text rather than the subject of others' therefore essentially decorporealizes her while demonstrating, through her emotional and intellectual vicissitudes, reversals, and uncertainties, that her selfhood is complex in the extreme, disparate and often contradictory, irreducible to the binary system into which Pleyel and Wieland seek to insert her.[29] Rejecting her externally imposed status as a solid, fixed, strictly coded image, she becomes instead fractured and all but invisible. She is, in this sense, allied to Wieland's vision of the truly divine (rather than the divine in human form) as unrepresentable and indescribable.

Vitally, however, the text itself never associates her with any specifically religious form of the supernatural. Outside of any theological framework, she is a numinous being, but not one that can be bound within a doctrinal structure of interpretation, as to do so would be to re-establish the form of ultimate authority that the text sees as spurious and dangerous.[30]

Indeed, she draws explicit attention to the fact that her "narrative [is] invaded by inaccuracy and confusion, asking rhetorically, "What but ambiguities, abruptnesses, and dark transitions, can be expected from the historian who is, at the same time, the sufferer of these disasters?" She goes on to say, "Now know I what it is to entertain incommunicable sentiments" (135), highlighting her position beyond representation, even when it is wielded by herself. Unlike the sharply Manichean stories about the people around them that Wieland and Pleyel have been writing in their heads, Clara embraces the chaos of her tale. Her refusal of her position as authority also constitutes a refusal on her part to impose artificial systems of cause and effect onto the events that she has narrated. She makes some attempt to provide a moral at the very end, but even this serves to divide responsibility up between villain and victim. Drawing in the apparently tangential story of the Conway family and the disasters that befell them due to marital infidelity, she states that "the evils of which Carwin and Maxwell were the authors, owed their existence to the errors of the sufferers. All efforts would have been ineffectual to subvert the happiness or shorten the existence of the [victims], if their own frailty had not seconded these efforts" (223), and she includes herself in this criticism. This becomes more significant when read in the context of her earlier assertion, "Let that man who shall purpose to assign motives to the actions of another, blush at his folly and forbear. Not more presumptuous would it be to attempt the classification of all nature, and the scanning of supreme intelligence" (134).

She is not, unlike Wieland or Pleyel, attempting to explain definitively the actions and motives of her family members; instead she is yielding up the authority inherent in her narratorial position, embracing the chaotic and the arbitrary rather than seeking to reduce or control it. To do so would be to perpetuate her brother's violence since, as Irving Malin says of the American Gothic hero/ villain, "Love for him is an attempt to create order out of chaos, strength out of weakness; however, it simply creates monsters."[31] It is precisely this disturbing overlap between villain and protagonist that the texts which come after *Wieland* exploit to its fullest, in the process, I would argue, repeating its thematic concerns but not its commitment to problematizing this particular form of epistemological authoritarianism. To a certain extent, it is possible to see Brown's novel as supporting and extending the increasingly influential late-eighteenth century Universalist and Unitarian rejection of Calvinistic doctrine on the basis that it seems to imply that God is somehow responsible for sin and has wantonly doomed the majority of his creation to eternal hell-fires.[32] As Scheiber puts it, "to believe in Theodore's claim of divine authority for his acts is to accuse the God whose decrees he has supposedly executed — a theory which leads to the conclusion that the gods themselves are hostile, if not actually insane[...]."[33] More than this, it implies that belief in a cruel and demanding God can transform the believer into an exact replica of his or her image of the divine — and specifically the negative aspects of that image. In other words, belief renders the believer tyrannical, authoritarian and capable of acts of unspeakable violence towards those who he loves most. (Significantly, in *Wieland* and its cultural afterlife, it is always a man who acts in this manner.) By extension, the novel functions as a strident critique of the surveillance fostered by Puritanism, of the sense that all must be scrutinized in order to uncover the moral "truth" lurking beneath the deceptive surface of good works and outward propriety — and it is both this and the claims to ultimate authority that Clara's problematized narratorial status allow her to side-step.[34]

However, as the example of Pleyel demonstrates, while the novel can therefore be aligned with the Universalist denunciation of the Puritan vision of God, as a whole, it rejects any system of belief and any form of authority as not merely specious but dangerous.[35] In particular, censure falls upon the very sentimentalization of family bonds and the increased sense throughout the eighteenth century in American culture that death tore families apart and separated the living from those dearest to them — the cultural shift which itself gave rise to the Universalist and Unitarian movements. *Wieland* shows how such thinking fetishized the family group to the point where paternal power became all but absolute and unquestionable.[36] As Rowe and Marietta argue, the emerging nation's loose (and often, in rural areas, non-existent) authoritative structures placed excessive pressure on the family to supply the absence, and to take upon itself all of the disciplinary and pedagogical functions that in Europe were carried out by established systems.[37] The result was a startling incidence of domestic violence and intimate murder in the early Republic. At the same time, the inviolable and self-sufficient nature of the American family allowed for, even enforced, the cultural invisibility of that violence. Consequently, "lawmakers and judges designed public policy and legal procedures to support male power by giving men tremendous discretion within households. For the most part, what happened in homes was private, and appointed judges were to arbitrate the most serious disputes that escaped their sacrosanct walls."[38]

Clara's narrative frames Wieland's confession and ultimately moves away from focusing exclusively upon the tragic events that have befallen her family, as she devotes considerable space to the story of the Conway family, her emigration to Europe, and Pleyel's relationship with Teresa, which ends in that lady's death and Clara's marriage to her brother-in-law. The novel therefore refuses to grant narrative primacy to Wieland and the devastation that he has wrought, a point given added weight by the fact that Clara's initial decision to haunt the house that was the scene of that devastation is reversed in the final pages. Though this may be the culmination of the spectralization that is itself a function of her position as first-person narrator, to allow it to stand as the ending of the novel would be to endorse Wieland's assumption of near-divine authority, and to acknowledge that his actions and their consequences should and do define the fictional space conjured up by the novel. However, it is precisely this endorsement that characterizes the later texts that draw on the basic material of *Wieland*.

John Neal's "Idiosyncrasies," published just under half a century after *Wieland*, also features a father figure who claims to be divinely inspired — indeed, the unnamed man who narrates most of the story seems to have been a famous preacher whose words were heard by thousands of devoted followers prior to the central events of the tale. His conviction of the utter rightness of his own thoughts and actions leads, with sickening inevitability, to a terrible accident on a snow-covered mountain which in turn results, sometime later, in the death of his son and seriously endangers his darling daughter. The son dies "perhaps of fright, perhaps of something else," and he goes on to add, "but however that may be — I never could bring myself to forgive his mother."[39] Through a logic that is clearly comprehensible only to himself, he blames his wife, Jenny, whose many beauties and virtues he delineates at length, for the accident. One day, as they are walking near a waterfall, he tells her that he believes that either of his children would have willingly hurled themselves into the snowy abyss that day had he demanded it of them, and that he could expect "such obedience" from "no other living creature," though to find such a one would render him far "happier." To prove him wrong, in an act of ultimate obedience, or possibly just so that she can escape from this perverse tyrant, she throws herself into the "whirlpool" crying, "*Be happier then!*"[40]

Having recounted his wife's death, the narrator asks rhetorically, "what business had she to drown herself without my leave! what a fool to do so at the bidding of a husband! and such a husband!" before going on to detail his indignation at his daughter's forthcoming marriage. Like Wieland, he views his family as possessions to be disposed of at his will, and expects nothing more from them than total subjection. While the contradictions inherent in his opinions ironically undercut his narrative, and while the visitor to whom he tells the story is given the last word, the text ultimately enshrines him as the voice of authority precisely because he is telling the story from inside an insane asylum, having been institutionalized following his wife's death, for which he was tried for his life. The interlocutor leaves him in his cell, informing us that he "now spends most of his time making speeches to the jury, and telling over the story you have just read, to every stranger that falls his way." The narrator therefore occupies for all textual eternity the position of figurative ghost that Clara eventually rejects, a narrator invisible to his own narrative gaze and perpetually engaged in a narrative act in which he is *the* voice of authority.[41]

The word "frailty" is used twice prominently in *Wieland*, and in both cases in relation to obedience to external authority. With startling similarity to its precursor texts, Paxton's *Frailty* centers upon yet another father figure, who becomes convinced that he has been ordered by an angel to rid the world of demons in human shape. In an evident allusion to *Wieland*, the unnamed Dad (played by Paxton) believes that when he lays his hand on those he has been told are demons, he can see *through* their external bodily form to the demon within. In other words, he commands the ultimate Puritan power, the ability to see people's souls and spiritual destiny, and it is this ability that legitimates what is, by any other standard, serial murder — again, since it is the soul, and not the body, that is important in his system of belief. Rather like the elder Wieland, whose doctrinal legacy is inherited by Theodore (and, indeed, like Jack Torrance, who seems to possess a lesser version of Danny's "shining"), he passes on this special sight, and the burden of carrying out "God's work" to his two sons, Adam and Fenton — though the latter is far from willing. Several years later, Adam once again begins the killings, and it is here that the film opens, as Fenton (played by Matthew McConaughey) walks into an FBI office in order to explain to an agent that his brother is the famous "Hand of God" killer.

The rest of the film vacillates between showing Fenton telling his story and flashbacks narrated by him, the latter accounting for the majority of the film. Where all of this begins to become significant, however, is when we gradually realize that the narrator is in fact Adam, the killer and fanatic. At the same time, in what amounts to a literalization of Clara's textual spectralization, it emerges that no-one in the office can quite remember what he looks like, and that he fails to show up on CCTV cameras, his face being obscured in every frame. He is, therefore, immune to external representation, because he claims the power of representation for himself. The film ends by intimating that Adam's legacy will live on; he is now a sheriff in a small town, still going under his now dead brother's name, and his wife is pregnant with what we can only assume is to be a son. (Adam had killed his brother because he became convinced that Fenton is also a demon — something their father had long suspected.) Again, his very literal position of authority may be heavily ironized, the viewer's desire to cheer his cunning escape from the law being undercut by his status as villain. The fact remains, however, that the film, in seeking to frighten us with a pessimistic ending, permits this authority to continue into the imaged future, never wresting control over representation — both of his own past and over the bodies and souls of others — away from the quasi-ghostly, and therefore invulnerable, Adam. Even when they die, as Jack Torrance does, these men remain immune to the violence, both literal and epistemological, that they themselves mete out to others, and are granted what amounts to eternal life by the texts they inhabit. Consequently, the texts covertly endorse — or at least perpetuate — the systems of representation that legitimate violent fanaticism and familicide.

While *Wieland* skitters away from ending on a note that immortalizes Clara's function as a living memorial to domestic violence and rationalism's failure, the later texts do not. Instead, we are presented with images of ultimate male authority — authority over representation, over memory, and over the lives and deaths of those under their immediate care and protection. In these later texts, what comes to the fore is the patriarchal nature of the nuclear family, and the manner in which the sentimental emphasis on family ties causes and permits violence.[42] Where Carwin's influence and the possibility of supernatural interference mean we can never fully blame Theodore for what happens, the later manifestations locate the source of fear in a single, patriarchal individual and, in doing so, accord him a far greater degree of power than ever occurs in *Wieland*. They, therefore, retrospectively draw attention to Wieland's own potential status as patriarchal psychopath but, equally, to the text's refusal to establish him firmly as such.[43] However, by placing the violent male protagonists both in the role of storyteller and of eventual ghost, that very patriarchal power is buttressed, legitimated and perpetuated, even as it appears to be denigrated, critiqued and reviled. However, somewhat predictably, it is this narrative, rather than Brown's arguably more subtle evocation of Clara's resistance to that power, that has sunk deepest into the American cultural psyche. I would not presume to assert what that tells us about the state of that psyche. Perhaps Jack Torrance puts it best when he defines "cabin fever" as

> "a slang term for the claustrophobic reaction that can occur when people are shut in together over long periods of time. The feeling of claustrophobia is externalized as dislike for the people you happen to be shut in with. In extreme cases it can result in hallucinations and violence — murder has been done over such minor things as a burned meal or an argument over whose turn it is to do the dishes."[44]

This trope's failure to die out in American popular culture seems to imply that better communications and a stronger network of legal structures have not exorcised the fear that normal family life has all too much in common with the experience of cabin fever. While Jack may be mocking his place of employment when he calls it the "bloody sacred Overlook," his bad language serves to draw attention to the frighteningly sacrosanct nature of the domestic setting and, even in a post-feminist world, to the godlike arrogance of the men who assume that the women who cook and clean for them are theirs to dispose of as they will.[45]

Notes

1. For a discussion of the burden placed on familial authority in the new Republic, see Barnes, 26.
2. Downes argues at length that democracy blurs uncomfortably with and repeats the operations of monarchy.
3. See Schmidt, 38ff; Kafer, 21ff; and Michaud, 55, for discussions of various individual hearing divine (or possibly satanic) voices in seventeenth- and eighteenth-century America.
4. King, 56.
5. Kafer, xvi, explicitly links *Wieland* with King's *The Shining*.
6. Brown, *Wieland*, 212–13. All future references to this work will be cited using parenthetical page numbers in the body of the essay.
7. See, for example, Bradshaw's comments (370) about "Wieland's lack of consistency, undeveloped plots and characters, and amazing coincidences"; Tompkins, xii, 42–43; and the contemporary reviews in the Charles Brockden Brown Archive and Scholarly Edition (brockdenbrown. ucf.edu).
8. See Michaud, 110, 113, for a discussion of the failure of cause and effect in early American Gothic texts.
9. See Tompkins, 51; and Barnes, 53, for a discussion of the indeterminate nature of the message or even the events of *Wieland*.

10. For an outline of earlier scholarship linking *Wieland* to both religious (specifically Calvinist) doctrine, see Hedges, 112.

11. Judson, 26. "Puritan" here is a somewhat tentative designation, considering its overlap with Calvinism in many central points and within a number of the critical frameworks offered as ways of explaining what happens in Brown's puzzling text. The terms will be used here more or less interchangeably, but with an awareness that a total conflation is neither desirable nor possible.

12. Hagenbüchle, 123. For examples of those who believe that they have been spoken to by Satan rather than God, who are given visions of hell-fire and damnation, or who were believed to be possessed by a or the devil, see Schmidt, 58f.

13. Judson, 26.
14. C.M. Davidson, 169–170.
15. Calvin, 297.
16. Chauncy, 4–5. See also Robinson, 12f; and Colacurcio, 36f.
17. Colacurcio, 3.
18. See Stannard, 76.
19. Bolton, 82–83.
20. Collins, 4–5. See Colacurcio, 70ff., for a discussion of the Puritan doctrine of relinquishing the material world in order better to know and understand the divine.
21. Stannard, 100.
22. Bressler, 13, details the theological battles and the rise of sentimentalism which resulted in the view of a vengeful, arbitrary God gradually fading from the American consciousness in the eighteenth century in particular.
23. Thayer, 91–92.
24. Kibbey, 2.
25. See C.M. Davidson (171) for a reading of *Wieland* as promoting a balance between and decrying all excesses of spirituality and rationality. Tompkins, 54, by contrast, sees it as a novel in which any attempt to decide on the primacy of one or the other is rendered impossible by the removal of authority effected by the Revolution.
26. Scheiber, 179.
27. Stevens, 27. See also Reis, 163, 165; and Schmidt, 39.
28. Lewis, 173.
29. See Wolfe, 431ff and Downes, 39, 129ff for discussions of inter-relationship between power, storytelling, the voice, the body and subject formation in Brown's writing and contemporary literature.
30. For an example of the critical tendency to conflate the supernatural and the religious, see Hedges, 119f.
31. Malin, 5.
32. See Bressler, 18, 56; Robinson, 11; and Tompkins, 55, for discussions of the Universalist view that the Calvinist God was "tyrannical" and "depraved." C.M. Davidson, 171, describes the Antinomian God as an "arbitrary sadist."
33. Scheiber, 183.
34. See C.M. Davidson, 167.
35. For discussions of the Universalist view that all doctrinal systems were tyrannical, see Bressler, 35–36, and Robinson, 18.
36. See Barnes, 10.
37. Rowe and Marietta, 37.
38. Cole, 162.
39. Neal, 45.
40. Ibid., 45–46.
41. Ibid., 46–47.
42. For a discussion of the status of Brown's novel as a violent re-appropriation of the tropes of sympathy, familial bonds and seduction/ eroticized death, see Stern, 117f.
43. See C.N. Davidson, 316, for a discussion of the overlaps between hero and villain in early Republican novels. Similarly, Barnes, 9–10, discusses the early Republic's conflation of patriarchy and tyranny.
44. King, 9.
45. Ibid., 204.

Works Cited

The Charles Brockden Brown Archive and Scholarly Edition. Web. 30 Sept. 2011. brockdenbrown.ucf.edu.
Barnes, Elizabeth. *States of Sympathy: Seduction and Democracy in the American Novel*. New York: Columbia University Press, 1997. Print.
Bolton, Robert. *Mr. Boltons Last and Learned Worke of the Foure Last Things*. London, 1635. Print.
Bradshaw, Charles C. "The New England Illuminati: Conspiracy and Causality in Charles Brockden Brown's *Wieland*." *The New England Quarterly* 76:3 (2003): 356–377. Print.
Bressler, Ann Lee. *The Universalist Movement in America, 1770–1880*. Oxford: Oxford University Press, 2001. Print.
Brown, Charles Brockden. "Walstein's School of History: From the German of Krants of Gotha." *Monthly Magazine* Aug. 1799 and Sept. 1799: 335–38 and 407–11. Print.
―――. *Wieland; or The Transformation: An American Tale and Memoirs of Carwin the Biloquist*. Ed. Emory Elliott. Oxford: Oxford University Press, 1998. Print.
Calvin, John. *The Institutes of the Christian Religion*. Trans. Henry Beveridge. Vol. 2. Edinburgh, 1845. Print.
Chauncy, Charles. *Enthusiasm Described and Caution'd Against*. Boston, 1742. Print.
Colacurcio, Michael J. *Doctrine and Difference: Essays in the Literature of New England*. New York: Routledge, 1997. Print.
Cole, Stephanie. "Keeping the Peace: Domestic Assault and Private Prosecution in Antebellum Baltimore." Daniels and Kennedy 148–171. Print.
Collins, John. "To the Reader." *A Discourse of the Glory*. Jonathan Mitchel. Boston, 1721. Print.
Daniels, Christine, and Michael V. Kennedy, eds. *Over the Threshold: Intimate Violence in Early America*. New York: Routledge, 1999. Print.
Davidson, Carol Margaret. "Calvinist Gothic: The Case of Charles Brockden Brown's *Wieland* and James Hogg's *The Private Memoirs and Confessions of a Justified Sinner*." *Le Gothic: Influences and Appropriations in Europe and America*. Eds. Sue Zlosnik and Avril Horner. Basingstoke: Palgrave Macmillan, 2008. Print.
Davidson, Cathy N. *Revolution and the Word: The Rise of the Novel in America*. Oxford: Oxford University Press, 2004. Print.
Downes, Paul. *Democracy, Revolution, and Monarchism in Early American Literature*. Cambridge: Cambridge University Press, 2002. Print.
Garris, Mick. *The Shining*. DawnField. 27 April–1 May. 1997. Television.
Hagenbüchle, Roland. "American Literature and the Nineteenth-Century Crisis in Epistemology: The Example of Charles Brockden Brown." *Early American Literature* 23:2 (1988): 121–151. Print.
Hedges, William. "Charles Brockden Brown and the Culture of Contradictions." *Early American Literature* 9:2 (1974): 107–142. Print.
Isenberg, Nancy, and Andrew Burstein, eds. *Mortal Remains: Death in Early America*. Philadelphia: University of Pennsylvania Press, 2003. Print.
Judson, Barbara. "A Sound of Voices: The Ventriloquial Uncanny in Wieland and Prometheus Unbound." *Eighteenth-Century Studies* 44:1 (2010): 21–37. Print.
Kafer, Peter. *Charles Brockden Brown's Revolution and the Birth of American Gothic*. Philadelphia: University of Pennsylvania Press, 2004. Print.
Kibbey, Ann. *The Interpretation of Material Shapes: A Study of Rhetoric, Prejudice, and Violence*. Cambridge: Cambridge University Press, 1986. Print.
King, Stephen. *The Shining*. London: Hodder, 2007. Print.
Kubrick, Stanley, dir. *The Shining*. Perrigrine Productions, 1980. Film.
Lewis, Paul. "Charles Brockden Brown and the Gendered Canon of Early American Fiction." *Early American Literature* 31:2 (1996): 167–188. Print.
Malin, Irving. *New American Gothic*. Carbondale: Southern Illinois University Press, 2003. Print.
Michaud, Marilyn. *Republicanism and the American Gothic*. Cardiff: University of Wales Press, 2009. Print.

Neal, John. "Idiosyncrasies." *American Gothic: An Anthology, 1787–1916*. Ed. Charles L Crow. Malden, MA: Blackwell, 1999. Print.
Paxton, Bill, dir. *Frailty*. David Kirschner Productions, 2002. Film.
Reis, Elizabeth. "Immortal Messengers: Angels, Gender, and Power in Early America." Isenberg and Burstein 163–175. Print.
Robinson, David. *The Unitarians and the Universalists*. Westport, CT: Greenwood Press, 1985. Print.
Rowe, G.S., and Jack D. Marietta. "Personal Violence in a 'Peaceable Kingdom.'" Daniels and Kennedy 22–44. Print.
Scheiber, Andrew J. "The Arm Lifted against Me: Love, Terror, and the Construction of Gender in *Wieland*." *Early American Literature* 26:2 (1991): 173–194. Print.
Schmidt, Leigh Eric. *Hearing Things: Religion, Illusion and the American Enlightenment*. Cambridge: Harvard University Press, 2000. Print.
Stannard, David E. *The Puritan Way of Death: A Study in Religion, Culture and, Social Change*. New York: Oxford University Press, 1977. Print.
Stern, Julia. "The Politics of Tears: Death in the Early American Novel." Isenberg and Burstein 108–122. Print.
Stevens, Laura M. "The Christian Origins of the Vanishing Indian." Isenberg and Burstein 17–30. Print.
Thayer, Thomas Baldwin. *Over the River; or, Pleasant Walks into the Valley of Shadows, and Beyond*.... Boston: Thomkins and Co., 1864. Print.
Tompkins, Jane. *Sensational Designs: The Cultural Work of American Fiction, 1790–1860*. New York: Oxford University Press, 1985. Print.
"Treehouse of Horror V." *The Simpsons*. Fox. 30 October 30. 1994. Television.
Wolfe, Eric A. "Ventriloquizing Nation: Voice, Identity, and Radical Democracy in Charles Brockden Brown's *Wieland*." *American Literature* 78:3 (2006): 431–57. Print.

From Bedford Falls to Punxsutawney: Refashioning A Christmas Carol

GRACE MOORE

What are you doing watching television on Christmas Eve?— Frank Cross, Scrooged (1988)

One of the best-known and best-loved stories of the nineteenth century, Charles Dickens's *A Christmas Carol* has such a pervasive influence that it has become what John Jordan, echoing Paul Davis, describes as a "'culture text' for the world at large" (xix). For Davis Ebenezer Scrooge, the miser who is reformed through a sequence of nocturnal hauntings, is a "protean figure" who is "always in process of reformation" (5). Furthermore, according to Davis, Scrooge has attained such mythical status that he is a part of our collective consciousness, known to those who have never read a word of Dickens's writing, and enjoying a rich extra-textual life. Since these afterlives shape our understanding of Dickens and frame our experiences of reading and re-reading *A Christmas Carol*, it is important to consider how Ebenezer Scrooge's character alters with time and responds to his changing context. If there is a "universalism" to Scrooge, then I would argue that it is one that has mutated in response to shifts in our context as well as our understanding and ministering of charity. Not only does Scrooge endlessly reform, he is also endlessly re-fashioned as Dickens's story has been reworked and updated over the years.

A Christmas Carol has been revised and adapted many times since the 1840s, and this essay will examine how its message of redemption has mutated and ultimately been diluted in twentieth-century adaptations. Drawing on sources including Capra's *It's a Wonderful Life* (1946), *Scrooged* (1988) and *Groundhog Day* (1993), I will examine shifting perceptions of charity and will argue that Capra's film speaks directly back to the concerns of both Dickens's novel and its source text, Philip Van Doren Stern's *The Greatest Gift* (1943). Capra and Dickens share fears regarding the vulnerability of families and communities in the face of risk, bank fraud and finance capitalism. However, as I shall demonstrate, later adaptations focus their attention on the rehabilitation of the individual Scrooge-figure, rather than what this person might do for his community once he has been re-claimed. I shall therefore begin by examining Dickens's Scrooge, his origins and his relationship to Victorian models of philanthropy, before considering how he has developed and altered in response to societal changes.

In March 1843, having digested two early versions of the Children's Employment Commission's report into child labor, Charles Dickens promised the social reformer Dr. Thomas Southwood Smith that he would write an article or pamphlet on behalf of the poor man's child. Having made this offer, Dickens wrote to Smith a few days later to defer delivery until the end of the year, suggesting, at the same time, that he had changed his mind regarding the format the piece should take. With characteristic enthusiasm and energy, Dickens urged, "*rest assured* that when you know them [the reasons for the change], and see what I do, and where, and how, you will certainly feel that a Sledge hammer has come down with twenty times the force — twenty thousand times the force — I could exert by following out my first idea" (Dickens, *Letters*, 3: 462).

The reasons behind Dickens's change of heart may not be entirely straightforward, notwithstanding his dramatic, forceful language. Dickens famously experienced a brush with poverty as a boy, when his father's chaotic finances saw him imprisoned for debt. The twelve-year-old Charles was employed — albeit temporarily — at Warren's Blacking Factory, where he worked pasting labels onto jars of boot polish. Rosemarie Bodenheimer has suggested that the trauma associated with this period left Dickens unable to write in any detail about the working poor, which might explain his sudden retreat from the promises he had made to Southwood Smith. Bodenheimer argues that, so moved was Dickens by the reports of young children toiling in factories and coal mines that, in spite of his "solemn pledges" to expose their plight in the *Edinburgh Review*, he found himself unable to chronicle their sufferings (Bodenheimer, 62–4). Instead of producing a pamphlet exposing the exploitation of children, Dickens wrote *A Christmas Carol*, a novella that has become virtually synonymous with the festive season and with the spirit of Christian charity, but a far cry from the hard-hitting exposé of his original pledge. From its very inception, then, *A Christmas Carol* was a mutating text that responded and changed according to the political climate.

Charity in Victorian Britain was not a simple matter.[1] While for Dickens reaching out to those in need was an instinctive part of human companionship, the climate in which his novels appeared was by no means so compassionate. The Poor Law Amendment Act of 1834 sought to centralize the distribution of aid by forcing those in need to apply to workhouses for assistance. Whereas in the past those who had fallen on hard times were able to receive aid that would enable them to stay in their own homes, the reorganization of poor relief according to the Utilitarian principle of the "greatest happiness of the greatest number" effectively led to the criminalization of poverty. More akin to jails than places of sanctuary, the workhouses came to be known as "Bastilles" after the notorious French prison, and were places to be avoided at all costs. Dickens attacked this austere system in his early novel *Oliver Twist* (1837–1839), where he exposed its abuses and corruption through characters like the avaricious beadle Mr. Bumble and the equally unsympathetic Mrs. Corney. Norris Pope has argued that, in writing against the brutalities of utilitarianism, Dickens revealed his complicated relationship with established religion. Pope comments:

> Dickens's own religious outlook was shaped by the staunchly Protestant conviction that religion was a matter of individual conscience, not something that depended significantly upon ritual, ecclesiastical authority, or abstruse theology.... [D]espite his irritation with aspects of evangelical philanthropy, he believed no less firmly than evangelicals did that charity and benevolence were essential and highly appropriate products of Christian faith [248].

While Dickens may have been deeply impatient with those who paraded their religion, charity was for him at the very core of a Christian life. The workhouses were, for Dickens, just one example of how basic humanitarian aid had become divorced from Christianity. Through *A Christmas Carol* he hoped to remind his readers of their duty to the poor, not just during the festive season, but throughout the year. Scrooge's desperate promise to the Ghost of Christmas Yet to Come demonstrates Dickens's belief that charity should not simply be seasonal. Scrooge declares, "I will honour Christmas in my heart, and try to keep it all the year. I will live in the Past, the Present, and the Future. The Spirits of all Three shall strive within me. I will not shut out the lessons that they teach" (111). Of course, not all readers are convinced by Scrooge's softening of heart, which G.K. Chesterton rather witheringly dismissed as a "softening of the brain" (quoted in Washington 564). However, the miser's radical change of character signals Dickens's belief that his readers, like the miser, were able to reinvent themselves and to assimilate the spirit of Christmas into their daily interactions.

While Dickens hoped that his little book would make him a fortune (the high costs of production soon dashed these aspirations), he also firmly believed that it could play an important role in bringing about social reform. Although the story ducked the representation of working children, it showed the extremes of poverty from the virtuous Cratchits to the horrifically wolfish children, Want and Ignorance. At this early stage in his career, Dickens still believed that by exposing social problems in his fiction he could bring about change. For him, it was a matter of faith that once his readers had seen the conditions in which the "residuum" was forced to live they would naturally intervene and offer aid. Indeed, such was his belief in humanity that it was not until the 1850s that Dickens began to doubt that graphic depictions of poverty and suffering alone could move his readers to pity for those less fortunate than themselves.[2] Although *A Christmas Carol* was not the politically directed piece of writing that Dickens had originally offered, he believed in its power to make a difference in society and, in particular, he trusted in what he came to describe in a letter to his friend John Forster as "*Carol* philosophy." While Dickens doesn't strictly define what he means here, it is safe to say that its values are partly connected to the "cheerful views, sharp anatomization of humbug, jolly good temper" that he outlines next to the phrase, and partly associated with the message of Christian salvation that underpins Scrooge's story (Letters, 4: 328). Such was the appeal of the little book that Dickens seems to have believed that readers would imbibe its message, like a bowl of Christmas punch.

Contemporary readers were swept away by the story's goodwill. The novelist William Makepeace Thackeray encapsulated the sense of community and togetherness fostered by *A Christmas Carol* when he commented,

> As for Tiny Tim, there is a certain passage in the book regarding that young gentleman, about which a man should hardly venture to speak in print or in public, any more than he would any other affections of his private heart. There is not a reader in England but that little creature will be a bond of union between the author and him, and he will say of Charles Dickens ... "GOD BLESS HIM" [Thackeray, *Miscellanies*: 5, 214].

Thackeray's generous response seems to have typified public enthusiasm for Scrooge's tale. Certainly, critics were eager to praise the novella, with Theodore Martin commenting that it was "calculated to work much social good" (*Tait's Edinburgh Magazine*, 129), going on to say that "it is a noble book, finely felt." The Victorians, with their appetite for the sentimental, were particularly drawn to Tiny Tim, although readers of today often voice discomfort at the child's overwhelming goodness and remarkable faith. Sally Ledger has argued convincingly that the story is so enduringly popular because of its combination of a "hard-hitting" attack on the draconian poor laws and the "Bacchanalian vision of plenty at Christmas time" (120), whereby the terror of Want and Ignorance is offset by the joyful domesticity of the Cratchits and festivities like Old Fezziwig's ball. *A Christmas Carol* remains a popular festive story, yet in the twenty-first century readers are not always drawn to its Christian message, identifying instead with its celebration of family and the domestic hearth and the more "Bacchanalian" aspects of the story. It is therefore little wonder that the novella and its protagonists have been adapted over time. Furthermore, as Christmas has become increasingly entwined with the commercial, adaptations have responded, presenting a critique of consumer culture and the self-absorption that it can generate.³

Ebenezer Scrooge (Michael Caine) stands menacingly above Bob Cratchit (Kermit the Frog) in *The Muppet Christmas Carol* (1992, Buena Vista), one of numerous adaptations of the Charles Dickens' novella, some of which are better than others at maintaining the progressive spirit of the original.

* * *

One of the most famous twentieth-century engagements with *A Christmas Carol*, Capra's *It's a Wonderful Life* is focused primarily around the character George Bailey. While this may seem inconsistent with Dickens's story, it actually reflects the focus of attention for nineteenth-century readers, who regarded Scrooge's beleaguered clerk, Bob Cratchit as the hero of the tale (76).⁴ Talented, restless, and eager to leave his hometown, Bedford Falls, George is repeatedly thwarted in his ambitions to travel and attend college. Although feistier than his Dickensian original, when the film begins George is on the brink of suicide, having been cheated by Henry Potter, the story's villain, and believing that he is worth more dead than alive to those who depend on him. This gesture encapsulates just how far the story has moved away from Dickens's original text; George is obviously thinking of others even when in despair, yet he is also contemplating a mortal sin and placing his soul in jeopardy.[5] At this early stage in the story it is difficult for the viewer to determine whether George is supremely selfless, or whether he has succumbed to selfish despondency.[6]

While *A Christmas Carol* is sometimes regarded as a time-travel story, with its combination of analepses and prolepses, *It's a Wonderful Life* offers a sequence of flashbacks, provided for the benefit of George's trainee guardian angel, Clarence. These glimpses of the past demonstrate how heroic and noble George has been throughout his life and show the many obstacles he has had to overcome. George's story is one of opportunities sacrificed for the good of others. In spite of the ambitions he voices when he declares, "I'm gonna see the world" and "I'm gonna build things," he is too closely enmeshed in both his family and his community to be able to follow his dreams. Each time he plans to leave, circumstances conspire and George's sense of duty compels him to remain behind. George might be considered to be something of a throwback, in that his decisions result from a sense of obligation that is at odds with the capitalist society he inhabits. Ebenezer Scrooge is, for much of *A Christmas Carol*, an upholder of the rigid boundaries between the public and private domains. Until he is visited by the three ghosts, his life revolves entirely around his money-lending business and he has no sense that his employee, Bob Cratchit, might have a life and a family beyond the world of the office. George, however, does not separate his business from his domestic life; he relinquishes his dream of a college education when, on his father's death, the shareholders of the Building and Loan society insist that George must remain behind to run the company. For George, the community is paramount and he feels a strong sense of duty towards the many friends and family members who have come to rely upon him. He is, in this respect, distinctly at odds with the modern professional.[7]

Part of George's emotional investment in the business is a result of its mission to provide affordable housing for the poor. In endeavoring to continue his father's investment in the community, George is pitted against the slum landlord, Henry Potter, who wishes to take control of the loan society and turn it into a ruthlessly profitable business. Throughout the movie, while George invests in people and their dreams, Potter shows himself to be a monopoly capitalist, interested only in money. Every misfortune is, for him, simply another opportunity to generate wealth, as he profits from the stock market crash and the Second World War. While the inhabitants of Bedford Falls are George's friends, Potter shows only contempt for them, refusing to allow them credit to buy houses and even at one stage declaring that George has been "trapped into frittering his life away, playing nursemaid to a lot of garlic-eaters." As this comment might suggest, Potter is intolerant of migrant communities and fails to see that they are part of America's future. George, on the other hand, embraces the newcomers and helps them to escape from living "like pigs in ... Potter's Field."

Potter dismisses George's father's impractical vision of a world in which all the residents of Bedford Falls might own their own homes, describing Bailey senior as a "starry-eyed dreamer." Mid-way through his characteristically impassioned riposte, George asks Potter why people should be forced to scrimp and save before they are allowed a roof over their heads:

> Wait for what? Until their children grow up and leave them? Until they're so old and broken-down that they.... Do you know how long it takes a working man to save five thousand dollars? Just remember this, Mr. Potter, that this rabble you're talking about ... they do most of the working and paying and living and dying in this community. Well, is it too much to have them work and play and live and die in a couple of decent rooms and a bath? Anyway, my father didn't think so. People were human beings to him, but to you, a warped, frustrated old man, they're cattle. Well, in my book, he died a much richer man than you'll ever be.

George's outburst here aligns him with the compassion that Dickens evoked through characters like Tiny Tim, yet it also points to a strategic, pragmatic relationship with community and aid that characterized Dickens's writing from *Bleak House* onwards. Dickens's point, like George's, is that if one cannot do good for the sake of doing so, then one should at least think strategically about appeasing the poor. The Scrooge-like Potter sees the inhabitants of Bedford Falls as so many cattle, whereas George's compassionate capitalism reconciles the need to make a living with his desire for positive change.

Unlike Ebenezer Scrooge, George does not need to be visited by three ghosts, but he does experience a vision that shows him how his town would look without him.[8] Andrew Miller has described this phenomenon as the "life unled," and identifies it as a significant characteristic in nineteenth-century realist writing, whereby characters consider what their lives might have become had they made different choices. Miller suggests that, given his own precarious path to success, Dickens was acutely aware of the serendipity of his life and endowed a number of his protagonists with a similar self-reflexiveness.[9] Miller is primarily concerned with *Dombey and Son* in his article (along with the fiction of Henry James), yet Scrooge engages with this process more dramatically than any other Dickens character, I would argue, because of the visions offered by each of the spirits and the intensity of his responses to them. Capra preserves this aspect of Dickens's writing, although instead of showing the saintly George his mistakes, he instead offers a bleak vision of what Bedford Falls and its inhabitants would be like without him.

Paul Davis has described *It's a Wonderful Life* as Capra's "quintessential American Carol," pointing to the director's use of the Victorian story to medi-

Frank Capra's *It's a Wonderful Life* (1946, Paramount Pictures) contrasts the generosity of spirit of the Christmas season and the self-sacrificing life choices of its hero, George Bailey, with the miserly actions of the Scrooge-like Mr. Potter. In this scene, newlyweds George and Mary Bailey (James Stewart and Donna Reed) sacrifice their $2,000 in honeymoon funds to end a bank run caused by the crashing of the stock market.

ate a tale of the Depression (165). In many ways, Capra and his team of writers were cavalier with their source text, Philip Van Doren Stern's short story "The Greatest Gift," but the changes they made to it were to make the story much more Dickensian.[10] Like its parent-text, *It's a Wonderful Life* directly engages with the political climate of the present day and of the recent past. As Davis expresses it, "The struggle of the American economy to free itself from the failures of the international bankers becomes the melodrama of George's efforts to keep his building and loan [company] afloat" (166). The message of the film is clearly that an individual life — no matter how apparently insignificant — can make an enormous difference and that George's generosity of spirit is what his nation needs (and what the viewers need) in order to recover from the draining years of Depression and war. According to Davis,

> George's story is never secondary to the historical panorama against which it plays, nor are his troubles ever suggested to be simply the result of historical

forces over which he has no control. The despair that George feels on the bridge may articulate such historical questions, but neither George nor the film makes the connection explicit [166].

I would argue, though, that George invites the viewer to draw these parallels when he is roused from his vision and, whilst apparently greeting the familiar surroundings of the town he has shaped, declares, "Merry Christmas, movie house!" thus breaking down the barriers between the imaginary and the real. In accepting George's salutation, the movie-goer becomes part of the film's community and therefore a part of its ethos of collective support.

George, of course, famously counts his blessings and learns to value his life once more and, while it may only be implied, the message to the viewer is clearly that hard work, perseverance, faith and neighborly values will always triumph in the end. Capra's film also accentuates the intersections of lives and the co-dependency that come with belonging to a community through Clarence's observation, "Each man's life touches so many other lives and when he isn't around he leaves an awful hole, doesn't he?" When he sees the misery of life without him and his wife a lonely spinster, George repeatedly declares, "Let me live again! I want to live again," even asking for God's intervention when Clarence appears not to heed his cries. George, of course, does not need to be redeemed like Scrooge, he simply needs to have the value of his efforts and many sacrifices affirmed so that he can continue to appreciate his family and the love that surrounds him. The film closes with a celebration of the power of the community, the "miracle" that Mary tells George of when preparing him to hear the news of the collection on his behalf. That George is positioned by the Christmas tree as he learns of everyone's contributions emphasizes that this is a seasonal "miracle" like Scrooge's change of heart. Henry Potter disappears from the plot altogether since this celebration of festive spirits and communal values cannot tolerate an unrepentant miser. Although not actively outlined by the script, Potter's misfortune, in addition to being thwarted in his plan to ruin George, is never to know the joys of mutual dependence and neighborliness.

* * *

The like of Henry Potter could not be banished for long, though. As its title suggests, Richard Donner's *Scrooged* owes a significant debt to *A Christmas Carol*. Tapping into the climate of corporate greed that characterized the 1980s, Ebenezer Scrooge is transformed into Frank Cross, the ruthless and demanding executive of a television network. While not a miser, Cross is, as his name implies, deeply misanthropic and amoral. Frank demonstrates his distance from the spirit of Christmas in an early scene, which rivals Scrooge's famous "Are there no prisons?" (38) speech in its nastiness. Overseeing an ambitious, live, multi-national production of *A Christmas Carol*, Frank rejects an advertisement prepared by his team as insufficiently sensational. He then screens an alternative advert of his own, encompassing war, crime and natural disaster, but without any references to Dickens's classic story. When an employee, Eliot Loudermilk protests "that looked like the Manson Family Christmas Special," Frank agrees that it has nothing to do with *A Christmas Carol*, insists on screening it anyway and has Eliot ejected from the building. Frank's assertion, "We'll *own* Christmas," demonstrates both his lack of interest in seasonal goodwill and his overwhelming ambition; it also shows the extent to which Christmas itself has been commodified since the nineteenth century. Christmas is, in the late twentieth century, no longer about togetherness and compassion; it has become about buying and selling, whether that is through merchandise or through the selling of network airtime to those peddling their wares. While Capra's adaptation sought to harness some of the magic of Dickens's original, reworkings from later in the twentieth century, like *Scrooged*, are considerably less cheerful in their outlook and increasingly critical of late capitalism.

Like *A Christmas Carol, Scrooged* attempts to identify Christian charity with the festive season. Frank Cross has little patience with philanthropy, yet while Scrooge is open about his frustrations with those who are unable to help themselves, Frank disguises his shortcomings through hypocritical performances of benevolence. Although he gushingly accepts his Humanitarian of the Year award, assuring the audience that he sometimes has to stop himself from giving too much, it is clear that Frank attaches no meaning to the honor. Having sworn that he will cherish it always, he absently leaves his statuette in the back of a cab, never pausing to think about it again. Thus, while the Victorian miser shows potential for redemption from the early stages in Dickens's novella, it is clear that the obsessive workaholic Cross will require a deeper shock to jolt him out of his selfishness. Like the viewers he imagines taking in his Christmas apocalypse advertisement, Frank has become desensitized to ordinary feelings and social interactions.

When Frank is visited by the story's Jacob Marley figure, his deceased former boss Lew Hayward, Frank again signals his complete isolation from humanity. He is spectacularly unafraid of the spirit and unmoved by his foreboding tone. Lew tells him, with great emotion:

Mankind should have been my business.
   Charity, mercy, kindness—that should've been my business. Don't wait. Get yourself involved. It's too late for me, but not for you.

Observing that Frank is unmoved by his entreaty, Lew asks, "Frank, you don't like Christmas, do you?" Frank responds effusively, "I love it! It's cold and people stay home and watch TV. These idiots are gonna be at home watching TV for me tonight. I'm a big fan of Christmas." Frank's cynical interpretation of Christmas is closely tied to commodity culture and even the apparently repentant Lew cannot completely abandon the rhetoric of his workplace as he wails to Frank, "My *business* should have been charity" (my emphasis). It would seem that repentance, 1980s style, is not as all-consuming as it was for Jacob Marley in the 1840s.

As with Scrooge, memory holds the key to Frank's personality, and flashbacks to his childhood and early adulthood reveal the underlying reasons for his ruthless determination. So emotionally detached is Frank, that he can only understand the experience when it is mediated through television. The Ghost of Christmas Past tells him of the vision from 1955, "This is not live, it's like a re-run." Nevertheless, as someone with a sophisticated understanding of how narratives work, Frank is able to recognize the conventions within which he is expected to operate. He tells the ghost, resignedly, "You've taken me back to show me my parents, and I'm meant to go all blubbery. Forget it. You got the wrong guy." Frank does, though, respond to the vision of himself as a lonely child, watching television as an escape from the uncaring father who gives him a pound of veal as a Christmas gift, rather than the toy train he covets. Although Ebenezer Scrooge is moved to pity through visions of himself as an abandoned boy, Frank has great difficulty in distinguishing events in his life from episodes of TV shows. The memories of his childhood turn out, for the most part, not to be *his* memories but are, instead, the recollections of the more interesting lives of a sequence of imaginary characters.

The most striking of Frank's recollections, though, are of his time as a young man, with his girlfriend Claire. Initially, we see a happy and idealistic couple and Frank responds to the young woman's generosity and warmth. Gradually, though, as his ambition takes over, Frank drifts away from his love. The flashback shows them separating on Christmas Eve in 1971 when Frank refuses to pass over a career opportunity (to play Frisbee the dog) to honor a longstanding commitment to spend the evening with Claire and their friends. Frank responds to the Ghost of Christmas Past's incredulous question, "You left Claire for Frisbee the dog?" with the defensive assertion, "I know who I am. I know what I want." This self-belief is increasingly shaken, however, as Frank is forced to contemplate his life in the present. Claire has become director of Operation Reach-out, a shelter for those in need, and she is clearly fulfilled by her work with the most desperate members of the community. Frank finds the shelter and its inmates offensive, abusing both the volunteers and those in need. He rants, "You wanna save somebody, save yourself!" and this bitter outburst encapsulates the difference between *Scrooged* and the earlier texts I have discussed.[11] Both *A Christmas Carol* and

It's a Wonderful Life show the importance of connecting with a community and demonstrate the joys of human fellowship. Scrooge achieves social and spiritual redemption and George is pulled back from the brink of despair by learning the value of the opportunities he sacrificed for those around him. Frank's reform is a much more individualistic affair, however, and the movie's closing scenes are primarily focused upon him, rather than any broader sense of what he might do for his large constituency of employees and viewers. We are left with little sense of how "mercy" and "charity" might become Frank's business, although it is very clear that he has embraced the celebratory aspect of Christmas.

The Tiny Tim plot is, to a small degree, retained in *Scrooged*, but it is, tellingly in my opinion, much less central to Frank's change in personality than it is to Scrooge's reform. Calvin, the son of Frank's long-suffering assistant Grace, has been silent for five years since witnessing his father's death. As with Scrooge, when the ghost of Christmas Present shows Grace's family at home, Frank has almost no knowledge of them and is shocked to learn that Grace has been widowed. While Dickens and Capra celebrate the family and the sanctuary it offers from the wider world of commerce, *Scrooged* shows it to be much more vulnerable — Grace is a single mother, struggling to balance her domestic and professional responsibilities and Frank has no respect for her personal time, keeping her late when she should be taking Calvin to see a specialist.

Since Calvin cannot speak, he is unable to play on the viewers' sympathies in quite the same way as Tiny Tim, but it is clear that Grace adores him and never loses her faith that he will one day talk to her again. Frank's vision of the future does not involve Calvin's death, but it does see him confined to a particularly austere looking institution. Frank's response to this scene somewhat cynically draws on his network of connections, as he yells, "I know the head of pediatrics at NYU. We'll get this kid out of here." Thus, while Scrooge understands that Tim needs basic goods that he can supply and is engaged by the little boy's faith and goodness, Frank's sense of what he might do for Calvin extends only so far as his high-flying contacts. Scrooge's change is driven by engagement and empathy, but Frank's is depicted as much more pragmatic — he wants to "fix" Calvin, rather than be a second father to him.

The Frank who emerges from the hauntings bears more than a passing resemblance to a televangelist. In a state of near-hysteria that leads some to question his sanity, Frank tells viewers that they'll "get greedy" for Christmas and the goodwill it inspires. This phrasing is curious in that it suggests that rather than being cured of his selfishness, Frank is instead preparing his audiences for a euphoric "rush" that they will experience — doing good becomes a type of self-gratification as Frank articulates it, suggesting that his redemption is far from complete — a critique that was leveled at the original Scrooge by critics including Chesterton and Edmund Wilson.[12] The responses to Frank as he hijacks the live broadcast to tell viewers to abandon their TV sets and spend time with their families range from discomfort to elation. At the same time, though, the movie undergoes a generic shift as Frank's embracing of yuletide allows him to be reunited with Claire. The plot gives way to romance and becomes entirely focused on Frank. His vision of Christmas is somewhat secular and although his predecessors look to Christ for guidance in their future, Frank is more caught up with the idea of families enjoying togetherness. His image of the festive season is perhaps, like his childhood memories, mediated by the television and the images it disseminates of people snuggled up by the fire, or romping in the snow.

* * *

If, as Paul Davis argues, "the *Carol* is the sum of all its versions, or all its revisions, parodies and piracies" (5), we must ask what is happening to this multi-layered text as it moves further and further away from Dickens's original and its religious message. While Frank Cross may laughingly tell Eliot Loudermilk that he's "scaring the Dickens out of people," the Harold Ramis movie *Groundhog Day* (1993) takes the Dickens out of the *Christmas Carol* story and even moves the plot away from the festive season, perhaps in a nod to the so-called "War on Christmas," which continues to seek the removal of religious festivals from public life. I would argue that a dialogue is established between *Groundhog Day* and *Scrooged* through the casting of Bill Murray (who played Frank Cross) as Phil Connors, a misanthropic television weatherman. Like Frank, Phil is hugely egotistical, declaring in an early scene, "I *make* the weather," and when he is introduced to the viewer, he is entirely focused on his career.

Ebenezer Scrooge and Frank Cross both reflect on their misdemeanors in response to ghostly hauntings, while George Bailey sees a vision of Bedford Falls, without him. Phil, however, undergoes a much more protracted lesson as he relives the same day over and over, implicitly at the whim of the groundhog whose name he shares.[13] Phil's interaction with his Groundhog Day shifts as he moves through a sequence of emotions; initially incredulous, he then experiments with robbing armored trucks, cynically extracting details from Rita about her perfect day, kidnapping the groundhog, and hedonistically indulging in any behavior that suits him. In short, he treats the recurring day as a license to do as he pleases and to act out his selfish impulses, rather than an opportunity to make amends for the many mistakes he made when he first experienced it. Over time, though, he becomes overwhelmed by the repetition and seeks escape through suicide, perhaps nodding back to *It's a Wonderful*

Life. Unlike George Bailey, though, Phil has not touched lives and seems only to have caused distress. Trapped in an endlessly repetitive existence, Phil experiences both mania and ennui as he tries to vary the events of his recurring day. Gradually, though, Phil begins to enjoy life in the little town of Punxsutawney and he undertakes an absurdly large number of good deeds, using his knowledge of the day's events to prevent tragedies. He repeatedly attempts to save an old man from dying in the snow, although the man continues to die regardless of how the day plays out.

It is only when Phil begins to value life and other people that his reenactment of the day's events can end. Towards the end of the film, still mistaking the groundhog's lesson as a blessing, Phil declares:

> I'm a god. I'm not *the* God, I don't think.... I didn't just survive a wreck. I wasn't just blown up yesterday. I have been stabbed, shot, poisoned ... frozen, hung, electrocuted, and burned.... Every morning I wake up fine, not a dent in the fender. I am an immortal.

He then proceeds to display his knowledge about the town and its inhabitants, but without any thought of how he might use what he knows for the good of the community. Rita, the producer with whom he has fallen in love, initially doubts him when he reels off a list of facts about the people surrounding them, but she then offers to spend the day with Phil as an "objective witness" and he diverts her with the many accomplishments he has gathered during his repeated day and ends by declaring his love for her. The scene then cuts to another repetition of the day, but this time Phil is "the most popular person in town" and Rita "buys" him in a bachelor auction so that she can spend the evening with him.

At the end of the evening, having produced an ice sculpture of Rita, Phil announces, "I'm happy now, because I love you," choosing to live for the moment, rather than anticipating the next iteration of February 2 with dread. When Phil wakes the next morning, it is finally February 3 and with an inarticulacy to rival Ebenezer Scrooge's whoops of joy, he stutters, "Today is tomorrow. It happened." The movie ends with Phil planning to settle in Punxsutawney. Although Phil has learned to help others, the movie ends by focusing on his personal fulfillment and, as with *Scrooged*, it provides resolution through the romance plot. Since the Groundhog has no voice, the purpose of his lesson is never fully apparent, but the story's closure seems to suggest that Phil has suffered in this purgatory in order to become worthy of Rita. Through separating Scrooge's story from Christmas, the writers Harold Ramis and Danny Rubin have also made its moral message much more nebulous. Certainly, Phil immerses himself in a community and finds himself unwilling to leave it, but the movie is ultimately concerned with him as an individual.

Furthermore, there is something a little unsettling in the idea that Phil cannot take his newfound goodness out into the wider world, instead choosing to confine himself to the quaint Pennsylvania town. The disappointing truth is, perhaps, that the new "good" Phil would be unable to function in the competitive world that he wants to leave behind, thus suggesting that charity and compassion are vulnerable indeed in the broader public sphere.[14]

In *Groundhog Day* (1993, Columbia Pictures), Phil Connors (Bill Murray) is a Scrooge-like television weatherman who is cured of his misanthropy through the magical intervention of a groundhog named Punxsutawney Phil.

* * *

In the closing scenes of *Scrooged*, Frank Cross declares to the studio and the viewers at home, "I believe in it now." Yet it isn't clear quite *what* it is that he has come to believe in. I would argue that the same is true of these late adaptations of Dickens's story. *A Christmas Carol* continues to mutate to reflect changing times and values, but it has become divorced from Dickens's social reform agenda. As the ongoing Global Financial Crisis demonstrates, families are just as vulnerable as they were in the 1840s and business values continue to threaten the community. Adaptations, however, no longer celebrate the misanthrope's re-entry into a world of neighborliness, but instead focus upon him as an isolated figure. It may be that society no longer has the patience for what Valentine Cunningham has termed "sermonic fictions" (272), or that in an age obsessed with self-improvement, readers and movie-goers are not able to look beyond themselves. Self-help books are, after all, among the top-selling titles reported by booksellers today.

Dickens regarded Christmas as a time for reflection and self-scrutiny, during which readers might take stock of the year that had passed, while thinking about how they might do better in the future. He outlines this process in a piece he wrote for his journal, *Household Words*, in 1851, "What Christmas is as we Grow Older":

Nearer and closer to our hearts be the Christmas spirit, which is the spirit of active usefulness, perseverance, cheerful discharge of duty, kindness and forbearance! It is in the last virtues especially, that we are, or should be, strengthened by the unaccomplished visions of our youth; for, who shall say that they are not our teachers to deal gently even with the impalpable nothings of the earth! [2].

Scrooge's story has become detached from Dickens's version of Christmas spirit and has instead become one of the accoutrements of the festive season. If *A Christmas Carol* is, as Davis says, a culture text, then recent re-workings like *Scrooged* and *Groundhog Day* should make us ask what they have to say about our culture, which seems, by comparison, so much poorer than the Victorian hearths celebrated by Dickens. Almost devoid of charity, lacking social and political commitment, these modern-day adaptations show the commodification of Dickens and of Christmas taken to an extreme. The characters offer diversion and entertainment, but compared to their originals they are pale specters indeed, and their emptiness should scare the Dickens out of us as readers and viewers.

Notes

1. See, for instance, John Waller, *The Real Oliver Twist: Robert Blincoe: A Life That Illuminates an Age* (London: Icon, 2005) and Ruth Richardson, *Dickens and the Workhouse: Oliver Twist and the London Poor* (Oxford: Oxford University Press, 2012) for details of the poor laws and their devastating effects on the underclass.

2. In *Bleak House* (1852–3) Dickens adopted a much sterner, more sinister tone and his narrative openly attacked those readers who refused to look beyond their own homes to engage with those who were, as his omniscient narrator chillingly proclaimed, "dying thus around us everyday" (734).

3. As Juliet John notes in *Dickens and Mass Culture*, there have been more than sixty-four screen adaptations of *A Christmas Carol* (212).

4. See Catherine Waters, *Dickens and the Politics of the Family* for a contextualization of the Victorian response to Bob Cratchit.

5. In many ways, this opening refers to Dickens's later Christmas story, *The Chimes* (1844), in which the central character, Trotty Veck, sees an horrific vision of the future, which stems from his lack of faith in the working classes. Believing himself to be dead, Trotty sees his friends and family fall into vice, culminating with a vision of his daughter Meg on the brink of drowning herself and Trotty's grandchild. Trotty learns to trust in the poor and recognizes that his faith in both God and humankind must be stronger.

6. This ambivalence is reflected in the film's reception history. While its combination of family values, patriotism and religion made it a favorite of Republicans (including the late Ronald Reagan, who was a close friend of Jimmy Stewart, the actor who played George Bailey), the movie's plot presents an overt critique of monopoly capitalism, and its New Deal politics continue to appeal to those of a more left-wing persuasion.

7. Dickens was extremely interested in how industrialism was changing human interactions and consciousness and he explored the fractured identities of professionals in a number of his later novels. Examples include the banker, Jarvis Lorry, in *A Tale of Two Cities*, English literature's first commuter, Mr. Wemmick in *Great Expectations*, and the unhappy schizoid schoolmaster, Bradley Headstone, in *Our Mutual Friend*.

8. See Adam Phillips, *Missing Out: In Praise of the Unlived Life* (London: Hamish Hamilton, 2012) for an extended discussion of how we live with the memories of the paths we chose not to take and the idea of the self who might have been

9. See Robert Douglas-Fairhurst, *Becoming Dickens: The Invention of a Novelist* for a detailed

analysis of the directions that Dickens's life and career might have taken and the extraordinary set of circumstances that combined to make Dickens the most popular novelist of his day.

10. *The Greatest Gift* is rather a surreal story that owes more to *The Chimes* than *A Christmas Carol*. It begins with a character named George on the brink of suicide, who then sees a vision of how the world would have been without him and learns that his friends and family would have been much less happy.

11. This phrase is echoed by Claire later in the movie when the Ghost of Christmas Yet to Come shows Frank what will happen if he doesn't change. We see a Claire who is mean and self-obsessed declare to a companion, "A friend said to me, 'Scrape 'em off, Claire. If you want to save somebody, save yourself'" and this scene recalls the vision Clarence offers to George in *It's a Wonderful Life*, when he shows him how the town would have been without him. The repetition of "save yourself" emphasizes its centrality to the plot of *Scrooged* and draws attention to the importance of individual agency and "self-help" in 1980s American society.

12. See G.K. Chesterton, *Charles Dickens* and Edmund Wilson, "Dickens: The Two Scrooges."

13. The device of the endless repetition of a day until it is lived out "correctly" was also used in a recent adaptation of *A Christmas Carol* (2000, dir. Peter Bowker) starring the British actor Ross Kemp.

14. In many ways this is an appropriately Dickensian conclusion. This retreat from the evils of the public world mirrors Esther Summerson's cloistering in the second Bleak House at the end of the novel of the same name. See Chris Brooks, *Signs for the Times: Symbolic Realism in the mid-Victorian World* for a discussion of Dickens's treatment of private world-building.

Works Cited

Bodenheimer, Rosemarie. *Knowing Dickens*. Ithaca: Cornell University Press, 2007.
Brooks, Chris. *Signs for the Times; Symbolic Realism in the mid-Victorian World*. London: George Allen & Unwin, 1984.
A Christmas Carol. Writer Peter Bowker, dir. Catherine Morshead, LWT 2000.
Cunningham, Valentine. "Dickens and Christianity." Ed. David Paroissien. *A Companion to Charles Dickens*. Oxford: Blackwell, 2008.
Davis, Paul B. *The Lives and Times of Eebenezer Scrooge*. New Haven: Yale University Press, 1990.
Dickens, Charles. *Bleak House*. Ed. Nicola Bradbury, intro. Terry Eagleton. Harmondsworth: Penguin, 2003.
_____. *A Christmas Carol and Other Christmas Writings*. Ed. Michael Slater. Harmondsworth: Penguin, 2003.
_____. *Great Expectations*. Eds. David Trotter and Charlotte Mitchell. Harmondsworth: Penguin, 2004.
_____. *The Letters of Charles Dickens, vol. 3, 1842–1843*. Eds. Madeline House, Graham Storey and Kathleen Tillotson. Pilgrim ed. Oxford: Clarendon Press, 1974.
_____. *The Letters of Charles Dickens, vol. 4, 1844–1846*. Ed. Kathleen Tillotson, associate ed. Nina Burgis. Pilgrim ed. Oxford: Clarendon Press, 1977.
_____. *Oliver Twist*. Ed. Philip Horne. Harmondsworth: Penguin, 2003.
_____. *Our Mutual Friend*. Ed. Adrian Poole. Harmondsworth: Penguin, 1997.
_____. *A Tale of Two Cities*. Ed. Richard Maxwell. Harmondsworth: Penguin, 2003.
_____. "What Christmas is as we Grow Older." *Household Words*, vol. XI, Christmas extra, 1851.
Douglas-Fairhurst, Robert. *Becoming Dickens: The Invention of a Novelist*. Cambridge: Harvard University Press, 2011.
Groundhog Day. Writers Danny Rubin & Harold Ramis, dir. Harold Ramis, Columbia Pictures, 1993.
It's a Wonderful Life. Writers Frances Goodrich, Albert Hackett, Jo Swerling & Frank Capra, dir. Frank Capra, Paramount Pictures, 1946.
John, Juliet. *Dickens and Mass Culture*. Oxford: Oxford University Press, 2010.
Jordan, John O. "Preface." *The Cambridge Companion to Charles Dickens*. Cambridge: Cambridge University Press, 2001.

Ledger, Sally. *Dickens and the Popular Radical Imagination.* Cambridge: Cambridge University Press, 2007.
Miller, Andrew. "Lives Unled in Realist Fiction." *Representations* 98.1 (Spring 2007), pp. 118–134.
Phillips, Adam. *Missing Out: In Praise of the Unlived Life.* Harmondsworth: Hamish Hamilton, 2012.
Pope, Norris. *Dickens and Charity.* New York: Columbia University Press, 1978.
Richardson, Ruth. *Dickens and the Workhouse: Oliver Twist and the London Poor.* Oxford: Oxford University Press, 2012.
Scrooged. Writers Mitch Glazer and Michael O'Donaghue, dir. Richard Donner, Paramount Pictures, 1988.
Stern, Philip Van Doren. *The Greatest Gift.* 1943. New York: Viking, 1996.
Waller, John. *The Real Oliver Twist. Robert Blincoe: A Life that Illuminates an Age.* Cambridge: Icon, 2005.
Waters, Catherine. *Dickens and the Politics of the Family.* Cambridge: Cambridge University Press, 1997.

Reclaiming the Relation of Religion, Politics, and Economics

JOERG RIEGER

The prevalent opinion still holds that religion possesses an identity of its own and that it can be defined as a discipline of study.[1] Many modern scholars have assumed that religion has its own distinct essence.[2] Many postmodern scholars no longer believe in such essences. Nevertheless, they also tend to agree that part of the definition of religion is that it is not politics and not economics, to name two other prominent disciplines. Religion is thus maintained as a discipline even once essentialist understandings of religion have been put to rest. However, such definitions of religion are not only too narrow; they cover up what is most interesting about religion today— namely the interaction of religion with other disciplines, particularly with politics and economics. In this essay, I am calling into question long-held assumptions that religious phenomena are related closest to other religious phenomena, that economic phenomena are related closest to other economic phenomena, and that political phenomena are related closest to other political phenomena. Often, the opposite is the case: certain economic notions of the "invisible hand of the market," for instance, are more closely related to certain religious understandings of divine omnipotence than to other economic understandings of how markets function.

New horizons open up if we set conventional disciplinary categories aside for the moment and examine some particular approaches to religion, economics, and politics in order to investigate what they have in common and what sets them apart. My hypothesis is that certain manifestations of religion have more in common with certain manifestations of economics and politics than with other manifestations of religion. If this is true, then scholars in religious studies, politics, and economics will have to deal in more serious fashion with the diversity of approaches to these three disciplines that prohibits narrow definitions of each of these fields. Furthermore, if this hypothesis is true, we will need to search for kindred spirits not only within our own fields but also across disciplinary boundaries. It is my hope that in the end this search will lead us to a broader and, hopefully, more constructive understanding of the various disciplines.

Broadening the Horizons of the Study of Religion

The basic observation that underlies my argument is that religion, economics, and politics—to name three prominent disciplines that mark our age—bleed into each other in more ways than is commonly recognized. In the United States, for instance, people subscribe to the principle of the separation of church and state, a principle that is anchored in the U.S. Constitution. The historical reasons for the development of this principle are clear: certain ways of relating church and state, as well as religion and politics, in the past have produced catastrophic results, including extensive wars of religion in Europe in the seventeenth century.

The truth is, however, that despite this principle of the separation of church and state there are few modern nations today where religion and politics are tied together more closely than in the United States. The Christian Religious Right, for instance, is deeply involved not only in politics as such, but in the politics of the Republican Party, the so-called Tea Party movement, and other conservative political enterprises.[3] At the other end of the political spectrum, progressive resistance movements like the Civil Rights movement, a newly emerging religion and labor movement in the United States, and the most recent Occupy Wall Street Movement find support in religious communities as well.[4]

The frequently unacknowledged relation of religion and politics in the United States is mirrored in the relation of religion and economics.[5] Classical capitalist philosophy noted the transcendent "invisible hand of the market" (Adam Smith), and neoliberal capitalism continues to be deeply linked to religious and quasi-religious assumptions. The tip of the iceberg in this regard can be seen in the seemingly trivial fact that prayer is often part of corporate board meetings in the United States. The relation of religion and economics is now investigated not only by scholars of religion but also by a growing number of economists.[6] This relation of religion and economics goes at least as deep as the relation of religion and politics, but it is even less acknowledged and reflected upon. When the separation of church and state became the accepted doctrine of the United States in the nineteenth century, there did not appear to be any need to state an explicit separation of church and economics or of religion and economics.

In this regard, it might be interesting to take a look at Europe, where religion is even less visible in relation to economics. While prayer or open talk about divine agency or God is frowned upon in the European context, I suspect that there is a religious moment built into the assumption that economics as currently practiced corresponds to the way things are, i.e., that economics "comes natural." I will come back to this later, arguing that what is linked here is not religion, politics, and economics in general but rather very distinct and particular forms of religion, politics, and economics, which share a set of family resemblances.

In the ancient world, the modern notion that religion is a reality that exists in separation from politics or economics, or that religion is a private affair that is restricted to civil society, would have been inconceivable. Operating on the basis of this modern notion of religion has, unfortunately, prevented both scholars and practitioners of religion from noticing some of the more interesting roles that religion has played in the past and is playing now. In the historical study of Christianity, for instance, the traditional modern opinion that the Emperor Cult of Ancient Rome involved the cooptation of religion (defined as a private/civic affair) by politics (defined as a public/political affair) has prevented generations of scholars from investigating its deeper significance and power.[7]

The narrow modern definition of religion has also prevented us from investigating the full implications and consequences of the rejection of this Emperor Cult by the early Christians. Was this merely a private act of faith, as has often been assumed, or were there larger political implications that were genuinely related to faith and religion? As a result, we have failed to understand significant components not only of ancient Christianity and what kind of religion it was but also of what made up ancient Roman culture and, thus, what is at the root of our Western civilization.[8]

Another example from the study of Christianity illustrates this issue further. The narrow modern definition of religion typically misses the point of Jesus's well-known response to the question of whether colonized Jewish people should pay the taxes levied by the Roman Empire. Jesus's famous statement to "give ... to the emperor the things that are the emperor's, and to God the things that are God's" (Matt. 22:21) provoked the amazement of his audience, according to Matthew's narrative, suggesting that something more interesting is at stake here than the mere distinction of religion and politics in two separate realms. For Jesus, like for his audience, it would not have made sense to assume that "the things that are God's" could be limited to religion and the private realm, while the rest of the world would belong to the emperor as a matter of course. As any righteous Jew would have known, everything belongs to God because God is the creator of the world, and so the request to give God "the things that are God's" sets the Jesus movement on a course of conflict with the political powers of the emperor. In this light, Jesus's execution on a cross as a political rebel makes sense and points to the deeper realties of religion. Modern religionists and much of modern Christianity, on the other hand, could only see Jesus's crucifixion by Rome as a terrible misunderstanding.[9]

Economics as Religion

Postmodern theories of religion have helped us to understand again that religion has never functioned merely in the isolated world of private affairs and that it has had broader implications all along, including implications for politics and economics.[10] Nevertheless, in a world where the modern academic disciplines are still in charge, there are still boundaries that appear to be in the way, despite an increasing number of interdisciplinary and transdisciplinary efforts. One of the current boundaries that separate religion from economics is that religion is seen as a venture that deals with the realm of ideas and values, while economics deals with material reality and the real world. Even when more complex definitions of religion and economics are used, these distinctions remain in effect, for instance when religion is considered a discipline that deals with matters of culture, while economics is considered a discipline that deals with matters of fact and thus shares some traits with the so-called hard sciences.

Based on these types of distinctions, some economists have argued that modern economics has come to function like a religion, as it moves from the analysis of economic phenomena and the calculation of numbers to the promotion of big ideas. Leading economists, in the account of economist Robert Nelson, function like priests in that they keep the big ideas of the discipline alive by preaching them in good and bad times, unconcerned by economic data.[11] The definition of religion operative in this context is tied to the promotion of big ideas and values, which takes place independent of empirical assessments of concrete situations and unaffected by scientific critique.

However, despite operating with a traditional definition of religion, Nelson's observations blur the boundary between religion and economics in some important ways, as economics is seen in a different light. Nelson's observation that economics has come to function like a religion, presented a decade ago, finds support in the context of the responses to recent economic crises. In the

United States, for instance, not even the harsh reality of the so-called Great Recession of 2008 and 2009 was able to dislodge the big ideas and values of neoliberal capitalism. Mounting evidence that these big ideas and values do not correspond to reality is rarely considered by the mainstream.[12] Core ideas of neoliberal economics, like that a rising tide will lift all boats or that wealth accumulated at the top will trickle down, are in tension with the observation that the rich keep getting richer, the poor keep getting poorer, and the middle class is thinning.[13] Still, the majority continues to believe with quasi-religious certainty the neoliberal creeds that economic deregulation is preferable to regulation, that economic privatization is preferable to other alternatives, that large corporations and banks need to be given special treatment by the government in order to promote economic growth, and so on.

In the United States this type of religion and the ideas it promotes is so effective that all major political parties continue to affirm the creeds of neoliberal economics without raising too many questions. The big ideas and values of neoliberal capitalism are so established that alternative economic analyses have a hard time rising to the surface and that potential debates are vehemently discouraged. There is little public awareness that alternatives exist. Moreover, alternative economic approaches are quickly branded with the ominous label of "socialism."

While Europe may be somewhat more open in this regard, similar dynamics of neoliberal economics as religion can be observed there as well, as both European corporations and governments continue to uphold neoliberal economic principles in pushing privatization, economic deregulation, and reducing checks and balances on free trade. Unfortunately, however, more often than not the religion of big ideas and values turns out to promote "pie in the sky"—an illusory hope that never becomes true in most people's lifetimes—and here both dominant religious and economic discourses share another set of family resemblances.

Religion scholars Jeremy Carrette and Richard King have shown the consequences of these dynamics for religion. As they have observed, under the conditions of neoliberal capitalism "religion is rebranded as 'spirituality'"— i.e., devoid of its material qualities and embodiment—"in order to support the ideology of capitalism."[14] Religion in this context loses some of its material qualities and rootedness in alternative ways of life that differ from the dominant paradigm. All that remains are free-floating ideas that seem to have little connection to what is going on in the real world.

What Carrette and King overlook, however, is that not only religion but also economics itself takes on the qualities of this free-floating spirituality in order to maintain the status quo of capitalism. Neoliberal economics as religion keeps promising "pie in the sky" to the public, whose savings and retirement accounts as well as house values have taken major hits, especially in the United States, while a small group of top investors makes more profits than ever before.

In this example a certain kind of religion and a certain kind of economics are moving in sync with each other. It is not that religion is merely used by economics here; economics itself functions like a particular type of religion, a religion that has adapted to economic conventions. At any rate, what ties these types of religion and economics together is the promotion of big and lofty ideas, which are not only devoid of material qualities and embodiment but which are constructed in order to defy any empirical evidence that reality might be different.

In the United States, these types of religion and economics are especially deep-seated, as they have made their way into the public psyche through the promotion of what is called "positive thinking," which is supposedly the key to the American Dream. The assumption is that thinking positive thoughts, against all odds, would create success at all levels. Barbara Ehrenreich's recent book *Bright-Sided* presents the troubling history of positive thinking in the United States. She notes its all-pervasiveness from the academy to religious communities and the world of business. Not only has this approach not worked, it has made things worse for those who believed the hype.[15] It appears, therefore, that these types of religion do not work for the majority of people, dubbed the 99 percent by the Occupy movement in view of the contemporary divisions in capitalist societies.

Reconceiving Religion and Consequences for Economics

As economics takes shape in ways that match what some have defined as religion, traditional definitions of economics are destabilized; economics is more than an account of reality and of the facts of finance. By the same token, we can now take another look at the definition of religion itself, which is not stable either. Although the description of religion as the promotion of free-floating ideas and values captures some forms of religion, it does not capture religion in general. To be more precise, what this definition appears to capture are particular forms of religions, which are endorsed and promoted by those who are in positions of power and control — dubbed the 1 percent by the Occupy movement — and who have an interest in covering up what is going on in the trenches where the real battles of life are fought.

The Emperor Cult in the Roman Empire, for instance, was designed to promote the big ideas and values of the empire, especially in situations where people would have raised questions. The notion of the divinity of Caesar is one of these big and free-floating ideas. Designed to promote the power and elite status of the emperor by eliminating the need to prove itself in real-life situations, this idea of divinity would protect him from the challenges of his peers who did not agree with his designs. Equally important, the idea of the divinity of Caesar would protect him from those who did not have much to gain from the empire and from those who were the victims of its conquests. If they could be convinced of his divinity, they would be more willing to follow his lead and opposition would appear to be hopeless. This big idea, proclaimed by the priests of the empire, was useful in maintaining the power of the status quo of the empire and in warding off questions about the reality of life in the empire, especially questions about the reality of life at its margins.

In the eighteenth and nineteenth centuries in Europe, the big idea of the superiority of the Christian religion was designed to ward off any challenges posed to what at that point was considered "Christian civilization," even by those who otherwise argued for religious pluralism and understanding. The work of German theologian Friedrich Schleiermacher (1768–1834) is especially interesting in this regard, as Schleiermacher provides arguments for the value of other religions while maintaining the superiority not only of Christianity in general but his own type of Prussian Protestantism in particular.[16] Empirical evidence of this superiority is not required, as those who hold to this religion seem to be in agreement about its qualities. In a discussion of miracles, which is not a small matter in Christian theology, Schleiermacher's response can presuppose that his readers agree "Even if it cannot be strictly proved that the Church's power of working miracles has died out..., yet in general it is undeniable that, in view of the great advantage in power and civilization which the Christian peoples posses over the non-Christian..., the preachers of to-day do not need such signs."[17] The big ideas of power and civilization trump even the divine agency itself. Religion, where it takes shape as big ideas and values that resist empirical assessment, has an important role to play in support of positions of power and control.

Today, the big ideas promoted by the so-called Gospel of Prosperity, which proclaims fantastic wealth and success for those of its adherents who engage in the right religious practices, are designed perhaps not primarily with the goal to make more people wealthy, as is often assumed. Just the opposite appears to be the case: the big ideas promoted by the Gospel of Prosperity help to fend off challenges from those who are not gaining the promised wealth and success. In this way, the Gospel of Prosperity contributes to the power and control of the 1 percent over the 99 percent. The losers can now be held in check and blamed for their own misfortune. The barely chastened promotion of big ideas by neoliberal economists fulfills a similar task, which is not primarily to increase the wealth of the community but the wealth of the economic elite, while blaming those who are unable to survive economically for their own exclusion from economic power.

What all these examples share in common is that free-floating big ideas and values serve to cover up and thus maintain the power differentials, and as such are designed to prevent closer investigations of economic and political realities, especially from the point of view of the 99 percent.

Nevertheless, this is not the only way in which religion functions. Religions that are not as strongly aligned with the dominant powers, or that resist these powers in some form or fashion, often display different dynamics. In the Roman Empire, for instance, alternative religious movements could not survive merely by promoting big ideas; rather, they had to prove themselves against the powers of the empire. These movements needed to demonstrate somehow that they made a difference. This appears to be the context of Jesus's response to John the Baptist in the Gospel of Matthew, as John began to have doubts about the Jesus movement.

Jesus's response is very different from those who promote big ideas, and it does not even seem to be particularly religious in terms of the dominant definition of religion: "Go and tell John what you hear and see: the blind receive their sight, the lame walk, the lepers are cleansed, the deaf hear, the dead are raised, and the poor have good news brought to them" (Matt. 11:4–5). Rather than demanding trust in great ideas, Jesus provides evidence of what difference his movement is making. Good news to the poor, in this context, cannot be pie in the sky or the proclamation that a rising tide will — eventually — lift all boats; good news to the poor only makes sense if it is the tangible transformation of reality.

Currently, the religiosity tied up with liberation theologies in Latin America and elsewhere is in a similar position. While often pronounced dead and outdated by those who promote dominant religion, liberation religiosity stays alive by being tied to movements that are making a difference in the lives of people. This happens, for instance, by raising levels of awareness about what is going on in real life, by organizing alternative communities not only religiously but also politically and economically, and by making it clear that religion takes a stand with those who struggle against oppression. Big ideas and values, in this context, are not necessarily off-limits but they need to prove themselves in some form or fashion in real-life contexts. If there is a disconnect, these ideas are bound to be transformed and reshaped in relation to the struggles of the people.

Here, religion assumes a different form. Rather than the promotion of free-floating ideas and values from the top down, religion is the negotiation of the pressures of real life in such a way that alternatives are nourished and become visible — the sort of alternatives whose existence the status quo refuses to admit. It is well known that the Christian Base Communities in Latin America in the 1970s and 1980s managed to form alternative bodies in their resistance against dominant religion, economics, and politics. What is less known is that these things are still going on in some shape or form. As these activities continue, they become more multifaceted and complex. As far as the projects of the Christian Base Communities in Latin America are concerned, other religious groupings have joined the resistance, including indigenous religions and some Pentecostal strands of Christianity.

In the United States, religious resistance movements have a history that goes back to the beginnings of the nation, from abolitionism to women's rights and Civil Rights movements. Today, a budding religion and labor movement is beginning to shape religiosity as it negotiates the increasing pressures that impinge on the lives of workers.[18] In addition, the current activities related to the Occupy Wall Street Movement are related to religion in less obvious ways, but connections exist. The Occupy Faith movement is only one example. The implications of the Occupy movement for religion and our understanding of the divine and of religious communities, as well as the implications of alternative religion for the Occupy movement are tremendous. My colleague Kwok Pui Lan and I are talking about a "theology of the multitude" that is emerging here.[19]

Talking about religious notions like, for instance, the work of Jesus Christ in this context is not code for unquestioning endorsements of the powers that be, as is often the case when the mainline invokes concepts like the "lordship of Christ." Talking about the work of Jesus Christ here demands a discussion of the difference Christ makes in the lives of those who experience the tremendous pressures of the labor market in a country like the United States, where the unemployed and the employed are played off each other in order to drive down wages and benefits.[20] The big ideas of wealth and success give way to considerations of Christ taking the sides of the people ("the last will be first," Matt. 20:16), taking a stand against Mammon and for God's care of the world (Matt. 6:24), and organizing an alternative way of life (riding into Jerusalem on a donkey, when the Roman governors rode on horses, Matt. 21:1–10).

Alternative ideas and values arise out of this engagement, grounding lofty ideas like the love of God and love of neighbor (Mark 12:28–34): when seen from the perspective of everyday labor, for instance, love of neighbor cannot be reduced to religious sentimentality and status-quo notions of charity. Love of neighbor means solidarity in the struggle, based on an understanding that self and other belong together, not giving in when the going gets tough, and seeing things through until reality and idea inform each other.[21] The idea of the love of God acquires a new meaning in this context as well.

In sum, religion does not necessarily have to be defined as the promotion of big ideas and values that are disconnected from everyday life. Another way of putting this would be to say that religion does not have to be defined by the common sort of "blind faith" that does not request evidence — or that is designed to resist it. Religion can now be understood in alternative fashion as testing and reshaping big ideas and values in relation to the struggles of real life under pressure. This broadening of the understanding of religion has implications for how we understand economics. Economics does not necessarily have to be a religion in the sense of the promotion of blind faith either. Economics, too, can be reconceived as testing and reshaping big ideas and values in relation to the struggles of real life under pressure. In this scenario, economic crises such as the ones of recent history can become opportunities to challenge the proclamation of lofty ideas in both economics and religion, and to reshape and redesign both economics and religion in new and interesting ways.[22]

That I am on track with these reflections is demonstrated by the fact that there are indeed new developments both in economics and religion that move in these directions, as they are driven by close attention to the struggles of real life under pressure, especially the struggles of the increasing numbers of those who are not benefiting from the status quo.[23] This should be common knowledge. Unfortunately, these developments are often overshadowed and covered up by the designs of dominant religion and economics, which are desperately trying to hang on to the big ideas and values of the status quo in order to ward off mounting challenges.

All these observations support my hypothesis: certain forms of religion share a greater affinity with certain forms of economics than with other forms of religion. The similarities and differences can be found in the basic structures: one structure promotes the proclamation of big ideas and values that are disconnected from everyday life as part of its design, while another structure requires hammering out ideas and values in the midst of the struggles of life. In this context, the question of power merits further investigation, since these structural differences seem to be related to the differences between dominant forms of religion and economics, which work for the 1 percent, and their subaltern variations, which work for the 99 percent.[24]

I must admit my own bias here for, after much deliberation, I have come to the conviction that scholars are ultimately better off not only when they test big ideas and values in reality, but when big ideas and values are developed in the context of real-life struggles that take into account the perspectives of those who are relegated to the margins of power. This perspective from the underside is valuable not only for those who are forced to dwell there but for all of us— and ultimately even for the 1 percent — as it forces us to deal with the destructive potential of detached ideas that know no limits and are ultimately unsustainable in a limited ecosystem. In small compass, this is the difference between the religion that supports the concerns of the 99 percent and the religion that supports the concerns of the 1 percent.

Complexity and Construction

In my argument so far it might appear as if there were only two options. The reality is, of course, more complex, as there are a variety of ways of relating big ideas/values and the struggles of life. The logical extremes are positions where big ideas/values are promoted in order to deny or reject the relevance of particular struggles of life. Some parts of neoliberal economics appear to function in this way, as particular problems like poverty or unemployment are believed to take care of themselves and do no not need to be addressed — must not be addressed, in Adam Smith's account[25] — so as not to disturb the big picture. On the other hand, there are a variety of grassroots approaches, where the big ideas/values of particular traditions are rethought exclusively in light of specific forms and shapes that particular struggles take.

In the developments that have often been described as "postmodernity," we have been forced to deal with difference, otherness, and pluralism in new ways. Postmodern thought has argued that there are usually more than two options. The greater openness that has resulted from this situation is welcome and much needed, and in some ways it undergirds my argument in some ways. Nevertheless, the postmodern situation has also led to some complacency, according to which pluralism now can be taken to mean everything is of equal value and that "anything goes." In this case, the religion of neoliberal economics or of the 1 percent would be just one more religion among others, which is just as valid as other religions. The sort of interreligious dialogue that emerges at this point has the advantage that it includes economics as religion by default,[26] yet the pluralistic creed of postmodernity favors all religions equally and so no decision can be made about value or validity and power relations are left out of the picture.

While this sort of postmodern pluralism is certainly preferable to the witch hunts of the past where only one position prevailed, I want to suggest a different approach. The dialogues between religion and economics that emerge when we question some of the traditional boundaries between the various disciplines might help us establish new, more productive boundaries. Rather than dwelling on the differences between religion and economics in general, we might pay closer attention to the differences between religions and economics that promote lofty ideas on the one hand and, on the other hand, religions and economics that negotiate ideas and values in the struggle against marginalization and oppression. Here, a new sense of disciplinary boundaries emerges, according to which the lines are drawn between some form of religion and economics and other forms of religion and economics. The feminist study of religion and theology, for example, might have more affinity to feminist economics than to the mainline study of religion and theology, and the mainline study of religion and theology may have more affinity to mainline economics than to liberation theology.

In this context, the classical insight of many oppressed people that the gods of the masters and the gods of the people are not the same begins to make sense. This insight has been expressed on many continents. In South Africa, it was a central discovery in the struggle against Apartheid. In Latin America, liberation theologians have addressed this issue, which is also expressed in José María Arguedas's novel *Todas las Sangres*.[27] What needs to be explored further is what difference religion and economics make in particular contexts—and whether and how they "practice what they preach."

As the lines that differentiate these approaches are drawn more clearly, constructive projects can also take shape with more rigor and vigor. On one side of the political spectrum this is already happening. Conservative think tanks in the United States, like the American Enterprise Foundation and the Institute for Religion and Democracy, encourage collaboration across the traditional lines drawn by current academic disciplines. Progressive voices might do well to consider how religious, economic, and political approaches that pay attention to perspectives emerging from the 99 percent might inform, reshape, and reinforce each other. These new kinds of interdisciplinary/interreligious dialogues will, no doubt, be more open ended and less homogeneous than their conservative counterparts, because of the open-ended nature of life in the diversity of the 99 percent and the varieties of pressures that are experienced here.

Another interesting question suggests itself at this point. In the complex situation of negotiating big ideas/values and the struggles of life, what would we find if we began to investigate particular struggles in particular contexts? For instance, what if we pursued the struggles in the world of labor in this way as one manifestation of the tension between the 1 percent and the 99 percent? How would our definitions of religion, politics, and economics be affected? To be sure, such an investigation would be a complex one, as it would necessarily have to address issues of race, gender, globalization, etc., as they are relevant to labor issues.

The approach that I am proposing would require some in-depth studies that have broader value beyond the world of a few specialists and that would have the potential to spawn collaborative projects between religious studies, economics, and politics, which are rarely happening now.

Notes

1. This essay is a rewriting of the keynote address given at the Southwest Commission on Religious Studies conference on March 11, 2012.
2. The most prominent modern examples, going back to the nineteenth century, are Friedrich Schleiermacher, *On Religion: Speeches to Its Cultured Despisers*, trans. and ed. Richard Crouter (New York: Cambridge University Press, 1996), and Ludwig Feuerbach, *The Essence of Religion*, trans. Alexander Loos (Amherst, N.Y.: Prometheus Books, 2004), but most modern scholars until recently assumed that religion had a distinct essence. Schleiermacher, of course, also made a major contribution to the self-understanding of the modern university in terms of fields and disciplines.
3. For an analysis of the landscape in the United States in the new millennium, see Mark Lewis Taylor, *Religion, Politics, and the Christian Right: Post 9/11 Powers and American Empire* (Minneapolis: Fortress Press, 2005).
4. See, for instance the formation of Interfaith Worker Justice (IWJ) and Clergy and Laity United For Economic Justice (CLUE) within the past 15 years, as well as the Occupy Faith movement.
5. As I have demonstrated in a recent book, see: Joerg Rieger, *No Rising Tide: Theology, Economics, and the Future* (Minneapolis: Fortress Press, 2009).
6. See, for instance, Robert H. Nelson, *Economics as Religion: From Samuelson to Chicago and Beyond* (University Park: Pennsylvania State University Press, 2001), and Duncan K. Foley, *Adam's Fallacy: A Guide to Economic Theology* (Cambridge: The Belknap Press of Harvard University Press, 2006).
7. See, for instance, See Günther Hansen, "Herrscherkult und Friedensidee," in *Umwelt des Urchristentums*, vol. 1, ed. Johannes Leipoldt and Walter Grundmann (Berlin: Evangelische Verlagsanstalt, 1967), 140, who assumes that "rational politicians" like Caesar and Augustus made use of these religious sensitivities in order to support their political aims and claims that living cults were (mis)used for the *"Loyalitätsreligion."* While Hansen admits "genuine religious yearnings and feelings of gratitude" (ibid.), he doubts that "real religious feelings" were at the basis of this cult (ibid., 141).
8. See, for instance, the discussion in Joerg Rieger, *Christ and Empire: From Paul to Postcolonial Times* (Minneapolis: Fortress Press 2007), chapter 2.
9. In this regard, the work of Richard Horsley and of John Dominic Crossan and others is instructive.
10. See, for instance, the work of scholars like Talal Asad, Tomoko Masuzawa, and Richard King.
11. See Nelson, *Economics as Religion*, xv.
12. See, for instance, John R. Talbott, *The Eighty-Six Biggest Lies on Wall Street* (New York: Seven Stories Press, 2009), and Ha-Joon Chang, *Things They Don't Tell You about Capitalism* (New York: Bloomsbury Press, 2010).
13. The numbers and the implications are discussed in Rieger, *No Rising Tide*, chapter 2.
14. Jeremy Carrette and Richard King, *Selling Spirituality: The Silent Takeover of Religion* (London: Routledge, 2004), 17. The consequences of this move have to do with "the tailoring of ... individualised spiritualities to fit the needs of corporate business culture in its demand for an efficient, productive and *pacified* workforce." Ibid., 29, emphasis in original. Yet simply "rethinking the ethical and social dimensions of tradition," as Carrette and King suggest, ibid., will not do since the traditions themselves were shaped in the midst of similar struggles and can thus easily be co-opted.
15. Barbara Ehrenreich, *Bright-Sided: How the Relentless Production of Positive Thinking Has Undermined America* (New York: Metropolitan Books, 2009), has written the history of positive thinking in the United States, noting its all-pervasiveness from the academy to religious communities and the world of business.
16. For the general context of this approach see Susanne Zantop, *Colonial Fantasies: Conquest, Family, and Nation in Precolonial Germany, 1770–1870* (Durham: Duke University Press, 1997); for an analysis of Schleiermacher in this context, see Rieger, *Christ and Empire*, chapter 5.
17. Friedrich Schleiermacher, *The Christian Faith*, ed. H. R. Mackintosh and J. S. Stewart (Edinburgh: T.&T. Clark, 1986), 450.
18. See, for instance, the work of Interfaith Worker Justice (www.iwj.org) and Clergy and Laity for Economic Justice (www.cluela.org; www.clueca.org), as well as some of the activities sponsored by Jobs with Justice (www.jwj.org). Accessed February 21, 2012

19. See Joerg Rieger and Kwok Pui Lan, *Occupy Religion: Theology of the Multitude, Religion in the Modern World* (Lanham, MD: Rowman & Littlefield, 2012).

20. Protection and support for workers is much worse in the United States than in most industrialized countries, and what little remains of worker rights is under attack.

21. For my own relation to the labor and religion movement see http://www.joergrieger.com/?page_id=17.

22. In *No Rising Tide*, chapter 2, I talk about this as the use of the "logic of downturn."

23. In the field of economic theory, for instance, feminist economists have introduced new and highly relevant reflections. See Marianne Ferber and Julie Nelson, *Feminist Economics Today: Beyond Economic Man* (Chicago: University of Chicago Press, 2003) and Nancy Folbre, *Greed, Lust, and Gender: A History of Economic Ideas* (Chicago: University of Chicago Press, 2009).

24. For a helpful discussion of the notion of subalternity see John Beverley, *Subalternity and Representation: Arguments in Cultural Theory* (Durham: Duke University Press, 1999).

25. According to Smith, a merchant who only intends his own advantage is "led by an invisible hand to promote an end which was no part of his intention." Moreover, "by pursuing his own interest he frequently promotes that of the society more effectually than when he really intends to promote it." Adam Smith, *An Inquiry into the Nature and Causes of the Wealth of Nations*, 5th ed., 1789 (London: Methuen 1904), bk. IV, chapt. II, par. IV.

26. For an argument that economics needs to be included in interreligious dialogue see Paul F. Knitter and Chandra Muzaffar, *Subverting Greed: Religious Perspectives on the Global Economy* (Maryknoll, N.Y.: Orbis Books, 2002).

27. Referenced in Gustavo Gutiérrez, *Entre las calandrias: Un ensayo sobre José María Arguedas* (Lima: CEP, 1990), 79.

Works Cited

Beverley, John. *Subalternity and Representation: Arguments in Cultural Theory*. Durham: Duke University Press, 1999.
Carrette, Jeremy, and Richard King. *Selling Spirituality: The Silent Takeover of Religion*. London: Routledge, 2004. 17.
Chang, Ha-Joon. *Things They Don't Tell You about Capitalism*. New York: Bloomsbury Press, 2010.
Ehrenreich, Barbara. *Bright-Sided: How the Relentless Production of Positive Thinking has Undermined America*. New York: Metropolitan Books, 2009.
Ferber, Marianne, and Julie Nelson. *Feminist Economics Today: Beyond Economic Man*. Chicago: University of Chicago Press, 2003.
Feuerbach, Ludwig. *The Essence of Religion*, trans. Alexander Loos. Amherst, N.Y.: Prometheus Books, 2004.
Folbre, Nancy. *Greed, Lust, and Gender: A History of Economic Ideas*. Chicago: University of Chicago Press, 2009.
Foley, Duncan K. *Adam's Fallacy: A Guide to Economic Theology*. Cambridge: The Belknap Press of Harvard University Press, 2006.
Gutiérrez, Gustavo. *Entre las calandrias: Un ensayo sobre José María Arguedas*. Lima: CEP, 1990. 79.
Hansen, Günther. "Herrscherkult und Friedensidee." *Umwelt des Urchristentums*, vol. 1, ed. Johannes Leipoldt and Walter Grundmann. Berlin: Evangelische Verlagsanstalt, 1967. 140.
Knitter, Paul F., and Chandra Muzaffar. *Subverting Greed: Religious Perspectives on the Global Economy*. Maryknoll, N.Y.: Orbis Books, 2002.
Nelson, Robert H. *Economics as Religion: From Samuelson to Chicago and Beyond*. University Park: Pennsylvania State University Press, 2001.
Rieger, Joerg. *Christ and Empire: From Paul to Postcolonial Times* (Minneapolis: Fortress Press 2007), chapter 2.
_____. *No Rising Tide: Theology, Economics, and the Future*. Minneapolis: Fortress Press, 2009.
_____, and Kwok Pui Lan. *Occupy Religion: Theology of the Multitude, Religion in the Modern World*. Lanham, MD: Rowman & Littlefield, 2012.

Schleiermacher, Friedrich. *The Christian Faith,* ed. H. R. Mackintosh and J. S. Stewart. Edinburgh: T. & T. Clark, 1986, 450.
_____. *On Religion: Speeches to Its Cultured Despisers,* trans. and ed. Richard Crouter. New York: Cambridge University Press, 1996.
Smith, Adam. *An Inquiry into the Nature and Causes of the Wealth of Nations,* 5th ed., 1789. London: Methuen, 1904. bk. IV, chapt. II, par. IV.
Talbott, John R. *The Eighty-Six Biggest Lies on Wall Street.* New York: Seven Stories Press, 2009.
Taylor, Mark Lewis. *Religion, Politics, and the Christian Right: Post 9/11 Powers and American Empire.* Minneapolis: Fortress Press, 2005.
Zantop, Susanne. *Colonial Fantasies: Conquest, Family, and Nation in Precolonial Germany, 1770–1870.* Durham: Duke University Press, 1997.

About the Contributors

Tim H. Blessing is a professor of history and political science at Alvernia University. Co-author (with Robert K. Murray) of *Greatness in the White House* (Pennsylvania State University Press, 1988, 1994), he is a frequent presenter on leadership in the United States, Europe and Latin America. His research interests also include the American presidency, political history and the early American republic.

Marc DiPaolo is an assistant professor of English and Film at Oklahoma City University. He is the author of *War, Politics and Superheroes* (McFarland, 2011, *Choice* Outstanding Academic Title 2011) and *Emma Adapted* (Peter Lang, 2007). He is co-editor (with Bryan Cardinale-Powell) of *Devised and Directed by Mike Leigh* (Continuum, 2013) and *The Conscious Reader* (Pearson, 2012). He has also published essays on the Beauty and the Beast fairy tale cycle, the Marx Brothers, and vampire movies.

Dara Downey is an occasional lecturer in the School of English, Trinity College Dublin. Her monograph on late nineteenth-century American women's ghost stories will be published by Palgrave Macmillan in 2014. She has published numerous essays on American Gothic writers and is the book review editor of the *Irish Journal of Gothic and Horror Studies*.

Katherine Brown Downey is the southwest region coordinator for the American Academy of Religion and teaches at the Hockaday School. A cultural historian and axiologist, she considers literary texts as artifacts that reveal the values of the culture that produced them. She is the author of *Perverse Midrash: Oscar Wilde, Andre Gide, and Censorship of Biblical Drama* (Continuum, 2004).

Tracy Floreani is a professor of English at Oklahoma City University, where she teaches American literature and writing. She is the author of *Fifties Ethnicities: The Ethnic Novel and Mass Culture at Midcentury* (State University of New York,

2013). While her scholarship focuses on ethnicity and immigrant identities in American culture since World War II, she enjoys exploring all facets of American cultural identities.

Marc Lucht is visiting assistant professor of philosophy and education coordinator for the Center for Peace Studies and Violence Prevention at Virginia Tech. A specialist in 19th and 20th century Continental philosophy, he co-edited (with Donna Yarri) *Kafka's Creatures: Animals, Hybrids, and Other Fantastic Beings* (Lexington, 2010).

Eric Michael Mazur is the Gloria & David Furman Professor of Judaic Studies at Virginia Wesleyan College, editor of *The Encyclopedia of Religion & Film* (ABC-CLIO, 2011) and *Art & the Religious Impulse* (Bucknell University Press, 2002), and co-editor (with Kate McCarthy) of *God in the Details: American Religion in Popular Culture* (Routledge, 2001, 2010).

Grace Moore is a senior research fellow in the ARC Centre of Excellence for the History of Emotions at the University of Melbourne. She also lectures in English and theatre. She is the author of *Dickens and Empire* (Ashgate, 2004), *The Victorian Novel in Context* (Continuum, 2012), and a study guide on *A Christmas Carol* (Insight, 2011).

Val Nolan is a lecturer at the National University of Ireland, Galway. His work has appeared in *Review of Contemporary Fiction*, *Irish Studies Review*, and *Nordic Irish Studies*. He writes regularly for the *Irish Examiner* and is completing a monograph on novelist and filmmaker Neil Jordan.

Joerg Rieger is the Wendland-Cook Endowed Professor of Constructive Theology at Southern Methodist University. His publications include *Traveling: Christian Explorations of Daily Living* (Fortress Press, 2011), *No Rising Tide: Theology, Economics, and the Future* (Fortress Press, 2009), and *Occupy Religion: Theology of the Multitude*, co-authored with Kwok Pui-lan (Rowman & Littlefield, 2012).

Gustavo A. Rodríguez Martín is assistant professor at the Universidad de Extremadura, Spain. A professional translator, he has published and lectured on cross-cultural studies, narratives in translation, and Shaw. He is a member of the International Shaw Society and the International Association of Paremiology.

Ruth Vanita is a professor in the Liberal Studies program at the University of Montana. A translator, poet, and Shakespearean scholar, she is the founding co-editor (with Mudhu Kishwar) of *Manushi*, India's first nationwide feminist magazine. Her many books include *Same-Sex Love in India: Readings from Literature and History* (with Saleem Kidwai, St. Martin's, 2000) and *Gender, Sex and the City: Urdu Rekhti Poetry in India, 1780–1870* (Palgrave Macmillan, 2012).

Gerald S. Vigna is an associate professor of theology at Alvernia University. He is a scholar in Catholic theology and ethics, and his interests range broadly over the span of Christian history with particular emphasis on early Christian history and literature. Vigna also teaches leadership studies and directs Alvernia's master's program in community leadership.

Matthew Yde teaches in the Department of Theatre at The Ohio State University. The author of *Longing for Utopia: Bernard Shaw and Totalitarianism* (Palgrave Macmillan, 2013), Yde has also published articles in *Modern Drama* and *SHAW: The Annual of Bernard Shaw Studies.*

Index

Numbers in **bold italics** indicate pages with photographs.

Abel 104
abolition of slavery 13
abortion 188
Abraham 103, 158, 210; *Abrahamic faiths* 168
Abrams, J.J. 163
The Action Bible 152
ad hominem 2, 84
Adam and Eve 96, 104, 106, 125, 174
Adamantius 80
Adams, Abigail 38
Adams, Dickinson 31–32, 36
Adams, John 25, 35–38, 40
Adler, Felix 156
Adonais 107, 110
adultery 188–189, 212
advertising 18, 196, 205
afterlife 51, 56, 63, 120, 158, 165, **166**, 168, 173, 176, 202, 213
agnosticism 2, 86, 115, 130, 139
Ahlstrom, Sydney 148
Alaric 95
Alastor 104
Alexander, Meena 99
Alexandria 3, 41, 79, 80, 85
Alighieri, Dante 3, 6, 15–18
All-Russian Congress of Peasant Deputies 38
Allah 127
allegory 84, 101, 140, 164, 176–177, 190
alms 67, 92
altar 102, 103, 105, 183, 210
ambiguous 152, 167, 175
American Enterprise Foundation 250
American Fascists: The Christian Right and the War on America 16
"American Monomyth" 55–56
American Museum of Natural History 154

American Revolution 26, 29, 36, 38, 40
America's "Post-Puritan" period 148
"Amnesty for the Devil" 79–97
amphibologisms 38
Anabaptist 85
anatomist 122
Ancoratus 84
Androcles and the Lion 4, 21, 117, 120
Angeli, Michael 172
angels 19, 33, 34, 43, 50, 53, 70, 81, 82, 94, 158, 169, 173, 182, 185, 188, 189, 190, 196, 209, 212, 215, 226
animals 15, 20, 62, 98, 99, 100, 101, 102, 104, 105, 108, 109, 139
animism 123
Anthony, Susan B. 1, 6
The Antichrist 65, 75
Anti-Defamation League 57
anti–Trinitarians 37
Apartheid 250
apocalyptic 34, 60, 181, 230
Apokatastasis 80, 84–86, 88, 93, 94
Apology (of Tertullian) 92
apostate 2, 108
The Apple Cart 125
the Archbishop of Canterbury 49
Ares 2
Arguedas, José María 250
ascetic 72, 75, 80, 115, 119, 122, 136
"The Assassins" 106
Atarbius 85
Athanasian Creed 41
Athanasius, Bishop of Alexandria 38, 41
atheism **2**, 8, 9, 98, 107, 115, 129, 130, 156, 157, 164, 167, 174, 182
atomic bomb 156
"Auguries of Innocence" 102

259

Index

Authentic Christianity 5, 15, 17, 18, 20, 64, 67, 68, 71, 77
The Authentic Letters of Paul 4

"baby boomer" generation 148
Babylon 5 163
Bach, Johann Sebastian 64
Back to Methuselah 21, 120, 124, 128, 130
Bailey, George 227, **228**, 233, 234, 236
Baka, Miroslaw 191
Baktin, Mikail 89
Baltar, Dr. Gaius 164, 169–***171***, 174–175, 177
Baptist Tabernacle of Los Angeles 53
barbarian 15, 127
Barcis, Artur 185
Barnard, Ellsworth 98
Barth, Karl 181–182
Bathsheba 48
Battlestar Galactica 162–164, 168–178
Baugh, Lloyd 185, 190, 197
B.C. 151
The Beatles 21, 144, 150
Bedford Falls 22, 223, 225–227, 229
Bellah, Robert 157
Benedict, Dirk 174
Bezukhov, Pierre 68
Bhagavad Gita 133, 100, 109, 156
Bible 3, 4, 6, 7, 19, 30–40, 44, 46, 47, 60, 69, 75–77, 80, 82, 92–94, 96, 104, 105, 116, 125, 130, 131, 143, 146, 151, 158, 181, 182, 192, 197–198, 206, 241, 246–247
Biblical literalism 116, 151
Bien, P.A. 43, 58
bigotry 26–27, 127
Biraghi, Guglielmo 54
Blake, William 86, 87, 102, 104
blasphemy 46, 49, 54, 57, 108
Bleak House 227, 237
Blessing, Tim H. 19, 25–42, 76, 255
Boanerges 125, 130
Bodenheimer, Rosemarie 222
Bolton, Robert 206
Bonhoeffer, Dietrich 187
Borowitz, Eugene 144, 149
Brahma 109, 127
Brahmin 101, 136
Bright, Bill 53
British Board of Film Classification 54
The British Empire 115, 130
Brooker, Charlie 177
Brown, Charles Brockden 200, 202, 204, 207, 213, 217, 218
Brown, Dan 3, 5, 13
Buddhism 67, 136, 155, 158, 168
Buell, Lawrence 139–140
bullshittery 167
Buñuel, Luis 8–9
Buoyant Billions 122
Burgess, Anthony 13, 14–15, 20
Burns, Frank 25, 147, 151–152

Bush, George W. 181
Butler, Jonathan 147

Caesar 244–245, 251
Cain 104, 125
California Academy of Science 154
Calvin, John 200, 204, 205, 208, 211, 213, 218
Calvin & Hobbes 152, 153, 158
Camissard 204
Canonical 19, 47, 130, 145, 150
Capra, Frank 22, 221–222, 225, 227–230, 232
capitalist 122, 195–196, 226, 240, 244
Carrette, Jeremy 243, 251
Cartesian 99
Carwin, Francis 204, 207–209, 211–212, 216
Catholic school 48
censorship 12, 45, 48–50, 53, 129
Ceylon 127
Charles I 15, 39
A Charlie Brown Christmas 4, 146, 151
Chaucer, Geoffrey 13, 16
Chauncy, Charles 205, 207
Chesterton, G.K. 121, 223, 233
the Children's Employment Commission's report into child labor 222
The Chimes 236–237
Christ 2, 3, 4, 5, 6, 7, 8, 9, 10, 11, 12, 19, 20, 37, 39, 43, 44, 47, 48, 49, 52, 56, 59, 62, 65, 70, 71, 73, 77, 81, 82, 83, 94, 96, 101, 102, 108, 120, 122, 125, 137, 147, 180, 181, 187, 190, 233, 246; *see also* Jesus
Christian Base Communities 247
the Christian Democratic Party of Italy 49
Christian existentialist 182
Christian Religious Right 240
Christie, Ian 53
Christmas 22, 146, 151, 221–238
A Christmas Carol 4, 22, 221–226, 229–231, 233, 235–237
The Church of England 114, 120
Church of the Holy Trinity v. United States, 1892 148
City of God 85, 92, 95
Civil Rights Movement 240, 247
A Clockwork Orange 13–14
Coetzee 58
Colacurcio, Michael J. 205
Coleridge, Samuel Taylor 98
Collins, John 206, 218
Communism 125, 181, 197
Cone, James 149
Constantinople 85
Coryphaeus 38
Council of Chalcedon decision in 451 48
Coupe, Laurence 16
Covenant 94
Cowper, William 102–105, 107
Cox, Harvey 144
Creative Evolution 119, 123, 124, 129
Cromwell, Oliver 39–40

crucifixion 20, 53, 65, 77, 101, 137, 158, 242
Cullen, Charles T. 32, 35
Cuse, Carlton 163, 165, 167
Cunningham, Valentine 236
Cylons 164, 168, 170, 172–173, 175–177
Cyprus 84

Dain, Norman 13
Daly, Mary 149
"Damned if you do..." 8–9
Dante and the Unorthodox 16
Dante's Inferno (video game) 18
Darwin, Charles 116, 130
Davidson, Carol Margaret 205
The Da Vinci Code 3–5
Davis, Jefferson 3
Davis, Paul 221, 227–228, 233, 236
"De Profundis" 4–5
The Decalogue 4, 16, 22, 180–198
Declaration of American Independence 25
"The Decline and Fall of Christian America" 153
deism 25, 36
Dement, Iris 95
Demogorgon 109
Descartes, René 99
The Devil 14, 33, 34, 44, 81, 82, 85, 86, 92, 107, 131, 138, 193, 209, 218
Dewey, Arthur J. 4, 7–8
The Diatessaron 34, 40–41
Didymus the Blind 85
Disney, Walt 150
Dobson, David 147, 152–153
Dogma 13
La Dolce Vita 9–10
Dombey and Son 227
Don Juan 120–121
The Donation of Constantine 3
Douglas, Frederick 13
Downey, Dara 22, 199–220, 255
Downey, Katherine Brown 19–20, 43–61, 255
Drew, John 100, 106
Drum-Taps 134
Dylan, Bob [Zimmerman] 21, 150

the Eastern Orthodox Church of America 49
Eastwood, Clint 79, 81, 86, 91, 95, 96
Ebert, Roger 9, 10, 21
Eden 55, 146, 155, 158, 173
Edinburgh Review 222
Edwards, Jonathan 13
Ehrenreich, Barbara 244
Eick, David 163
"1829 Report on the Subject of Mails on the Sabbath" 28
Einstein, Albert 14
Eliot, T.S. 16
Elson, John 144
Ely, Ezra Stiles 28
Emerson, Ralph Waldo 133, 136

Emmanuel 103
Emperor Decius 80
Encyclopedia of Religion in Film 16
"The End of Christian America" 153
Enfield, William 36–37
English Civil War 40
Epiphanius of Salamis 84
Esau 94
The Eternal Word Television Network 53
Eucharist 92
Eudoxia 125
Evagrius Ponticus 85
ex nihilo 81
Ezekiel 82

Facebook 133
Falwell, Jerry 53
The Family Circus 151
Family Guy 157
"Fanaticism and Familicide from *Wieland* to *The Shining*" 22, 199–220
"Fantasy's Power and Peril" 3
The Far Side 22, 153, 154
"The Far Side of Science" 154
Fellini, Federico 9–10
Ferrovius 118
the Fifth Ecumenical Council at Constantinople in 553 85
The First Amendment of the U.S. Constitution 49, 148
Fitzfassen, Epifania 125–126
The Five Gospels (Jesus Seminar text) 7
Floreani, Tracy 21, 133–142, 255
For Better or for Worse 153
Forbes, Bruce 147
Forster, E.M. 110
Forster, John 224
Frailty 22, 200, 202, 215
Frankenstein 154–155
Fraser, Andrea 12
Frederiksen, Paula 57–58
Freeman, Morgan 12, 79
French Revolution 40
"From Bedford Falls to Punxsutawney: Refashioning *A Christmas Carol*" 221–238

Galilei, Galileo 3, 45
Gandhi, Leela 100
Gandhi, M.K. 99, 106–109
Geisel, Theodor Seuss 152
Gibson, Mel 9, 10, 11, 20, 44, 45, 57, 58
Gide, André 45–49, 51–52
Gilmour, Michael 154–155
Gita Govinda 100
Globalization and Theology 18
Gnosticism 81–83
God 1–3, 6–7, 9, 11, **12**, 13–16, 28–29, 33, 35–36, 38, 40, 43–44, 46–48, 51, 52, 55–56, 58–59, 62–63, 69–72, 76–85, 87–89, 91–96, 98–99, 101–108, 110, 115–116, 118–119, 121,

123–125, 129, 130, 135, 137–141, 143, 144–145, 148–149, 155–157, 164–165, 168–175, 177, 180–189, 192, 197, 203, 205–206, 213, 215, 218, 224, 229, 234, 236, 240, 242, 247
Godspell 151
The Golden Rule 137
The Good Samaritan 128, 131, 181, 192
"The Gospel According to Comic Strips: On Peanuts, The Far Side, and B.C." 143–161
Gospel According to Dr. Seuss 152
The Gospel According to Peanuts 17, 21, 145, 146, 148, 157
The Gospel According to Saint Matthew (film) 9–10, 151
Gospel Harmony 35
Gospel of Prosperity 245
The Gospels 2, 7, 10, 19–20, 31, 35, 37, 41, 47, 52, 57–60, 75–77, 105, 116, 118–119, 136, 143, 145, 147, 150, 151, 157, 158, 180, 181, 189, 191, 192, 197, 246; see also the Bible
Gould, Stephen Jay 26, 154
Graham, Billy 145
Grasmick, Harold G. 93, 95
The Great Depression 228
The Great Divorce 86–88
Great Expectations 236
Great Recession of 2008 and 2009 243
The Greatest Gift 222, 228, 237
Green, Asa 27
Grimshaw, Mike 157
Groundhog Day 22, 222, 233–236
Gutiérrez, Gustavo 149

Hackman, Gene 79
Hal 9000 183
Hammond, Phillip 148
Handel, George Frideric 64
Harry Potter 21, 150
Hart, Johnny 151
Hatch, Nathan 147
Hathorne, John 3
Hayman, Greg 152
Heaven 16, 19, 33, 40, 69, 80, 81, 83, 86, 87, 88, 93, 102, 106, 109, 110, 121, 125, 130, 139, 158, 184, 207
Hedges, Chris 16
Hell 1, 19, 33, 81, 86–89, 93, 96, 103, 105, 121, 155, 209–210
Herberg, Will 149, 156
heresy 1–2, 4–5, 16, 40–41, 49, 77, 83–85, 92, 114, 118–119, 127, 129, 156, 162
heterosexuality 138
Hexapla 80
Higdon, David 154–155
Hindu 20, 98–101, 104, 106–107, 109, 127–128, 155–156, 158
Hindu Pantheon 106
Hippie 133, 139
Hitopadesha 100
Holloway, John 99

Hollywood 10, 44, 54, 56, 60, 177
Hollywood vs. America 49, 54
Holocaust 144, 156
Homosexuality 3, 138
Hoover, Roy W. 4
Hume, Basil Cardinal 54
Hume, David 105
Hunt, Leigh 103
Hutchinson, Anne 208
Hymers, Reverend R. L. 53

"Idiosyncrasies" 200, 214
Ilych, Iván 68
Immigration Act of 1965 149
The Index Librorum Prohibitorum (Roman Catholic Index of Prohibited Books) 47
India and the Romantic Imagination 100
The Institute for Religion and Democracy 250
Internet 157, 177
"Internet Movie Database" 150
Isaac 103, 158, 210
Isaiah 43, 82, 105, 158
Islam 155, 168, 45 see also Muslims; "Revolt of Islam"
"Israel" (definition) 43
Israel (place) 46, 53, 54, 60
It's a Wonderful Life 4, 22, 221, 225–228, 232, 237

Jackson, Andrew 19, 28
Jacob 43, 94, 158
jails 223; see also prisons
Jainism 104
James (disciple) 125, 130, 131, 158
James, Henry 227
Jefferson, Thomas 4, 5, 19, 25–42, 76
The Jefferson Bible 3, 4, 19, 30–32, 34–40; see also Bible
Jehovah 51, 115, 135
Jeremiah 2
Jerome 84, 85, 92
Jerusalem 51, 84, 85, 130, 247
Jesus of Nazareth (person) 1–4, 6–11, 15, 18–20, 22–23, 30, 33, 35–40, 43–45, 47–53, 56–60, 62, 64–77, 90, 102, 105–106, 116–119, 121–123, 125, 129–131, 137, 143, 144, 155, 156, 180–182, 189–191, 197, 241–242, 246–247
Jesus of Nazareth (television miniseries) 20, 54
The Jesus Seminar 4
Jewett, Robert 55–56
Jews 3, 29, 30, 33, 36, 37, 39, 40, 51, 52, 144, 148
Joan of Arc 123
John Bull's Other Island 128
John Knox Press 150, 158
John of Jerusalem, Bishop 84
John the Baptist 85, 246
Johnston, Lynn 153

Index 263

Jonah 155, 158
Jones, Kenyon 101
Jones, William 100
Jordan, John 221
Judas 48, 51, 52, 53, 59, 89
Judson, Barbara 204, 218
Julian and Maddalo: A Conversation 108

Karalis, Vrasidas 47
Karataev, Platon 68, 70
Kazantzakis, Nikos 20, 43–61
Keane, Bil 151, 155, 158
Keats, John 102
Kennedy, John F. 14, 148
Kent, James 29–30
Kibbey, Ann 208
Kieślowski, Krzysztof 180–199
King, Martin Luther 4, 14, 145
King, Richard 243, 251
King, Stephen 22, 199
King David 48
The Koran 136
Krishna 100, 110, 156
Kubrick, Stanley 14, 184, 199, 201, 202

Lamb of God 101
"Lamb Unslain: Animals and Shelley's Panentheism" 20, 98–113
Larson, Gary 21, 153, 154, 155, 156, 158
The Last Temptation of Christ 4, 19, 20, 43, 44, 45, 46, 47, 51, 53, 54, 55, 56, 57, 58, 59
Lavinia 117
Lawrence, John Shelton 55–56
Lazarus 50
Leaves of Grass 21, 134, 137
Lee, George Vandeleur 114
Lennon, John 8, 16, 144
Lentulus 117–118
Leonidas 80
Lewis, C.S. 86–89, 91, 95–96, 180–181
Lewis, Paul 210
Liberation theology 56, 149, 250
The Library of Congress 27, 145, 157–158
Lieber, Jeffrey 163
Lincoln, Abraham 30
Lindelof, Damon 163, 165, 167
Lost 162–179
Lucht, Marc 62–68
Luther, Martin 4

MacDonald, George 87
Madison, James 38
"Madness and the Stigma of Sin in American Christianity" 13
Magdalene, Mary 48, 50, 51, 190
the Magi 156
Mahan, Jeffrey 145, 147, 157
Mahony, Episcopal Archbishop of Los Angeles Roger M. 53
Mammon 2, 15, 180, 247

Man and Superman 21, 120
Man in Black 176, 165
The Manga Bible 152
the Manhattan Project 156
Manichæan/Manichean 41, 100, 212
Marcionite 33
The Marriage of Heaven and Hell 86
Martin, George R.R. 167, 174
Martín, Gustavo A. Rodríguez 114–132
Martin, Steve 154
Marty, Martin 145
Martyr, Justin 34, 35, 40
martyrdom 80, 118, 119
Mary and Martha 50
Mason, John B. 140
Mather, Cotton 2
Mazur, Eric Michael 16, 21, 143–161
McGaughy, Lane 4
Medved, Michael 49, 54, 56
ménage à trois 114
Mere Christianity 180
metanoeo 190
Meyers, Robin 17
Middle Ages 35, 60
Middle East 3
Midrash 45–48
The Millionairess 125
Mohammed 45
Moloch 103
Moor, Edward 100
Moore, Grace 221–238
Moore, Episcopal Bishop of New York Paul 53
Moore, Ronald D. 163
Mormon 148
Moses 155, 158
Moslems 29; *see also* Muslims
Mother Angelica 53
Mother Teresa 49
Munny, William 79, 89, 90, 91
Murray, Bill 233, 235
Murray, John Courtney 156
Muslims 128
Myth 16

the National Catholic Conference 49
National Council of Catholic Bishops 49
National Endowment for the Arts 12
Native Americans 3, 137
Nature's Way 154
Nazianzus, Gregory 85
Neal, John 200, 214
Nelson, Robert 242
The New Deal 236
The New Testament 4, 41, 56, 57, 81, 83, 155, 189 *see also* Bible
New York v. Ruggles 29–30
Newcome, William (Bishop of Dromore) 35
Newton, Frank 101
Nietzsche, Friedrich 4, 5, 8, 9, 20, 21, 62–78, 144

264 Index

"Nietzsche and Tolstoy on Authentic Christianity" 62–78
1968 Medellin Conference 145
Nixon, Richard 14, 39–40
No Rising Tide: Theology, Economics, and the Future 18
Noah 155
Nolan, Val 21, 162–179, 256
"Nones" 153

Obama, Barack 18
Occupy Wall Street 18, 22, 240, 247
Ochs, Phil 145
"Ode on a Grecian Urn" 102
Oedipus Tyrranus; or, Swellfoot the Tyrant 108
Ofili, Chris 12
Old Woman (Doña Ana) 120–121
Oliver, Mary 110
Oliver Twist 223
On First Principles 70, 80–81, 85
Oppenheimer, J. Robert 156
The Oriental Renaissance 100
Origen of Alexandria 3, 14, 79, 80, 81, 82, 83, 84, 85, 89, 90, 92, 95, 96; *see also* universalism; Vigna, Gerald
The Origenistic Controversy 92
Our Mutual Friend 236
Over the River 206
The OverMan 63, 65, 75

pacifism 2, 6, 62, 67, 76
paganism 16, 41, 62, 69, 73, 108, 118, 127, 149
Paine, Thomas 105
Palestrina 64, 75
Panarion 84
Pantheistic 101
Parables 7–8, 56, 114, 147
The Parables of Dr. Seuss 152
Paradise Lost 88
Parker, Dorothy 14
Pasolini, Pier Paolo 9–11, 151
A Passage to India 110
The Passion of the Christ 4, 9, 11, 20, 44, 57, 58
Peanuts 17, 21, 145, 146, 148, 151, 153, 157
Pentecostal 247
"The Pet Lamb" 102
Phantastes 88
Pharaohs 170
Pharisees and Sadducees 51, 71, 189
Philadelphia Bible Institute (now Philadelphia Biblical University) 94
Phillips, Adam 236
Philocalia 85
Piesiewicz, Krzysztof 184, 186, 195
Piss Christ 12
Pitman, Randy 49–50, 54
Plate, S. Brent 152
Poor Law Amendment Act of 1834 223
Pope, Norris 223
Pope John Paul II 197

Pope John XXIII 10
Pope Urban II 3
Portinari, Beatrice 16, 19
Pratt, Henry John 152
Preisner, Zbigniew 182
Presbyterian 145
Priestley, Joseph 36–37
Prince of Tyre 82
private property 62, 77, 122
The Problem of Pain 88–89
Profiles of Jesus 7
"Prometheus Unbound" 106, 109
prostitution 50–51, 79, 90, 137; *see also* whores
The Protestant Ethic and the Spirit of Punishment 93
Protestantism 28, 85–86, 93–95, 114, 133, 136, 144–145, 147–149, 158, 205–206, 208, 210, 223, 245
purgatory 88, 234
Puritan 12, 136–137, 148, 204–206, 208–210, 213, 215, 218
Pythagorean 92–101

The Quarterly Review 103
Queen Mab 107
Qur'an 39; *see also* Koran

Rabbi 149, 158, 193
Radical Reformation 85
"The Radical Theology of Krzysztof Kieślowski's *Decalogue*" 21–22, 180–198
Radicalism of the American Revolution
Ramis, Harold 233–234
Reagan, Ronald 153, 236
"Reclaiming the Relation of Religion, Politics, and Economics" 23, 239–254
relativism 120, 127
"Religious Discourse in *Lost* and *Battlestar Galactica*" 21, 162–179
Religious Speeches of Bernard Shaw 119
The Republican Party 236, 240
Return to Nature or Defence of Vegetable Regimen 101
Revolt of Islam 103–106
"Revolution by Other Means: Jefferson, the Jefferson Bible, and Jesus" 19, 25–42
Reynolds, David 137
Reynolds v. United States, 1878 148
Rieger, Joerg 17–18, 23, 239–254, 256
The Rime of the Ancient Mariner 98–106
Robbins, Ruth 6–7
Robespierre, Maximilien 38–40
Robinson, William, Jr. 29
Robinson Crusoe 58
Roman Catholic Church 44, 80, 86, 182
The Roman Empire 3, 6, 7, 9, 41, 51, 80, 117, 155, 241, 244, 246, 247
Romantic movement (Romanticism) 98, 99, 100, 101, 102, 135
Roof, Wade Clark 149

Index

Rubin, Danny 233–234
Rufinus 84–85, 95
Rush, Benjamin 27, 36
Russian Revolution 40
Rust, George 85

Saint Augustine 4, 34, 35, 41, 85, 92, 93, 94, 95, 96
Saint Francis of Assisi 10
Saint Paul 4, 6, 38, 50, 52, 59, 65, 69, 71, 76, 82, 158
Saint Symeon the New Theologian 1
Salem witch trials 3
Salt, Henry S. 98, 108–109
Samson 155
1 Samuel 46
Santa Claus 155, 189
Satan 53, 80–81, 85, 90, 200, 205, 217–218; *see also* the Devil
Saul 46, 47, 50, 103
Saul (play) 46
Saunders, Ben 17
scepticism 29, 119, 164, 208
Scheiber, Andrew 209, 213
Schleiermacher, Friedrich 245, 251
Schmidt, Daryl D. 4
Schulz, Charles 145–147, 151, 153
Schwab, Raymond 100
scientology 155
Scott, Bernard Brandon 56
Scott, Nathan 145
The Screwtape Letters 87
Scrooged 22, 221, 229–237
the Second Comings 51
"second disestablishment" 148
"Second Great Awakening" 148
Second Temple Period 36
The Second Vatican Council ("Vatican II," 1962–1965) 145, 156
secular humanism 1
The Sensitive Plant 107
separation of church and state 149, 240–241
Sermon on the Mount 6, 67, 71
"sermonic fictions" 235
Shakespeare, William 108, 114, 130
Shakuntala 100
Shaw, George Bernard 5, 14, 114–132
"Shaw's Subversion of Biblical Language" 114–132
"Sheilaism" 157
Shekhinah 182
Shelley, Mary 155
Shelley, Percy Bysshe 98–113
Sherbert v. Verner 1963 148
The Shewing-up of Blanco Posnet 129
The Shining 22, 199–203, 215, 217
The Shinning: *The Simpsons* "Treehouse of Horror V" 199
Shiva 106

Short, Robert 145, 146, 147, 148, 150, 152, 153, 158
Short, William 33, 36, 37
A Short Film About Killing 191, 192
A Short Film About Love 190
Simon Peter 119
"Sinners in the Hands of an Angry God" 13
Sixbey, George 135
Slavery 3, 13, 108
Smith, Adam 240, 249, 252
Smith, James 38
Smith, Kevin 13
Smith, Margaret Bayard (or B. Harrison Smith) 37
Smith, Thomas Southwood 222
Smith, William S. 38
Smithsonian Institution in the United States 32, 154
Snoopy 146, 157
Snyder, T. Richard 93–95
Socialism 8, 16, 18, 38, 98, 108, 122, 130, 243
Society for Ethical Culture 156
Solid People 87–88
Solidarity Movement 197
Solomon 152
Son of Man 6, 33
"Song of Myself" 4, 133–142
"'Song of Myself': Teaching Whitman's New Bible Today" 21, 133–142
"Sonnet to Byron" 108
Southern Baptists 49
Southey, Robert 98
Spinoza, Baruch 105
Spiritualism 155
Springsteen, Bruce 150
Stalin, Joseph 39
Stam, Robert 57–58
Star Trek: Deep Space Nine 163
Star Wars 150
Starhawk's *The Spiral Dance* 149
The Statute of Virginia for Religious Freedom 25
Stein, Edith 86, 153, 154
Stern, Philip Van Doren 222, 228
Stevens, Laura M. 210
Stewart, Jimmy 228, 236
Stiles, Ezra 28, 33
Sufism 136
The Supreme Court 148
synesthesia 140

A Tale of Two Cities 236–237
Taoist 158, 168
Tatian 34–35, 40
The Tea Party 240
Ten Commandments 16, 22, 181, 184, 188–189 195, 196
Tertullian 92
Thackeray, William Makepeace 224
Thayer, Thomas Baldwin 206

the "third disestablishment" 148
Thomas, Keith 100
Thompson, David 53
Thoreau, Henry David 133, 136
Three Colors Trilogy 181
Thus Spoke Zarathustra 63
Time "Is God Dead?" issue 144, 148
Tintern Abbey 98
"To Edward Williams" 108
Todas las Sangres 250
Tolkien, J.R.R. 21, 150
Tolstoy, Lev (Leo) 20–21, 62–78
Too True to Be Good 119
Torah 39, 52, 158
torture 3, 9, 69, 77, 105, 119
"Touro Synagogue Letter" 27
transcendentalism 133, 134, 137
"The Treaty of Peace and Friendship" with the Pasha of Tripoli 26
Trinity (and Trinitarianism) 37, 41, 81, 94, 151
Trotsky, Leon 38–39
Twain, Mark 144–145

unemployment 247
Unforgiven 79, 86, 89–91
Unitarianism 136, 205, 213
the United States Conference of Catholic Bishops 57
United States v. Ballard, 1944 148
Universalism 56, 86–89, 91, 94, 205, 213, 218, 221; *see also* Apokatastasis
Uriah 48
utilitarianism 223
utopianism 106, 110, 137, 199

Vahanian, Gabriel 144
Valley Forge 27
Van der Kemp, Francis Adrian 31, 37
Vanita, Ruth 20, 98–113, 256
Vanzetti, Bartolomeo 14
Vanzetti, Luigia 14
Vaux, Sara Anson 89, 91
Veck, Trotty 236
vegetarianism 92, 99, 100, 101, 104, 111
Verheiden, Mark 172
Victorian era 7, 8, 100, 116, 123, 127, 129–130, 222–224, 227, 230, 236
The Vietnam War 14, 45
Vigna, Gerald S. 20, 79–97, 256
Virgil 16, 19
Virgin and Child 183
Vishnu 106
von Balthasar, Hans Urs 80, 86

wages and benefits 247
Wagner, Richard 63–64

Walden Pond 136
Wall Street 2
war 3, 23, 26, 67–69, 72, 76, 95, 139, 169, 172, 175, 194, 197, 208, 228, 230
War and Peace 4, 68, 72
War on Terror 168, 175
Warner, Marina 3
Warner, Stephen 149–150
Warren's Blacking Factory 222
Washington, George 19, 25–27
Watterson, Bill 152–153
Wells, H.G. 14
"What Christmas Is as We Grow Older?" 235–236
What Is Art? 63
Whitehouse, Mary 54
whores 30, 137; *see also* prostitution
Why the Christian Right Is Wrong: A Minister's Manifesto for Taking Back Your Faith, Your Flag, Your Future 17
Wicca 155
Wieland, Clara 200, 202–204, 207–209, 211–217
Wieland, Theodore 202, 204, 208, 213, 215–216
Wiesel, Elie 156
Wilde, Oscar 5–8, 17, 45–49, 51–52, 63, 77, 110
Wildman, Donald 53
Wilkins, Charles 100, 109
Wilson, Edmund 233
Wilson, Edward O. 154
Winfrey, Oprah 21, 150
Wood, Gordon 26, 29
Wood, Michael 9
Woolf, Virginia 110
Wordsworth, Dorothy 102
Wordsworth, William 98
World and Person: A Contribution to Christian Truth Seeking 86
World War I 95, 148
World War II 156, 187, 226, 255
worms 107–109
worship 15, 17, 27, 28, 69, 70, 76, 77, 103, 105, 106, 100, 110, 127, 136, 162, 164, 168, 186, 187, 204, 208, 209
Wuthnow, Robert 148, 155
Wycliffite heresy 16

Yde, Matthew 21–22, 256; "*The Radical Theology of Krzysztof Kieślowski's Decalogue*" 180–198

Zarathustra 71–75
Zeffirelli, Franco **20**, 54
zombies 155, 158n20
Zoroastrianism 3

www.ingramcontent.com/pod-product-compliance
Ingram Content Group UK Ltd.
Pitfield, Milton Keynes, MK11 3LW, UK
UKHW041931140426
5217IPUK00014B/423